THE FOUR SHIELDS:

THE INITIATORY SEASONS OF HUMAN NATURE

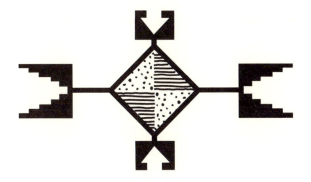

STEVEN FOSTER
WITH MEREDITH LITTLE

ILLUSTRATIONS BY JAMES WRIGHT

Lost Borders Press
P.O. Box 55
Big Pine, CA 93513
e-mail: lostbrdrs@telis.org

© 1998 by Steven Foster and Meredith Little

All rights reserved. Including the right of reproduction in whole or in part in any form

Lost Borders Press and colophon are registered trademarks of The School of Lost Borders, Big Pine, CA 93513

Library of Congress Cataloging-in-Publication Data

Foster, Steven, 1938—
    The four shields: the initiatory seasons of human nature / Steven Foster
  and Meredith Little. — 1st. ed.

    p. Cm.
Includes bibliographical references
ISBN   0-9667659-0-7: $19.95

1. Ecopsychology (Wilderness Therapy)   2. Developmental Psychology
3. Rites and ceremonies. 4. Spiritual life (nature). 5. Initiation
      I. Little, Meredith, 1951 — . II. Wright, James. III. Title

LCCN: 98-92065

Manufactured in the United States of America

10 9 8 7 6 5 4 3 2

      Front/Back Cover by Emerald North
      Moon Tree Series: acrylic on canvas
      Sun Tree Series: acrylic on canvas
First Edition

This book is dedicated to those who sit in council

within the circle of the self

What have I learned but
the proper use for several tools?

The moments
between hard pleasant tasks . . .

Seeing in silence:
never the same twice,
but when you get it right,

you pass it on

— Gary Snyder

THE FOUR SHIELDS
TABLE OF CONTENTS

Preface i

The Four Shields of Human Nature 1

The Summer Shield of Human Nature .... .29

The Fall Shield of Human Nature .... .43

The Winter Shield of Human Nature .... .61

The Spring Shield of Human Nature .... .79

Four Shield Dynamics .... .93

Four Shield Therapy .... .119

Summer to Winter: The Rites of Fall .... .139

Fall to Spring: The Rites of Winter .... .171

Winter to Summer: The Rites of Spring .... .203

Spring to Fall: The Rites of Summer .... .229

The Yellow Brick Road .... .255

Appendix I: Shield Impersonation .... .275

Appendix II: The Four Shields of a Woman .... .289

Appendix III: The Four Shields of a Man .... .315

Bibliography .... .347

PREFACE

> I want the strong air of the most profound night
> to remove flowers and words from the arch where you sleep,
> and a black boy to announce to the gold-minded whites
> the arrival of an ear of corn.
> -- Federico Garcia Lorca, "Ode to Walt Whitman"

The basic teachings of this book come from a series of meetings with a remarkable man that took place over twenty years ago. We met with him no more than a dozen times over a span of years, and then we parted to go our separate ways. Yet the teachings stuck to our hides. We never forgot. A new, yet very old, perspective was conceived in us. As the years passed, the perspective significantly altered our lives.

This remarkable man, who we shall call "I Am a Ghost," was half Northern Cheyenne and half German. When he came into the room you smelled alkali dust and ozone. He seemed to have a hundred faces: demon, angel, alien, poet, story teller, sorcerer, witch, dictator, little boy, warrior, little girl, mother. . . . He claimed to have been through highly sacred initiations among the American Indians, and to be the holder of sacred teachings passed down through generations of initiates. The teachings of the four shields, he said, came to his people from "the south." By south we understood him to mean the Aztec and Mayan civilizations of Mesoamerica. But the teachings did not necessarily originate there. They had come to "the south" through contact with other primitive cultures throughout the world.

I think the teachings of I Am a Ghost stuck so tenaciously to our consciousness because he was, indeed, a sorcerer. His "impersonation" of the four shields of nature (and his own nature) made a profound impression on us. The ways in which he taught us could be harsh and manipulative, but his aims were valid. We did not suffer his methodology without the richest of understanding. The most important thing he ever said to me concerned his desire to become "fully human." "What," said I, "aren't you already fully human?" "No," he said. "I am still in the process of becoming five." "Five?" I asked. "What about four, as in the four shields?" "Five," he said. "The four shields make the fifth, the whole. Number five means fully human."

The years passed. Our work with wilderness passage rites prospered. The simple metaphor given to us by I Am a Ghost was filtered through our own awareness and experience. The original seed grew into a vast discipline that at times seemed hardly related to its origins. Our restless imaginations leaped beyond the basic framework originally presented to us, and we began to explore every nook and cranny of our Anglo-European heritage, measuring whatever came to consciousness with our four shields ruler, "putting it on the wheel" to see where it fit. At the same time we began to explore the natural world around us with the same measuring tool. The more carefully we measured, the brighter shone the mystery of its aptness. The four faces of "self-thus" stood out ever more clearly, and their self-evidence rang of truth.

Those who came to the School of Lost Borders were invaluable reminders of the four shields "masquerade." Through them we became familiar with the impact of the initiatory experience on the shields of human nature. The impact was enormous. Their everyday masks were ripped away by a process that seemed strange and new, yet somehow anciently remembered, and the drama of the four shields was revealed. We saw the stuff of which the shields were made. We saw the fear of the child, the dark inwardness of the adolescent, the maturity of the adult, the illumination in the eyes of the mythic one who had been confirmed. We listened to thousands of stories and learned to track the psyche through the mazes of inwardness. In every story we came upon the spoor of initiatory confirmation. In every precious individual, we traced the outlines, no matter how vague, of a shield system, a unique manner of expression/defense, a personal mythos.

It was the initiatory experience "in a natural setting" that really did the trick. Nature opened the people. That is, their own Nature opened them, slowed them down, gave them solitude and emptiness to fill with a self-conscious knowing. The simplest thing, like learning how to stay warm, or cool, or to keep dry in the rain, involved a mythical journey through the kingdom of initiation, to the realms of understanding, mastery, and creative insight. How quickly we learned that our job was not to "therapize," but to be witnesses, to mirror back our version of "meaning," and to confirm the change in life status represented by each journey.

The four shields metaphor became a private language between us, a way of referring to the particular shield structure of a person. With time, we fashioned a more formal version of the private language. It became the regimen by which our students were trained in the psychology of human nature.

We often wonder if I Am a Ghost had any idea of the lengths to which we would take his metaphor. And now it has reached the form of a book -- a book that has been most difficult to write. If the subject is psychology, it is also "common sense," natural science, history, anthropology, sociology, philosophy, epistemology, the arts, religion, and theology. It seems to engulf the whole kit and caboodle of primitive and modern culture. No matter which direction we faced from the center of the seasonal circle of the self, we were confronted by a thousand windows, each begging to be opened. Ultimately we realized, as we had to, that what we were trying to describe was nature itself. Our nature.

The vastness of the metaphor belied its fundamental simplicity. The formula itself was easily understood. The applications to which the formula could be put seemed infinite. Again and again I had to pull myself back from the brink of a kind of insane fascination with such questions as: "What are the four shields of a stone?" Or "What are the four shields of the AIDS virus?" The sirens called to us from the kingdoms of limitless speculation. We stopped up our ears with mugwort. We lashed our feet to the solid ground. We went on a fast and embraced the rough desert earth. We held tight to the trusting, innocent children that we were, are, and will be. The madness passed. The metaphor became simple again.

Writing this book has brought me to the door of the Castle of Doubt. The "doing of it" was profoundly related to my own sense of inadequacy. Although I was professionally trained in scholarly pursuits, I had left that life over 25 years ago, vowing never to return. I went into the marketplace, where the lonely, the desperate, and the depraved rubbed elbows with the fanatic, the addicted, and the lost. I went into the desert, where I grew infinitesimally small and insignificant in comparison to the kit fox. I forgot all the approved methods of reasoning, even how to phrase a sentence. It seemed more direct, more real, to personally experience a thing, than to theorize or write about experiencing it.

But the call was there. Write the book! We discussed the possibility for many years. But I was afraid. I didn't know enough. I would never know enough. I would not be able to rescue what I had learned professionally so many years ago. I lay awake at night, looking out at the stars shining through our bedroom window, wondering if my reluctance to take on the project had anything to do with my fear that I would die not having accomplished what I was supposed to do.

Once I was well into the first draft, the toll that would be exacted became evident. I would have to become obsessed with the doing of it. My life would have to be so arranged that I could balance long hours of working with people in nature at the School with long hours of research, staring into the console late into the night. My family life would suffer. My son and daughter would graduate from high school remembering their father as the guy in the back room who came out for dinner and the late news. My wife would have to cover the phone for me night after night and find intimacy at odd moments, when my head wasn't crammed with anxiety over the condition of a paragraph. I would become something of a stranger to my most important source of inspiration, the natural solitude that lurked just outside the boundaries of our tiny town.

For eight long years I carried this book in my womb, measuring each contraction with whatever language I could draw from our desert aquifer.

Now, the end is in sight. My daughter recognizes my face and my sons call me on the phone. Meredith and I find space to play. I can take the time to spend entire days out in the wind-swept mountains. I read what I have written with the eyes of an intimate friend who knows the author only too well. Mostly, I like what I see. Limitations, yes. But the subject was too vast. Everything was relevant. The author had to pick and choose, to plot his course and walk it as simply as possible, to remain faithful to the original metaphor. He was quite unable to take up every possible objection to the scheme he was presenting. He did not intend to write a polemic. He wanted to advance a new, yet very old, "psychology" of human nature. He wanted to write something on which others more skillful and knowledgeable than he could build. He wanted to write something that could be used by the culture to rectify the terrifying imbalances developing within the caged human psyche.

Above all, he wanted to write something that might benefit the expression of nature that is human. Despite his limitations, he modestly succeeded, at least in his own eyes. Having completed the book, he would be the first to admit that it raises far more questions than it did when he began.

If the book reads, feels, looks a little strange, it is. Having experimented with several possible outlines, I finally had to organize and develop the concepts of the four shields in the form of a main theme and four variations. The main theme is: The Four Shields of Human Nature. Each of the variations explores the dimensions of one of the four shields. There is a certain amount of redundancy, as the wheel turns around. This can't be helped. We learned it by repetition, by "going around the wheel" thousands of times. So the variations whirl into each other as the perspective changes, and they all prefigure the theme, the one, the whole.

As we circled around and around the wheel of the four seasons of human nature, we began to notice how they began to blend into each other, like colors on a whirling, spectral wheel. We noted the interplay and tension of opposites, and listened to the echoes of one shield in the other three, or the three other shields in the one. We marvelled at the shades, the nuances, the subtleties, the seemingly infinite combinations, gradations, and permutations of this "primitive" psychology and wrung our hands in despair. How could all this be contained in one book? The only way was to hold true to a design that held true to itself, yet was suggestive of all the possibilities. This, I trust, has been done.

For a long time, I felt stymied by matters of pure style. In what sort of language should the metaphor be phrased? So much ground to cover. So many metaphors. How could I please everyone? No matter, I allowed myself to be pulled into a sea of self-knowledge. My own experience as a human being became a kind of authority, dictating style and content. You will discover that the book is "Western," enriched by the root system of our own Anglo-European heritage. The basic paradigms sprung semi-automatically to the lips of perception, and resisted expulsion, despite the fact that we studied with Native American teachers for fifteen years. I tried to let the dark, neolithic, ancestral soil of me do the thinking and the talking. When I did, the dark earth talked in the languages of Anglo-Saxon, Germanic, Jewish, and Celtic. I couldn't resist adopting all four voices: an earthy one, a psychological one, a mental one, and an imaginative one. I couldn't keep the poetry out. The four shields metaphor -- and surely metaphor is *all* -- aches for the caress of imaginative truth. Surely, if our species is to survive, the poetry must be strong.

This book has been written for certain kinds of people. I could not please everyone. I presume my reader to be educated, aware, professional, active in the fields of education, social science/service, and ecology. I have deliberately kept away from psychological controversy. The metaphor itself calls for a peculiar kind of concentration. Once the circle has been drawn, all the psychologies can find their place inside it. This ancient wisdom of the four shields establishes psychology as one of the oldest sciences. It identifies the main psychological season as fall, the dark shield. The initiation place. The place where the sun goes down and we go inside and turn on the light.

I also write to the ecologist and the true conservative, to those who in their lifetime share an abiding love for all other life forms. I presume that there are many kinds of ecologists and I speak directly to those who seek the basic truth of our oneness with our environment. These are the ones who know in their bones the organic relationship between nature and human, the ones who seek to build the bridge across the illusionary chasm between human and nature. I have known many of you. You are brave enough to admit that nature wears more than just a physical dress. You are also aware of her inward, psychological dress, her web-like mental dress, and her shining spirit dress. You comprehend her holistically. And deep down you really care what happens to *homo sapiens*.

Last but not least, I write to the average, intelligent adult of any race, gender, or sexual persuasion, who cares for the earth and the fate of the human species, who wants to preserve our home for the grandchildren. I offer you a gift, an understanding that can heal, a knowing of how you might go about it for yourself or even what you might do within your own neighborhood.

My graceful, intrepid wife Meredith went with me through those obsessive years. She helped shape every thought, every concept, every symbol. A good deal of that which is presented here comes from the trainings, seminars, and courses the two of us have developed and conducted at the School of Lost Borders. She is my partner. We made this "wheel" together. I am merely the writing component of our private and professional union. Her interests lie elsewhere, in her love for the land, in her gifts of listening and hearing, in her balanced wisdom and caring heart. But I tell you this -- she picked this crazy old man off the asylum floor so often she might as well have written the book all by herself. How can I express my love for her, my gratitude for her for being both muse and teacher, not to mention lover and psychotherapist.

She is the first to read whatever I write. So gracious and loving a soul she is, so reluctant to hurt a feeling. Invariably, her response has spurred me on, even when I couldn't quite agree with her positivity. Her marks and comments in the margins were precious stones with which this necklace was strung. Ten years of marriage passed. This book is an expression of our love.

James Wright has been with us faithfully, shouldering his own share of the burden, sifting through changes in the manuscript, suggesting alterations here and there, arguing this or that point, matching his drawings to the text. All the while he was engrossed in his own writings, his passage rites of hopping freights, his gods and goddesses, his bestiaries. For every minute he spent on the drawings for this book, may his reputation as a genuinely gifted and insightful "eco-psychologist" and writer increase. When the final production of the book was undertaken, James and his wife Hannah were dancing with the arrival of a second child. The dear fellow was working on his own book, working on ours, counseling at-risk adolescents, living the life of lover and house mate to his woman, and actively fathering his baby son.

Because of the work of Marlow Hotchkiss (one of the authors of *The Box*), the book exists in its present form. His editorial assistance was incisive and appropriate. His enthusiasm for the ideas suggested by the basic metaphor inspired me again and again. At a crucial point in its development, he disassembled the book so adroitly I was able to see how far from the mark I had strayed. I could not have found a keener, richer intelligence to see the implications of what I was trying to say and guide me on my way. God speed to him, his wife, Leslie, and their daughter, most appealingly named Meredith.

For reasons only understood by reading the book, I want to thank in particular Selina, Russell, Tom, Emerald, Roger, Steve, Doug, Dan, Clara, Colleen, Mike, Selden, Char, Alan, Nicolai, Kate, Rusty, Sharon, Pamela, and Paul.

Gratitude goes to Kathy de Reemer, M.D. for her interest and guidance through the medical implications of the four shields metaphor. She supplied me with hours of research into the relationship between body and psyche as evidenced in neurotransmission and the hormones. Her active interest in my health touched me deeply, and I knew I had an ally for life.

Gratitude also to a very beautiful, matter-of-fact woman who appeared out of nowhere and offered to lay out the contents of the book into a form acceptable to the printer. This she did, but not before she went into the mountains of the Eureka Valley and fasted for four days and nights. When she returned there was a ground squirrel in her hands, a snake in her pocket, and a story about love. Thank you, Nancy Wells.

Ms. Irmtraut Sheaffer, of Munich, Germany, a Jungian-expressive therapist and a long time student of the vision fast process, has been a constant source of inspiration while the book was gestating. An accomplished concert pianist, she does not deign to get down in the dirt to fast and cry and listen to her neolithic ancestors. It was she who first brought to our attention certain crucial connections between primitive psychology and the research of C.G.Jung.

Much gratitude goes to Sue Lamb, for reading and commenting on the MS at an early date. She has performed this service for me more than once and has always turned my energies toward vital, realistic directions. And to Howard Lamb, for *Child of Fortune*.

Nor can I forget to mention Emerald North, a keen student of the shields, a vision fast midwife, and a member in good standing of what Virginia Coyle calls "the Dark Institute." How many hours have we spent discussing the roots of the creative impulse and the multicolored dimensions of that shield in which she is most gifted -- the spring. To us, she is a visible symbol of the self-initiated, illumined woman.

That goes also for our friend and colleague, Virginia Coyle (*The Box, The Council Process*) whose vision and energy and beauty has bewitched us into seeing what is possible. Now that we live with her, our boundaries have become truly lost. There are few women like her in the world. As she has grown, she has realized the full potential of all four of her shields, and is truly a human paradigm to whom we refer when we seek to understand the four shields of a woman. Thank you Gigi, now and forever.

Nor must I neglect to mention certain individuals who have inspired us, loved us, and touched us with their magic. Elias Amidon, Elizabeth Roberts, Natalie Rogers, Joan Halifax, Ralph Metzner, John Davis, Jed Swift, Jeffrey Duvall, Mary McHenry, Win Phelps, Deborah Bradford, Joseph LaZenka, Derham Giuliani, Robert Greenway, and for special reasons, Brian Sorokin and Silvia Talavera.

Last but not least, I must thank the man who first introduced us to the Wheel – and publically acknowledge my indebtedness to him. After the dust devil came through, we picked up the pieces one by one and lo! they fit into the puzzle that became this book. As I recall, he was the first American Indian to tell us that we too were native American. He was giving us permission to love this land as our land, all of us together, like a rainbow. He knew this was the only way to save our species and our environment. His name? Lightning Bolt.

The real writers of this book are the people who came to The School of Lost Borders with their lives and their stories. We could but stand aside and watch, our mouths agape, as they demonstrated, through their crises and resolutions, the healthy, whole rudiments of ecopsychology. Nor could we have continued without their support. Their continued interest in the practical use of four shields process has lured us back to the wheel of the seasons, finding answers in continued study.

Meanwhile, the seasons came and went. The summer sun parched the lost borders of the Land of Little Rain. The fall chilled the air and the Range of Light hulked somber and snowless. Winter came with piercing winds and scattered snows. The great range was muffled in a cloak of white. Starving coyotes screamed at the dawn of a freezing sun. Then came spring, in a gush of wildflowers. Spring after spring after spring. Fall after fall after fall. Ever so slowly, the spark in the tinder pile began to glow, to spread out. When these smoldering flames consume the last of the pile, this book will be done.

> Steven Foster with Meredith Little
> School of Lost Borders
> Big Pine, CA
> 1998

DRAWING OUT THE SHIELDS

The four shields system is an abstraction derived from patterns in the natural world. It is the winter ruminating on the physical body of summer, evolving thought forms from palpable experience. In the body of this particular text that form is verbal because only language can teach the subtleties of shield meaning. But working with the shields brings forth more than words. Images, too, will emerge and display a kaleidoscopic cycle, rotating around the shield wheel with endless variation. This imaginal emergence is spring's creativity drawing deeply from the dark well of fall's introspection. Word and image form a whole representing the pivotal balance of the shield system, the evolving cross which symbolizes the movement of life on earth.

I have tried to illuminate the text with imagery which not only illustrates the ideas but also evokes non-verbal experience of the shields. In this endeavor I seek to stir the archetypal waters of the psyche, thereby promoting an engagement with the text that is more than intellectual, perhaps even irrational. To this end I have rummaged through the antique dustbin of symbols, adopting and adapting various forms to depict qualities of the shields as I see them.

The folly of this approach is that it is idiosyncratic at heart, and my interpretations of symbols and shields is the product of my own perceptions into the archetypal realm. This is a quirk of the method but does not negate the intent to evoke soul. Although we float in the sea of soul, soul is also the fluid of our inner being. I have tried to encourage this work by allowing the images to rise out of trance, dream, airy inspiration and other depersonalized states. My hope is that these images will further encourage the reader to fall back into his or her own soul, digesting the shield material at an unconscious level.

A few words should be said about the swastika. At some point in my doodling, graphing endless dizzying circles of shields, I realized I was making swastikas. This shouldn't be surprising since the swastika is a cross in revolution, a symbol of the fourfold cycling around itself. A multi-cultural symbol which spans time and place, it has now become fixed foremost in our consciousness as the symbolic embodiment of the Nazi regime. The Nazis were clever in many ways, but perhaps none more than in their dramatic use of symbols. They appropriated the swastika because it was a symbol of power. The swastika is a mesmerizing mandela, an ideal focus for those weary of crisis and looking to the promise of revolutionary change and a new world order. We all know the outcome of this promise. Amongst the major losses is one yet to be tallied -- the loss of the swastika itself as a vital, life-affirming symbol.

I appreciate the opportunity to conjure images out of Steven and Meredith's work. They have indulged many fanciful notions of mine which bear only distant resemblance to their ideas. They have also endured persistent carping on differences of opinion or emphasis. Despite all this, they have maintained good humor, encouragement, and provided me with a chance to study with them. When I accepted their initial challenge to try my hand at these graphics, I had no clue where it would take me. It seems that no sooner would I send them a batch of sketches, feeling that I had truly exhausted the imaginal possibilities, than Steven would write back asking for more. I had little choice but to drag myself back to the symbolic well and dredge for more. So it has gone around and around the wheel, frequently thinking I have seen all there is to see, only to go around again and see it completely anew. I guess that's what it's all about.

James Wright
Matrix Borne
Cape Porpoise, Maine

THE FOUR SHIELDS OF HUMAN NATURE

> The Chinese word for nature, zi-ran (Japanese shizen) means 'self-thus'. . . . For those who would see directly into essential nature, the idea of the sacred is a delusion and an obstruction: it diverts us from what is before our eyes: plain thusness . . . No hierarchy, no equality. No occult and exoteric, no gifted kids and slow achievers. No wild and tame, no bound or free, no natural and artificial. Each totally its own frail self. Even though connected all which ways; even because connected all which ways.
>
> This *thusness*, is the nature of the nature of nature. The wild in wild.
>
> — Gary Snyder, *The Practice of the Wild*

> Heaven is my father and earth is my mother, and even such a small creature as I finds an intimate place in their midst.
>
> Therefore that which extends throughout the universe I regard as my body and that which directs the universe I consider as my nature.
>
> — Chang Tsai (1021-1077)

Once upon an ancient time there lived a human being. This individual could be anyone, but let's imagine this person was you — or me.

Wait a minute, you say. Do you mean us as we are now? Yes and no. I mean us as we are now *and* as we were then. Perhaps you know what I'm getting at. Our kind was born a million years or so ago, when our ancestors forsook the trees. We may think we don't remember very well, but if we listen very closely to the beating of our hearts, we will hear the roaring of our ancient home. We can no better escape who we were then than we can stop being who we are now.

The fact is, despite all the fancy trappings of "modern civilization," we never stopped living close to nature, and only comparatively recently in human history have we bought the lie that we do not. The lie has belied our actual experience of human life — which is closer to the "primitive" than we might care to admit. All it will take is a good natural catastrophe, an earthquake, famine, tornado, or flood to remind us how profoundly we depend on our natural environment.

Let's also imagine that many thousands of years ago our lives were premised by a shared basic assumption that formed the foundation of formal (and informal) education. This assumption was often, if not always, connected with rites, ceremonies, and ritual gatherings involving the family, neighborhood, or community at large. Perhaps you can remember how easily you accepted this shared premise. After all, there was no escape from the seasonal reality of your natural home.

SELF-THUS

The basic assumption went something like this: You and I are "self-thus." Our people are all self-thus. All the animals, plants, birds, insects, are self-thus. The sky, the wind, the rain, the snow, the mountains, the sea, the lightning, the thunder, the shadows, the night are self-thus. The sun, moon, and stars are self-thus. Everything is self-thus. Because we all share the same mother and father, we are all made of the same self-thus. We all share the basic nature of our mother and father.

Of course, there are a thousand other names for self-thus. But regardless of what we call this *unus mundus,* this essence, it exists at the center of all life and death. Without it, there would be no life, no death, no *nature.*[1]

So we must begin our discussion of the psychology of human nature with a clear statement about what we are, for we will never escape our essential nature. We are earth-born, children of nature, and related to every living thing. We are self-thus in human form.

We are "self." My self, your self, every self — the self of all things, the self that we all share — the self of the earth, the self of the universe. For our species, self is conceived via our own human perceptions. We are the human version of self. I am a human self. You are a human self. But that furry creature sitting on your lap is a cat self. And the tiny shadow it chases every night is a mouse self. And that piece of rind the mouse snatches from the compost is an orange self. Through their "selfness," the orange, the mouse, the cat, and the human are related. By their selfness, all selves are related. By their relatedness, all selves are one in Self.

We are also of "thus." Consider the word, "thus." It implies a kind of narrative. "And thus . . . it happened," "and so it went," "events transpired." The events of the moment, the year, the century unfolded. "Thus" implies time passing, aeons rolling — and how it all happened was like "thus." "Thus" is the history, the process, the "outcome" of nature. It is the passage of the seasons. The succession of night and day. "Thus" — as I type the word — is also the human version of thus. The body, to this extent. The psyche, like this. The mind, in this manner. The spirit, likewise.

As human versions of self-thus, you and I are altogether human and altogether natural: we are "human" (with all the characteristics of the species) "nature" (living within a natural cycle marked by growth, decay, regeneration, and interdependence). As such, we share in the evolutionary processes, the drama, of nature.

If you want to look for self-thus, you will have to remove the masks and costumes it uses to express and defend itself. You will have to peel away the color, form, and species. You will have to remove the flesh, the bone, the blood, the cell, the chromosome, the molecule, even the quark. Underneath it all you would find the center of the circle of life, the "essence," the "force," the "intelligence," the "spirit" — the self-thus.

Ancient people liked to describe and draw pictures of self-thus. Modern people do too, although not always as consciously. Although there were always differences in detail, the ancient descriptions tended to bear striking resemblance to each other. The meanings also tended to be similar. Although there were many different ways to cook it, self-thus always boiled down to the same truth.

The intersection of two lines at right angles. A four directions mandela.

The four directions (space).

The four seasons (time).

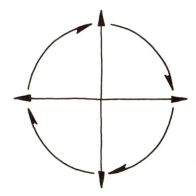

Two constants: direction and season^2 (self and thus). From the union of these two spring four opposites. South (summer) and north (winter) and west (fall) and east (spring). These opposites compose one whole, as represented by the circle. Each opposite is connected by the clockwise movement of the wheel.

This clockwise movement is, in fact, the movement of the seasons, the circular path of the sun in the northern hemisphere, as it circles toward the north in the summer and inclines again toward the south in the winter.

The circle or boundary around the cross identifies its inner content as human self-thus. The content outside the boundary is also self-thus, though not necessarily of the human variety. The boundary is there because self-thus makes boundaries.

These boundaries exist so that self-thus can *express* and *defend*, act and react, project and introject, reach out and pull in, expand and contract, and they represent interaction and cooperation between what is inside and what is outside. The human mandala is only one of billions of living circle boundaries of self- thus.

Express suggests "extend." Defend suggests "pull in." Extend and pull in. Give and take. React and watch response. Act and recoil into memory. Sow and reap. Express and defend. Exhale and inhale. And so the seasons pass from body to memory to mind to death and renewal — and the in-out, give-receive, express-defend of human self-thus dances its intricate dance of cooperation with the self-thus of all living things.

The human boundary is like a shield, or a mask, or a persona. We were taught to see it as a shield structure, a painted shield that both expresses the "medicine" of the human self-thus and defends it from disease and other threats of the natural world. A shield says "I am this" or "I am that." The shields project themselves beyond their boundaries and cooperate in four different ways with nature through intent and action. The shields also say: "I am not this or that." They defend themselves from the encroachments of nature by cooperating in four different ways with whatever touches the circle.

As human beings, you and I inhabit a unique space/time at the center of turning seasons of nature, changing as they change. All the other versions of self-thus occupy space/time in the same fashion. As the seasons pass, the basic grid of the directions, two straight lines in tensioned opposition, remains the same. No matter how wildly the ship of self-thus bounces on the stormy seas of time/space, the mandala, or tetrad, remains constant.

The four seasons, faces, personas, shields of human self-thus correspond to and consist of the four seasons, faces, personas — shields of the earth. In humans, the four faces are: summer (the emotional, instinctive, physical, reactive, body-child), fall (the inward, self-conscious, psychological soul of transition), winter (the rational, responsible, controlled, interdependent mind of maturity) and spring (the regenerating, healing, creative spirit of that which is born from death). Body, psyche, mind, and spirit. The same four faces are worn by all living forms of self-thus: the physical, the psychological, the rational, and the spiritual.

Our human brand of self-thus is born on the eastern horizon — where the sun rises in the spring of life — and takes on the body of human as the sun moves into the summer shield of childhood. Ideally, childhood is high noon, a pleasure garden, warm. innocent, emotional, erotic, and vivid with sensations. As we grow older, the sun begins to decline in the west, and a shadow creeps into our awareness. Soon the time will come when our initiation into womanhood or manhood will commence. We will enter the fall shield, where our perceptions are focused inwardly and we have to endure challenges that signify the end of childhood.

In the fall shield of adolescence, the innocence of our ancient ancestors becomes experience. We remember, as did Adam and Eve, the old human curses of self-consciousness and death. We are helpless to arrest our fall from the garden of innocence. We can only surrender and accept the terms of severance — which is the inevitability that the descending darkness in the west will swing toward the absolute zero of midnight and the north star. We enter the dark passage because we know that the time has come to work, marry, become parents, join the community, and take on elderhood. It cannot be otherwise. We have to become adult if the community is to survive the long dark hours of winter. Come spring, the sun will come around again to the birthing of a new cycle. We who still live will emerge from the earth like babies from the womb, alive and hungering for summer.

Our own brand of self-thus, then, grows into advanced life stages of maturity through successive initiatory experiences. Again and again, summer's child has to be initiated via fall's adolescent so that we can become adult (winter). Fall's adolescent has to be initiated into winter's adulthood so that we can become regenerated (spring). Winter's adult has to be initiated by spring's regeneration so that we can become summer's child. And spring's newly born has to be initiated through the physical body of summer so that we can remember and feel inwardly who we are (fall).

The four directions of human self-thus are found all over the world in medicine wheels, mandalas, and the like, and are symbolized by colors, elements, fields of force, concepts of dimension, compass directions, and other natural phenomena. If we were to assign colors to the four seasonal directions, we would choose the red-black-white-gold color scheme associated with traditions as disparate as the Australian aborigines, the Sanskrit Hindus, the ancient Egyptians, the alchemists of medieval Europe, the religious savants of China and Japan, and the Maya/Aztec of Mesoamerica.

South, the direction of summer, would be red, the color of the pumping blood, of rage, lust and desire. West, the fall, would be black, the color of night, of shadow, of the underworld, of the absence of color, of the screen on which dreams and feelings play. North, the winter, would be white, the color of snow and ice, of chastity, reason, and the mature mind. And spring, in the east, would be gold, the color of the rising sun, of the hair of the muse dancing at dawn on the eastern rim of the world.

Tradition has assigned more than color to the four seasons. There were the four directions, the four elements, the four races, the four ages, the fourfold deities, the four winds, the four dimensions of space (length, height, volume, time), the four dimensions of time (past, present, future, space), the four gates of Heaven, the four humors (sanguine, phlegmatic, choleric, melancholic), the four corners of the earth, the four cardinal, fixed, and mutable signs of the zodiac, the four apostles, the four basic geometric figures (circle, line, square, triangle), the four basic operations of arithmetic (addition, subtraction, multiplication, division), the four "qualities" (warm, dry, moist, cold). Indeed, fourfoldedness is fundamental to almost every depiction of human self-thus.

The planet earth herself, the radiant spinning globe as seen from outer space, might be the most obvious symbol of the four seasonal/directional metaphor. From any perspective from which you view her, she has an up and down (north and south) and a right and left side (east and west). On the other hand, from any perspective she has no up and down, no right and left, but is a continuously spinning, seamless surface, a sphere. One might conclude that she is all one — or that she is four in one, that she possesses volume, like a ball — or that she is empty, like a circle drawn upon a flat surface of eternal space.

Now let us descend to her surface, Here we stand on dry land. How do we see her now? She stretches all around us in all the gradients and vectors of the six directions (south, west, north, east, skyward and earthward). That radiant globe so separate from us in outer space now surrounds us, undergirds us. It would almost appear as if we were at the mid point — that anywhere we stood we would be at the center of it all. Appearances can be both deceiving and absolutely necessary. The fact is that there is no center — that the entire earth is not the center, that our home galaxy is not the center. Nevertheless, we must persist in perceiving ourselves at the center, for without this perception there would be no means of balancing. We would not be able to stand on our two legs.

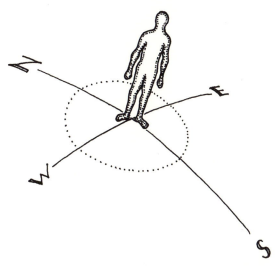

This picture of self-thus is certainly no abstract, one dimensional construct. At the center of the circle is a vertical pole, stretching upwards and downwards, adding two more dimensions to the circular four. This vertical, combined with the horizontal of the compass or clock, suggests volume — height, depth, width, roundure. A ball or bubble like the earth, at the horizons summer, fall, winter, and spring. If you will, a humming gyroscope of direction and time — a biosphere.

The center pole is self-thus — unbridled, wild self-thus. It reaches skyward and earthward, up toward the life giving sunlight and down into the dark roots. It yearns toward birth even as it is pulled towards death. This up-down, yin-yang paradox is at the heart of self-thus. Opposites bound together into one still point at the center of the circle of shields. Forever they have intercourse.

Upward and downward, sacred and profane, increase the volume of the shields as they turn around the center. Seconds or years pass. Every time the spring comes around again there is an increase in the size of the "polar field."

Every time fall comes around again there is a decrease in the size of the "polar field." The "magnetic" influence of the poles upon each other exerts a kind of tide-line, an interlapping and parting of the sacred and the profane. The land is the sea, and the sea is the land — and nature, at the still point of the turning wheel, is all.

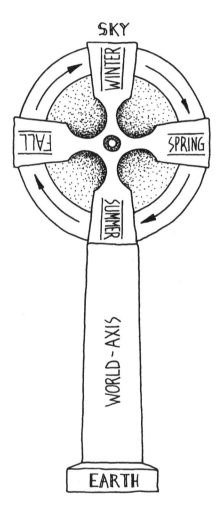

THE SHIELDS OF THE CELTIC CROSS

THEME AND FOUR VARIATIONS

> Women and men (both dong and ding)
> summer autumn winter spring
> reaped their sowing and went their came
> sun moon stars rain
>
> — e.e. cummings, "Anyone Lived in a Pretty How Town"

Listening once again to one of the finest pieces of classical music ever written — Beethoven's piano sonata, "Twelve Variations on a Theme from Handel's 'Judas Maccabeus'" — I was struck by the idea that human nature is composed of music. The universe itself is one big symphonic theme in four movements: matter, psyche, mind, and energy/spirit. The earth, with her sub-variations of the four seasons, is itself a variation on the theme of the universe.

The human beings of the earth are sub-variations on the theme of the seasons — which in turn is a variation of the theme of earth. The variations are endless. The human variation of the earth theme may not be any more important than any of the billion others, but it is ours, and we have grown very attached to it. All the creatures have their own unique rendering of the main theme, and together we share its common properties.

In Beethoven's "Variations" the main theme is almost completely buried by the constant birth of new expressions of itself, yet it remains, and surfaces here and there to remind us that indeed, the theme will never die. As the sonata progresses, one becomes aware that one of the ways in which the original theme is preserved is by timing. Every variation follows the same time length and pattern. Not a beat is lost. Thus the pattern, and the content, reflect the main theme. Each season, as a variation of the theme of earth, keeps time with the theme and reflects the content of "self-thus."

In another sense, the innocent theme enters the passage of variation, where it is initiated into ever more complex forms of itself until it emerges mature, triumphant, and changed. The child of birth, the highest expression of the theme, undergoes the changes of growth, only to emerge into its fullest expression at death. The initiations — the variations — are vitally necessary for the survival of the theme. Otherwise it will die, a victim of its own inability to grow. The initiatory process involves being torn apart so that various parts can be affirmed, or rewoven into new expressions. Thus the human initiate undertakes the dismemberment of variations that result in new growth.

The seasonal passage, then, is a theme of earth. The four seasons are variations of the theme. The summer persona (the summer shield as described in these pages), is the human variation of the earth sonata. It is one of the movements in which the main theme is expressed. Fall, winter, and spring are also human variations of the theme. Together they compose the symphony that is the natural human experience. They sing out by themselves, they blend, they cooperate, they contrast, they oppose, but always they are one, always bringing forth the theme, the main, the four stranded thread, the life, the self that is ever "self-thus."

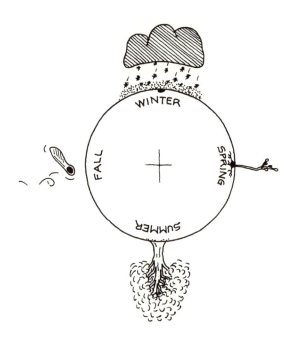

MAPLE SEED'S JOURNEY

THE WEATHER

> Though trees turn bare and girls turn wives,
> We shall afford our costly seasons;
> There is a gentleness survives
> That will outspeak and has its reasons.
>
> — W.D. Snodgrass, "April Inventory"

For centuries, poets and artists have tracked the dimensions of human weather with metaphorical anemometers and vanes. Reactive emotions are hot; the mind is cold; the feelings are dark; the spirit is bright. In the summer of childhood, conditions are optimal for growth; the barometer reads "high." In the winter of adulthood, life is hard, suffering great; the barometer has fallen to "low." The "fall" from high to low is chronological, a veering off into the dark regions of change. Sooner or later, the winds are buoyed by the rising spirits of spring. The body is renewed. Fair weather comes again. But not for long. Nothing changes so much as the weather. And always, the hurricanes, the droughts, the floods, the thunderstorms, the twisters, the invisible radiations of happenstance, riding the jet streams of energy through the skies, continents, and oceanic currents of human sentience — the winds of human self-thus descending and rising between hot and high, and cold and low, like a hawk gyring through shifting thermal regions of brightness and shadow.

We are not only profoundly dependent on the "weather," but the weather is profoundly dependent on us. Together with all the other species that exist in this particular mixture of gasses and electromagnetic radiations called "earth's atmosphere," we co-create the weather, and so insure our common survival. Without all of us there would be no weather. Without weather, we would not be. How rich the idea! That we are, in fact, weather systems whose purpose is to maintain the survival cycle of summer, fall, winter, and spring.

As the weather changes from season to season, direction to direction, so changes human nature, always in tune, always in cooperation with self-thus. And as the seasonal weather changes, disturbances occur: highs and lows, inwardness and outwardness, droughts and floods, hots and colds, squalls and doldrums, earthquakes and healing rains. In human terms, these disturbances are like complexes, crises, upheavals, dreams, and other intense experiences that determine motivation, behavior, personality, and character.

The weather shield of today, June 5, is warm and windy. Dust devils swarm across the valley and there's a tornado watch in western Nevada. Spring came as a changeling, a shape-shifter, a trickster wearing a coat of many colors. Ten times the average amount of rain and snow. Ten times the usual number of clouds. Wild flowers came forth with unbelievable force. Bird and reptile populations exploded. Insects thickened the air. The shield of spring has indeed been rich and strange.

Even so, the spring shield of human nature is rich and strange, a harlequin clown, a walking, talking coyote. The old forms cannot contain this birth force. Today it is fiercely hot. Tomorrow it will snow. Then the big winds will come. The people know what is happening because it is happening within them. These are the pangs of labor. Spring is here. Tomorrow will be summer.

AS THE WORLD TURNS

> Within the circles of our lives
> we dance the circles of the years,
> the circles of the seasons
> within the cycles of the moon
> within the circles of the seasons,
> the circles of our reasons
> within the cycles of the moon. . . .
> The circles turn,
> each giving into each, into all.
> Only music keeps us here.
>
> — Wendell Berry, "The Peace of Wild Things"

By the time humans arrived a few million years ago, life on earth had long since acquired an infinite number of interconnected, related awarenesses that cooperated with the environment to provide optimum conditions for survival and completion. Humans were no different than the others. We all lived within the laws of nature, or we did not live. And the laws of nature lived within all life, within all life awareness, within all consciousness of unitary being. Among humans, the self was aware of its "thusness." This awareness made it possible for our species to survive, to live with all our relatives and to join them in the song of life. Despite gigantic upheavals, sudden appearances, unaccountable disappearances, and mass extinctions through millions of years of human evolutionary history, that song never died. The relationship of human to its only home holds fast.

It is not far-fetched, then, to suppose that for many thousands of years in the temperate regions, the human version of self-thus wore the four aspects of its home: a summer mask, a fall mask, a winter mask, and a spring mask. These masks were both distinct and blended, even as the seasons came and went, and were directly and personally related to natural phenomena, the cycling of the earth, the motion and relative positions of the sun and moon, and the balancing dance of day and night.

Obviously, the human species would never have survived without this relationship to the seasons. Yet we have come to a point where this obvious truism has lost some of its veracity in the mass consciousness of the modern human world. Life in technological cages and increasing ignorance of natural processes lull us into thinking that we no longer depend on the earth for our survival, that technology is our protector and savior, and that the four faces of human nature don't exist.

To humans, the seasonal masks are ways of perceiving ourselves and our environment. We look through the eyes of the mask of summer and we see summer reflected in ourselves. Through summer eyes we see what we were, are, and will be. Likewise, we perceive ourselves through the eyes of fall, winter and spring. Like the seasons themselves, space/time is blended into any one of the seasonal masks we wear.[3] The summer perception retains a memory of past summers, in the genes of all its children, that determines the present summer and predicts future summers. And so on: "the circles turn,/ each giving into each, into all."

Moving from season to season, however, is not usually as abrupt as putting on another mask. The dynamics of the comings and goings of human seasons require that there be an almost infinite number of seasonal variations. Much of the time the masks are superimposed, blended, shading toward or away from the archetype of any given season. Elements of the summer linger on into the fall. Elements of the fall persist into winter. Elements of winter shadow the spring. And elements of the spring mingle with the summer.

Likewise, elements of any given season are found in its opposite: summer in winter, or winter in summer, or fall in spring, or spring in fall. Today (June 2), the local weatherman agreed. In his forecast for tomorrow he joked, "Well, folks, we're back into winter." At any time any given season contains elements of the other three, and, in fact, wouldn't even exist if not for the other three. This interdependency of the seasons is not a fanciful notion. Without all four, life in the temperate zones (as we know it) would not exist.

A metaphorical construct of a complex life system, such as *homo sapiens*, with optimal chances for survival on the planet Earth, would first of all be capable of cooperative oneness with the natural environment. On paper, human and environment might look like two superimposed circles moving from oneness to separation back to oneness, dancing a mutually regenerating electromagnetic *pas de deux* from summer to fall to winter to spring. It would be quite difficult at times to determine which circle was which. For purposes of identification, this system of dancing circles might be called human nature, or the human version of "self-thus."

A second characteristic of this life system would be the ability of the species to grow, to flourish, to sense its environment, to defend itself from predation, to copulate instinctively, to learn by imitation, to inherently grow toward its adult form (i.e. the summer shield of human nature). A third characteristic would be the ability of the species to possess self-consciousness and a memory both personal and generational, to be aware of what it is doing, to experience itself from "within" itself in such a way as to be able to correct and direct itself (i.e., the fall shield of human nature). A fourth characteristic would be the ability of the species to conserve resources, to survive through hard times and retain its evolutionary form, to expend energy in useful interrelationships with the environment, and to control its adult form in order to nurture its own kind (the winter shield of human nature). A fifth characteristic of such a system would be its ability to regenerate itself, heal itself, and be drawn to the Spirit of which the universe is an expression (the spring shield of human nature).

Take a further step. We *are* that anthropomorphic metaphor. Quite literally, we *are* the physical, psychological, mental, and spiritual stuff of the seasons. Sometimes we wear the summer face of the child. Sometimes we wear the fall face of the passageway from child to adult. Sometimes we wear the mature winter face of the adult. Sometimes we wear the spring face of regeneration. Usually these faces blend with each other, like summer blends with fall, fall with winter, winter with spring, etc. But no matter how well-blended, at any given time one face tends to predominate. That face is the seasonal shield.

ANCIENT ECOPSYCHOLOGY

> For what is inside you is what is outside of you and the one who fashions you on the outside is the one who shaped the inside of you. And what you see outside of you, you see inside of you, it is visible and it is your garment.
>
> — Terry Tempest Williams, *Refuge*

The four shields is an ancient paradigm with psychological implications. It posits the circle of human self-thus within the context of nature and shows how the outside of the circle reflects the inside of the circle, and vice versa. It may be that in the earliest times, there was no human sense of differentiation between inside and outside, or as Jung put it, between "subject" and "object." Nature's four shields were conceived to be equal to — the same as — the four shields of human nature.

This non-differentiation of human and nature gave rise to "primitive" "applied psychologies" based on the seasonal changes of nature. These are known to modern anthropologists as "rites of passage," or "rites of initiation." In their earliest forms, these rites mimicked the initiation and passage of the seasons. The gods and goddesses of vegetation who participated in these rites died and were reborn again as thousands upon thousands of years passed and successive human generations inherited the land. To secure the well being and survival of our kind, we imitated the seasonal cycles of our gods and goddesses. We initiated each new generation in passage rites that insured the growth of human self-thus to its full capacity — thus we also insured the return of the seasons.

Life depended on the return of life. Human health was based on seasonal health. Seasonal health was based on human health. Anthropocentric? Of course, but nevertheless true as far as our survival was concerned. Only when we were able to grow into fullness through our own seasons, were we in harmony with our environment. When we survived and prospered nature itself was healed.[4]

THE IMMUNE SYSTEM

> If, then, we would restore mankind by truly Indian, botanic, magnetic, or natural means, let us first be as simple and well as Nature ourselves, dispel the clouds which hang over our brows, and take up a little life into our pores.
>
> — Thoreau, *Walden*

Our primitive ancestors had their own conception of the human immune system. It bore little resemblance to the modern medical model. To them, the physical body was only one of the shields of self-thus — the summer. Not just the body but the psyche or soul (fall), mind (winter) and spirit (spring) were vulnerable to disease. Healing took place on four levels, each of them of equal importance to the well being of the whole that was human self-thus.

Like all natural life, humans passed through seasons, transitions, passages, as they fulfilled their destiny. The journey began as the body (summer) undertook the memnonic passage (fall) to maturity (winter). The completion of this passage led to the rejuvenation of spring. The spirit of spring reentered the body, bringing with it the psychological, mental, and spiritual health of the other shields.

This particular depiction of human self-thus considered how the body (summer) grows by remembering (fall) and learning (winter) how to reach spirit (spring) so that it can return to a body growing by remembering. The body cycles through seasons of initiation/transition (fall) so that it can attain the maturity of mind that leads to enlightenment — so that the body, and the whole, can be fructified.

Nature itself can be diseased, the carrier of viruses and bacteria, the bearer of famine, flood, and drought. So the body. In order for human self-thus to survive, it must follow, interact and cooperate with that of which it is made. The seasonal stuff of human nature requires that a diseased body (summer) contract itself into the inwardness of memory and self-consciousness (fall) so that it can attain clarity of mind, will and action (winter). Clarity of mind then leads to the healing impulses of spring. These impulses will enliven the body/child and healing will be done.

The immune system of our ancestors encompassed four kinds of vulnerability to disease. The body was vulnerable, and so were the other four. Acting in concert, the shields defended the self against malaise. If one of the shields was weak, or absent, or over-zealous, the chances for survival were reduced. A healthy shield system responded freely and fluidly to growth-events, and was not afraid to enter the psychological passage. A healthy adolescent did not turn away from the portals of maturity. A healthy grown-up accepted the conditions of aging and looked forward to deeper initiation into the mysteries of the spirit.

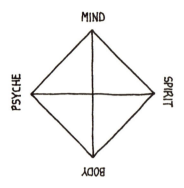

THE IMMUNE SYSTEM OF THE SELF

NEUROSIS

> I can't remember
> where this happened but I think
> it was late summer when everything
> is full of fire and rounding to fruition
> and whatever doesn't,
> or resists,
> must lie like a field of dark water under
> the pulling moon,
> tossing and tossing.
>
> — Mary Oliver, "Music"

Neurosis (as a phenomena, not as a psychoanalytic concept) was known to "primitive" people. Certain individuals exhibited signs of neurosis at one time or another in their lives. Sometimes the causes of the neurosis were known, sometimes they were not. Psychological sickness could be caused by ailments in the body shield, the psychological shield, the mind shield, or the spirit shield. Usually, the body, or the child shield, was suspect. Some kind of sickness resided in the flesh and bone, or the child had foundered in the swamps of the dark shield of psyche the soul — or the passageway between the body and the soul (between the child and the psyche) was chocked with debris.

In order to be healthy, human self-thus must successfully negotiate the passage between summer and winter. This passage is crucial. Without it there will be no survival. The body must be initiated by the soul if the body is to survive as mind. The child must be initiated by the fall shield if the people are to be enlightened.

Even so, in order for nature to be healthy, summer must be initiated by the fall so that it can survive the winter. Fall must be initiated by winter if its shrinking body is to expand in the spring. Winter must be initiated by the spring so that the mind can be enfleshed, so that the elder can be the child. And spring must be initiated by summer so that light can become darkness, and outwardness inwardness.

Neurosis and psychosis can be defined as deriving from incomplete initiations ("passages"), not only between summer and winter, but between fall and spring, winter and summer, and spring and fall. These incomplete initiations cause shields to be exaggerated, weak, or repressed. Neuroses and psychoses arise.

Psychotherapists are undoubtedly correct in pointing out the importance of giving safe expression to primal urges (summer shield). When these instinctual needs are denied, the child persona loses the power and direction required to navigate the dark waters of the psycho-mnemonic fall shield. Initiation is incomplete. Adult maturity (winter) and enlightenment (spring) are never fully attained. The child "tosses and tosses under the pulling moon."

Inherent weaknesses in the body shield, like inherent weakness in nature, can be genetically transmitted. Our distant ancestors probably understood this. They certainly understood that psychological sickness was sometimes related to bodily sickness. They may not have understood "hormone" or "neurotransmitter," but they were familiar with maps of psycho-organic pathways between body and psyche. They discerned the same pathways in nature. They lived in the world of the physical but were completely at home in the "psychosphere."[5] It was important to teach the young that they had more than a body.

The fall shield of human nature is a neurotransmitter. It sends, receives, modifies, reroutes impulses between itself and the body. In this switching yard, the neurochemical body (the physical) is transformed into an intricate web of self-consciousness and memory. From this web emerges something quite the opposite of the body — the power of thought, form, self-control, and appropriate action. In humans, no two switching yards are exactly alike. The roads, tracks and trails from the body to the psyche and back again are breathtakingly intricate. In their workmanship can be seen the influence of the mind and spirit shields.[6]

WHOLENESS

> Air, fire, water, and
> Earth is our dancing place now.
>
> — Gary Snyder, "All the Spirit Powers Went to their Dancing Place"

If there were a measure of "mental health," it would involve the ability of individuals to grow into the fullness of each season — that is, the ability to fully become, or enact, the contents of each shield.

The summer shields of basically healthy persons would be athletic, earthy in a physical sense, instinctive, playful, emotional, sensual, innocently erotic, with a strongly developed sense of the child within. There would be a good deal of skin-skin contact with the earth.

The fall shield of such persons would be capable of deep introspection, would crave solitude in the psychosphere, feel deeply and empathetically, love self, possess a conscience, and dream the dreams of the sacred ancestors. Such persons would be severed from their childhood. Having internalized their mother and father through rites of initiation, they would have adopted a greater mother and father. They would be people of inner character and possess a soul.

Their winter shield would be capable of mature judgment, self-control, appropriate action, marriage, parenting, working, with a strong sense of community and family. Actions would be in tune with the mind of nature as evidenced by the natural laws with which self cooperated. Social behavior would be marked by responsibility, diplomacy, foresight, and tact. The biggest concern would be the welfare of the children.

The spring shield would be imaginative, creative, inventive, spiritual, capable of awe and reverence. All life would be seen as holy, sacred, and saturated with signs of spirit. The springs of inspiration and regeneration would flow through every event. The experience of nature would include the mystical and non-ordinary.

More often than not, most of these attributes can be found in "primitive" people. Living in close proximity to the nature of which they are composed, they do not entertain fears or doubts regarding separation from it. Such well-roundedness is not so common in the modern age, although there are many who, like their archaic ancestors, have developed into their full potential. Such persons are capable of survival in the fullest sense of the word.

THE MODERN IMMUNE SYSTEM AND THE BIG LIE

> For man has closed himself up, till he sees all things through narrow chinks of his cavern.
>
> — William Blake, "Marriage of Heaven and Hell"

Although the origins of the Big Lie are too complex to address here, the fact is that somewhere along the way our ancestors gradually lost the tendency to grow into the full maturity of human nature. Our development was arrested at some point between childhood and adolescence and we found ourselves on a detour in the developmental process that has resulted in the loss of our relationship to the four faces of nature.[7] We stopped growing into full adulthood. We stopped taking responsibility for the condition of the earth and of ourselves. As the centuries passed, the illusion that we were separate from nature, and at war with our essential nature, grew stronger, even as we grew more childlike, more dependent on technobiotic wombs that promised safety and security from the howling cold.[8]

Many seek the roots of the Big Lie, for they hope to identify its causes and apply the cure. Some claim the Lie is the result of our ancestors' ancient decision to settle down in one place, till and sow the land, domesticate animals, and "own" property. In this view, "I have" gradually became as important as "I live."[9] Others point their finger at the evolution of language, the proliferation of symbols, the linguistic phenomenon of displacement, or the invention of historical time.[10] Still others hold ancient patriarchy, or ancient matriarchy, responsible. And the psychoanalysts and others reason that the development of laws, institutions, and social values shaped the human psyche into complexes and neuroses.[11]

Some say it all started with Adam and Eve. They were expelled from the Garden of Eden because they had sinned. They had eaten of the knowledge of good and evil and Jehovah decided to banish them for all time. After that, they had to labor and sweat and suffer the pains of childbirth and child rearing — and they had to die. No longer would they be immortal. No longer could they live the life of innocent childhood, sucking blissfully on the tits of mother nature.

It was their banishment that surprises me, the forced separation from the beautiful garden of nature. Surely the great and only god must have had something else in mind. To bump them out of Paradise because they disobeyed his orders, because, like healthy children, they were tempted by the very thing that was forbidden? There sat the cookie jar up on the second shelf. Dad said "don't touch." All they wanted was one cookie from that jar — just to know what was good and what was evil. They found out what evil was, all right. Evil was disobeying Dad's orders.

The knowledge of the difference between good and evil, as the Biblical account maintains, could have had a great deal to do with what we call the Big Lie. This lie may have begun with the notion that there are some things in nature that are good and some things that are evil. This relatively innocent idea, however, developed into fixed doctrines regarding what was sacred and what was profane. The quaint idea that the body was corruptible and mortal and therefore profane and that someday we would be free of it is doubtless one of the main roots of the lie.

Banishment from our earthly paradise because we are sinners is not a particularly sane view of human self-thus. But the truth is that somehow we banished ourselves and all those attempts to get back into the Garden have only resulted in a deeper estrangement from our own nature. We seem to have forgotten that the Garden is within us, as well as without, and that we never left it in the first place. Every day the sun shines on the Garden. Every night the moon teases the roots. Summers come with riotous life, dying back in the fall, holding on in the cold wind of winter, and budding with renewed vigor in the spring. The plants and animals that we named are there — or what's left of them. The Garden seems to have fallen into disrepair. It must be that we are walking around in it without being aware that it is all around us and in us and that in the form of self-thus, it — we— are immortal.

Today we are raised in cultures without passage rites into adulthood. Our own attempts to confirm the attainment of maturity have gone largely unrecognized. Still we are expected to find our places in the sun, our sources of health and healing, and to make sense of our life stories. We grope our way through the seasonal transitions and crises of our lives and try to find meaning in them. The human environment, with its incredible array of technological umbilicals, has become a reality unto itself.

The true reality, that we are, in fact, nodes in the vast network of nature, has been overlooked, ignored, forgotten. There is little to tempt us to remember. And only rarely does it occur to us that our separateness from ourselves, from that which we truly are, is the root cause of our dis-ease. Only rarely do we sense that a deeper harmony is possible, a balance, a wholeness, a relatedness that comes from living a life attuned to the cyclical and transitional seasons of self-thus.

Even as we live with the illusion of separation, the reality of non-separation dictates our days and ways. The sun rises and sets on the empty desert and the crowded city alike. The snow falls on the great ranges and our tiny flower boxes. The night creeps into the canyons and our bedrooms. We continue to be born, to be children, to enter adolescence, to lose our virginity, to bear children, to marry, to parent, to divorce, to work to survive, to enter middle age, to go through menopause, to pass our climacterics, to become crones and elders, to die. The essence of our self-thus has not changed from the earliest of human time. Our genes are still composed of the original DNA. Our seasons pass. We are like all our brothers and sisters on this earth. We come into this world, we fluoresce, we mature, we decay, we die.

Modern human immune systems look much the same as they did thousands of years ago. But the shields don't seem to be as strong as they used to be. Nowadays, we see more damage done than in the days of yore. There are more of us to contract and carry disease. The crowded conditions in which many of us live breed a sicknesses of epidemic proportions. Huge numbers of us grow up in broken, abusive, or loveless homes. We grow up without passage rites and take our places as adults without even knowing what it means to be mature. The simplicity of "primitive" life has been replaced by a complexity of laws, machines, technologies, to which we must render daily obedience or we will not survive. Distracted from the truth of who and what we are, our shields take some pretty good whacks. Without a doubt, they are more threatened, even as nature is more threatened, in these challenging times. The innocent little boy that I was grew up without rites of passage into manhood. The raw Christian kid had to initiate himself. This process took twenty years. Even now, I can't be sure the job is completely done. But I was able to step into the dark enough times to finally get a handle on the meaning of self-love. By age 58, my shields are battered but reasonably intact. Others have taken beatings beside which my feeble attempts at initiation pale. Some of the life stories we have heard in our elders' councils have curled our hair. Stabbings, beatings, rapes, suicidal depressions, tragic accidents, hate blows, nightmares, failures — major blows to the shield system — somehow endured, lived with, and even made over into what the American Indians call "medicine power."

Yes, our shields are battered. Yes, some of them seem battered beyond recognition. Yes, many of them seem to run on fumes. But all is not lost. Large numbers of us have survived the onslaught. Our shields are covered with initiation cuts and we are the better for it. We know now what our culture did not tell us, that the path of summer leads to fall, that the fall inevitably succumbs to winter, and that winter cannot hold back the spring.

We may be neurotic; we may be unbalanced now and then; we may have our quirks; we may not always be in tune with nature or our essence; but we are reasonably intact. We may have unknowingly followed the initiatory path of nature, but we learned and grew anyway. Generally, we feel ready to face the consequences of our actions.

We're not afraid of our bodies; we like to use them, especially in the outdoors. We don't mind being children, appreciating life from a child's point of view. Hence we are playful and innocently erotic and quick to vent our emotions. No doubt we sustained injuries in childhood. Terrible as these woundings were, we can still experience childish wonder.

We may be a little weird, but we've come to love and accept ourselves regardless of our pain. The path to this self-love wasn't easy. We had to find it in the darkness of our adolescent selves, in feelings like guilt, shame, self-disgust, boredom, anxiety, fear. Ever so gradually, we disengaged from our mother and father and began to piece together a face inside the hall of ancestral memory, the face of an inner man or woman, who symbolized this self-love. We watched ourselves suffering and had compassion on ourselves. We learned empathy with the plight of others here, at the wailing wall, and experienced the strange feelings of forgiveness. Nature haunted us with dark shadows and deep memories hidden in the shrinking leaf. Death came to us like a feeling.

We may be a little strange, but we're basically mature. We care for our children, our mates, our friends, our neighbors, our neighborhood, our town, our world. We have taken roles of responsibility within it. We are willing and able to work hard at whatever necessary task is set before us. We are, as a rule, capable of rational and appropriate action. We do not tend to overindulge our "little boy" or "little girl." We look ahead, so that we can plan ahead, always aware how proper planning means being in synch with the natural order. We observe and celebrate the seasonal passages of our lives and the natural world. We are willing to undergo deeper initiations into the mystery of aging, including our own death.

We may be pretty dense at times, but we are, after all, reasonably enlightened. Some of us would like to be more so. We are acquainted with the Muse. Some of us have an intimate relationship with her, or him. Maturity has brought the desire to look into the life of things, and when we look carefully we can see the spirit infusing all forms self-thus. We sense the spirit within. We know that when we die the spirit will bring us to spring. Hence, we are visionaries, and we seek to find our way to the sacred mountains of the heart. We know the sun will rise on a new tomorrow.

Now, to get the whole picture of the modern immune system, put it all together into one discrete unit of human self-thus — you or me. Surround this dear soul with the slings and arrows of modern life, with the incredible realities of the technobiotic age. Watch the shields go up and down, watch the wheel spin.

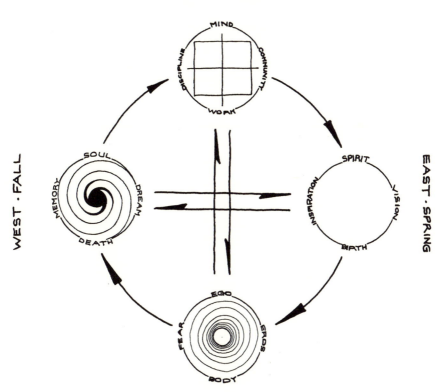

THE FOUR SHIELDS

ENDNOTES: THE FOUR SHIELDS OF HUMAN NATURE

[1] The English word, "nature," is one of those crazy abstractions that must be used within an expression in order to make sense. The Oxford Dictionary of English Etymology lists these definitions: "essential qualities or innate character *of*; vital powers *of*; inherent power dominating one's action; creative and regulative power in the world; material world." For the purposes of this discussion, all of these definitions are implied, particularly "inherent power dominating [human] action." This same "power" dominates *all* action.

[2] Or vector and velocity.

[3] In primitive cultures, "Past, present, and future are conceived of as cyclic phenomena, and the pursuit of the cycle . . . remains subjectively sustaining." Stanley Diamond, *In Search of the Primitive* (New Brunswick: Transaction Publishers, 1993), p. 66.

[4] "And as they . . . explained the fluctuations of growth and decay, or reproduction and dissolution, by the marriage, the death, and the rebirth or revival of the gods, their religious or rather magical dramas turned in great measure on these themes . . . To them the principle of life and fertility, whether animal or vegetable, was one and indivisible. To live and to cause to live, to eat food and to beget children, these were the primary wants of men in the past, and they will be the primary wants of men in the future so long as the world lasts. Other things may be added to enrich and beautify human life, but unless these wants are first satisfied, humanity itself must cease to exist. These . . . were what men chiefly sought to procure by the performance of magical rites for the regulation of the seasons." Sir James Frazer, *The Golden Bough: A Study in Magic and Religion* (New York: Macmillan, 1963), pp. 377-8.

[5] Rupert Sheldrake's work on morphogenetic fields draws a relationship between human memory and the memory or electromagnetic resonance of natural fields. "Field" is defined as "something" that exists around an object that produces it": ". . . the structure of fields depends on what has happened before. They [fields] represent a kind of pooled or collective memory of the species." Lovelock defines memory as "the capacity to store, recall and compare information in order to self-correct and self-direct the system." Lyall Watson refers to memory as "the self-referencing capacity of a system, its identity." See *Earthmind: Communicating with the Living World of Gaia*, Paul Devereax, John Steele and David Kubrin (Rochester, VT: Destiny Books, 1989). For our purposes,

the "psychosphere" refers simply to the psyche of nature, an inwardness that surrounds an object.

⁶ What is commonly called "neurosis" can often be a unique kind of gift, especially if the shield system is reasonably healthy.

⁷ How long did our oneness with nature last? If we reach way back into prehistory we will find the remains of cultures quite similar to the American Indians or the Australian Aborigines, peoples with sophisticated mythologies, rites, and value systems. Despite their post-Christian reputation for savagery, our sacred great-ancestors nurtured their kind and our species for at least 50,000 years. One might reason that, as far as species survival was concerned, the "primitive" types did pretty well. Look at what the "civilized" era has brought us. How can we continue without a home? We *are* our home.

⁸ It is possible that our shift in attitude to our home was, and is, a kind of evolutionary defect, a built-in self-destruct mechanism over which we have very little power. It is also possible that this alteration in perspective represents a "dangerous opportunity" for us to readjust our bifocals, to dispel the deadly illusion, and to recognize that human and nature are and have always been one and the same.

⁹ The brilliant work of Paul Shepard has conceptualized several shifts in thought and perspective that gradually occurred among our archaic ancestors, primarily as the result of agriculture and the domestication of animals. Paul Shepard, *Nature and Madness* (San Francisco: Sierra Club, 1982), pp. 19-46.

¹⁰ Loren Eisley, *The Invisible Pyramid: A Naturalist Analyzes the Rocket Century* (New York: Scribners, 1970).

¹¹ Sigmund Freud, *The Future of an Illusion,* Ed. James Strachy (Garden City: Doubleday, 1946).

THE SUMMER SHIELD OF HUMAN NATURE

> Oh, hours of childhood,
> when behind the symbols was more than merely
>   the past,
> and before us was not the future. Sure, we were
>   growing,
> and often we strove to grow up sooner, half
> for the sake of those who had nothing but being
>   grown-up.
> Yet we were content in our going alone
> with things that last, and we stood there in the breach
> between the world and the plaything, on a place
> founded from the first for a pure event.
>   — Rainer Maria Rilke, *Duino Elegies,* IV

> I have to acknowledge that the sea is a cup of death and the land is a stained altar stone. We the living are survivors huddled on flotsam, living on jetsam. We are escapees. We wake in terror, eat in hunger, sleep with a mouthful of blood.
>   — Annie Dillard, *Pilgrim at Tinker Creek*

Before we get further involved in applied methods and processes, we need to move away from the main theme and examine the variations. The whole can be known through an understanding of its parts.

The time has come to get more intimate with the summer shield of "human nature," especially that which pertains to psycho-ecology, the ancient underpinnings of human health. We will have to take a good look at the summer and how it is manifested in human experience, culture and mythology, and how deeply it influences our lives.

Leave the house and take a walk with me along the creek above our little town on a midmorning, just after the sun has entered the sign of Cancer. You might not want to wear a lot of clothes. Shoes are optional, though the ground sizzles. We can always stop and dangle our feet in the cold, clear flow of the creek. As we walk we'll notice how the web of life, of which we are a part, has responded to the long, hot days and brief, warm nights.

No ignoring the feeling of swarming restlessness in the air, in the bright green foliage, even in the creek, which is cresting with the force of melting snows from the mountains high above. The world is alive with instinctual life. Like a swarm of bees we are a part of that life, raging toward a completion of which our present form is but the faintest suggestion.

> I don't know what it is about fecundity that so appalls. I suppose it is the teeming evidence that birth and growth, which we value, are ubiquitous and blind, that life itself is so astonishingly cheap, that nature is as careless as it is bountiful, and that with extravagance goes a crushing waste that will one day include our own cheap lives . . . . I can play the devil's advocate and call it rank fecundity — and say that it's hell that's a-poppin.[1]

The fittest will continue to propagate themselves. The weaker will succumb to the "law of the jungle" and become part of the cellular structure of whatever creature chooses to devour them. An adult female lacewing will devour every egg she lays (a few escaping by chance). Larvae emerging from eggs *inside the body* of the adult gall gnat immediately begin to devour their parent. Hunger. Hunger to live, hunger to copulate, propagate, replicate, be born. According to Edwin Way Teale, a lone aphid breeding "unmolested" for one year, would give birth to offspring which, stacked end on end, would extend themselves 2500 *light years* into space.[2] Ten percent of all the world's species are parasitic insects: scales, beetles, borers, weevils, flies, thrips, wasps, cutworms, lice, skippers, mosquitos, gnats, mites, and mealy bugs, not to mention flukes, leeches, and worms. The mindless body of nature froths and ravens — and survives.

As we walk we see the evidence of the fundamental flight or fight instincts governing the survival of self-thus — the lizard running for cover, the robber fly impaling its victim in midair, the mantis gorging itself on carpenter ants, the ground squirrel running for cover. These patterns of behavior, stored in the genes, insure the survival of the species. Let's not forget the humans in this scene, the frightened, visceral, unpredictable, wily, human animals. We belong here as well. Like the other animals, we feed on the abundance of the web in which we are enmeshed, and are equipped with the same instincts: prey, defend, flee, freeze.

As we labor uphill, panting and sweating in the hot sun, we're reminded of the "withness" of our bodies. Truly, summer is the time of the physical body of things. At no other season is it more apparent. All are young, raging to live, to become mature, to ripen. Like a child, physical existence is innocent, heedless, seemingly without a care. Herein lies the paradox of summer. The innocent body of the child must survive in a world of violence and destruction. You can see this paradox in the play of children. Let's play war. Let's be cruel to the new kid on the block. Bang bang, you're dead.

But the same kinds of play take place in the animal worlds as well. Coyote cubs and lion kittens pounce on each other in mock kill. Chipmunk young play at standing sentry for the colony. The young instinctively know that the summer world is not benign. They seek safety in home and family, especially the mother.

Death may be lurking in the shadows. Monsters stalk the land. Wars are being waged. Blood is being spilled.

Blood — another central metaphor for the summer. For if there is abundant death here, there is also abundant life, with many shades in between. The blood is healthy, or anemic, or strong in killer cells, or weak in killer cells, or deficient, or polluted, or poisonous, or dried up. Whatever its condition, it plays host to life that is abundant or crippled, healthy or sick, commensal, or parasitical. And there, amid all these conditions, qualities, and types of bloodiness, birth and death are playing hand in hand, like children in the Garden of Eden. There is a kind of psychology here. Good blood, bad blood, hot blood, cold blood, sweet blood, poisonous blood, inherited blood — as though the very stuff that infuses us with life can melt into the cells of self-consciousness, feeling, and memory, forming character, personality, and individual uniqueness.

We stop, panting, and look down at the creek. That roaring thing isn't water; it's a crooked vein of blood running through the earth, teasing the roots of things with the fulfillment of living flesh. Here in the high desert, the importance of earth blood to the continuance of life could never be clearer. Even as the web of interconnection wells up with fluid, secretions, saliva, the sun is sucking it dry. But the blood of summer is not conscious of its deathwardness. It beats in the veins with the headlong song of life, with the simmering 98.6 of summer.

The breeze touches sweat on the back of our necks and we shiver with delicious coolness, reminded of another aspect of the summer body. Flesh. The senses. Sensation. Physical pleasure or pain. Michael Cohen has identified over 49 "sensory fulfillments" created by the interface of natural and human.[3] The skin itself is a kind of ego that hungers to excite itself.[4] Summer is well characterized by the skin surfaces of things, the outermost layers, the ponds and soils covering the naked self-thus. Summer is what takes place in, on and among all those surfaces — all the bendings, swayings, shimmerings, touchings, all that push and pull of sheer palpability.

Summer's flesh harbors the erotic impulse, the play and interplay of sensuality and desire that insures the propagation of the species. The coming of warmth requires the removal of winter's clothing. The flesh is revealed, and becomes the subject of desire. The love poems of Dafydd ap Gwilym, a Welsh poet of the 14th century, typify the popular attitude found in May Day and summer solstice ceremonies celebrated all over medieval Europe:

> Is it true, girl that I love,
> That you do not desire birch, the strong growth of summer?
> Be not a nun in spring,

> Asceticism is not as good as a bush.
> As for the warrant of ring and habit,
> A green dress would ordain better.
> Come to the spreading birch,
> To the religion of the trees and cuckoo.[5]

A modern poet of the 20th century, has her own way of putting it:

> I will be you be the flower
> You have found my root you are the rain
> I will be boat and you the rower
> You rock you toss me you are the sea
> How be steady earth that's now a flood
> The root's the oar's afloat where's blown our bud
> We will be desert pure salt the seed
> Burn radiant sex born scorpion need
>
> — May Swenson, "Untitled"

The child demands to possess the object that gratifies its need to eat, drink and multiply. Morality does not exist. Instinct, urge, desire, lust — such as these take precedence over questions of right and wrong. If the body hungers, it must be fed. Anything standing in the way of attainment of the needed or desired object is to be ignored, eluded, battered through, destroyed, or tricked by secrecy or fabrication. Nor are feelings of guilt or culpability a part of the summer shield. Even as the fox gets into the hen house or the raccoon into the back pack, so the human child gets into the pantry. The summer contains all the goodies stacked on the shelves. Only in the memory of fall come such feelings as guilt or conscience.

Daylight rules. Hence all seems revealed. But exactly what is revealed? The light cannot penetrate the masks worn by everyone in this masquerade. The light illuminates the skin, not the nakeder body. We see life, the body alive and breathing. We don't see the invisible veins of death running through it, or the psyche of it, or the idea of it, or the spirit hiding within. When daylight rules, Maya rules. Illusion rules. The body appears as all in all, strong, flexible, and seemingly invincible. In the summer shield the body rules the mind, the soul, and the spirit. It calls to us with the pull of gravity: the texture of dirt, sand and stones, the pungency of green foliage, the flesh of grass, and the scatter of birds, and we cannot help but respond and call it beautiful, and accord it innocence, and give it to the growing, wondering children.

> Early early
> That simple time
> When eyes knew
> The shine of seals;
> Ditches at noon
> Swarmed with stars;
> The hills hummed;
> The moon came out
> Bright on the shells
> Wet from the water
> Of slacking waves.
> O how could early
> Otherwise be?
>
> — Theodore Roethke[6]

 Children all over the world play the same games, share a similar sense of the world. They all respond to love and are afraid of hate. They all hide from danger behind their mother's skirts. They are all innocently capable of being contrary, nasty, sly. Yet the song of light hums like honey on every child's lips. How can there be a world of homogeneity? The body is of many parts, and the body is all. The god worshipped by summer's children is the harlequin god, the goddess of license, the pipe player, the love dart archer, the deities who cannot keep from falling in love with mortals. Life is a circus of variegated delights, a super-market, a shopping mall where gods and humans intermingle and play.

 The essence of human summer is characterized by the sentence, "I have." Like the triumphant sun in the sky, the ego stands in full possession of the field. Contained in ego are the primal, reactive emotions: rage (fight) and fear (flight or freeze), and that complex surrounding sources of nurture, protection, gratification, and the ego's need to possess. Though science may not allow us to assign "emotions" to any other creature but humans, the child suspects otherwise. A yellowjacket wasp, angered by the swipe of her hand, stings her in a kind of revenge. A kit, separated from the mother fox, whines and cries like a lost child. The little girl understands. The little fox is afraid. Surely, all the children of summer recognize these reactive emotions in other species. Now the roaring of the creek drowns out all else. Listen carefully to its song. Can you hear the sounds of rage, fear, lust, happiness, and loss?

 The time has come to turn back. Our footsteps retrace the dusty path. Big sage exhales a pungent, smoldering odor. Seed tops are beginning to form. The brush crackles with the rattle and hop of lustful grasshoppers. A jackrabbit, flushed from cover by our wandering footsteps, explodes in a fearful dash for the safety of a distant copse. A kingfisher flashes like a twisted thread through the cottonwoods along the creek. A robber fly clings to a sunburned stone. Red paintbrush and yellow encelia border a copse of wildrose, its veiled pink petals withering into swollen hips. A copulating pair of blue belly fence lizards lie as still as the stone upon which they pleasure themselves.

Let's detour over to the spot where the creek is captured by a small reservoir. From a distance we can hear the laughter of children. Bikes, lunch sacks, T-shirts, line the path. At the edge of the water, Paiute kids are swimming and diving in the pool. Whooping and hollering in their king of the mountain game, they don't notice our approach. We stand and watch for a while, remembering our own childhood, the endless days of summer.

How easy to forget that we are still that child we once were, that summer was never lost, even in the deepest winter. Is it not a fact that, in the death-trance of winter, all living things also retain an inner image, a memory, an imprint of their childhood? Could it be that winter's desire for the ardent, physical body of youth actually gives birth to spring? Could it be that childhood recollected in the tranquility of maturity actually gives birth to poetry?

SUMMER

In ancient times the arrival of summer was associated with the advent of irrational and childlike (as opposed to rational and adult) behavior, and was duly celebrated by orgies, games, contests, and festivals presided over by or dedicated to gods and goddesses or heros and heroines. In *Le Chevalier de la Charrette* by Chretien de Troyes, during the May festival of Ascension the queen is won in combat by a prince from a land of eternal youth.[7] An early Welsh version of

"Trystan" has Esyllt, wife of March ap Meirchion, elope with Trystan to the woods of Kelyddon. She is attended by her maid, Golweg Hafddydd ("aspect of summer's day"). While the two lovers feast on each other, March seeks out the vile seducer with his army. Brought to justice at King Arthur's court, Trystan agrees to a compromise. March shall have Esyllt when the trees are leafless. Trystan shall have Esyllt when the trees have leaves.[8]

SUMMER & WINTER, LOCKED IN
STRUGGLE ON THE WHEEL OF
THE CELTIC YEAR

There are many variants to this old story. We know it so well, with an ancient, bodily sensing. The basic plot goes like this: winter and summer are at odds for the self. Summer will steal her away from winter. But then winter will steal her back. And no matter how greatly we might desire the innocent freedom and plenitude of summer's Eden, we must inevitably accept the yoke of winter. Once a year we can go to the summer land of leaves and childhood. But we can't stay there. A battle will have to be waged. Summer will lose and we will fall from our innocent state. We will have to go back to our leaflessness. But that doesn't mean that we have lost our youth. All winter we reap the benefits of our summers. The winter never quite claims us. On the longest night of the year, Tristan rides up to the castle walls and calls out a challenge to the frozen trees.

To properly grasp the literary ethos of the endless summer of human nature we must open the books marked "Childhood." There we will find much to pleasure us, entice us, tease us with nostalgia.

Mainly, our literary tastes would slide along the surface of what is currently popular or "in": harlequin romances, mysteries, splatterpunk, tales of corruption and vice, westerns, doctors and nurses, monsters and pretty girls and boys, sex and love, gangsters and drugs, hot worlds and cheap thrills. We'd be drawn to subjects involving war toys, soldiering, violence, revenge, and genocide. We'd gobble up magazines about health, fashion, fitness, dieting, gourmet dining, and staying young — all the glitter and glamour of Maya. We'd frequent the dance hall, the singles bar, the strip joint, the restaurant, the video games arcade, the shopping mall, the furniture store, the car dealership, the super market, the body shop, the hairdresser, the MTV, the health food store, the workout gym. Engrossed in the gods and goddesses of pleasure in the moment, our special effects would be excellent, if not miraculous. We'd leave the theater having been served an entertainment orgasm. Before long, we'd be seeking another.

The summer shield comprises the body and all the mythic components of athletic activity: the passion of the blood, the frenzy of supreme effort, the grace and dynamics of motion, the tragedy of defeat, the ecstasy of victory. The midsummer Pythian, Delphic, Delian, and Olympic games of classical Greece began with a dramatized wrestling match between Zeus and Cronus, the outcome of which established the new kingship. The king always died in the contest, but was revived in the rites of midwinter.[9] The symbols of such sport remain much the same today as thousands of years ago: the uniform, the ball, the bat, the headgear, the hoop, the running shoe, the javelin, the goal, the prize. Likewise, competitions for honor, contests between egos, between humans and gods, between families, tribes, regions, nations, flags, totems — much of what gives birth to history, regionalism, factionalism, or nationalism — are the stuff of the summer persona.

The summer's ego seeks to preserve, defend, expand, aggrandize, revenge, satisfy itself by murdering, pillaging, raping, conquering, winning, in order to acquire fame, allegiance, subjects, booty. War gods and goddesses have been around for a long time. Legendary and historical heroes, heroines and villains of warfare such as Achilles, Cuchulain, Beowulf, Freya, the Amazons, the Shogun, Arthur, Modred, Lancelot, Morrigan, Alexander the Great, Caesar, Genghis Khan, Hotspur, Napoleon, Hitler, Stalin, the Green Berets, etc., are human expressions of the same bloody shield. How the mighty are fallen — and how many innocents have been slain? Will the carnage ever cease?

What is gained seems never enough. The mythical summer ego is irrepressible, a bottomless pit. It may be raped, beaten, harassed, buried, defeated, or killed. But it will glow again in the forge of flesh, bursting into green fire when the growing season returns. Morality? The child does not understand morality. Life is overabundant; the pickings are easy. The strongest and meanest will survive. The predatory instinct to physically endure, and the emotional complex that surrounds it (defensiveness, fear, rage, pleasure in killing and eating), can be found in all of summer's mythical children. They squabble with and even murder their siblings (Cain and Abel), pick on the most favored (Joseph and his brothers), denigrate the weakest or stupidest (Grimm's "The Two Brothers,"), commit incest with siblings (*The Kalevala*), plot against and kill their parents (Orestes, Modred). Pelias' daughters cut their father up into thirteen pieces and boil them in a cauldron.

The hothouse of summer grows all forms of family life. In wild nature it is not unusual for the mother to eat the scrawniest, or drive the weakest from the den, or deliberately ignore one or more of her offspring. The father is known to kill the rival son, commit incest with the daughter, or refuse to share the kill. These things are done easily, for the summer shield is ignorant of values or morality. Hansel and Gretel are abandoned by their father. The ugly duckling's mother refuses to accept him. Snow White is poisoned by her stepmother. Phaedra falls hopelessly in love with her son. Othman buries his little daughter alive rather than to bear the disgrace of feminine offspring. Zeus cheats on his wife. Hera plots to humiliate and rob him of his power. Apollo murders a mortal in cold blood simply because the fellow plays the flute better than he. Heracles goes on a rampage and murders his wife and children. Amphitrite changes a rival mortal into a barking monster with six heads and twelve feet. And just because she was surprised while bathing, Artemis transforms poor Actaeon into a stag. To add insult to injury, she tears him into little pieces.

The strongest tendency to be found among ancient deities, however, is their proclivity toward matters erotic: Aphrodite, the "foam born" goddess of desire, is caught with Ares in the jealous net of Hephaestus. Eos, fatuous goddess of the dawn, is cursed with a constant longing for young mortals. Eros of the golden wings hunts mortals with barbed arrows. Apollo tricks Thalia, Dryope, Daphne, Hyacinthus, and how many others, into bed. Cybelle, whose festival was held at the beginning of summer, incites humans to extra-marital love. Io, the white cow in heat, suckles the lustful Zeus. Pan, the human god, instigates riots and endlessly pursues lovely nymphs.

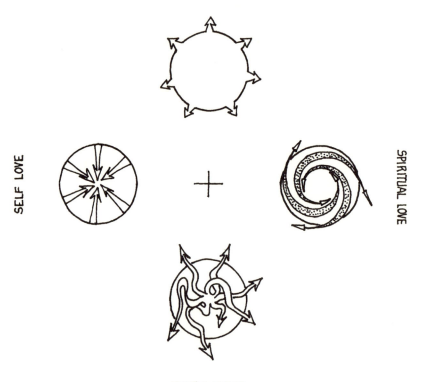

THE SHIELDS OF EROS

The erotic bond is often associated with violence and death, as in the fate of Adonis, or the crippling of Anchises, or the hog-spells cast by Circe. Aphrodite suffers a "fatal attraction" that is, in fact, a "fatal compulsion." Mortals who cannot escape her advances are usually killed. On May Day, "Aphrodite Urania" ('queen of the mountain') or Erycina ('of the heather') mates with the king. Then she destroys him, as a queen-bee destroys the drone, by tearing out his sexual organs.[10]

If I were to list the pertinent or meaningful symbols of the mythos of the summer of human nature, I would have to include the entire body of the physical world, all that is seen, tasted, touched, smelled, and heard. Clearly, that is impossible. The infinite variety of potential symbols is but an indication of the infinite variety of unique and discrete human interactions with the physical environment.

Here are a few pieces of the body, snatched from an infinitude:
the tumescent genitals and their secretions, the hoisted skirt, the flashed
        erection, the bow and arrow of Desire (eros)
the bomb, the rocket, the tank, the supersonic fighter, the semi-
        automatic, the hand gun (the "toys" and primal fears of
        childhood made physically real)
the snake, the shad, the pinecone, the date palm, the heifer, the weed
        (natural fertility)
the bull, the ram, the goat, the Satyr, (lust, brute procreative strength)
the scallop shell, the sea anemone, the throats of flowers (vulva)
lemmings, rabbits, sparrows, quail, locusts, mosquitoes (summer's
        plenitude)
the mare and the stallion (animal sexuality)
the dolphin (sensuality, play)
the feast, the orgy (gluttony, loss of inhibition)
the flood light, strobe light, spot light, stage light, light show (sensation,
        illusion)
the boar (savagery, violence)
the Song of Solomon (romance, eros)
the ripe ear of corn (phallus and seed)
wine, mead, the Maenads (intoxication)
eyes, nose, mouth, fingers, ears (the "outlets of the senses")
currency (material value)
the pentacle (material world)
the corpse (physical death)
clay, mud, moss (flesh of the earth)
the southern wind (physical warmth and well being, "the long, hot
        summer")
the mosquito, the flea (blood-sucking, lechery)
the gadfly (anger)
the worm (mortality)
the rival twins (competition, ego survival)
the pack, the gang (group violence, dominance hierarchy)
the bad girl, the vixen, the macho woman (faces of the feminine
        summer)
the berserker, the thug, the heel, the gigolo, the macho male (faces of
        the masculine summer)
Midas' gold (lust for material goods)
the prostitute and her "mark" (illicit love)

the Emperor's new clothes (illusion, pride)
Caliban (elemental, mortality-bound)
Falstaff (love of pleasure)
the tattoo (fleshly icon)
Barbie and Ken (childhood romance)
the sports star, the Hollywood star, the rock star (fantasy icons)
the "drink," the "toke," the "snort," the needle-sting (sensual pleasure)
the Rolls Royce, the BMW, the limousine, the sports car, the Harley
      (cultural dominance hierarchy)
the "honkey," the "nigger," the "redskin," the "spic," the "infidel," the
      "fag," the "dyke," the "nerd," the "bastard," the "wimp," "them"
      (childish intolerance based on fear and ignorance)

Now that we have come to what we call the "21st century," the summer shield is no less in evidence. In fact, this particular shield may be considerably more amplified by the presence of billions of humans multiplying themselves into oblivion, having long ago left behind rites of passage into adulthood.

>   Caught in that sensual music all neglect
>   Monuments of unageing intellect.
>
>   — W.B. Yeats, "Sailing to Byzantium"

ENDNOTES: THE SUMMER SHIELD OF HUMAN NATURE

[1] Annie Dillard, *Pilgrim at Tinker Creek* (New York: Harper and Row, 1974), p. 160-1.

[2] As quoted by Dillard, p. 167.

[3] "Integrated Ecology: The Process of Counseling with Nature, *The Human Psychologist*, Autumn, 1993.

[4] "The skin is both permeable and impermeable, superficial and profound, truthful and misleading. It is regenerative, but caught up in a continual process of desiccation. It is elastic, but a piece of skin detached from the body shrinks greatly. It sets off libidinal cathexes that are as much narcissistic as sexual. It is the centre of emotional well-being and also of seduction. It gives us pain and pleasure in equal parts. It transmits to the brain information from the outside world, including certain 'impalpable' messages which it is precisely one of its functions to 'palpate' without the Ego being aware that it is doing so.
 . . . . Its nudity is a token of our destitute state, but also our sexual excitation." Didier Anzieu, *The Skin Ego: A Psychoanalytic Approach to the Self.*

[5] Alwyn and Brinley Rees, *Celtic Heritage: Ancient Tradition in Ireland and Wales* (London: Thames and Hudson, 1961), p. 287.

[6] Untitled. Theodore Roethke, *Straw for the Fire: From the Notebooks of Theodore Roethke*, 1943-63 (New York: Doubleday, 1974).

[7] Alwyn and Brinley Rees, p. 287.

[8] Ibid, p. 383-4.

[9] Robert Graves, *The Greek Myths*, I (Baltimore: Penguin, 1955), p. 187.

[10] Graves, *The Greek Myths*, I, p. 71.

THE FALL SHIELD OF HUMAN NATURE

> Fall. descent; lapse into sin; falling from an erect posture; downward motion (see WATERFALL); autumn (orig. *fall of the leaf*, ME); 'falling' article of dress; death in battle, downfall; OE. trap (as in pitfall).
>
> — *Oxford Dictionary of English Etymology*

> O Rose, thou art sick!
> The invisible worm
> That flies in the night,
> In the howling storm,
>
> Has found out thy bed
> Of crimson joy:
> And his dark secret love
> Does thy life destroy.
>
> — William Blake, *Songs of Experience*

A change is in the air. A constriction has occurred. The days are getting shorter and cooler. Migrating birds fill the skies. "We had gone to bed in summer, and we awoke in autumn; for summer passes into autumn in some unimaginable point of time, like the turning of a leaf."[1] Life is turning inward, toward hibernation and self-preservation. Deer herds migrate downward from the heights toward the lowland fields. The green abundance of vegetation ceases to spread, bears fruit or seed, begins to shrivel. The first frost bites into the leaf. The flesh turns yellow, brown, falls from the bones.

Summer lied. It was not eternal. With the core of our being, we feel this lie. Yet in our rage to live we had chosen to believe it. A late medieval English poet, Thomas Hoccleve, reflected on the coming of fall:

> After Harvest had brought in its sheaves, and brown Michaelmastide had come and robbed the trees of their leaves, which had been green and delightful in vigor, and had dyed them a yellowish colour and cast them underfoot, that transformation affected me to the depths of my heart; for it reminded me once more that there is no stability in this world. There is nothing but change and mutability. [The world] is not going to last. Man must forgo it. Death will thrust him down to the ground under his foot. That is everyone's end.[2]

The innocent physicality of summer must change if life is to survive the winter. The role of the fall will be to initiate and prepare the summer to live in the winter. The instruments of initiation will be change and mutability. Look to the west where the sun sets. Soon it will be dark. It's time to go inside and switch on our feeble light.

Come with me into our late fall garden. Apples, strawberries, tomatoes, corn, cucumbers, and peppers have all been picked. The stalks darken and wither. The praying mantises have already constructed their egg caskets. An abandoned finch nest has blown down from the top of the mulberry. Locust seeds litter the bare ground. The lizard who basked all summer long on the twisted juniper snag has disappeared. Our cats patrol the outer perimeter of the garden, plumper, thicker-furred. Everywhere, signs of decay. The shadow of death has fallen over the bright swarm of summer. The furious beat of vegetable and animal blood has slowed. What was so pleasing to the senses now tastes spare, austere, empty. A different kind of body is evolving, a transitional body. Eventually, it will become cold, immobile, frozen into a trancelike death.

The summer shield has turned toward the passage shield of autumn. The child of summer has ceased to be innocent. The child is being initiated into the mysteries of death. Innocent homo sapiens has become like "one of us," as the "Creator" of Genesis put it, knowing the existence of both good and evil. Physical nature has become, for want of a better word, psychological or "inward." Even as the summer seems to withdraw into the earth with the first frost, so the ego, the innocent one, withdraws into its private darkness and "I have" must confront "I don't have." Instinct and sensation must become experienced feeling, a memory which tells us there will always be a fall. There will always be a lapse into self-consciousness, a seeing of self as being separate from a childhood mother, or father — even an identification of self with evil. Eventually we will entertain thoughts like Annie Dillard's: "Either this world, my mother, is a monster, or I myself am a freak."[3]

Somehow we will survive this lapse into inwardness, this helpless shriveling under the freezing shadow of winter. We cannot hold death back. The only way to survive what is sure to come is to go where the senses cannot go, to blindly lapse into the realms of feeling (as opposed to emotion), to finally sleep in the arms of dreams, tides, and the collective unconscious.

In the fall, the child of summer severs from the paradise of Eden and psychologically reflects on the meaning of life's greatest initiation:

Now that the leafy branches are growing bare, often I sigh and sorrowfully mourn when I consider how all this world's joy comes to nothing. One moment is here, and the next, gone as if it had indeed never existed. What many people say is true: Everything is transient except the will of God. We all have to die, however little that may please us. All that grows green in the grove is now withering all at once. Jesus, help to make that [teaching] clear, and protect us from hell, for I do not know where I must go, or how long I must remain here.

— Middle English lyric[4]

The time has come to harvest the grain, to winnow and fan, to thresh and thrash. The seed (the survivors) will fall to the earth. The chaff (the weak ones) will be snatched away by the wind. The seed must be ground in the mill to make flour for winter's bread.[5] So with humans. To survive the winter, the grinding must take place inwardly. With the arrival of fall, Thoreau "withdrew further into my shell, and endeavored to keep a bright fire burning both within my house and within my breast."[6] Annie Dillard did it another way: "You wait in all naturalness without expectation or hope, emptied, translucent, and that which comes rocks and topples you; it will shear, loose, launch, winnow, grind."[7]

FALL

In terms of the developmental cycle, the fall shield is the time of initiation — a dangerous phase — when the child of summer is prepared to become the adult of winter. The child must willingly submit to the death shadows of the fall. The connection to a physical mother and father must be severed and the child given to anima, animus, and the Mother who rules the lost self:

> Not till we are lost, in other words, not till we have lost the world, do we begin to find ourselves, and realize where we are and the infinite extent of our relations.
> —Thoreau, *Walden*

If the fall shield were assigned a power of human nature, it would be introspection — the ability to in-spect oneself, to be self-aware, to feel the pathos of mortality. The fall shield confers the ability to name emotions, to say, "I *feel* angry." "I *feel* sad." Though the one who introspects is powerless to do anything but watch events unfold on an inner screen, the germs of incipient self-transformation ferment in the retort of memory — even as they seethe within the rotting husk of the seed or the exhausted pulp of the chrysalis or placenta. In the fermenting stillness lurks the power to turn grapes into wine.

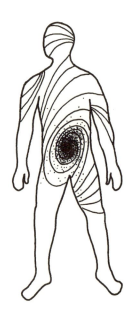

THE FALL OF HUMAN NATURE

Darkness. The absence of sunlight. The shadow land inside. The cellar. Where the fruits of experience (the fall from the summer Garden) ripen in the vat of memory. The deep forest, the swamp, the poppy fields of dreams, the rotting undersides of personal karma, spellbound pools of narcissistic feeling, sirens of evil, chasms of separation, exposure, loneliness, disintegration, chaos, and death. The karmic quicksands of memory, the shifting tides of guilty, shameful, awkward feelings. All these characterize the fall shield of initiation. But something else lies embedded in uneasy darkness. A flake, a gleam, a flame, a gift, a knowing, a way of holding on in the flux of unknowing. The fall initiate finds this thing. It is the means with which she will transform herself:

> Only he whose bright lyre
> has sounded in shadows
> may, looking onward, restore
> his infinite praise.
>
> Only he who has eaten
> poppies with the dead
> will not lose ever again
> the gentlest chord.
>
> — Rainer Maria Rilke, "Sonnet to Orpheus," I, ix

In ancient times, the darkness of night crowded in without artificial impediment. Despite their fears, our ancestors lived with it, for there was no other alternative. The time had come when there would be more darkness than light. Mother Earth would have it her way. One of the marks of maturity was knowledge of the night and its associated maps and spirits. This knowledge has been lost to inhabitants of the modern urban world.

As befits a season where action turns toward inaction, when the physical turns toward the psychological, those "liminal entities" who enter the initiatory passage of winter are socially neither here nor there. They are betwixt and between the positions assigned by culture and community. Even as the children of summer must die, so must the erased ones (neophytes) sacrifice their identity because they are in transit from here (childhood) to there (adulthood). Inhabitants of a season of memory and mutability, they "elude or slip through the network of classifications that normally locate states and positions in cultural space." Thus, the "liminality" of the fall shield "is frequently likened to death, to being in the womb, to invisibility, darkness, bisexuality, wilderness, or an eclipse of the sun or moon."[8]

Walking home along a darkened lane, we come across two teenagers necking in the shadows. Again we are reminded that initiation is also sexual, that "loss of virginity" is related mythically and linguistically to "the fall" from Eden. We remember our own adolescence, the innocent hunger to know the secrets of our own sexual nature, the very secrets by which our own kind have persisted through the millennia. We remember how self-conscious we are, how torn with feelings and fantasies we cannot name. Innocently, we discover that we are no longer innocent. A brief moment of panting, fainting desire. A lifetime of feeling and remembrance. First we don't know — then we know. Hopefully, from that knowing spring self-acceptance, and confidence in the magic of our own way. And with the aid of that same inner knowing, a uniquely secret companion takes a developmental leap within us, a shadowy archetype through whose eyes we see ourselves — an anima or an animus with the power to determine the course of our love and our choice of partners.

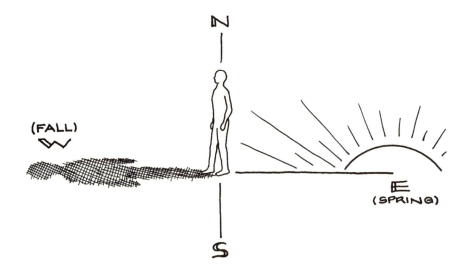

The light of the rising sun casts the deepest shadows in the west. One of the shadows cast is the anima or animus, the inner feminine or inner masculine. The young man is seduced or entranced by the goddess. The young girl is tricked or ravished by the god. These events take place inwardly, where there is no escape, where memory thunders like fate, where self-acceptance must be found amidst the rubble of rejection, loss, trauma, accident, and karma. The psyche cannot elude the blandishments of spirit any more than shadows can elude the light. But the light only makes the psyche more conscious of its earth-bound existence, of its mortal body, of its shadow, of its deepest longing to be united with that which it is not — the spirit or god — in which dwells the spark of immortality.

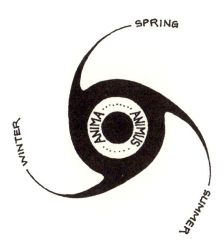

IN THE HEART OF THE FALL SHIELD

    Enough of this. Feel the cold north wind reaching for the back of our necks? The harvest is in and already it's All Hallows Eve. A great feast must be held to celebrate the names of all the saints, known and unknown, to insure protection for the winter. Now the hobgoblins and spooks of the unconscious will rise in an attempt to thwart the life-giving vigor of the invoked saints. Innocence has come to the center of the battle of good and evil forces for possession of a soul. Yes children, there is evil in the world, and trials galore. If you're prepared to face the monsters, you're prepared to last the coming winter. Go inside and warm yourself over the fire of darkness.

> Folly is an endless maze,
> Tangled roots perplex her ways,
> How many have fallen there?
> They stumble all night over the bones of the dead;
> And feel they know not what but care . . . .
>   — Blake, *Songs of Experience*

    When there is no light, we cannot see. And when we cannot see, we must go inward and remember. What do we remember? Is it really possible to remember way back to the beginning of human time? Certainly, in that dark shield, we remember that we are, and always have been, mortal, separate, and alone, that we feel or do not feel afraid, that we are or are not in control, that we have or have not entered chaos, that we are or are not victims of life, that we are or are not hurting. The dark shield of fall forces us into self-assessment, and ultimately, self-love or self-rejection. It forces us into a kind of psychic death, from which we emerge newborn or self-rejected. Sometimes, in the Hall of Memory, we get lost in an endless maze of mirrors, and succumb to madness.

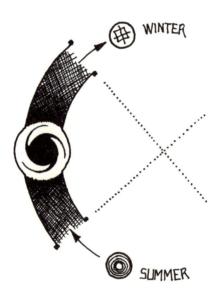

THE METAMORPHIC PASSAGE OF FALL

Summer's leaf falls to the ground and slowly decomposes. This process of decomposition, how what is dying becomes the stuff of birth, is the mythos and the mystery of the fall shield, and must be viewed within the greater mystery of ego-psyche-mind-spirit. In a mythical sense, ego must give way to psyche, even as summer must give way to fall, or the physical sphere to the "psychosphere."[9]

The shift from material to consciousness necessitates a descent into the nether regions — to Erebus, Hades, Adlivun, Amenti, Avalon, Kur, Lethe,

Limbo, Chaos, Niflheim, the Asclepion, the black hole of narcissism, the snake cave, the forest of the witch, the cauldron of the warlock, the nightmare, the fearful wilderness, the sacred mountain of confusion, the kingdom of the rapist, the trance of crucifixion, the ordeal of abduction, the sacrifice of self, the inevitable blood-letting, the magic sleep, the trial by intercourse, the passage of dis-ease, the curse of blindness, the vale of prostitution — even the twilight zone of sex change.

The coming of fall announces the ancient story. The story is woven with memory — what childhood is always becoming: the "inner life," the reflective within-ness of the psyche — the adolescent. The adventures to be had here unfold on an inward stage, an *underworld* journey. They are not visible to the naked eye except as they are reflected in the behavior of the body. Who can predict where the initiate, the candidate, the heroine, the hero, the wandering soul will sprout in the fallow shadowlands of psycho-memory? Wherever she/he goes will be found the stuff of mind and maturity. The collective will be blessed.

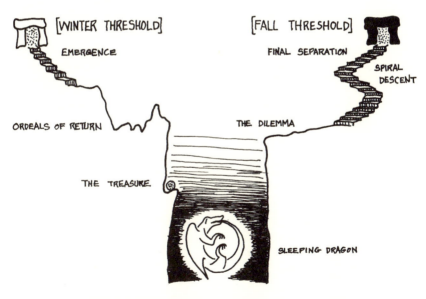

THE UNDERWORLD JOURNEY (FALL SHIELD)

Dramatically, the west shield is the stuff of tragedy. The protagonist must fall. The mythic memory knows this. Every human must be held accountable for his/her deeds (karma), or counter the moves of fate with his/her fatal flaw.

There is a dark side to every coin. The fall shield cannot be cheated. Sooner or later it will extract its due. The innocent one must finally go into the dark and see.

Often, what waits in the dark is connected to or symbolizes the uniting of man with inner woman, or woman with inner man. The overtones of this encounter can be passionate, terrifying, erotic, and deadly. Because these anima/animus scenarios take place in the vast reaches of the collective psyche, where self-love is learned and practiced, what is encountered is often culturally taboo. The god/goddess Hermaphroditus, son/daughter of Hermes (winter) and Aphrodite (summer), resides in the persona of fall. And Janus, the two-faced god of beginnings, stands at the threshold of every passage.

The coming of the season of fall and the onset of fall-winter darkness was celebrated, as in the Anglo-Saxon world, with seasonal rites of passage typical of All Hallow's Eve. At the moment when summer constricted into fall, the border between day and night, light and dark, body and soul, eros and thanatos, physical and psychical, instinct and dream, innocence and experience, summer and fall, was blurred. Anything could happen. The door was open to a shifting world thronging with shadows of memory, dreams, and the collective unconscious. The body encountered the sacred/profane world of the soul, where demons and unidentified things roamed the vast steppes of the psyche. Spirit lovers, savage strangers, *incubi, succubi, lamias,* sorcerers, sorceresses, dragons, gods and goddesses in disguise, and other anima/animus entities lurked in shadows and dark water, to ravish, devour, or trick the psyche into a living death. The burial mounds opened and the souls of the dead walked upon the land.[10]

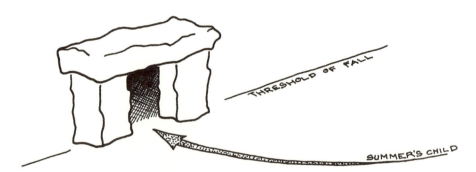

THRESHOLD CROSSING

The "mono-myth," as identified by Joseph Campbell in *Hero With a Thousand Faces*, can be found in almost every culture the world over. Quite simply it is the story of initiation via the western shield, told in a thousand languages in a thousand versions. CuChulainn must pass through the Land of Shadow, cross the Bridge of Leaps, fight the giant CuRoi, copulate with the formidable lady Scathach, and return to Ireland with an "initiation scar" on his arm. Ishtar must descend into the underworld and be torn asunder if she is to rescue her lover Tammuz and return as his triumphant bride. Bacab must be scourged, crucified and resurrected. Gawain must undergo the perilous test of the lady's bed. Osiris must return each day to the kingdom of the dead. Perseus must face the Medusa if he is to be united with Andromeda. Hercules must become the slave of Omphale. Tiresias must accidentally stumble into the clearing and see the goddess bathing nude, the last thing he will ever see. Persephone must be ravished and carried off to the underworld for the corn to come up in the spring. Briar Rose must prick her finger on the spindle of sleeping death so that the kingdom will be regenerated. Hansel and Gretel must leave home and wind up in the witch's oven if they are to grow up and be man and woman. Odin must enter the dark cave of the giantess to find the kettle of inspiration. God must be nailed to the cross of the four directions, die, and be entombed in the cold earth, before the son/sun can rise from the dead. The stories go on and on.

> O happy gate of blackness, cries the sage, which art the passage to this so glorious change. Study, therefore, whosoever appliest thyself to this Art, only to know this secret, for to know this is to know all, but to be ignorant of this is to be ignorant of all. For putrefaction precedes the generation of every new form into existence.
>
> — Paracelsus[11]

The darkness and decay of death is where the soul ("psyche") lives. It lives here because it is self-aware, and it knows that it is part and parcel of a body (summer shield) that must ultimately die. Indeed, it is up to each individual soul to decide, given what it remembers there in the darkness, whether or not it wants to live. In ancient times, the initiate in rites of passage was expected to go into the vale of soul-making and remember and dream the will of the sacred ancestors to live, to take a responsible role in collective survival, and to seek to become one with the spirits of all things. The function of the psyche in initiation is to prepare the candidate for a regenerating birth. But first he/she must experience the deepest feeling of all — the feeling of death — in order to become a whole adult. Thus the initiate is led through the rite of passage "by steps timed to his inner development, coinciding with his abandonment and rejection of childhood, affirming his desire for wisdom and understanding beyond the tangible reality he knows so well. . . ."[12]

The legend of Eros and Psyche (Apuleius, second century A.D.) takes place primarily in the fall shield. The mortal soul, doomed to wander lonely on the earth, is initiated into divine love — but not without earning it via an animus lover, a lonely pilgrimage, an initiatory task, a descent into the underworld, a poisonous sleep of death. By dint of perspiration (and inspiration), the soul completes its earthly tasks and even, almost, tricks death. Unfortunately, Psyche is in love with her body as well, and appears to fall victim to its inevitable fate. But she is not dead. She was only sleeping. She is sacred and divine, even when she is falling head first into Hades. Eros transports her from the spell of the box. The dark fall of human nature is forever wedded to the spirit light of spring. Psyche and spirit are one.

The current interest in chaos theory and "dark matter" is related to certain important aspects of the fall shield mythos, aspects which involve the tension between physical and psychic existence and its psychosymbolic "resonances." Take the idea of darkness. Certain schools of astrophysics have turned their attention to the fact that 90% of the mass of the universe is in the form of matter that gives off no visible light or radiation at any wavelength. "Dark matter" they call it, or the mass in a "shadow universe." Indeed, great voids separate planets, solar systems, stars, and galaxies, voids dark and invisible yet a kind of "gravitational glue" holding the evolving whole together. This 90% "formless no-thingness," is absolutely essential, for it gives form to the other 10% — and gestalt to the whole.

Scientists wonder what this dark stuff is all about. Is it produced by entropy, is it filled with WIMPS (weakly interacting massive particles), or axons, or superstrings, or hyperspace, or aether, or simply chaos?[13] We can but applaud their noble efforts to see into the murky dimness of the fall shield. Could it be possible that actually they are looking into a smoking mirror in which they see the human psyche reflected? And is the human soul anything if it is not part and parcel of the soul of nature?

"Our psyche is part of nature, and its enigma is limitless," (Jung).

The psyche of nature is chaotic and dark, rife with fermentation and putrefaction. It dwells between body and mind, between organism and design, between sensation and purpose, between "I have" and "we are." It is composed of voids that separate stimulation from logic, instinctual emotion from rational order. But these voids are thick with tensions of nonlinearity and feedback loops of memory that transmit, like echoes of energy through the neurotransmissional network, the original impetus of the body toward its "opposite," the mind.[14]

> Our layered consciousness is a tiered track for an unmatched assortment of concentrically wound reels. Each one plays out for all of life its dazzle and blur of translucent shadow pictures; each one hums at every moment its own secret melody in its own unique key. We tune in and out. But moments are not lost. Time out of mind is time, nevertheless, cumulative, informing the present.[15]

Phrased in the four shield metaphor, organism (summer) and mind (winter), are bound into a positive/negative memory feedback loop called fall, which is characterized by shrivelling (shrinking inward), turning color, falling, lying fallow, decomposing, hibernating, and apparently ceasing to grow. But profound changes are fermenting in the vat of dying. The seeds dreaming in their husks and the larvae sleeping in tight curls, are surrendering their bodies to the transformative powers of the nature's psyche. This surrender is absolutely necessary if they are to survive and attain maturity.

If immortality lies in the direction of the rising sun, the only way to get there is to go the opposite direction, toward the setting sun. The vale of soul-making bears a rich harvest of myths, archetypes, symbols, images, feelings, and concepts. For example:

the threshold (from the Anglo-Saxon, "thrashing hold"), the doorway, the
    passage (liminal state in the initiatory process)
the alchemist's retort (the psyche as container of the unconscious)
the hypnotic suggestion (within the body and its brain lies the psyche)
the living dead, zombies, the phantom of the opera (souls without spirit)
the body/sex as shameful/disgusting (culturally instilled guilt)
Narcissus (psyche in love with self)
addiction in all its forms (guilt, obsession, conscious self-destruction)
the "sin," the "evil" (result of Judeo-Christian "fall")
the bear (hibernation)
the scorpion (What's underneath the rock?)
hypochondria, melancholia, Epstein-Barr, somatoform disorders, chronic
    fatigue syndrome, seasonal affective disorder, (de-pression, the
    unconscious)
the captivity, abduction, exile (symbols of the liminal state)
the pilgrim, the supplicant, the Grail quester (the initiate)

homosexuality, bisexuality, transsexuality, heterosexuality (sexual expressions of
    anima/animus)
skeletons in closets (memories that determine character, soul)
suicide (extreme self-abnegation)
solitude, loneliness, blindness (liminal state marked by predominance of
    psychic activity)
Andromeda (woman helpless in chains)
Prometheus, Sisyphus, Tantalus (the endless torture of memory)
existential "nausea" (human consciousness of existence)
the ash tree, the oak, the owl, the bat, the loon, the raven (symbols of
    the underworld)
the bull roarer (god of initiatory death)
The Book of the Dead, The Popul Vuh (underworld journeys)
Dionysus and the Maenads (initiatory death and dismemberment, the vines
    pruned in the fall)
Hecate, Kali, Circe, Morgan le Fay, Lillith, *vagina dentata,* witches and
    sorceresses in general (personal and collective anima)
the black widow spider, the female praying mantis, (male-devouring
    anima of natural self-thus)
Kala, Dionysus, Merlin, Bluebeard, the nightmare (lit. "death man"),
warlocks and woman-eaters in general (personal and collective animus)
demon possession (the dark side of the force)
Gaia (the dark earth, incomprehensible creatress of the Delphic Oracle)
Sir Gawain, Sir Percival (initiates)
"dream time" (collective ancestral dream of life and death)
circumcision, *jus prima noctis* (initiatory perforation of the genitals)
leaving home, going off to college, loss of virginity, first job (initiatory
    severance from the parents, new stage of individuation)
the river Styx, Limbo and other borders of chaos (the threshold of liminality)
the periodic tides and phases of the moon, menstruation (relationship
    between moon and psyche)
"fate" (the role of memory in the making of karma)
the Hanged Man (the initiatory state, hanging between heaven and earth)
separation, divorce, midlife, retirement, dying (initiatory passages, new
    stages of individuation)
rites of purification (inward preparation for liminal state)
the Via Negativa (taking the dark road in order to reach the light)
entombment in the bowels of the earth (liminal state of initiation)
the color black (absence of all light)

the roots (that which is beneath the surface, inner self, the unconscious)
the digestive system (the fermenting vat from which conscious volition is
       distilled) entropy (dying toward a state of equilibrium)
the "weak force" (decay working inward)
the vulture, cannibalism (living off death)
deadly nightshade (poison from a flower that blooms at night)
the fen or bog, the Slough of Despond (the vale of stagnancy)
the wailing wall (the memory place where the self changes)

    The fall shield, then, is composed of the psyche of natural self-thus, the ethos of human adolescence, and the presence of ancestral memory that has informed human culture from the very beginning. The fall shield is the soul of nature. We live in this soul and it lives in us. Because self-consciousness is imbedded in the physical body of nature, the soul is aware of its mortality. Down through the ages, this awareness — that we are not God, that we do not live forever — has given rise to the great human myths of initiation, transformation, and the afterlife. The deepest memory, perhaps deeper even than birth, is the memory of death:

> And here, face down beneath the sun
> And here upon earth's noonward height
> To feel the always coming on
> The always rising of the night . . . .
>
> — Archibald Macleish, "You, Andrew Marvell"

THRESHOLD OF HIBERNATION
THE BARROW RETREAT

ENDNOTES: THE FALL SHIELD OF HUMAN NATURE

[1] Henry David Thoreau, "On the Concord and Merrimack," *Walden and Other Writings*, Ed. Brooks Atkinson (New York: Random House, 1950), p. 414.

[2] Marie Collins and Virginia Davis, *A Medieval Book of Seasons* (London: Sidgwick and Jackson Limited, 1991), p. 96.

[3] Annie Dillard, *Pilgrim at Tinker Creek*, p. 177.

[4] *A Medieval Book of Seasons*, p. 122.

[5] Granted, this metaphor is drawn from agriculture. It is also true that in pre-agricultural cultures there was no "fall" from the Garden of Eden, no loss of paradise. (See Lawlor, *Voices of the First Day* (Rochester, Vt: Inner Traditions, 1991, p. 74) There was, however, a turning inward toward the darkness and chaos of the initiatory state, as represented by the marked difference between childhood and adolescence.

[6] *Walden*, p. 223.

[7] Dillard, p. 259.

[8] Victor Turner, *The Ritual Process: Structure and Anti-Structure* (Chicago: Aldine, 1969), p. 95.

[9] The "morphic fields" explored by the biochemist Sheldrake have led to the recognition of ELF, ESP, or *psi* fields that, it is surmised, comprise a "psychosphere." See Paul Devereux, John Steele and David Kubrin, *Earthmind: Communicating with the Living World of Gaia*, pp. 82-5.

[10] Alwyn and Brinley Rees, *Celtic Heritage: Ancient Tradition in Ireland and Wales*, pp. 89-94.

[11] *Hermetic and Alchemical Writings*, 1: 153, as quoted by Manly Hall, *The Secret Teachings of All Ages* (Los Angeles: Philosophical Research Society, 1969).

[12] Paul Shepard, *The Tender Carnivore and the Sacred Game* (New York: Scribner's, 1973), pp. 205-6.

[13] See James Trefil, *The Dark Side of the Universe* (New York: Scribners).

[14] John Briggs and F. David Peat, *Turbulent Mirror: An Illustrated Guide to Chaos Theory and the Science of Wholeness* (New York: Harper and Row, 1989).

[15] Dillard, *Pilgrim at Tinker Creek*, p. 84.

THE WINTER SHIELD OF HUMAN NATURE

> Winter all eats
> That summer begets
>
> — Middle English aphorism

> All that summer conceals, winter reveals.
>
> — Annie Dillard, *Pilgrim at Tinker Creek*

> Meaning, not space and time, connects all things.
>
> — Robert Lawlor, *Voices of the First Day*

Circling the seasons of human nature, we have come to summer's opposite. Look around. What is there to see? A cold lifelessness has settled over all. Few life forms appear. A dazzling whiteness has shrouded everything in numbing sameness. The bare bones have been picked clean. The north wind has eaten it all.

> It is pleasant while spring lasts with bird song; but now the wind's blast and rough weather are approaching. Ah! Alas! how long this night is! And I am most unjustly sorrowing, mourning and fasting.
>
> — Anonymous lyric, Middle Ages[1]

Summer's children could not survive without the aid of winter's adults. The hunger to have it all, sense it all, eat it all, is hardly appropriate in a world where famine stalks the land. Now the child must eat of the fruits of the adult's labor, or he doesn't eat. And the adults must reap the fruits of their adolescents' initiatory passage or the people don't survive.

Survival is accomplished only by effort. Those who live through winters in northern climates understand this only too well. If the work is not done, if one lacks the proper foresight, there's a frigid hell to pay. Take, for example, some of the simple precautions necessary for winter driving in Montana:

> Put stumps in the back of your pickup to give weight and bite to the rear axle, to keep from fishtailing in deep snow. Tack cardboard in front of [your] truck's or car's radiator to keep the engine heat in.

Back-up parts for the generator . . . extra points, spark plugs, oil filter, fuel filter.

Battery charger and extra charged battery to carry out to ailing truck, like a replacement heart.

Snow chains.

Sleeping bag, ax, in all vehicles.

Gloves, flashlight.

Snow shovel in all trucks.

Don't set emergency brake when parking in really cold weather — it could freeze that way and you'd be stuck.[2]

When hard times are at hand, something must always be done, some kind of coherent plan employed. Seeds must be stored, dried meat and fat accumulated, roots tied up and preserved, excess baggage shed. Sometimes food must be found in inhospitable surroundings. In the ugliest blizzards the fires of life must be ignited and kept alive. But food implies work and cooperation, at least among humans and other creatures of their gregarious kind. Cooperation implies discipline, tooling, language, communication, and congregation. Without active love for the welfare of the whole, the family unit, tribe, or community will not survive. As Thoreau put it, "We belong to the community. It is not the tailor alone who is the ninth part of a man; it is as much the preacher, and the merchant, and the farmer. Where is this division of labor to end?"[3]

WINTER

During the winter, honeybees — nature's miracles of cooperation — use their own honey for fuel. They "buzz together in a tightly packed, living sphere. Their shimmying activity heats the hive; they switch positions from time to time so that each bee gets its chance in the cozy middle and its turn on the cold outside."[4] Likewise, ants hibernate in great social globs, and ladybugs take shelter in group clusters half a foot in diameter. In winter's scheme of things, "the illusion that the individual is an independent entity threatens the internal integrity of the organism [in this case the community] which is rooted in interdependence. The individual is an arrangement of ways of relating."[5]

The reactive, emotional ego of the summer shield is of little use in the winter. "I" cannot exist apart from "we." And "we" cannot exist without those who compromise and sacrifice. Because we share the fear of death, we share the will to live. Mothers labor to give birth. Parents labor to care for their children. Elders labor to keep the community intact. In winter, "I have" (summer) and "I feel" (fall) become "I work." The muddled, inward adolescent has grown into a clear thinking, civic minded citizen who matures, ages, and finally dies. Even as the elder's summer body of earth appears to disintegrate, the mind continues to be of service to the greater good.

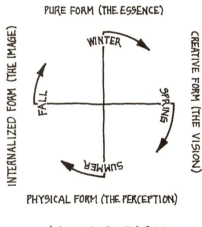

MAKING FORM

With the arrival of winter, the physical child of summer and the psychological adolescent of fall enter still another dimension — the realm of mind, design, and order — the very forces that hold sway over the fate of the seed or organism sleeping in suspended animation. The random energy of summer has frozen rigidly into an essential form inherently guided by abstractions: the laws of mathematics, physics, cellular biology, chemistry, and the natural sciences. The cosmic unified field theory. The "primary mathematical intuitions" (Jung). *Axiomata* concerned not with appearance (summer shield) but with mental structure. The Mind. The Plan. Without the mind function, life would never survive the death of winter. The plan would not exist by which the web of life effects its own continuance. So it is that the intellect, the powers of observation and description, the wits, common sense, the hypotheses and deductions of logic, rule the behavior of the winter shield of human nature.

Mind — not as in brain, but as in all the different kinds of brains and how they are similar and dissimilar. Mind — not just "deduction," but "induction." Mind — not just logical, but meaningful.

THE MIND ...

is an enchanted thing
        like the glaze on a
katydid-wing
        subdivided by the sun
        till the nettings are legion.
Like Gieseking playing Scarlatti. . . .

It has memory's ear
        that can hear without
having to hear.
        Like the gyroscope's fall,
        truly unequivocal
because trued by regnant certainty. . . .

— Marianne Moore

In the summer shield, the body commands the mind. In the winter shield, the mind controls the body. Control is vital. (Latin: *contra* — "opposite"; *rotulus* — "to roll"). Restraint must be exercised over the tendency to pitch and yaw. Restraint requires energy. Energy requires fuel, of which there is precious little to burn. Self-control is one of the gifts the adolescent brings out of the fall shield. To go out of control is to revert to the summer shield, most inappropriate in the middle of winter. Other forms of irrationality and/or irresponsibility are likewise inappropriate. Like the hive, the community must care for its own. Those who cannot exercise restraint will become parasitical or die. Hence, laws exist by which the collective controls itself and maintains its balance. Such laws are ultimately concerned with the conservation of energy. There is no greater need than to practice conservation in times of famine or chaos.[6]

Of course, emphasis on law and order, rules, regulations, and doctrines can itself go unrestrained, resulting again in harm to the people. Too much cold can kill the sleeping, germinating seed. Even so, too much rigidity can kill the human spirit. In penitentiaries, the law tears the soul from the body, leaving a gutted, vindictive shell. Likewise, the system of values, mores, and ethics (and the corresponding divine punishments for transgressors) as practiced by many religions, can kill or sterilize the germinating seed. Nevertheless, the frozen grip of winter can never quite kill all the seeds. The fires of revolution/regeneration are unquenchable. Eventually, spring will come, and the survivors will arise: "Intense! naked! A Human fire, fierce glowing, as the wedge/ Of iron heated in the furnace" (William Blake, "America: A Prophesy").

Take a walk with me along the creek, the same walk we took in the summer. Before we go out the door, we better be wearing the appropriate clothing. We don't want to die of hypothermia. How nice to have remembered to bring foul weather gear and stout boots. Thus shielded, we start out, boots crunching in the icy snow, breath condensing into clouds of frost. About the time we reach the edge of town, a lone raven flies into the bare trees above the creek, settles down on a limb, and croaks three times. We joke that she's quoting "Nevermore." And that's how it seems. Winter will never relent its icy assault on the land. Pickings are slim. Even Mrs. Raven looks gaunt, haggard, cut out from the shadow of death.[7]

Drawing closer to the creek, we notice that the boisterous voice of summer has quieted. Only the slightest murmur betrays the passage of a small channel beneath the muffling ice. Everything seems dead, killed by the cold, yet still alive in a host of hidden forms: egg, seed, pupa, spore. The mountains that feed the creek song are locked in stony white. We look into the translucent depths. Trout are lurking down there, safe in their cold-blooded envelopes, while we warm-bloodeds stamp and blow and layer ourselves with woolen defenses that would be useless if we were immersed for more than a few minutes in the trout's abode. The very thought that it would not be a good idea to jump into that water is a gift of the winter shield, as is the layered clothing. Still, the water is flowing, a warm shadow of summer running sinuously through the rigidity of form. It reminds us that with the aid of memory (fall), we can have summer in December, roses in winter.

As we turn away from the creek, I feel the old bones creaking. Not so spry as I used to be. As the years passed, I've had to find alternatives to youthful vigor in elements of the winter shield — values, work, home, the exercise of wit (presence of mind), and a respect for wisdom such as found in the old Anglo-Saxon lament:

> Earthly glory ageth and seareth.
> No man at all going the earth's gait
> But age fares against him, his face paleth,
> Grey-haired he groaneth, knows gone companions,
> Lordly men, to earth o'ergiven,
> Nor may he then the flesh-cover, whose life ceaseth,
> Nor eat the sweet nor feel the sorry,
> Nor stir hand nor think in mid heart. . .
>
> — "The Seafarer" (Trans. Ezra Pound)

THE WINTER OF HUMAN NATURE

The cold wind takes our breath away. We stumble and turn our backs to the worst of it. Boreas will howl in our faces all the way home. If we have lived a life of fidelity to the best of that which winter brought forth from us, and if we have watched the other creatures die, then we know that we must die. It will occur to us that we must not need life anymore. We will climb one last time into the frozen mountains of the north and give away all we have left to the wind. Alone, we will enter the circle of our life's purpose, a purpose defined by a restless search for answers to the ultimate question: How can the people survive? We will die there, at the center of the shield of winter.

> A kind of northing is what I wish to accomplish, a single-minded trek toward that place where any shutter left open to the zenith at night will record the wheeling of all the sky's stars as a pattern of perfect, concentric circles. I seek a reduction, a shedding, a sloughing off.
>
> — Annie Dillard, *Pilgrim at Tinker Creek*

The *Secretum Secretorum* of the middle ages depicts winter as an old woman naked, bent and twisted with age. Though the mind may remain sharp, the body molders, aches and reaches for the grave. The elder gives the body away so that the people may live. Summer is depicted as a lusty young child, ruddy-cheeked and well-fed. The winter gives itself away to the children, and what it gives away is what it has harvested from the summer. That which is reaped is that which is given away.

> Oh! Blessed rage for order, pale Ramon,
> The maker's rage to order words of the sea,
> Words of the fragrant portals, dimly-starred,
> And of ourselves and of our origins,
> In ghostlier demarcations, keener sounds.
>
> — Wallace Stevens, *"The Idea of Order at Key West"*

"The maker's rage for order" is the evolved form of rage. Though "the maker" is invisible, "the rage for order" is everywhere apparent in nature and in the human species. The season of winter marks the last step in the life cycle. So the mind of "the maker" marks the last step in the human life cycle. Even as the human body degenerates into old age and death, its psyche gravid with memories, "the maker" persists, stands clear of the wreckage, and knows what is good for the self, for the people, and for the environment. It knows because it is of the mind of nature, of the essence of its brothers and sisters, of the consortium of personal, social, planetary, and cosmic orderers.

The Tao of Lao-Tzu, one of the greatest works of the human mind contemplating the mind of nature, contains an incomparable description of "the maker's" mind:

> There is something formless yet complete
> That existed before heaven and earth.
> How still! How empty!
> Dependent on nothing, unchanging,
> All pervading, unfailing. . . .
> One may think of it as the mother of all things under heaven.
> I do not know its name,
> But I call it "Meaning."

The invisibility of mind makes it appear to be nothing in the eyes of the physical senses, but "nothing" is actually a way of establishing order, meaning and purpose:

> We put thirty spokes together and call it a wheel;
> But it is on the space where there is nothing that the utility
>   of the wheel depends.
> We turn clay to make a vessel;
> But it is on the space where there is nothing that the utility
>   of the vessel depends. . . .
> Therefore just as we take advantage of what is, we should
>   recognize the utility of what is not.[8]

Perhaps the most striking attribute of "the space where there is nothing" is that it can only exist between parts or components ("somethings") that are interacting or relating as a whole. Such interrelated aggregates can be said to be "a mind."[9] Without the "nothing" that organizes and holds interacting parts together, there would be no whole. The nothing of mind is an adhesive, an invisible bonding in things that has the ability to retain its shape or proportion even as it grows and changes. All living things and their biosystems seem to possess this nothing.

How do the parts and the nothing between them interact to create mental process? According to Gregory Bateson, interaction is triggered by the ability of mind, through the interrelationship of its parts, to draw distinctions (boundaries, borders, thresholds) between this/that or then/now.[10]

Such boundaries are also cast around the natural self in the form of self-definitions or self-limitations that can either inhibit the interrelationship of parts to the whole or enhance their ability to harmoniously interrelate, alter their boundaries, and adapt to environmental changes.

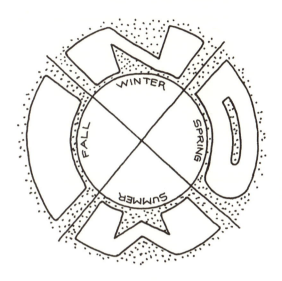

MIND = THE "NOTHING" THAT ORGANIZES AND HOLDS INTERACTING PARTS TOGETHER

Mental processes require collateral energy. That is, the mind (nothing interacting between interrelated parts) must be hitched to something (input, stimulus-event, environment) in order to become a process.

> Tao never does;
> Yet through it all things are done.

Natural stability or order is achieved through the continual repetition of a cycle of changes which always returns the system to a status quo. I.e., the winter must undergo a cycle of changes before it can again become winter. In such a fashion, winter survives. In Bateson's quadripartite diagram of the circular chain of determination that composes a "machine," the "governor"(in the north) represents the place of the winter mind within the seasonal cycle of the natural self: the cylinder (south), the flywheel (west), and the energy input, or fuel (east). Winter is the season that "governs" the dynamic of the entire seasonal system. Without it, the "machine" will "go into a *runaway*, operating exponentially faster and faster" until it breaks down.¹¹ The fury of summer growth must be controlled (balanced) by a dispassionate period of no growth. So the mind is the invisible governor in the four shield system. It insures, or attempts to insure, that the whole wheel turns as one.

To understand the mythos of the winter of human nature, one must examine social interaction: family, society and culture. "Society" has manifested itself in ways that have insured the survival of the whole system over the span of a couple million years. Undoubtedly, there were several ice ages — and periods of uncomfortable thawing as well. Yet our species persisted. The "nothing" of the natural mind controlled runaway, set boundaries, made distinctions, saw patterns, found meaning, acted out plans, and otherwise provided for the balance of the whole organism (individual and social) through the periodic wintercycles of no-growth. The evolving human mind (and the minds of all living systems) is the response/adaption of the human species to the seasonal governorship of winter.¹²

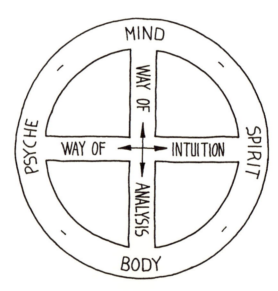

THE FOUR SHIELDS OF LEARNING

The mind of winter is mature, as opposed to childish, rational, as opposed to emotional, considered, as opposed to instinctive, conciliatory, as opposed to warlike, responsible, as opposed to frivolous, nurturing, as opposed to selfish, wise, as opposed to foolish, intelligent, as opposed to ignorant, and persevering, as opposed to distracted.¹³ Such qualities as these make for stability and order within the community. The mythos of winter, then, means cooperation between the parts, interrelationships between borders, peaceful coexistence, interpersonal/interspecies communication, the rites and institutions of marriage, childbirth, child rearing, education, initiation, profession, aging, dying, and death, law and religion, science and theology, and all the means by which the human species controls its runaway body and all-consuming psyche in order to insure its collective survival.

The abstract mind that molds the physical world into the wonders of technology first manifested itself in the ancient arts of tooling, shelter and fire making, stalking and hunting, herbal medicine, basketry, pottery, tanning, agriculture, the domestication of animals, blacksmithing, and the invention of the wheel. That same mind continues to absorb itself in the practical uses of mathematics, astronomy, physics, biology, chemistry, game theory, etc., for weather prediction, navigation, communication, transportation, artificial intelligence, medicine, and of course, the dispassionate manufacture of instruments of mass destruction.

There is no lack of patriarchal and matriarchal deities associated with the winter shield of human nature. Most of the creation gods and goddesses brought the order of mind to the earth. According to Christianity, in the beginning the living god, whose name was Word, made the universe. According to the Romans, the God of All Things appeared suddenly in Chaos and divided the earth from the heavens, the water from the earth, and the upper air from the lower. He set the elements in order, divided the earth into zones, and assigned stations to the four winds. Under the leadership of Anu, Mesopotamian god of heaven, the cosmic order was established out of primeval chaos as an organized whole. Anu's queen, Mother Earth (Inanna/Ishtar), was responsible for the great round of the seasons, delivering the earth each year from the blight of winter by returning in the spring. In Egypt, Isis the "goddess of many names" who protected agriculture, cattle, sailors, medicine, midwives, and pregnant women, collected the dismembered fragments of her slain husband Osiris and restored him to life, thus insuring the seasonal inundations of the Nile.

Through the winter labor of childbirth, all the great mother goddesses (Inanna/Ishtar, Ninlil/Ningal, Isis/Hathor, Ashtoreth/Astarte, Cybelle/Magna Mater, Rhea/Gaia, Kuan Yin/Padmapani, Demeter/Ceres) gave life to the kings and queens of antiquity. Divine or sacral monarchies became means of consolidating and stabilizing the dynamics of civilizations as diverse as Chinese, Minoan, Babylonian, Assyrian, Grecian, Roman, Egyptian, Anglo-Saxon, and

Mayan. These monarchs and high potentates governed their secular/sacred realms in order to maintain the order of creation. In Egypt, the Pharaoh reigned as "the shepherd of the land, keeping the people alive," coordinating natural and social forces "for the well-being of mankind, maintaining the divine order of society, and championing justice (Maat) of which he was the source."[14] Kings such as Arthur, David, or Alexander exemplified the truth of the answer to the riddle of the Holy Grail: "The king and the kingdom are one." When the king was stricken, the sickness weakened the order that maintained the kingdom. Even so, when the mind is stricken, the spirit, body and soul are affected.

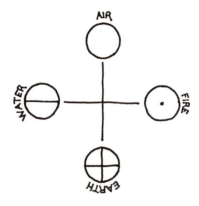

SPANISH ALCHEMICAL SYMBOLS

Among the mythical gods/goddesses and heroes/heroines who personified the mind shield of human species survival, one might find Spider Mother of the Hopi, Corn Mother and Awl Man of the Tewa, Iztat Ix of the Inca, Danu of the Celts, Isis and Thoth of the Egyptians, Hermes, Artemis, Demeter and Athene of the Greeks, Padmapani of the Buddhists, Adapa of the Babylonians, Noah, Abraham, and David of the Hebrews, Sophia of the Gnostics, St. Paul, St. Augustine, Quetzalcoatl of the Mayas, Tahmurath and Zoroaster of the Persians, Concordia of the Romans, Ullr of the Teutons, Fu-hsi, Nu-kua, Kuan Yin of the Chinese, and many others who manifest the cornucopia of arts, trades, crafts, services, liturgies, theologies, tantras, and other cultural utilities spawned by the human mind.

The nothing of mind cannot be sensed, or even understood, without its referents, and can best be characterized either with abstractions or nouns which denote or connote usefulness or meaning. In a sense, the symbols mentioned below represent means of holding together interrelated parts in the physical, psychological, and spiritual worlds, and serve to maintain and nourish the well being of the human collective and its place on the earth:

the prime minister, the president, the king and queen, the leader, the senator, the representative, the director, the CEO
the state, the kingdom, the nation, the congress, the parliament, the government, the corporation, the council
the institution, the court, the school, the agency, the foundation
the law, the ordinance, the constitution, the crime, the punishment, the enforcement, taxation
the composition, the form, the genre, the classification, the context, the grammar, the syntax, the plot
the conversation, the communication, the letter, the phone call, the telegram, the FAX, the Internet
the rite, the ceremony, the custom, the tradition
the church, the liturgy, the minister, the priest, the bishop, the congregation
the community, the neighborhood, the homes, the streets, the shops, the services, the utilities
the plan, the design, the diagram, the blueprint, the map, the cipher, the gestalt
the fractal[15]
the science, the art, the discipline, the profession, the practice
the decision, the deed, the act
the meeting, the conference, the schedule, the appointment
the time
the object, the subject
the teaching, the learning
the diagnosis, the prognosis, the theory, the treatment
the museum, the library, the conservancy, the trust, the preserve
the commitment, the vow, the duty, the responsibility
the marriage, the childlbirth, parenthood, elderhood
the last will and testament
the value, the ethic, the principle
the product, the quality, the quantity, the cost, the market, the buyer
the environment, the ecosystem, the biosphere, the national forest, the land trust

Various concrete symbols typify the manifestation of mind in the human world. Such symbols are like "minds," sufficient unto themselves, yet interrelated with all the other minds to form the Mind of Earth.

mother's milk, the pelican, the spring (nourishment)
the edible seeds, roots, fruits, and vegetables (rewards of labor and
    cooperation with the earth)
rabbit, cotton, flax, the silk worm (clothing)
the bow drill, the fire board, the tinder (warmth and light)
the willow, the cedar, the juniper, the clay (shelter)
the silica stone, the hardwood, the bone shard, the skin, the gut (tools)
sage, yarrow, willow, dock, mint (the healing herb)
the Great Bear (orientation, navigation)
the evergreen (sturdy, long lived, unchanging)
the buffalo, deer, bighorn sheep, turkey (who give themselves away for
    the life of the people)
the stop sign, the red light, the turn signal, the center line (safety and
    order)
the forge, the kiln, the mill, the wheel, the kitchen, the lab, the sheet of
    paper, the dynamo, the keyboard, the console (technological
    mind matrix)
the cathedral, the temenos, the ceremonial circle (sanctuary)
the ant, the bee (community as one)
the platoon, the private, the sergeant, the general, the rules and
    regulations (military discipline)
the convent, the cloister, the seminary (spiritual discipline)
the midwife, the teacher, the mentor, the guru, the guide (teaching function)
the driver's license, the marriage license, the gun license, the car license,
    the dog license (regulated behavior for the good of the whole)
the book, the disk, the tape, the chip (information, history)
the clock, the schedule, the log, the routine, the itinerary (management
    of time)
the dam, the nuclear plant, the wind generator, the solar panel
    (management of energy)
the toilet, the sink, the gutter, the sewer, the dump, the junk yard
    (management of waste)
the mechanic, the electrician, the plumber, the carpenter, the engineer,
    the truck driver, the super market checker, the housewife, etc.
    (installation and maintenance of life-support systems)

the one who: washes dishes, does laundry, cleans house, wipes the baby's
    ass, cooks meals, chops wood, waters the garden, pays the bills,
    hauls the ashes (domestic survival)
the dove, the olive branch, the plowshare, the lamb (peace, accord,
    harmony among the people)
"taking on the veil," "getting on the wagon," "going straight" (chastity,
    sobriety, self-control)
St. Nicholas, Santa Claus (the compassionate generosity of maturity)
the Crux Ansata (the four seasons, winter as the head)
the waning moon (hard times, dim light)
the proverb (the wisdom of maturity)
the bag of fertilizer (survival via cooperation with the earth in
    anticipation of spring)

The mythos of winter has always evoked a response (culture), that has for thousands of years guaranteed the survival of the human species as individual-family-community-tribe-nation. Only recently have we begun to understand the extent to which we have damaged our environment and our species by the misapplication of mind. A balanced mind is the invisible adhesive that holds the seasonal cycle together. Without winter, the child of summer would never pass into adulthood. Without winter, there would be no death, and therefore no regeneration.

> If Winter comes, can Spring be far behind?
> — Percy Shelley, *"Ode to the West Wind"*

THE WEB OF MIND

ENDNOTES: THE WINTER SHIELD OF HUMAN NATURE

[1] Marie Collins and Virginia Davis, *A Medieval Book of Seasons*, p. 122.

[2] Rick Bass, *Winter: Notes from Montana* (Boston: Houghton Mifflin, 1991), p. 151.

[3] *Walden*, p. 41.

[4] Edwin Way Teale, as quoted by Annie Dillard, *Pilgrim at Tinker Creek*, p. 47.

[5] Philip Slater, *Earthwalk* (Garden City: Doubleday, 1974), pp. 55-6.

[6] This is particularly true of modern civilization. Overpopulation has brought famine. In the face of global famine, those who have enough practice little self-restraint.

[7] "The year was rolling down, and a vital curve had been reached, the tilt that gives way to headlong rush. And when the monarchs [butterflies] had passed and were gone, the skies were vacant, the air poised. The dark night into which the year was plunging was not a sleep but an awakening, a new and necessary austerity, the sparer climate for which I longed." Annie Dillard, *Pilgrim at Tinker Creek*.

[8] *As quoted by C.G. Jung, Psyche and Symbol* (Garden City: Doubleday, 1958), p. 247.

[9] Gregory Bateson, *Mind and Nature* (New York: Bantam, 1979), p. 102.

[10] Bateson, pp. 104-111.

[11] Bateson, 116.

[12] On the relationship of bioregion to the human mind, see Barry Lopez, *Crossing Open Ground* (New York: Vintage, 1988), pp. 64-5. The fact that we have not yet completely self-destructed is due to the continued presence of the winter mind in our shield system. The fact that we are indeed flirting with species extinction can be explained in two ways: 1. We are rapidly approaching the state of runaway because our species governor is weakening; and 2. The governor-mind of nature, in order to keep itself in balance, is in the process of eliminating (controlling or setting limits to) the runaway growth of the human species. In either case, we can act in such a way as to insure the continuance of *homo sapiens*, or we can turn our backs on our apparent weakness and fall victim to a runaway summer (population explosions, mass epidemics, wars and

genocide on a vast scale) in which only the fittest will survive. See also Lyall Watson's argument in *Dark Nature: A Natural History of Evil* (New York: Harper Collins, 1995), that in order for the human species to survive we must overcome our own programming (summer shield naturalism) and attain a new maturity.

[13] I am reminded of the story of the New York City mama cat who repeatedly went back into a burning building to rescue her kittens, emerging finally with the last one, her eyes burned shut, her hair gone. Some might call this the maternal "instinct." Perhaps instinct is the wrong word. The mother cat obeyed a fundamental law of nature: the parents give of their bodies so that their children can live. "Instinct" alone doesn't account for her behavior. Instinct would have prompted her to flee the raging inferno. Instead she acted from the winter shield, from the mind of Nature, according to the natural law of the preservation of species.

[14] E.O. James, *The Ancient Gods* (New York: Putnam's, 1960), p. 108.

[15] Mandelbrot's "fractal" employs a means of measurement that embraces both order and chaos, from objects thousands of light years across to objects that can be encompassed on the head of a pin. Scientists today "are discovering how an immense number of diverse shapes can be characterized by their fractal dimensions. Everything from the winding of rivers to the convolutions of human brains, from the structure of galaxies to the patterns of metal fractures yields to the fractal measure." John Briggs and F. David Peat, *Turbulent Mirror: An Illustrated Guide to Chaos Theory and the Science of Wholeness* (New York: Harper and Row, 1989), p. 105.

THE SPRING SHIELD OF HUMAN NATURE

> Spring. A. place of rising, as of a stream; B. action or time of rising or beginning; C. young growth; D. first season of the year; E. rising of the sea to its extreme height; F. elastic contrivance (fig. impelling agency)
>
> — *Oxford Dictionary of English Etymology*

> One becomes two, two becomes three, and out of the third comes the one as fourth.
>
> — *Maria Prophetissa*

Turn to the east! The sun is rising like a golden shield. Shadows of the long night of winter have faded like dew. Dawn arrives in stark outline, in visionary relief. Everywhere things are being born, quietly at first, then with a shout. The web takes a breath, quivers, and expands. The earth stands forth, clothed in the nakedness of light. Suddenly, we can see things as they are, and they are more than we ever sensed, felt, or thought. We see through the eyes, we fly through the body, of Imagination. William Blake was right. If birth is threaded through the primal DNA of life, then Imagination is too.

> If the doors of perception were cleansed every thing would appear to man as it is, infinite.
>
> — *Marriage of Heaven and Hell*

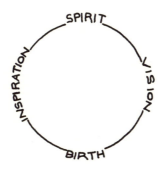

SPRING

The ardent body of summer, the psychological darkness of fall, and the abstract order of winter have brought us to the brink of a mysterious quantum leap. This miraculous coming forth of life enriches and vitalizes all the other shields of nature. Without birth, nothing can grow. Without growth, nothing can die. Without death, nothing can be born. With the birth of spring, all the other seasons are born. The four originate in the one. The circle of the self completes itself by returning to, and beginning with, the source from which all things flow. Some give a name to this source — Spirit, Creator, Transformer, Matrix, Holy Ghost, Muse. Surely you have a name for it, even if the name cannot be uttered.

Call it infancy, but it is very old. Call it ancient, but it is always new. Call it imagination, inspiration, illumination, vision. "We are led to believe a lie, when we see with, not *through*, the eye." Blake is talking here about the vaginal eye, through which the world is born. If you don't believe me, look *through* your eyes at spring. But we must leave our cages, indulge our human nature-and not fall under the illusion that we are separate from what we are. Look at all that green stuff exploding in the garden. Migrating birds cluster in the skies. Snakes are oozing up from dens of hibernation, hungry and blind. Horses are foaling, sleepy bees nosing around for the first scents. Doesn't all this remind us of who we are? Can't we feel it rising within us, an intoxication like wine? Can't we feel how our eyes are co-creating it? Are we so blind as not to recognize ourselves as a part of all this?

The shield of the new born stands in startling contrast to the shield of adolescent fall. Instead of darkness and shadows, there is light, illumination, enlightenment. Instead of inwardness and introspection, there is ecstasy and creative expression. Instead of psychological feeling there is spiritual knowing. In the fall, the self must learn to love the self. In the spring, the self must learn to love the spirit. In the fall, human nature sees with the eye of self-consciousness. In the spring, human nature sees through the eye of Imagination — the Big Picture. In the fall reside the dangerous conscience-monsters — guilt and regret. In the spring, conscience is but an illusory obstacle to freedom. In the realms of dawn, there are no fetters, no prisons. To the new born infant anything is possible. "So our human life but dies down to its root, and still puts forth its green blade to eternity" (Thoreau, *Walden*). The rising sun stirs the heart of the pilgrim with dreams of setting forth on a new life:

> Yet longing comes upon him to fare forth on the water.
> Bosque taketh blossom, cometh beauty of berries,
> Field to fairness, land fares brisker,

> All this admonisheth man eager of mood,
> The heart turns to travel so that he then thinks
> On flood-ways to be far departing . . . .
>
> — *"The Seafarer"* (Trans. Ezra Pound)

Don't be deceived. All is not sweetness and light. As long as it is bound to the great wheel of the seasons, human nature cannot take flight into some alien dawn and never return. The spirit energy must assume the bodily proportions of summer, and then in the fall turn inward and prepare again to be initiated for winter.

The expansion of spring always incorporates the constriction of fall. The brightest illumination produces the darkest shadows. Spring cannot exist without fall. Illumination requires a prior state of blindness.

A symbol central to the spring shield is fire — the spark that bursts forth from the mind of winter — the kindling, arousal, quickening. The electrical spark in the chromosomes is the fire in the star. As sperm seeks the egg, so nothingness leaps for fire. From the ring of fire leaps light. From the light leaps body and shadow. From body and shadow leaps mind. From the mind leaps fire. And from fire leaps body and shadow. And so, with the application of the spark, the whole round is enlivened, like yeast, and the body is enlivened by the spirit.

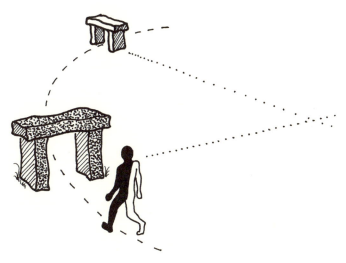

DEATH : THRESHOLD INTO THE BIRTH SPIRIT WORLD

The mystery of birth comprehends all. Under the aegis of the spring shield we worship, pray and express reverence, devotion, awe, and mystical love. Quickened by such power, our lives can be transformed and enlightened, the metaphysical plane apprehended. Even when the cosmic trickster leads us to an unexpected *contretemps*, even when we must "suffer the slings and arrows of outrageous fortune," we arrive again at the birth gates of spring, all swollen and golden with potential, hungering for the passage into summer. Does there need to be stronger proof of immortality? Light is all. "O Death, where is thy sting? O Grave, where is thy victory?"

So leave the house and walk into the fields of wildflowers. Was there a dying? It is so easy to forget the rigors of winter when the sun climbs the sky like the Philosopher's Stone. All creation is turning to watch and donning clothing of light. All are divine, all are enlightened, all are holy. In the ebbing blood of the dead god the anemone is blooming. "If there is not another life, there is at least another way to live."[1]

You don't need to know the names of the yellow ones, or the purple ones, or the icy blue ones. Give them your own names. You say you don't have the ability to do that? You'd rather leave that function to the poet? *You* are the poet. *You* are the singer. *You* are the wildflower. Name it after yourself. Call it Blue Eyes, or Tooth Wart, or Long Legs, or Falling Hair, or Purple Vulva, or Bald Shine. If, in fact, you are Nature, and Nature is you, then the season to create yourself, to name yourself, to heal yourself, to send hatched egg letters to yourself, is now.

Notes taken by a fasting woman during her time alone startle with a truth that is already familiar. Access to the spirit shield of nature comes naturally:

> "Massed before me the tangled roots long dead of a fallen tree still clutch dark moist earth in a death grasp. 'What am I holding on to that needs to be let go?' I ask the roots. 'Being nice for approval, for acceptance sake,' they answer."
> "Suddenly I see a wild rose bush growing modestly in front of the massed tangle of tree roots. 'The thorn and the flower.' Thorny issues. Love grows out of owning one's thorns." "The question rises, 'What should I do?' A jay suddenly squawks raucously, unhinging the peace. 'Ah, so I need to put up a squawk early on,' you say."
> "Suddenly, high up, a squirrel begins an irritated sputter of sounds. I've intruded on him. 'How clear and direct you are,' I say. 'I'm learning.'" And I see a tree trunk, so rotten it's close to sawdust. Like this old pattern, falling apart.

> "Across, on the other side of the stream, a young tree, stands in the foreground, growing straight up. Behind stands another tree, bent at a right angle.

Together they form an upside down figure four. And behind these two, two other trees rise close together, red brown trunks in a long, slender slight curve . . . in a quiet, slow, steady dance. Feelings of tenderness and devotion come. Behind the four dancers is one whose trunk is shaped like a harp. A harp needing strings. Sun suddenly out. Obscuring clouds opening — to a cornflower blue sky."[2]

The spirit of nature answers the questions of the heart. The wind *does* speak. The trees *do* have a voice. Does the voice belong to nature or to us? What's the difference?

So put away the axe, the chainsaw, the wedge, the kindling hatchet. Stack the firewood in next winter's corner. You have no need for these tools now. The work of death is complete. All that frozen white stuff dripping from the eaves is thawing the Great Mother's heart. The fist that held you in the trance of suspension is loosening its grip. A warmer wind slobbers all over the edges of your frozen mind. The winter coma has passed. Its end is spelled with the color green.

> Dust as we are, the immortal spirit grows
> Like harmony in music; there is a dark
> Inscrutable workmanship that reconciles
> Discordant elements, makes them cling together
> In one society.
>
> — Wordsworth, *The Prelude*

One might wonder where Wordsworth's music comes from. The ancients were intrigued by the question thousands of years before we came along to ask it. According to the Egyptians, Hermes created music when he fashioned the first lyre. But they begged the question. Music existed before the lyre, before any physical means of expressing it. The Pythagoreans surmised that music (and its attendant arts) came from the diapason, the perfect harmonic interval between the mundane earth and the enduring stars. The multitudinous parts of creation were divided up into tones, harmonic intervals, numbers, names, colors, and forms. But the Pythagoreans' mathematical, universal, musical instrument still begged the question. Whose fleshless fingers pluck the Mind that quivers into music? Only the act of listening to music can answer the question, and the answer is indeed ineffable.

Of course, it is quite easy to tell the truth when truth is so slippery. And the truth is that all living and dying things have a voice, all sing, all are prompted to make music. That which plays upon the body, soul and mind of all things is that which propels them through the gates of life. Once they have crossed this threshold, they can do aught else but sing. The songs may not always be pleasing, especially to the reactive and psychological ear, for it knows that music may be found in violence and death. The hammer "sings" against the anvil. The wildfire "rips" through the underbrush. The flash flood "roars" like a locomotive. The cougar "snarls" over its kill. The music erupts, fed like magma from the Source. Best not to ignore it. "Beauty and grace are performed whether or not we will or sense them. The least we can do is try to be there" (Annie Dillard, *Pilgrim at Tinker Creek*).

That same music is on the poet's lips, in the painter's brush, in the human apprehension of the ghostly fingers that play upon the strings of summer's body, fall's soul, and winter's mind. Just when we think the music has ceased, when the rigid gloom of winter stifles even the breathing of the seed, that's when the music bursts forth.

> While with an eye made quiet by the power
> Of harmony, and the deep power of joy,
> We see into the life of things.
>
> — Wordsworth, *Intimations Ode*

Metaphor. The spring shield is metaphor. Because we cannot look directly into the face of God, we must avert our eyes and grope for metaphor, similitude, likeness. Even if we are magically enabled to look, like the man who would be king, into the storehouse of eternity, we cannot normally see exactly what is there. Primary forms, elements, symbols appear, all of which seem to be related through dissimilarity. Music and fire are not the same. Yet in the poetry of the east shield, they are identical. Music is fire. And fire is bird, and bird is angel, and angel is spirit, and spirit is prayer, and prayer is imagination, and imagination is birth.

The universe is glued together with metaphor. The metaphor is an endless loop, a mobius strip, a skein of light travelling through warped space that tucks back in on itself like a snake on its tail. With metaphor all things are sewn together through the miracle of intercourse, interrelationship, interpenetration.[3]

Why do we seek the spring? We could be creatures like the mole, the worm, or the owl, preferring darkness and night. We could be happy with brute existence, clinging mindlessly to the host like parasites. Why do we insist on drinking from the Source, from the Pyrrhian Spring, Connla's Well, the cauldron of regeneration, the wildflower? The teaching of the four shields says that we seek the spring because we are of the body, memory and mind of the universe, because the body, memory and mind seek spirit — nay, *are* spirit. Yes, we are powerless — to resist the inrush of power — as powerless as the earth to the forces of renewal, as powerless as darkness in the naked dawn.

.... Which brings us to certain secrets of initiation:

If the eyes are blinded, the mind "sees through" to the light.

If the child of oneself becomes lost in the darkness of the threshold passage, the adult of oneself will find him, and bring him to the light.

Enlightenment must dissolve into the body. The body must become lost. The lostness becomes a path that leads to enlightenment.

Initiation and rites of passage are not social forms that have been imposed on the community by whimsical autocrats. Initiation follows the way the body takes to become spirit. It follows the seasons.

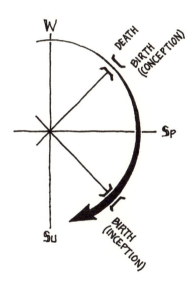

SPRING: THE INFANT OF IMAGINATION

When we cannot forsake our own darkness, we are powerless to recognize the light, even when it blinds us with the truth. Conversely, when we are powerless to recognize the light, we cannot forsake our own darkness. The child who never grows out of adolescence is cast away on the seas of memory and feeling. She resists change, feels trapped by labyrinths of possibility, becomes a wandering soul attached to a dying body. Though winter is always just around the corner, the season is always fall.

Initiation, then, is the means by which mortals attain immortality. Via the birth-gates of winter, the body of earth is revitalized, renewed. The spark of life returns. Via the birth-gates of death, the body seeks consummation in spirit. Summer dies into fall. Fall's memory darkens into winter and there, where the mind holds sway, the body dies. This is necessary if the spirit within the body is to be revived. With the birth of spirit (spring) comes bodily existence (south), memory (fall), and mind (winter). Thus the whole is enlivened by the arrival of spring. Open your eyes!

> He who despairs of spring with downcast eye steps on it, unknowing.
> He who searches for spring with his knees in the mud finds it, in abundance.
>
> — Aldo Leopold, *Sand County Almanac*

There is no dearth of symbols depicting the revival of spring. The mythos of regeneration, rebirth, transformation, metamorphosis, and the like is found in every human religion, in a myriad of folktales and myths. The best-loved folktale of China, the story of Meng Chiang Nu, illustrates the regenerative power of the spirit:

> The Mengs and the Chiangs were separated by a wall. One year the two families each planted a pumpkin, whose vines climbed up both sides of the wall and met at the top, where they joined and fruited into an enormous pumpkin. When the pumpkin was divided, they found inside it a beautiful little girl. They called her Meng Chiang.
>
> Meng Chiang grew up in a time of war. The Chinese emperor was building a great wall along the frontier, from north to east. To insure that it did not collapse, he buried a living victim at each mile of the wall's ten thousand mile length. His empire recoiled in terror as his demand for sacrifices increased. Finally, a sage came to the emperor and suggested that only one sacrifice was needed, the life of a man called Wan (whose name meant "ten thousand"). This alone would satisfy the spirits. When Wan heard of this plan, he fled.
>
> It so happened that Wan was hiding in a tree in the garden of Meng Chiang's house when she went out naked in the moonlight to bathe in the garden pool. "If any man were to see me now, as I am, then I would happily belong to him forever," she said out loud. Overhearing, Wan called out from the tree. "I have seen you."
>
> So Meng Chen and Wan were married. But in the middle of the wedding feast, soldiers burst in and carried Wan off to be sacrificed. His bride was left to weep inconsolably.

After a while, Meng Chiang undertook a perilous journey to the Great Wall in search of her husband's remains. But when she reached the wall, she despaired of knowing where, along its great length, to find his bones. As she sat and wept, the wall took pity on her and collapsed, revealing the remains of her husband.

The emperor learned of her devoted search. He sent for her and, astounded by her beauty, resolved to make her his wife. Meng Chiang agreed to his proposal, subject to three conditions: that a forty-nine day funerary feast for her husband be held; that all officials of the high court should attend; and that an altar forty-nine feet high should be erected by the riverbank where she might make offerings to the dead Wan. The emperor consented.

When all had been prepared, Meng Chiang mounted the altar and reviled the emperor in front of the officials and high court. In the name of Wan she cursed and shamed him for his cruelty. Then she threw herself into the river.

The angry emperor dragged her body from the water and cut it up into little pieces. He ground her bones into dust and cast the dust into the river. The little particles of dust turned into little silver fishes. To this day these fishes nourish the river and the people with the everlasting love of Meng Chiang.[4]

Ground into powder by the millstones of the body's passage through love, separation, and death, the human returns to the earth transformed and transforming, bearing the Grail, the bleeding lance and the silver plate into a barren winter-bitten land. We are crucified with the gods and goddesses, we descend into the sea of dark unknowing and suffer a sea change into something rich and strange. We return as Vishnu, Oannes, the Lady of Dolphins, the Daughter of the Swan, or Jesus-ICTHYS. We return as nourishment, in the little fishes, in the tall grass, in the budding cherry, in the swarm of dancing flies — as the spirit of that in which we are embodied. The fact that we return is the fact of spirit.

But first, like Melampus, we must find the nest of snakes and rear their young. We must sleep with the coilings and slitherings of nightmares, passions and sufferings. We must accustom ourselves to the night of fear and wrest from it an inner rigor, a plan, a way, a stratagem. Only then will the snakes lick our ears clean so that we can understand the language of birds and animals. We must build the nest, shadow by shadow, in which we will be immolated, and suffer ourselves to be delivered of eggs. Only then can we taste immortality. Like Amaterasu Omikami, we must allow the solar mirror to lure us through the gates of death to enlightenment. Like Eos, we must marry the mortal even as we long to be free of it. Like Meng Chiang, we must caress ourselves with the moldering bones of lost love until we gain the courage to die nobly. Only then can we realize the dawn.

Among the ancient Greeks, Demeter (Mother Earth) consorted with her daughter Persephone (female, woman) in the summer, when the grain and the corn waxed and the animals grew sleek and fat. When harvest was done, Persephone descended into the underworld to dwell with Hades, her gloomy husband, through the six months of fall and winter. But with the coming of spring, Helios thawed the frozen earth and Persephone returned to the living arms of her Mother.

Adonis ("the Lord") was condemned by the circumstances of his birth to spend one half of the year with Aphrodite (eros) and the other half with Persephone (thanatos). While biding his time with Aphrodite, he was killed by a wild boar. Aphrodite revived his spirit in the form of a blood-red anemone. A variant of the myth says the love goddess prevailed on Persephone to restore Adonis to earth for four months every spring.

The *Bardo Thotrol* (Tibetan Book of the Dead) makes the meaning of the initiatory passage very clear. In the death passage toward spring, the summer body that must die encounters the ghosts of its karma in the dark shield of memory (fall). But if it holds true to its purpose to be reborn, exercising the discipline of the Bardo (winter), it will not be sidetracked into a premature birth (which is only a kind of death), and will emerge into the fullness and completeness of spring's enlightenment.

Another kind of expression typifies the spring shield: trickster tales, such as found in every culture, traditional and modern. The Trickster, another name for God — or the Devil — exists in order to express the quixotic, random, unexpected quality of human experience, especially that kind of experience that leads to enlightenment and/or life-changing catastrophe. If life, like a coin, has another side, the Trickster is the other side — the side not seen — until too late. In one sense, the Coyote or Zen master tales, or the pranks and blunders of shamans, magicians, crows, ravens, raccoons, magpies, hyenas, and Brer Rabbit are means of tricking us into seeing the other side of the coin, the karma we knew was there, but chose to ignore — the spring on the flip side of the fall.

Aha! Spring came after all — whether we welcomed it or not. With a similar persistence the magician, or is it the fool, seeks to go where death is — for that is where birth can be found.

Once ensnared by the briefest look into eternity, we must go there again, and again, as often as spring follows winter. In the spring shield of human nature, death and birth, mortal and divine, nature and spirit, are inseparably one. The trickster knows this, and does not know it, and all the while is inexorably drawn to the light. That ageless boy reclining on the lotus; that lovely young girl rising from the bed of aged Tithonus — are they gods and goddesses, or are they idiot savants? Ask the morning star.

If the spring shield is the spirit shield, you may ask, what is "spirit?" Within the nomenclature of the four shields, the spring shield is the vital principle that births all things ("spirit"), as opposed to the fall shield, which is the inner psyche or individual memory that dies ("soul"). In this sense, the Christ who prayed in the Garden of Gesthemane (fall shield) that the burden might be lifted from Him would be defined as soul. The Christ who descended upon the apostles in tongues of fire might be defined as spirit. Soul is connected with death, spirit with birth.

Spirit: the breath of life, of immortality; incorporeal vitality; vital power. See: spire, spirant, spiral, aspire, inspire, transpire. God (spirit) breathed into the lump of clay "and man became a living soul." Even so, the spirit of nature breathed into the empty featurelessness of space/time and all things became living flesh.

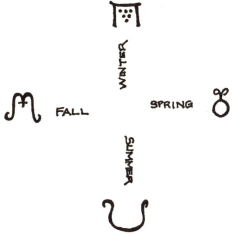

ANCIENT GERMANIC TIME SIGNS

Images, symbols and concepts of spring abound without number. The very idea of symbol (a representation of associated qualities and essences) involves the expressive function of the eastern shield, where the sun (Heimdall, Horus, Mithra, Eos, Aurora, Dawn) rises with rosy fingers and all things praise their "Maker." The poise, the dance, the posture of praise of *everything*, even the "meanest flower that blows," gives birth to intimations, reveries, awareness, recognitions, understandings, imaginings that lie too deep for tears. Hence it would be difficult to list every living entity or its dance of separateness/interrelatedness, for in itself that is a symbol, metaphor, or similitude of spirit. Among those symbols in human parlance that have come to represent the qualities of the spring shield are the following:

the wind (breath of infinity or creativity)
birds of all kinds, their songs, migrations and feathers, especially the
    eagle, hawk, nightingale, swan and dove
the sudden power and illumination of lightning (Zeus, Thor)
the oracle (the Pythia, the runes, the mouth of the prophet)
the lyre (Apollo), the flute (Kokopelli), the pipes (Pan)
the magic wand, staff, stick, cauldron, broom, potent, touchstone, ball,
    glass, herb, ladder, ring, basket
the Muses, the Charities, the angels
the rainbow
the alchemist's gold
the lotus, the rose
the magician, the fool
the prayer, the praise
the spark (tinder box, flint stone, match, hot coal)
the supernova born from the collapsing star
the song line (of the Australian aborigine)
the budding cherry (Japan), the budding hazel or hawthorne (Celtic)
May Day (Beltaine, Anthesteria, and all rites of spring)
Easter (as governed by the goddess who rules the menstral cycle, Oestre)
the Tarot
the shining path
the local spirits of "primitive" animism
the touch of the doctor, nurse, healer, shaman/ess, medicine person
the quantum leap of the electron
the idea of spontaneous mutation, combustion, transformation, shape-
    shifting, the act of making sacred (consecration)
the goal of any quest, pilgrimage, or spiritual journey (grail, treasure,
    temple, river, mountain, holy place)
the spiritual envelope in which the physical body is enclosed (halo, aura,
    shekinnah glory)
the new shoot, sprout, bud, or blossom
the nativity of humans and other mammals and/or invertebrates
divine messengers (seraphim, ofanim, arelim)
the pure knight (Sir Galahad)

the Holy Ghost, indwelling spirit, totem animal, inner voice
the new moon

    The mythos of the spring shield, then, suffuses all entities in natural self-thus. The spirit of spring has infused the human version of nature with imagination, creativity, and the impulse to regenerate and heal. The wrinkled, red, ageless little thing that comes wet and screaming from the mother's womb is merely one of the infinite number of infants born from the Source of human nature, of which spring is merely an earthly example. Forever may the spark fly out from the flint.

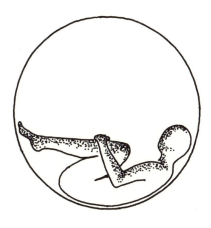

IN THE BIRTH SPIRIT WORLD OF SPRING

ENDNOTES: THE SPRING SHIELD OF HUMAN NATURE

[1] From an untitled poem by Theodore Roethke, *Straw for the Fire: From the Notebooks of Theodore Roethke, 1943-63* _____.

[2] Courtesy, Selina Sweet.

[3] "But it occurred to me that I could no more catch spring by the tip of the tail than I could untie the apparent knot in the snakeskin; there are no edges to grasp . . . . The power we seek, too, seems to be a continuous loop" Annie Dillard, *Pilgrim at Tinker Creek.*

[4] From Anthony Christie, *Chinese Mythology* (Middlesex: Hamlyn, 1968), pp. 96-7.

FOUR SHIELD DYNAMICS

> The summer does it without thinking.
> The fall does it in the dark.
> The winter does it with premeditation.
> The spring does it with the lights on.
>
> — School of Lost Borders Training Paradigm

What causes the self to assume the seasonal shields? Since humans belong to "all things" they must also, at any given time, impersonate one of nature's faces in the masquerade.[1] Any stimulus-event can activate the self to change the shield, to put on another seasonal mask. If the shield system is more or less intact, the first shield impersonated is invariably that of childhood — the summer persona. The child reacts first because, in the seasons of human nature, the child's mask is reactive, instinctive, and primally attuned to raw experience. Once the summer shield has been assumed, the subsequent seasonal changes (shields) come up naturally, but not always in an orderly fashion. Sometimes the fall, winter, or spring shield gets stuck in the "up" or dominant position and the turning dynamic of the seasonal masquerade halts, usually to be resumed after an hiatus, sometimes, never.

SCENARIO

A man goes to work and is told that he has just been laid off. The child of him reacts with emotions of anger, fear, and resentment. His blood pumps faster; his adrenalin count goes up. He pounds his desk, sprains a knuckle. But he doesn't care. The sensation of pain suits the situation.

This childish reaction, typical of the way he acted when he was a boy, is normal, if not appropriate. If the summer boy's reaction were the *only* reaction, if he could not get a grip on himself, he would be in for more trouble than he really wanted. The earth cannot sustain herself on endless summer. There would be no inwardness, no maturity, no harvest, no birth — only endless copulation and predation, emotion without feeling, sensation without thought, warfare without peace, growth without spirit or control. If he is healthy, this man's story will continue through the succeeding variations of fall, winter, and spring.

Having performed, acted, expressed, defended himself through the shield of summer, the man will become constricted, inward, and self-conscious (fall).

Memories will plague him. He will look back on his days of employment and ask himself, "What have I done to deserve this? He will remember all the times he acted like a child. He will see himself through his mother's or other women's eyes, perhaps in a shameful or depressed light. He will feel helpless, victimized. His mistakes will parade across the screen of consciousness to make him feel like a failure. He may even consider suicide.

The natural self cannot, should not, evade this impersonation of the fall persona. The man must go to this dark place where summer's child is initiated. How else can he be prepared to endure the rigors of winter (unemployment) as a mature adult? Initiation is preparation. Fall exists to confirm that summer's child no longer rules. If, however, he gets mired in the shield of fall, he will become a liability to himself and the family for whom he seeks to provide. A boy-adolescent in crisis cannot handle the rigors of winter, at least not until he has completed the fall passage.

If his shields are reasonably healthy, he will eventually arrive at winter — the rational man. Adolescent feeling will become thoughtful action. From feelings of helplessness will come a plan, a course of action, a determination to do what has to be done. He will reason with himself, consider and weigh assets and liabilities, and ponder a future course. He will take control of himself and do what is necessary to end his relationship to the company. The ability to swallow hard times, to weather physical and psychological blows, to hold on, to continue somehow, is what will bring him to spring. There is no other reliable way.

Illumination is a reward, not a piece of luck. If the adolescent shield of fall longs for the spring, the only way to get there is through the dead of winter. If, however, the man should become stuck behind the shield of winter, he will become cold, rational, hiding any pain he might feel with a brittle mask of self-control. Survival will become a grim battle waged with an unending winter. The seed of rebirth will die of the cold.

When he takes up the spring shield, he will understand why such misfortune entered his life. Apparent defeat will become victory. Life will burst forth from the dead ground. He will see through the eyes of imagination, beyond the pale of his current predicament. He will see what he can do to enhance his life and the lives of those he loves. These understandings may come as revelations, and seem related to matters of faith and regeneration.

Much as he might wish, however, he cannot indefinitely wear the mask of illumination. He must take care to survive the onset of summer, the return of childish emotions, the hard realities of life without a job, or the need to relocate in a very physical world where predators prey and sirens of distraction sing sweetly. Should he become stuck behind the mask of spring, he will be of little use in an existence that requires the participation of the other three shields: his body, psyche, and mind.

How long does it take for the natural self to revolve through the seasons — to move from stimulus to memory to thought to regeneration? An instant, a few minutes, a few days, a few months, a year, a lifetime. A single revolution can sometimes be abbreviated (or elongated) by simultaneously donning more than one shield at a time. The flow of consciousness is often dominated by all four impersonations coming and going, like minor and major themes in a symphony, rising and falling alone or in combination. This kind of interlayering or superimposing, often experienced as chaotic or disorderly, is, in fact, the stuff with which the natural self becomes complete.

The amount of time spent in any shield-impersonation is also relative to the strength of the given shield system. When the stimulus event is strong, such as the death of a loved one, several masks may be employed within a relatively short time. A death can also mire the self in a single shield, such as the fall shield of mourning, for a considerable length of time. Some people mourn for years. This impersonation might be considered inappropriate in a life drama where the eventual participation of the other shields is also required.

SCENARIO

A 30-year old married woman gets a phone call at work. Her beloved father has died unexpectedly. The shield of summer comes up: shock, disbelief, outrage, grief, loss. Blood pounds through her veins. She feels faint, fights for control, wants to be comforted. The little girl, daughter of her father, comes profoundly alive. But then she puts on the mask of the fall and retreats inside to the universe of feeling. She becomes the adolescent she was, the nearly grown daughter of her father. Through her father's eyes, she watches herself grieve. She feels helpless, at the mercy of implacable death. Suddenly, the phone rings. A customer wants to place an order. Automatically, she puts on the mask of winter and takes the order. She hangs up and bursts out crying, realizing how life goes on, even in the face of tragedy. Within a short span of time, she has employed four shields, the summer, fall, winter, and spring.

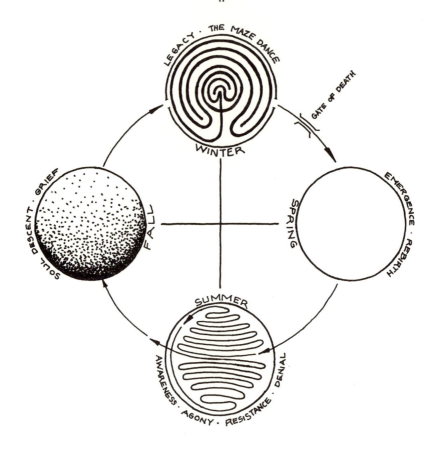

THE FOUR SHIELDS OF DYING

As night comes on, the physical reality of death will give way to another movement in her sonata of grief, called "the psychological." The innocence of the little girl has been invaded by the realities of death. Her empathetic husband comforts her through a rocky night. Crushed by sadness and memory, she wanders slow-motion through feelings of guilt, regret, anxiety, love. She weeps for the little girl she was. Disturbing dreams flit in and out like bats.

By morning, the fall theme of dark feeling fades into a minor key, and the theme of the winter shield surges into a major key — the duties of funeral, memorial and burial arrangements. She takes her place on stage as the competent, intelligent, worthy, 30-year-old daughter-mother of the man who died — a unique and independent adult in her own right. She stands beside her widowed mother and makes necessary adjustments in her own life to accommodate the unexpected loss, all the while coping with the emotions of the child and the psychological vagaries of the adolescent. But she must not wear the shield of the winter indefinitely. By absorbing herself in duties, arrangements, and expectations of others, she may prevent herself from experiencing the necessary grief appropriate to the fall shield.

Even as she acts and reacts to the social and private demands of death, she may contact some of the benefits of the spring shield — a sense of personal expansion, a new found wisdom, even a transformed life. She will see more clearly the relationship between herself and death. The death of her father will become not only a learning experience, but a revelation and a setting free.

Of course, the little girl will meet crisis again and again in the summer shield. The next stimulus event could be anything from the breakdown of a household appliance, to an unfaithful spouse, to the death of her mother. Every time, she will have to come around to the adolescent, the adult, and the illumined one, only to return again to the child.

SCENARIO

Let's take a look at *your* shield system. You're driving down a country road, your stereo purring mellow sounds, when all of a sudden you are riveted to what your eyes are telling you. A car lies upside down in the road. A bloody victim sprawls nearby. Others are still in the car. Dust and the stench of burning rubber still hang in the air. You are the first one to reach the scene. You notice, as you automatically apply the brakes, that gasoline is spilling from a ruptured gas tank — and that there is an open lane off to the side that you can drive through.

Your first reaction is that of the child of summer. You see the blood. You smell the presence of death and shock. Your stomach sinks. Your palms sweat. You feel nauseous, weak, and panicky. You're afraid to look too closely. It would be easy to innocently slip past and drive on, letting the driver behind you deal with the carnage. So what do you do? Do you roll up your window, pump up the radio, and pass?

No, you wouldn't do that. I'm only describing what the child of summer would do. It's not an appropriate persona with which to deal with the situation. Nevertheless, it's the first shield that comes up. You cannot avoid it.

Even as your childhood persona reacts in horror, your fall persona withdraws into the constrictions of self-consciousness. You're watching yourself react. You're aware of your emotions. You're assessing your ability to lend help, remembering your last course in first aid. Though you may tend to see yourself negatively, you also realize you have some strength. You always knew you had it in you. No doubt you have at least entertained the fantasy that you would "act" (play the role) responsibly in such a crisis. Nevertheless, you cannot impersonate action while under the passive influence of the fall shield. You can only impersonate inwardness. You live in a world of self-consciousness.

Ah yes, the car wreck. You put on the mask of winter. You consciously apply the brake. You have become the self-disciplined adult who gives of self so that the people may live. Knees shaking and sick to your stomach with fear and adrenalin (child shield), profoundly self-conscious (adolescent shield), you get out of the car and face the unknown. As you look into the visage of violent injury and death, you see what you can do to help the victims (adult shield).

Because the winter shield acts appropriately — does what needs to be done at the scene of the car crash — you are illumined. The spiritual aspect of the accident will become apparent when your part in the rescue is done. It will move you to profound realizations, perhaps bringing tears of relief and self-acceptance. As you shake in the throes of after-shock, you will realize you have made a quantum leap in growth. What you have just done will well up inside you — the stuff of poetry, song, and spiritual conviction.

Did I place you in too flattering a light? All I gave you is an intact shield system. That doesn't mean you aren't neurotic, burned out, or having your share of troubles. You just happen to be one of the more balanced ones. You are capable of acting from the appropriate shield. You can put on all four of the personae necessary for your survival and the continuance of your species. You can reasonably operate on all four levels of human nature: body, psyche, mind, and spirit.

SUMMER TO FALL

> Why cannot the Ear be closed to its own destruction?
> Or the glistening Eye to the poison of a smile:?
> Why are Eyelids stored with arrows ready drawn,
> Where a thousand fighting men in ambush lie? . . .
> Why a tender curb on the youthful burning boy?
> Why a little curtain of flesh on the bed of our desire?
> — William Blake, *The Book of Thel*

Nature, as it is experienced by humans, passes from sensory reality to remembered reality, i.e., from raw experience to reflected experience, or memory.[2] As raw experience (sensation, instinctive reaction) becomes reflection, it contracts, implodes, into a psychological persona, where there is no action, no behavior. That which has just happened (the summer), becomes the stuff of memory (fall). The stimulus event, first experienced in the summer shield, goes into a shadow realm, a dark ocean of interrelated memory events. The reactive emotions become the stuff of remembrance and feeling: the "psychosphere."

AUTUMN'S CRUCIBLE
THE ALCHEMY OF EXPERIENCE

THE SENSATIONS & EXPERIENCES OF SUMMER DISAPPEAR INTO FALL'S CAULDRON OF MEMORY WHERE THEY ARE DISTILLED INTO THE ACTIONS & DECISIONS OF WINTER

Summer is the urge of things to be remembered in the fall. But fall's memory must become winter's mind. Winter's mind must give way to the spirit of the spring. The spring must become embodied in summer. And when the body of summer turns inward to prepare for winter, it falls again into memory. Fall stores away all the memories of the seasons. The memories form complexes within the fall shield. These complexes have a great deal to do with the psychological makeup of human nature.

The fall, then, is a place of sublimation and translation, where raw sensation, emotion, or dis-ease settle into a kind of psychological memory-sorting chamber that sooner or later conveys it to the mind of winter so that a kind of regeneration will occur. Obviously, the fall shield is where childhood must be initiated into adulthood. The fledgling body and its attendant sensations, emotions, drives, encodings, must negotiate the labyrinth of memory and self-perception in order to manifest as mind-in-action. The "tender curb" must be lifted. The hymen must be removed. Only then will spring come.

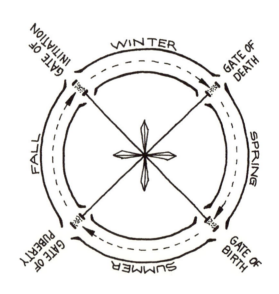

SHIELD AS PASSAGE
THE COURSE OF INITIATION

The fear of imminent death that characterizes many forms of initiation produces a memory trance. The child remembers childhood vividly even as he is being torn away from it — remembers, but cannot re-live, and is helpless to act. At that point, there is a surrendering to the inevitable, even a kind of relaxation, into a profoundly psychological ("soul logical") condition, an inward dying diametrically opposed to the outward birthing of the spring shield. This "vale of soul-making" is an absolutely essential step toward the birthing of spring. What lies between the soul and the spirit is the passage of winter.

FALL TO WINTER

> The individual mind is imminent but not only in the body. It is imminent also in pathways and messages outside the body, and there is a larger mind of which the individual mind is only a sub-system. The larger mind is comparable to God and is perhaps what some people mean by God, but it is still imminent in the total interconnected social systems and planetary ecology.
>
> — Gregory Bateson, as quoted by James Lovelock (*The Ages of Gaia*)

Fall initiates raw bodily experience into the realms of mind (winter) via the sacred contexts of chaos, remembrance, flux, self-consciousness, feeling, soul, and psychological death. Fall is the preparation place, the individuation place, the coming of night, the test of adaptability to the power that is not merely physical, the test taken on the dark side of the universe. The test can be failed. The child can die in the first hard frost. The child can become lost in memory. But if all goes well, raw experience will be alchemized by fall into the activating mind of winter.

The mind of winter is exactly what the brain of summer is not. It is immaterial. It has no physical form, shape, or property. As Bateson put it, "Mind is empty; it is no-thing. It exists only in its ideas, and these again are no-things. Only the ideas are imminent, embodied in their examples."[3]

The presence of mind is traced in the behavior of the untold numbers of species that make up the organism called Gaia. Nursemaiden of sentience, guardian of ancestry, mind is immanent in all living creatures and determines their evolutionary form and progress.[4] Mind is Lovelock's "Daisyworld," an image of the living earth in which one species can never grow unchecked, where the basic design is diversity and interrelationship between earth, atmosphere, and life cycles.[5] Mind seeks to manifest the absolute simplicity and complexity of essence and completion. Of course, it cannot attain this completeness until the winter turns into spring. By then, mind has died so that spirit can regenerate old forms.

Mind, as it is manifested in the natural world, can look dead to the physical eye. Nothing is there. The stems are bare. The rivers are frozen. Potential for physical life appears at a minimum. Life forms seem cast into a cold rigidity. At the absolute zero of winter thought moves, like a killing wind, like a white shroud, like the cold unreachability of galactic space. Thought awakens the seed buried in the cold earth.[6] Thought, and its cousin "Will," tremble in the frozen fingers of the trees. The emptiness of mind enters the seemingly inert matter of the summer persona and warms it with the will to live, to care for its own, to intend, purpose, think, or make orderly. In the face of the blizzard, the mind holds to its purpose — is true to the Idea, the principle, the tradition, the form, the ecology.[7]

WINTER TO SPRING

> O be inspired for the flame
> in which a Thing disappears and bursts into something
> else;
> the spirit of re-creation which masters this earthly form
> loves most the pivoting point where you are no longer
> yourself.
>
> — Rainer Maria Rilke, "Sonnet to Orpheus," II

The passage of winter ends in birth. Under the influence of this shield there comes an awakening, an opening, an expansion, a surging of potential, a transformation. Trailing clouds of glory the infant of imagination comes forth squalling and primordial from the adult mind that consents to death so that the baby can be born. The winter shield can be likened to the cold ground. The spring shield can be likened to what comes up from it. Now we have come full circle. The summer shield grew the seed; the fall shield sowed it in the ground; the winter shield froze the seed into the labor of death; the spring shield broke forth from the dying husk and found the light.

The ancients knew that old forms must be shattered so that new growth could fructify the people and the earth. In spring celebrations they burst the chains of winter with contrariety, lawlessness, sexual license, and intoxication (i..e., Beltane, May Day, Mardi Gras, Fasching, etc.). Such occasions were sacred and inviolate to the people. The birthing season expanded the profane, infusing it with the spirit of divinity. In the land of springtime, sacred and profane were one.

It seems perfectly reasonable to assume that on the great wheel of compensations the summer should be opposite the winter, the materiality of things should be opposite the immateriality of things — that they should be, in their opposition, related — and that the road from youth to maturity, from emotion to thought, from summer to winter, should be called the dark passage. But the journey of raw sensation through the seasons of human nature is not complete. We must turn toward the east, where the brilliant star of death is rising like water condensing into clouds. Here, in the spring shield, we experience the synthesis of the physical, psychological, and mental, and we realize we are spiritual beings as well, capable of stirring to life again in a shower of bright rain.

When the laboring mind dies, spirit is born. When the mind of summer's blade of grass finally succumbs to spring, a new blade of grass is born. Like its opposite, the fall shield, spring is a passage. It stands opposite psychological death. These opposites produce a tension between spirit and psyche (soul). Whereas the fall is a turning inward toward the darkness, the spring is a coming outward toward the light. The two are of course related.

If summer is the larvae, fall the pupae, and winter the adult, then spring is the egg. The egg hatches. What comes forth is spirit in a fledgling body. The regenerated entity possesses not only a body, but an incipient memory and mind. The memory is absolutely essential if the mind is ultimately to bring forth another egg. Hence the coming of the egg is a synthesis of all four shields.

The transcendent spirit shield (spring) is connected to the deathwarding soul (fall), by the physical world (summer), and the mental world (winter). The egg, then, begins with a spirit (spring) that descends into a body (summer), acquires a soul (fall), and a mind (winter), all of which combine to make, to give birth to, another egg.

Why should mind seek to be reborn in spirit? Form must be continually shattered so that fledgling new form will come forth. The mature growing thing must give itself away to the children. The old order must die. The king and queen must die. Long live the king and queen!

Perhaps it is easier now to understand the meaning of Yeats' famous lines: "Nothing can be sole or whole that has not been rent." The rending happens in the fall from innocence, in the influx of raw sensation into memory, and in the breakdown of the form of winter. Only then can the soul mature the mind that labors to give birth to completeness.

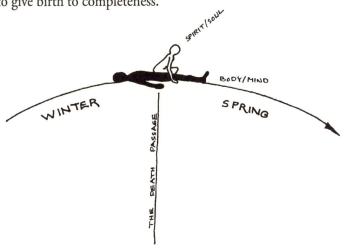

IN DEATH THE BODY IS GIVEN AWAY
WHILE THE SPIRIT COMES TO LIFE

THE STUCK OR EXAGGERATED SHIELD

Nature moves around a wheel of the seasons that rarely if ever reaches equipoise. Sometimes there is hardly any winter, sometimes hardly any summer. Sometimes summer passes into winter with barely a hint of fall. Sometimes spring is so brief that summer is already here.

Even so, the four shields of modern human nature are not always in balance, or of the same size and weight. Some are lighter, less developed. Others are heavier, over-developed. Some come up more often than others. Some come up less often than others. The exaggerated shield is heavy, over-developed, and often stuck in the up position. During the initiatory process, the exaggerated shield is the one most likely to be seen, regardless of whether it is appropriate to the occasion.

Imagine a lopsided wheel turning through muck. Every time the lopside comes down, the wheel sticks, collecting a load of muck. If we pull hard enough, the wheel will turn, only to hang up again in the same way. So an exaggerated shield will get stuck, collecting the muck of karma. The more often it gets stuck, the more karma it collects and affects the other shields. Sucking in energy from the other shields to maintain itself, the exaggerated shield (the summer shield, for instance) overbalances its opposite (the winter shield) in order to protect it or compensate for its weakness or absence. Thus, whenever there is an exaggerated shield, the opposite shield will be undernourished, weak, one or two dimensional, or apparently absent.

Why does a shield become exaggerated? The causes are often found in the summer shield, in the experiences of childhood, or in the fall shield, the initiatory passage. Growth was inhibited, essential experiences were denied, love was absent, security and shelter were inadequate, violence and/or abuse occurred, severance was incomplete or never attempted, gifts went unrealized . . . the list seems endless, especially in the light of every child's unique experiences in this modern world. In a more general sense, a shield often becomes exaggerated because the summer persona dislikes becoming the fall. The tendency toward stasis — refusing or unable to budge from the shield — is the bane of a healthy shield system that moves with balance and ease of motion from one seasonal persona to the next.

THE WEAK OR IMMATURE SHIELD

The weak or undernourished shield develops concurrently with the development of an exaggerated shield. In many cases, the exaggerated shield is attempting to protect or compensate for its opposite, the weaker shield, but its dominance simply causes more harm. The more it overshadows the weaker shield, the less chance the weaker shield has to grow. Without proper exercise, the weak shield atrophies, cannot hold its own weight within the shield system. It turns away from stimulus-events, even when its response would be appropriate, and allows the exaggerated shield to predominate.

Whenever you find a weak shield, you find an opposite exaggerated shield. Sometimes, there is more than one weak shield — and more than one exaggerated shield.

In our culture, the tendency is toward exaggeration of the summer and fall shields, and undernourishment of the winter and spring shields. This might be expected in a society obsessed with youth that has no formal rites of initiation into adulthood.[8]

OVER-DEVELOPED SUMMER SHIELD

SHIELD LAYERING

Shields are composed of layers, complexes, composites of emotions, feelings, thoughts, ideations, feedback loops — different kinds of weather systems or "disturbances" — that as a whole or in part determine the relative strength or weakness of the shield system. Any particular shield can be weak in some areas, strong in others. These patterns of subordination and dominance characterize the uniqueness of any particular shield system, the way it responds to stimulus-events, its ability to express and defend itself.

No two persons with shields exaggerated in any particular season can be expected to exhibit identical symptoms. For example: a man who is afraid of change, a woman who is addicted to material things, a father who beats his children, a mother who panics at crisis, a man who is addicted to pleasure, a woman afraid of the dark — all of these typify exaggerations of the summer shield. Like the atmospheric climate, their masks are constructed of the same substance, but there are many versions of the same mask.

To be precise, it is not the shield itself that becomes exaggerated, but clusters or complexes within it. These clusters form patterns of hypersensitivity and habit — buttons to be pushed by stimulus-events. When the buttons are pushed, the persona-shield acts or reacts, expresses or defends itself habitually in certain ways — with a certain mask or profile. This profile tends to remain a reliable means of identifying any particular self. Changes, alterations, recombinations of shield ingredients are, of course, always possible, sometimes by the dint of hard work, sometimes seemingly by spontaneous transformation.

The complex infra-structure of any given shield cannot be ignored any more than the complex infrastructure of nature. The incredible diversity and interdependence of natural life is what human is made of. When the natural is invested with three other dimensions beyond the physical (psychological, mental, and spiritual), the complexity is compounded. The summer shield is physical, biological, electrochemical, sensational, emotionally instinctive, and genetic. But it is never summer alone. When considered as a whole, the summer shield — or any other shield — is like a thick, rich web or net, with multicolored, interlayered threads extended to three other webs. Such webs comprise the unique seasonal persona of any given individual.

Not only are the shields layered, but they commonly overlap, or blend, so that at any given moment, more than one is engaged in the business of expression and defense.

Though we may be looking at outward, visible signs of one shield, the next shield may be already engaged, though not apparent in outward behavior. This overlapping process takes place naturally, as air currents flow from low to high and back again. In effect, there are no boundaries that separate one shield from the next. The boundary lines are there merely to facilitate discussion.

Experience of the initiatory process is a means of diagnosing disturbances and complexes in the shield system. Initiation induces a crisis. The crisis is a passageway. The way in which the initiand does or does not negotiate the passage is a means of assessing the strengths and weakness and anomalies in any given shield-web. If the initiation takes place in the wild, the four faces of nature evoke and reflect patterns in the human shields.

THE INTERRUPTED PASSAGE

The passage from one season to the next can be aborted. For one reason or another, the intervening shield inhibits rather than facilitates movement. The passage shield may be injured in some way. When this occurs, healthy movement through the seasons backs up, like water behind a dam. There is a stagnancy, a festering, sometimes a surging back and forth between shields. The stimulus, rather than being processed, appears to be sent back to its source. This condition can be likened to the transitional phase between seasons. Out here where we live, the interface between summer and fall is often quite indistinct. One day it will be fall, the next day summer. Our high desert "Indian summers" often present a condition in which both summer and fall seem to dwell uncertainly together.

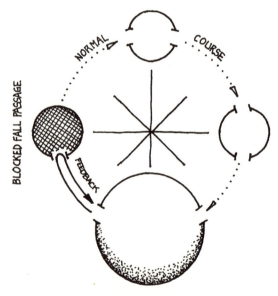

INFLATED SUMMER SHIELD

EMOTION TURNED BACK AT FALL

The transition from emotion (summer) to self-consciousness (fall) can become inhibited to such an extent that a dissonance (negative feedback loop) results. The emotion of anger (south) can experience difficulty reaching the consciousness of "I am angry" (fall). Even if the self does realize it is angry, it may not be able to find appropriate or suitable means of communication (north). If the anger is not able to pass through self-consciousness to the controlled action of mind, it backs up into the source from whence it came, further troubling the waters. "I am angry" moves backward into pure anger, which surges forward into "I am angry," which surges backward into pure anger, and so on. The relationship between anger and violence is well known. In this case, the anger is unable to make its way through a stubborn fall psyche that, for reasons of nature or nurture, refuses to make way for winter (i.e., the anger is never "initiated"). The summer shield becomes exaggerated.

Rapid cycling bipolar affective disorders, such as manic/depression, hyperthyroidism and other childhood hormonal deficiencies, are often typical examples of an interrupted passage between the body and the psyche. Instinctive and reactive hormonal emotions fail to clear the psychological passage to thought. They are sucked up by a bottomless depression that finally spits them out back where they started. The child cycles endlessly from child to adolescent and back to child. The passage of body to psyche to mind is imperfectly completed. The weakened governor (winter shield) is unable to control the combustion or the fly wheel. And the weakened imagination fixates on obsessional goals impossible to achieve.

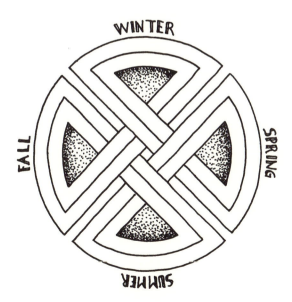

THE INTERLOCKING NATURE OF THE SHIELDS

THE FOUR OPPOSITES

> The bones connected by joints are at once a unitary whole and not a unitary whole. To be in agreement is to differ; the concordant is discordant. From out of all the many particulars comes oneness, and out of oneness come all the many particulars.
>
> — Heraclitus, 112

Balance among the shields is effected first by identifying the undernourished shield. This shield requiring the healing is always found opposite the exaggerated or stuck shield. Therapeutic attention is therefore removed from the apparent "problem" — "Why do I keep feeling this, doing that?" etc. — and is placed on the dynamics of balance. If one shield is predominant, then its opposite must be subordinate. The therapeutic objective is to nourish that subordinate shield, to give it weight and health. In order to bring the "patient" into contact with the opposite, weaker shield, the adjacent shield (the intervening season) must be encountered. Each seasonal shield is a healing passageway to the following season.

Balance is a tension. Disturbance in the south will effect the north. The adherent, or glue, that holds the opposites in a state of equilibrium is the adjacent season. Fall and spring adhere to each other through the agent of winter. Spring and fall adhere through summer; summer and winter through fall, and so on.

The act of adjusting the balance between two opposites by opening the passageway of the adjacent shield will always adjust the balance of the entire system. Again, the natural metaphor seems appropriate. Mother Earth herself does a superb job of adjusting her balance as she rolls along the great circle of her planetary existence. Eons of drought are followed by eons of rain. Eons of heat give way to eons of ice. One day is sunny, the next is cloudy. As the seasons roll past, she stays in balance, if only by being constantly in the state of seeking equilibrium. Fret not the storm; there will be blue skies again. Gloat not over the blue skies; a storm looms on the western horizon.

Just as it might be hard to remember the difference between this fall and last fall, so healing adjustments within the shield system may seem imperceptible to the unpracticed eye. In a healthy person, they occur all the time. Hopefully, over a period of time, the adjustments become obvious. The scar is covered up with vegetation. You have to get down on your hands and knees to find bits of ash and charred wood. The fire may still be alive somewhere down there, but it may be a while before it flares up again.

In some ways, Jung's twentieth century theories point to the more ancient four shield dynamics of the natural self. In his view, the laws of opposition in nature reflect the laws of opposition inherent in human nature: "the psyche is . . . a self-regulating system . . . ." for "there is no balance, no system of self-regulation, without opposition." All things flow into their opposites:

> "The transition from morning to afternoon means a revaluation of the earlier values. There comes the urgent need to appreciate the value of the opposite of our former ideals, to perceive the error in our former convictions . . . . Energy necessarily depends on a pre-existing polarity, without which there could be no energy. There must always be high and low, hot and cold, etc., so that the equilibrating process — which is energy — can take place . . . . The point is not conversion into the opposite but conservation of precious values together with recognition of their opposites."[9]

The four seasons dynamic is a good illustration of Jung's contention that energy (i.e. expression/defense) is created by the dynamic equilibrium of opposites, such as the bi-polar tension/balance of his famous mandala of the four functions of consciousness: feeling, sensation, thought, and intuition.[10]

The seasonal paradigm undergirds Jung's mandala concept. Summer must ultimately flow into its opposite, winter, and back again. Fall must ultimately flow into its opposite, spring, and back again. Without this compensatory, contradictory motion, there would be no body, no psyche, no mind, and no spirit — no balance. As the sun tips toward the south on the day following the winter solstice, so the sun tips toward the north on the day following the summer solstice. And as the hours of darkness lengthen on the day after the fall equinox, so the hours of light lengthen on the day after the spring equinox.

At summer solstice, the body of the human self begins to yearn toward the mind of winter — to become the not-body of mind. And at the winter solstice the mind of the human self begins to yearn toward the body of summer. At the fall equinox, the inward psyche begins to yearn toward the spirit of spring. And at the spring equinox, the outward expression of spirit yearns toward the dark, introspective regions of the psyche.[11]

If we imagine the four season mandala as a vertical-horizontal construct, then south to north represents an up/down flow between opposites. Summer (the body) would be down, and winter, the bodiless mind, would be up. The tensional flow between them, between physical growth and mental form, is illustrated by the ways in which the natural world, including humans, grows and changes and yet retains its ideal form.[12] Fall and spring, opposites on the horizontal plane, are also related enantiodromically by the tension between the body-bound psyche/soul and the mind-bound imagination or spirit.[13] The four particular opposites compose the whole, the one, the unitary four-in-one.

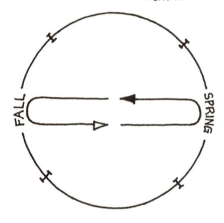

ENANTIODROMIA OF SPRING AND FALL

THE FULCRUM AS PASSAGE

To put it simply, summer and winter turn (balance) on fall. Fall and spring turn (balance) on winter. Winter and summer turn (balance) on spring. Spring and fall turn (balance) on summer. If the child is to become adult, she must pass through fall. If the adolescent is to become enlightened, he must pass through the winter. If the adult is to become a child again, she must pass through the spring. If the enlightened one is to incorporate the vision within, he must pass through the summer. Hence, in initiatory rites of healing, the passage "ordeal" or "trial" is determined by the season through which a person must pass in order to reach the desired shield. This concept forms the basis for various kinds of "initiatory therapies" involving nature.[14]

The time element is significant here. How long does it take for summer or winter to tip back and forth on the fulcrum of fall or spring? How long does it take for fall or spring to slide across to their opposite on the fulcrum of winter or summer? A microsecond. A minute. A day. A year. A lifetime. Some of the above. All of the above. The amount of time taken to wheel through the seasonal shields is relative to the datum of experience being processed.

The prick of a pin is nothing. It spins its way around the wheel of the seasons (body, psyche, mind, spirit) in no time at all. Likewise, the touch of a fly against the cheek. But the touch of two lips against each other in a kiss can launch a cycle that may last a lifetime. There are, then, cycles within greater cycles within even greater cycles, each cycle-duration relative to the magnitude/dimension of stimuli, and each cycle balanced on the fulcrums of adjacent seasons: body and mind balanced on psyche; psyche and spirit balanced on mind; mind and body balanced on spirit; spirit and psyche balanced on body; and so on, around and around the wheel.

ENDNOTES: FOUR SHIELD DYNAMICS

[1] "Impersonation." See Appendix I.

[2] William James proposed that psychological states are derived from physical states (pre-synapse). Freud, on the other hand, considered psychological states to be primary to bodily states (post-synapse). Four shield theory agrees with the former. The body, the sheer physical reality of things, is stimulus, the psyche is response. Summer precedes fall. But the seasonal paradigm is also circular, and does not end with the fall, or any season. Winter comes, then spring, and then summer. Each season determines the shape and condition of the other three, and so changes itself with each revolution of the seasonal wheel. Turning, turning, there is no stasis. On the wheel, as Rilke put it, "Abiding is nowhere."

[3] *Mind and Nature*, p. 12.

[4] Lamark, *Philosophie Zoologique*.

[5] J.E. Lovelock, *The Ages of Gaia* (New York: W.W. Norton, 1988). See also Paul Devereux, John Steele, and David Kubrin, *Earthmind: Communicating with the Living World of Gaia* (Rochester, Vt.: Destiny Books, 1989).

[6] An entomologist friend reminds me that there is a tiny, fragile moth living in the windswept valleys of northern Nevada that hatches and flies only on the coldest days of the winter, when the blizzard howls and the icicles hang from the sagebrush. Something else entirely, something akin to natural laws of which we cannot conceive, guides all life through the winter.

[7] Among humans, the workings of mind can be discerned in the structure of society itself, which mirrors the "natural order." Sanctified by customs, expressed in ceremony, ritual, and rite, and buttressed by tradition, human society in its "primitive" form is conservative (changing essential form only under the impact of institutional decay and chronic disorganization). In its "civilized" form, society is split off from the natural order, yet retains a semblance of it. Laws have replaced custom, rituals and rites have decayed into proceedings, formalities, and doctrines, and tradition has become politics and the nationalistic state. Cf. Stanley Diamond, *In Search of the Primitive*, pp. 137-8.

[8] Hereditary diseases or predispositions affect not only the summer shield but also, and particularly, the fall. Such "blights" de-energize the fall shield

and render the child less capable of coping with the shadowlands of the west. When the child cannot blaze an adequate trail through the dark jungle of the psyche, the winter shield is stunted.

[9] C.G. Jung, *Psychology of the Unconscious*, Trans. by Beatrice M. Hinkle (New York: Moffat Yard, 1916), pp. 60, 74f.

[10] The difference between four shield theory and the Jungian mandala is in the south and west poles. Jung places feeling in the south, sensation in the west. Four shield theory places sensation in the south, and feeling in the west.

[11] Even as Eros, languishing in the celestial city of immortal spring, longs for his beloved Psyche, who stumbles about in the darkness of fall, despairing of ever finding him.

[12] See *entelechy* (Aristotle).

[13] Mathematically, the four shields are a periodic or oscillating system: "two coupled oscillators" in a "multidimensional torus attractor. " Imagine the back-forth motion of a summer-winter pendulum — a "limit cycle." Add to the first pendulum or limit cycle a second fall-spring pendulum, with its back and forth limit cycle. These two pendulums, or limit cycles, interact with each other by swinging not only back and forth, but from side to side. To plot the phase space trajectory of the two coupled systems, one must calculate the position and momentum of each oscillator: The summer pendulum swings toward fall, gaining momentum as it passes the zero point between summer and fall. At the same time, summer swings toward winter, gaining momentum as it passes the zero or "fixed point attractor." Meanwhile, the fall pendulum swings toward winter, passing the zero point (between fall and winter). At the same time, the fall swings toward spring, gaining momentum as it passes the center zero, or fixed point attractor. The winter pendulum swings back toward summer, gaining momentum again as it passes the fixed point attractor (between winter and summer) — and at the same time swings toward spring. And so on. A full explication of torus attractors can be found in John Briggs and F. David Peat, *Turbulent Mirror: An Illustrated Guide to Chaos Theory and the Science of Wholeness*, pp. 31-41.

This seeming impossibility — that an oscillator can swing back and forth and from side to side at the same time — is rendered quite understandable when one considers the oscillations of the earth in relation to the sun. At the solstice, summer begins a long swing toward winter. To get there, i.e., in order to fulfill one-half of its "limit cycle," it swings toward the fall. At equinox, fall begins its long swing toward spring. To get there, it swings toward winter.

[14] See the chapters subtitled "The Rites of Fall," "The Rites of Winter," "The Rites of Spring," and "The Rites of Summer."

FOUR SHIELD THERAPY

> All things come in their due seasons.
> — Heraclitus, 12

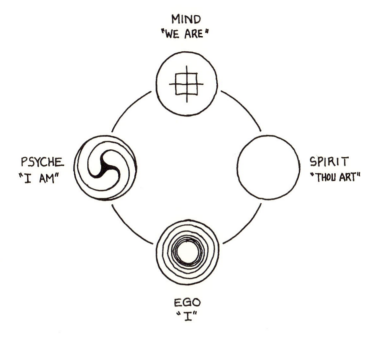

THE IDENTITY WHEEL

In the stark of night, lightning gropes down into the chasm and touches a tree. The tree explodes. Then the fire dies — but not completely. Down in a bed of needles, it smolders. Wisps of smoke escape now and then from the buried core. Life goes on. Months, maybe years later, in a high wind, the ground collapses in on itself and the starving flame leaps for the air.

So it is with human nature. Injuries, traumas, accidents cut into the quick and wound the body, the psyche, the mind, and the spirit. Something hurts profoundly. In a healthy shield system, this hurting is a way of staying alive. The destructive element smolders and eventually leaps forth as "medicine power," a kind of personal magic sometimes identified as charisma or character.

"Wounds and scars are the stuff of character. The word *character* means, at root, 'marked or etched with sharp lines,' like initiation cuts."[1]

The woundedness can usually be traced to the summer, or child shield. Any physical, emotional, or psychic hurt affects first the reactive child, then the psychological adolescent, then the rational adult, and finally the spiritual persona. Each of the shields suffers the hurt in its own way, according to its own composition. The agent causing the wound, like the lightning spark, smolders in the dark shield of the fall, in the labyrinths of memory.

The Post Traumatic Stress Disorder has educated us to the need of many "victims" to relive and express (re-dramatize) the pain/fear/horror/helplessness of a traumatic event in order to heal the wound. That is, the fire must not, cannot, be smothered. It must be allowed to smolder, as it were, in remembrance of the event, until tendrils of flame grope toward the fresh air.[2] Whenever the story is told, there can be a purging, a burning of unhealthy psychic tissue.

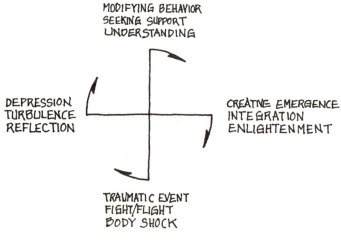

THE 4 SHIELDS OF TRAUMA

In a healthy shield system, the lightning burn does not become a severe handicap. A teenage girl gang raped in Central Park refused to become a victim for the rest of her life. The rape flowered into a vision, a life crusade against sexism in the mass media. A man who caught his wife sleeping with another man became a psychotherapist for men in divorce. A woman who survived her tension filled childhood by having asthma attacks took on physical challenges until the childhood disease disappeared. A young man afflicted with dyslexia became an expert tracker of animals and humans in the wild. An American Indian suffering from alcoholism and unemployment became an elite blizzard pilot driver for the highway department. A woman sexually abused in her childhood expressed her vulnerability, anger and fear in exquisite paintings.

A decently healthy shield system will eventually assimilate the fire burning deep in the folds of the fall shield by taking up a course or means of action in the face of adversity (winter) that will utilize burned tissue as fertilizer for new growth (spring). To paraphrase Nietzsche, "That which doesn't kill me enriches me." This inward resolve accounts for the persistence of life on earth to adapt and survive.

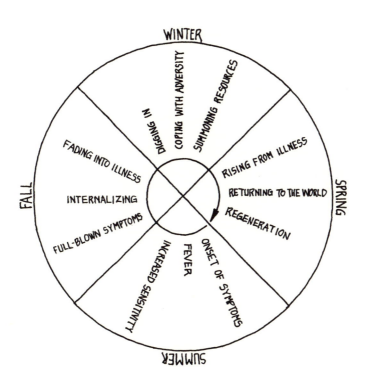

How many are there among us in the process of healing such wounds? Any ordinary life brings more than one wounding. It is as though our shields become battered as we grow through the seasons of our days, and no matter how expertly we bang the dents out and refinish the surface, it's never quite the same. The dents and whacks still show. Why can't we heal ourselves completely? "There is a crack in everything," Leonard Cohen sings, because "that's how the light gets in."

Our battered shields wear the truth. We can bliss out on eros and a billion and one distractions; we can practice various forms of egolessness and Buddha-mind, but we must always return to pay the experiential toll exacted by the seasons, transitions and traumas of our days. The payment can be high. It is important that we occupy ourselves with the repair of our shields, so that they can continue to smolder and leap for the air amid the storms of seasonal life.

It would be erroneous to assume that every human is born with the potential for a healthy shield system. It would also be erroneous to assume the same for any non-human species. Many traits and tendencies inherent to shield structure are inherited. The twin rivers of heredity and environment converge with a meshing of currents and eddies that congeal into the shifting personas in the circle of self. Nevertheless, few individuals are predestined by inheritance to live a crippled life due to shield inadequacies. Although the culture militates against it, people have been known to overcome great obstacles to self-healing. Invariably these people speak of their experience in terms reminiscent of the ancient metaphor: the child must pass through the inward darkness of the initiatory passage so that the adult may be enlightened. Summer must yield to fall so that winter may be transformed into spring.

SHIELD HEALING

> What, if not transformation, is your insistent
>   commission?
> Earth, dear one, I will! Oh, believe it needs
>   not one more of your springtimes to win me over.
>
> — Rainer Maria Rilke, *Duino Elegies*, IX

There is more than a little truth in the old adage that a poor summer blights the stalk, the fruit, the seed, and the sprout. Yet the recurring seasons can bring better weather. The tree can, through the years, develop into the fullness of its purpose, despite its battered condition. It can remember the bad seasons, and compensate by growing more slowly or quickly. The fruit that comes from it can be wholesome, delicious, and mature enough to make tougher, plumper seeds to endure the winter. From these seeds can come sprouts inherently ready to challenge the vicissitudes of the seasons of life.

Most healing occurs slowly, almost imperceptively, even as the seasons pass. Humans are no more capable of instantaneous, long-lasting transformations than any of their animal kin. There can be great leaps in growth that come like sunrise or healing rain. But there can also be long periods of fallowness, where growth seems almost non-existent, or drought parches the landscape. Even as the seasonal shields turn predictably from now to now to now, the weather within them copulates with their environment, giving birth to an infinitude of variations. However gradually, the blackened scar left by the burn is covered by a blanket of green. The burned stuff has sunk into mulch for the natives and exotics crowding up through the wound. Trees grow tall. After a while, only practiced eyes can differentiate the burn from the surrounding cover.

An understanding of seasonal balance is a basic key to the healing of the shields. If the child of summer is to be healed, then the adult of winter must do the healing. This can be accomplished only if the child is willing to undertake the initiatory passage of the fall. Only then will the adult child be illumined in the shield of spring. The initiatory journey can take a long time to complete its healing course. Rarely does one immediately arrive at the mature kind of understanding that results in illumination or transformation. These things take time. One must be strong, patient, and self-disciplined if one is to survive the passage of fall.

INITIATION IN THE WILDERNESS

Applied four shields theory involves the immersion of human in nature in order to effect a reciprocal healing process. Because there is a two-way permeable boundary between the two, the entire whole — the self-thus — is healed. If I sleep beneath a creosote bush for four days and nights, the bush and I draw from the same Source and are healed. The healing is effected by the body, soul, mind, and particularly the spirit, of nature.

The healing is therefore "wholistic," and does not exclude the violence, chaos, contradiction, and death inherent in self-thus. The "negative" elements of nature (and human nature) also become agents in the healing. The healing process is reciprocal. This fact was of course well known to "primitive" peoples, but has since been forgotten by modern culture. The big lie (that we are separate from nature) has conceived the misconception that we can control, manipulate, and plunder self-thus. But by doing so, we find that instead we are endangering ourselves and other species.

Therefore, if I, a human, sleep under a creosote bush and dream a dream, that dream nourishes the bush and all the species around me. If I feel thirst and drink water, the bush and all the other species drink also. If I am sad, and the tears flow from my eyes like rain, the bush and all the species feel a healing pang in their soul. If I sing and pray to the rising sun for the power to be reborn, I and the bush and all the species around me are each in their own way reborn. The creosote bush and its surrounding environs (extending to embrace the entire universe) heal me because I belong here. And I heal them because they belong here. We who belong here heal each other even if it means we have to die for each other — and we do. But death itself is never final:

> In the book of the earth it is written:
> *nothing can die.*
>
> — Mary Oliver, "Ghosts"

Because four shields theory is "initiatory," the fall or psychological shield is primarily responsible for conveying the child to adulthood, the body to mind, emotions to thought, and sensation to maturity, and contains much that "civilized" humans tend to see as negative. Nightmares, addictions, depression, autism, suicide, and all the death-fears of the soul reside here. The road to full self-consciousness teems with slimy monsters that must be recognized as a necessary part of the self, and therefore as agents of healing. But the initiatory process applies to the other shields as well. Each shield acts as a passageway, or means of transition, from one shield to its opposite — from one season to the next: from childhood to adulthood, from soul to spirit, from mind to body, from spirit to soul.[3]

Although van Gennep did not specify rites of passage and initiation according to seasons, such rites can be classified, described, and adapted even in modern times, given the alterations in human shielding wrought by the Big Lie (that human and nature are not one and the same) .

Various seasonal rites of transition form the basis of an applied psychology which, when used in conjunction with nature and human, can be of great therapeutic benefit. In other words, there are practical methods of effecting seasonal transitions in humans, moving them from one persona to its opposite (e.g. summer to winter or fall to spring) through the initiatory or transitional persona of the adjacent season. Through fall, summer becomes winter. Through winter, fall becomes spring. Through spring, winter becomes summer, and so on.

The training curriculum at the School of Lost Borders provides such transitional rites in natural settings, during which time therapeutic modalities specific to each of the four shields is prescribed. These modalities form the substructure of a new, yet very old, "nature-based psychology," or "initiatory psychology," that has far less to do with theory than with the raw contact of human and nature. The "therapy" done here is invariably accomplished in the natural world and has been arranged into four basic strategies. These strategies are like musical variations on the single theme called the four shields.

SEVERANCE FROM THE CHILD SHIELD

In order to grow, human nature must be initiated. We must sever the cord that binds us to the physical world (summer shield). This does not mean that the summer shield must become immaterial. It must become psychological. It must detach itself from strictly physical concerns and accept the burden of soul.

No doubt, nature does exactly the same. The body of summer turns into the fall, where it begins to die off, fall away, shrivel, constrict, shed its leaves, scatter its seed, turn inward, harbor its resources, and live in the memory of its species, the memory of winter and returning spring. Its "soul," if you will, is the memory that it will die, or at least undergo a kind of death.

The initiand is prepared to enter that memory: "I am mortal. I am attached yet somehow not attached to a dying body. I must enter my species and collectively feel our fate. I must plant myself in the dark soil of death. I must accept myself and my lot in life, and hibernate in the dens of dreaming." Preparation to enter this vale of soul-making involves vital instruction from elders and mentors. The physical body must be prepared for self-consciousness.

At the School, this preparation is short-term, as compared to the preparation time required by primitive rites of initiation. This has been necessary, but not preferable. Our ancestors knew that preparation was an all-important phase in the initiatory process. The body must be readied to initiate a love affair with the psyche. The child must sever from mother and father; the candidate must leave a former life behind. The initiand must enter an inward stage of growth in order to mature. These things take time and care. The body is attached to the habits and routines it knows. The child is attached to security and egotism. He is quite happy not being introspective.

The brute fact is that if the initiand is not adequately prepared, she may die a physical death. She will not be able to face the rigors of the fall and will wither too far and perish. This fact is usually more perceived than real, for the elders and mentors have no desire to allow an unprepared initiand to enter the threshold arena. The suggestion of death is usually sufficient.

The substance of the elders' instruction varies, of course, from culture to culture. Usually the teachings cover such matters as the definition of manhood or womanhood, or the new life stage that is being confirmed. Certain "secrets" are imparted, such as how to get through the maze, or the names of the monsters that imperil, or ways of behaving in order to survive, or the whereabouts of helping spirits, guides, and deities. The candidates are physically, psychologically, mentally and spiritually prepared for the ordeal of the threshold.

At the School, the severance or preparation phase begins when the student declares his/her intent to participate in the course. The pace intensifies when the students and elders meet. On site preparation time can be four days to two weeks. Students are prepared physically for the specific trials of the threshold phase. They are asked to assess and clarify their feelings, intentions, and spiritual longings. They talk about what they are leaving behind and what they see ahead. They are given tools: the model of the four shields, and the symbols, archetypes, and ceremonies pan-culturally associated with the threshold rite which they are soon to undergo. They spend time alone in nature carrying out assignments or tasks related to their preparation. When the moment comes for them to enter the threshold passage, they are pronounced ready.

DESCENT INTO THE SOUL

The child of summer nature enters the dark shield of initiation (fall). The initiation is a certain kind of trial or time of taboo. It lasts a prescribed amount of time and usually takes place in the wilderness. This soul descent takes many forms. It can be a sudden and overwhelming fear experienced in one incandescent moment — or it can be a long year of seclusion. Invariably, there is some form of self-denial, helplessness, exposure, anonymity, or threat that brings the reality of death to self-consciousness.

At the School, the threshold phase takes the form of fasting, seclusion, and exposure. Natural darkness is often used in conjunction with these rites of fall. We have watched thousands of candidates enter the threshold time. The child in their eyes is afraid. Innocence is about to become experience. Soon they will know.

Whatever happens to the initiand during the threshold ordeal is half-determined by the individual, half by the natural environment. The quality of the environment changes as the candidate changes, or stagnates as the candidate stagnates. This "mirroring" of self by nature and nature by self is a basic eco-psychological function of the fall shield. If nature mourns, I mourn. If I mourn, nature mourns.[4] The soul-soul bond between human and nature is the cradle of true maturity.

We welcome the candidates when they return from their threshold experience. They have learned something during their sojourn in the fall shield. We ask them to wait, not to tell their stories until the following day. The return can be a dangerous time. Considerable care must be taken by the elders to insure that the returnees are well grounded, that they are willing to let their inner struggles and ecstasies gestate within even while they put on their social bodies. When the time of taboo ends, this fact is celebrated with feasting and social merriment.[5] The candidates have returned. They have confirmed their readiness to assume a new life station. It was good. There was no failure.

THE FOUR SHIELDS OF MEMORY

Every winter, Meredith and I go down to Death Valley with a few close friends and fast alone for four days and nights. We walk away from the vehicles, each in his or her own direction, and we don't see each other for a while. That we be allowed this alone time is an issue of utmost importance to us. How can we enact the complex roles of midwives if the threshold experience were not always fresh in our memories?

Memory — a key concept. It unlocks the therapeutic cupboard. For what the candidate brings back from the threshold is a story. And the story is a narrative based entirely on remembered events, both inner and outer, and as such it comprises an altered version of "the real." What is real and what is remembered are two different — yet related — realities. Indeed, it could be safely stated that the reality of memory can be more "real" than what actually, physically, happened. Memory reality has a great deal to do with health, adaptability, survival, and growth into fullness of self.

Last winter, as I fasted in Death Valley, I was aware as never before of the relationship between memory and threshold ordeal. When I left the others and hiked alone into the desert, I started swimming in a sea of memory. Inwardly, not a single idea, thought, image, feeling, emotion, sensation arose that was not a part of my own memory field. Outwardly, not a single encounter, event, symbol, species marked my travels that was not a part of the memory of nature. Literally, a sea of memory. For how can you draw distinctions between human memory and natural memory? The borders become lost in the whole.

I was remembering and nature was remembering. Together we were remembering how to survive, grow, perpetuate, nurture, and evolve. We were remembering who we were and where we were going. Remembering together, as one, we became God remembering. God putting himself back together. God regenerating.

Specifically what did I remember? I remembered in my body. I lived with all the experiences I had accumulated there, from childhood on — the sensations, tensions, hungers, and needs.

I remembered in the dark rainbow chambers of my psyche, the consequences of my deeds, acts of omission and commission, memories rich with conscience, insight and feeling. And I remembered with the dreams and daydreams of my sacred ancestors.

I remembered my place in the ecosystem, in the scheme of things, in the nurture and maintenance of my species within the cosmic field of memory — in which my puny little memory was but a mote — but a necessary mote — in the unfolding design of the cosmos.

And I remembered whenever my memory was jolted, whether the impetus to remember came from within or without. I would be walking along and wup! Something in the path would catch my eye — a stone, a plant, a stretch of dappled shade, a patch of sky, a bird song, the drone of a fly. And suddenly, without warning, I would be swimming in the lands of memory.

The four seasons and the four directions exist because God keeps "re-membering" nature. Nature exists because all the species, including us, keep remembering birth and death and everything in between. We remember in the body, in the psyche, in the mind, and in the spirit. And because we remember, we collectively create our destiny. Somehow our destiny is more than the reality we remember. What is remembered has the power to change us. Memory alters all.

When the candidate brings a memory story back from the threshold, we treat the memory as if it were the reality. And what we mirror back to the story teller comes from our own remembered reality. Memory mirrors memory, and from this fortuitous commingling a new reality, a new future is born.

THE FOUR SHIELDS OF MEMORY

THE MIRROR OF THE ELDERS (INCORPORATION INTO WINTER)

The experience of the ordeal comprises a shield story, not only of the fall, but of all four. In primitive culture, this story formed the basis of community acceptance, appreciation, and respect. The candidate was welcomed into the neighborhood, the existing social order. She/he had earned this place (winter shield). Now it was the labor of the elders to insure that the story, particularly its spiritual content (spring shield), was channelled back into the physical world, and into the community, so that the people would prosper.

The response of the winter shield "elders," "midwives," "guides," or "medicine teachers" during the incorporation of the candidate is profoundly important. The story is told. The child encountered the dark in order to become mature and enlightened. There are a thousand variations of this same story. The elders listen carefully, and employ a method called "mirroring."[6]

"Mirroring": the elders turn a collective mirror to the person who is narrating the story. The mirror with which we are concerned is not the mirror in the bathroom or bedroom. It depicts far more than the physical proportions of the one looking into it.[7]

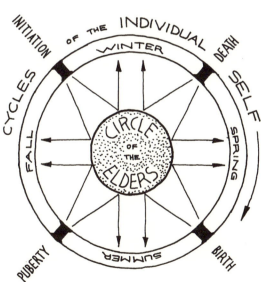

THE MIRROR OF THE ELDERS'
CIRCLE REFLECTS MEANING
AT EACH PASSAGE

The mirror of the elder's council is composed of the eyes and ears of the elders. The "impressions" which it reflects are emotional, psychological, rational, and spiritual, and have less to do with physical reality than personal reality. The elders' mirror is a means of answering questions such as "Who am I?" "Where am I?" "How am I?" "Where am I going?" "What are my means of getting there?"

The elders listen to the story and combine its elements with what they have already discerned in the narrator. They ask questions by which the initiands can define themselves and the "problem" under scrutiny. And they mirror back their observation of how the initiands have gone about defining themselves. This self-definition is the "medicine."

The "medicine" is composed of the gifts, symbols, emotions, feelings, thoughts, pretensions, desires, deeds, values, imaginings, dreams, social attitudes, and life situations that the dark shield passage has jogged into the story told to the elders. The medicine is the fabric in which personal mythology is being stitched. Sometimes the elders see themes, patterns, potentialities that are not obvious in the story. Their life experience gives them the right to look ahead, and to respond soul to soul. Their mirror is almost always "positive" as opposed to negative, for they know that their validation is the stuff of health and vitality.

Mirroring defines the well being of the individual in four dimensions:

1. The summer, or physical shield: The body, the senses, the needs of the instinctive, emotional one;

2. The fall, or "dark shield": The psyche, the feelings, the dreams, the vulnerabilities, the inner life of the adolescent one;

3. The winter, or mature shield: The rational, the cognitive, the responsible, interpersonal one;

4. The spring, or "spirit" shield: The gifts and visions of the creative, transpersonal, enlightened one.

As such, the medicine has a great deal to do with the immune system. That is, it has to do with the means by which persons govern and defend themselves against the inroads of disease (on all four levels), and the means by which they "express" (project, advertise, display) themselves on the same four levels. The mirror of the elders discerns areas where healing can occur. Usually, the healing can be effected in the shield opposite the exaggerated or stuck one.

The initiatory story is a rich "body" of information for the elders' mirror. It is a microcosm of the narrator's life played out on the stage of nature. The story is interlarded with the four dimensions of nature: the corporeal body, the psychosphere, the mind (intents and purposes), and the spirit. At certain points in the narrative, the human and the natural become interlinked. These linking moments are an important part of the personal myth being expressed.

A man who was earning a living illegally brought back a story from the threshold that included a meeting with a chuckwalla that scuttled away to safety. These big grey [and tasty!] lizards of the eastern Mojave are masters of escape and defense. If they sense themselves to be in danger, they immediately withdraw to a crack or crevasse in the rocks and puff themselves up like a balloon. Their tenacious, scaly hides swell into the crack and the lizards become like the rock itself, immovable, seemingly invulnerable. Unfortunately, they are easily removed from their fortress with a hooked, sharpened stick. The point of the stick deflates them; the hook pulls them out to dinner.

Because they knew the habits of the chuckwalla, the elders were able to hold up the mirror. "You are the chuckwalla," they said. "You think you are safely defended. You are badly deluded. The law has a long sharp stick with a hook on the end of it."

Another story involved a woman hanging on to a husband who kept having affairs with other women. During her threshold fast a brilliant, iridescent hummingbird flew into her face several times, startling her. At other times she watched it turning circles in the air and whistling. She wondered what it all meant. Identifying her visitor as a male, the elders pointed out the faithless habits of the male hummingbird, how he loves 'em and leaves 'em, how he makes all the ladies' hearts go pitty pat with those incredible aerial acrobatics. She laughed and said yes, she knew that deep down inside, but just didn't want to confront her choice. The crossroads stood clearly before her. Either she decided to love him as he was, knowing he would never change — or she would leave him and go her own way.

The elders see natural mirrors in the shield story. In these mirrors the initiands are themselves reflected. Chuckwalla is a mirror. Hummingbird is a mirror. A mountain climbed, a ridge walked, a clearing entered, a deep forest explored, a creek crossed, a dry wash slept in, is a mirror. A scorpion under an overturned rock is a mirror. The constellations of the night sky are mirrors. The wind says "Look into me. What do you see?" The elders help the initiand to look into the mirror and see how the wind is of his body, psyche, mind, and spirit — in him, around him, of him. They help him to see how is is inseparable from natural law. Then they help him recognize how the wind, or the ant, or the setting sun, is part of the mythic aspect of himself.

The narrative itself reflects the myth of the teller. As the person tells the story, she tells it in such a way as to reveal how she sees herself — or wants to see herself. To a certain extent, the narration is always a kind of "lie." Indeed, how does one ascertain the "truth" of any story one tells about oneself? Once experience passes into memory, it easily becomes "falsified," "colored," "retouched," incompletely remembered, changed by how the narrator wants it to be heard. The mirror of the elders comprehends the "lie." It recognizes how the lie is significantly linked to the development of self-esteem, social behavior, and visionary action. Thus the elders support what the self wants to say about itself.[8] In such a fashion, the reflected medicine of their mirror empowers the narrator to become and enact the "myth" they tell about themselves.[9]

By exploring the psychological shield, the child has aged. The story of the passage is both treatment and cure — and more than that. It is a "creative self-definition" beginning with the words "I am . . . ." This mythos is so powerful that when it is yoked to a balanced shield system, it can benefit our species and nature in general.

Some cures last, others fade into the need for vaccinations or additional doses. The most balanced shield systems are constantly in the process of moving through the seasonal weather of the shields, including the child's need to continually reencounter the monsters of the initiatory passage — so that the adult can be nourished, so that the story, in all its variants and sub-plots, can again be told.

There is no therapeutic substitute for a body of empowering elders. I did not say "judging" or "examining"; I said "empowering." The empowerment process is an art in itself. As a function of the incorporation phase of a rite of initiation, the telling of the story and the empowerment of the elders carries within it the seal of approval of the communal north shield, approval that confirms our mythical value to the earth and our fellow humans. Obviously, we don't see much of that kind of empowerment today — or those kinds of elders. Because the culture lacks meaningful passage rites into mature (and maturer) stages of life, there are few adults capable of recognizing and honoring those who, by dint of self-initiation, attain levels of maturity that benefit the community.

THE SHIELD STORY (SPRING)

A shield story is about how "self" fared "thus." It is a story about human nature. It is told to the elders at the end of an initiatory experience. It is long or short, trivial or momentous, comic or tragic. It is a bucketful snatched up from the river of experience, a sample taken from a core, an intense vignette drawn from an autobiography. Invariably the fabric of it is deep and rich with information about the condition of the four-fold immune system of the self who is telling the tale. The natural setting is all-important. Wild nature spirit reflects back and elicits shield behavior and perception.

A shield story is not necessarily a success story. Though it may end in enlightenment, it rarely if ever means "happily ever after." A shield story usually signifies the growth, decay, death, and rebirth of a particular person. This cyclical motion accumulates experience, memory, understanding. and all the other stuff of human nature.

A shield story is about how one fashions myths about oneself, stories about how the self can become fulfilled, or how the self can survive, or how the self can communicate itself.

"Success" within a shield story might be defined as the protagonist's ability to convert the experience of a seasonal passage into personal enlightenment — or the ability to accept the experience as worthwhile. But the enlightened one must always return to the body, to the child, to the innocent beginnings of new shield adventures. The protagonist seeks through all this to balance the shields, to find his/her place in nature.

The plot of a shield story is always different and always similar to other shield stories. Though every story is unique, every story is always about the shields, the personas, the masks employed by the individual self in order to cope with the experience. Therefore, the shield story always involves four basic characters — the child (summer), the adolescent (fall), the adult (winter), and the enlightened one (spring). The plot can be a perfect example of "the story of my life," or it can be a window through which one or more aspects of the life story stands clear.

All plots taken together compose a mono-plot, an archetype of initiation. The child went into the dark to become mature, to take her place in life, and to be enlightened. Against this archetypal backdrop the individual shield story spins itself out. Multi-layered shields peel back to expose strengths, weaknesses, fears, dreams, and gifts that are the stuff of growth and self-acceptance.

Elders do not moralize about the relative worth of this or that story. Each story is instructive, representing a unique means of coping with the givens of change and survival. Each story is honored and given its rightful place in the history of human nature.

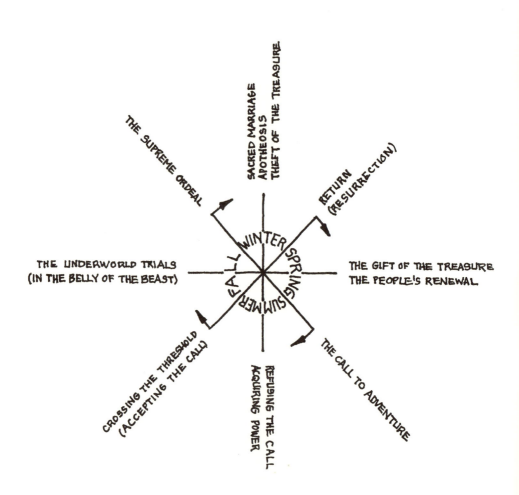

THE MONOMYTH (JOSEPH CAMPBELL)

ENDNOTES: FOUR SHIELD THERAPY

[1] James Hillman, *New Age Journal*, 1992.

[2] One's nose, however, should not be pushed back down into the trauma against one's will.

[3] Arnold van Gennep, *The Rites of Passage* (Chicago: University of Chicago Press, 1972), p. 182. Van Gennep suggests that "the phenomenon of a *transition* may be noted in. . . biological activity in general, in the applications of physical energy, and in cosmic rhythms. . . . that one of the most striking elements in seasonal ceremonies is the dramatic representation of the death and rebirth of the moon, the season, the year, vegetation, and the deities that preside over and regulate vegetation." These seasonal rites, which celebrate "the transition from one state [or season] to another, are virtually equivalent to giving up the old life and 'turning over a new leaf.'"

[4] As in the classic elegy. See: "Adonais," by Shelley, or "Elegy on the Death of Yeats," by W.H. Auden.

[5] Almost always we include a bathing at a nearby hot springs as an important step in the return. People strip down to bathing suits or the buff and sit in the hot waters together. The dust of the desert threshold is washed away and everybody sees everybody else "in the body," as it were. Thus the visionary content of the initiand is channelled into the next shield, the body of summer.

[6] The elder does not "therapize." The elder is more like a favorite uncle or aunt, or a wise person who lives next door, a person with considerable life experience, a respected older person, or a person who has learned from being in nature. In this sense, it is very important for any "therapist" to be an elder, that is, to have experienced various kinds of "initiations" into maturity.

I much prefer the term, "elder." And we "elders" do not work alone but in the company of other elders. See *Sitting in Council: An Ecopsychological Approach to Working With Stories in Wilderness Rites of Passage*, a Ph.D. Dissertation by Linda Loos, Institute of Transpersonal Psychology, 1997.

[7] Of course, even the ordinary mirror is not perfectly "physical" about what it reflects back. The one looking into the mirror usually sees subjective hopes, desires, and fears in its quicksilver surface. What is mirrored has a great deal to do with "self image" — my body, my personality, my character, how I am seen by others. Adolescents on the verge of adulthood gaze into the mirror not just to look for pimples or blemishes. They are trying to formulate their "myth" or

"story" about themselves. They are asking the mirror for an answer to the question, "Who am I?"

[8] Unless, of course, the vision is quite inappropriate, irresponsible, dangerous to self or others, or otherwise out of touch with reality.

[9] An 800 pound man went on a diet and exercise regimen in order to save his life. After two months and an initial weight loss of 300 pounds, an essential part of his treatment became a mirror which distorted his image to that of a 250 pound man. The mirror image was a "lie," and he knew it. But the lie gave him the incentive to continue to lose weight until, indeed, he did look like a 250 pound man. Even so, the mirror of the elders reflects back to the person the essential health of the myth so that it can be "owned" and emulated.

SUMMER TO WINTER: THE RITES OF FALL

> Don't try to control a wild horse by grabbing its leg.
> Take hold the neck. Use a bridle. Be sensible.
> Then ride! There is a need for self-denial.
>
> — Rumi, "Zikr"

THE MALADY

    Summer's child (of any age) was hurt or never quite grew up and has turned away from the fall passage of inwardness and feeling. The winter shield is undernourished and the other shields are also affected. The child is given over to tantrums, anxiety, fear, hypertension, hysteria, jealousy, violence, sexuality, cheap thrills, greed, game-playing, attention-seeking, manipulation, parasitism, gluttony, irresponsibility, materialism, etc. Self and self-serving have become all important. Without the modern conveniences of the technological cage, and the goods and services on which (s)he is dependent, (s)he is at the mercy of the environment, and incapable of acting appropriately or self-reliantly in the face of crisis.

THE RITES OF FALL

What kinds of initiatory rites help to accomplish the child's transition to adulthood? Because it is the seasonal weather adjacent to the desired goal of winter, the fall shield is brought into play. The series of psycho-physical experiences comprising the rites of fall take place in the natural world, focusing on growth events that evoke inward dimensions — solitude, set-apartness, exposure, loneliness, helplessness, boredom, fear, impatience, helplessness, and dreams. From these spring the ability to maintain the winter shield. The rites of fall introduce powerful new earth-images of anima or animus to replace the archetypes of the parents (particularly those of the opposite sex), from whom there must be severance.

How ageless is the human understanding that the child must risk the darkness and uncertainty of self in order to know the meaning of maturity! How easily we forget that we are all children, that we are always being called on to risk that darkness, and so it will be when we stand at the brink of death. The "child" can be any one of us, for there are many "grown-ups" who are afraid to risk this darkness. There are many adult children whose winter shields, or portions thereof, have never been realized because they never set their feet on the "yellow brick road" and completed the dark journey of puberty.[1]

The rites of fall emphasize severance and individuation. The child (of any age) must be taken away from home and parents, or from work or daily routine, or from the situation that exacerbates the crisis. Fear blocks the passageway. The fear must be turned into an ally, a means of gaining entrance. Fear is the badge of courage. All the myths and legends agree. Nothing is accomplished without turning from the easy road toward the deep forest of the psyche. The threshold crossing must be anticipated, committed to, voluntarily attempted, knowing that physical, psychological, or spiritual death may result. This death risk evokes the powers of inwardness that guide us to maturity.[2]

At the end of the passage of fall lies a status change — maturity. If this change is witnessed and acknowledged by a community which also confers the rights and privileges of adulthood, the attained shield takes on weight and energy, counter-balancing the childhood shield, creating a healthy tension between the north and south poles. When the emergent adult is thereby enlightened, the same kind of tension is established between the introspection of the adolescent shield in the west and the creative expression of the adult in the east. The incorporation of the initiate into a new life station, status, or phase, accomplishes such a balancing of the shields.[3]

Even though it is currently impossible to obtain communal participation in the incorporation and/or validation of the initiate within a new life stage, it is still possible to prescribe specific initiatory activities for specific problems within the summer shield. Shield healing can occur if elders willing to perform a maieutic function are there to receive the initiates at the end of the passage. The healing is intensified if the initiatory experience is conducted within the ceremonial guidelines of a rite of passage or confirmation: *By this act you have attained a mature life station; you have confirmed that this is so. The act is binding. It cannot come undone because the story has been told to a council of elders and witnesses. And this council has empowered you by assuming that indeed you have changed your life status.*

At the School of Lost Borders, the "rites of fall" are prescribed for exaggerated summer shields and are conducted as passage rites, or initiatory-style ceremonies. Van Gennep's three phases — severance, threshold, and incorporation — are duly observed. The fourth phase — enlightenment, is celebrated within elders' councils. Appropriate precautions are always taken to insure the safety of the student.

RITES OF DAY: The Day Walk

Rise at dawn, leave your life behind you, and walk alone, without food, into the natural world.[4] Chose an intuitive course that takes you to whatever elicits your interest. If you are currently dealing with a crisis or problem, take the problem with you and allow it to inform your steps as you wander. Do not think you have to cover as much ground as possible, or to needlessly expose yourself to danger. Walk with all your senses open. Imagine yourself as an animal. Be wild. Try not to be heard or seen. Don't consult your watch. Find places to rest where you feel welcome. Practice being perfectly quiet, in a state of alert repose. If you need to, take a nap. Perhaps you will dream an important dream. Talk to yourself or to any other wild thing. Pray if you feel the urge. At sunset your walk is finished. Return to the elders' council and tell your story.[5]

The Man Who Hadn't Made Love in Three Years

Dave, a 44 year old married man with two teenage children went on a day walk as a means of preparing for a subsequent four day and night vision fast. He was not a particularly happy man. For the last several years he had been "an ogre" to his wife and children. Although his computer parts business was growing, his love affair with his wife had come to a full stop. Three years before, with the aid of a hypnotherapist, his wife had accessed vivid memories of physical and sexual abuse when she was a child. Since then they had been unable to make love.

Dave loved his wife and had never been unfaithful to her. He empathized with her plight and understood her therapeutic need to refrain from intercourse. "I have no intention of hurting her," he said. "She's the light of my life. I couldn't live without her." But he was desperate — the way people are when they keep changing the subject, only to come back to the main theme. His body craved contact with a woman — specifically his wife, more generally with anyone wearing a skirt. He said he felt as though he had been forced to live a life of fantasy. Masturbation was unsatisfying. He wanted the real thing. And he couldn't have it.

Dave left camp early in the morning carrying an emergency kit, a gallon of water, a raincoat, and a knife. He headed west, into the foothills of the Sierra Nevada. It was a spring day, cloudy but warm and breezy. Patches of lupine, paint brush, and desert gold dotted the hillsides. By late afternoon, the clouds had dissipated. By nightfall, Dave had not returned.

We spent a restless night wondering what had happened to him. By early morning light, I set out to find him. Just before noon, I spotted him coming down an east facing ridge of the main massif of Birch Mountain. When I reached him, all my fears for his well being dissolved. He looked and talked just fine. But his story, told in its entirety to the elder's council that afternoon, raised the hair on the backs of our necks.

Instead of setting his feet on a wandering, random course, Dave had set his sights on the summit of Birch Mountain, a 13,900 foot peak. All day, he climbed steadily upward, gaining thousands of feet in elevation. Before he stopped a thousand feet short of the summit, he had climbed 5,000 feet, almost a mile high, without food or companionship. He had passed through three life zones: high sage desert, sub alpine, and alpine. Looking neither to the left nor right, he had simply climbed, and climbed, trying by sheer physical effort to quench the fires that burned so fiercely within him.

It was no use. He never made the summit. Even if he had, he would not have quenched the fire. By the time he stopped climbing, it was late afternoon. He realized he would not make it down before dark. He knew he had to get down off the exposed ridge. He would have to spend the night somewhere. He headed down a steep arroyo, looking for shelter. At nightfall, he had reached a small seep, around which grew a profusion of willow and aspen. He stopped there, hastily gathered some wood, and built himself a fire. As he warmed himself in the bright flame, he suddenly realized how tired he was. He put his raincoat and wool camp on and lay down near the fire. It occurred to him as he drowsed off that for the last several hours, he hadn't been thinking about his wife.

He slept badly. He had to keep waking up to throw more wood on the fire. At one point he was startled by a violent thrashing in the brush nearby. At first he thought it might be another human. He called out. There was no answer. The thrashing sounds increased. Something was coming toward him through the willows. He fumbled in his day pack for his knife, and couldn't find it. He screamed a fearful warning. The thrashing stopped, then moved off at right angles, away from him. The night was quiet. The stars shone down impassively. There was only the sound of his own harsh breathing. He threw another stick of wood on the fire and sat wide-eyed for the next several hours. At dawn, he erased his fire and moved out, feeling rested somehow, and less anxious about his problem.

The mirror of the elders reflected the way in which Dave had danced with his sexual energy during his medicine walk. He had aimed for the highest peak (of himself), in the hope that he could surmount his bodily needs with a climax of another sort. But he had simply burned out. Forced by circumstance to spend a dark, cold, lonely night with himself, the little boy had been awakened by a sign, an unidentified creature (probably a deer) thrashing in the thicket. The creature in the thicket was Dave in his own thicket. The willows, with their roots deep in the soil of his life-generating "seep," had caught him for a while. Eventually he would work his way free. He wouldn't forever dwell in the dark shield regions of frustration and incapacity. There were good signs in the north shield — his ability to take care of himself, to survive a fearful night of exposure, to clean up after his own mistakes. The elders considered his medicine walk to be confirmation that he was ready to carry his sexual needs into a four day and night vision fast.

RITES OF NIGHT: The Night Walk

Go to a place where you can be absolutely silent and alone, surrounded by the mingled shadows of inward human nature.⁶ Invite the darkness in. Walk and sit all night with your feelings, your memories, the daily traffic on the streets of your psyche. Listen to the night, to the beating of your heart, to the rasping of your breath. Listen to your fear. Listen and wait. If you should fall asleep and dream, remember your dream. You have been separated from the light so that you can pass through a dark place. If you feel led, raise your voice to scream, moan, shout, or otherwise give vent to whatever feels trapped within. Practice ways of walking, standing, sitting that characterize your power to express and defend yourself. The night walk will give you character, soul, and credentials to be revealed later in the elders' council.⁷

The Woman Who Hallucinated What Was Good for Her

Elise and I drove our cars separately up to the McMurray Meadows turnoff. She parked her car there and got in with me. I took her up the road about three miles, stopped, smudged her off, and drove back home. She would walk back down the road to her car in the dark.

It was 9:00 on a moonless, weekday, September night. The road was remote. People rarely traveled it after dark. Her biggest fear had been of encountering human predators in the dark. We were confident she would be safe. If, perchance, a car should come up the road as she was going down, she would see it coming a long way off. It would be easy for her to get off the road and hide behind the big sage brush off to the side. The people in the car would be looking straight ahead, into the tunnel of their headlights. They wouldn't see her.

Elise had visited the School over a period of years in order to explore her initiatory shield in ways that would lead to self-discovery. She was troubled by memories of childhood sexual abuse, the sudden, tragic death of a lover, and a mountain of self-doubt. She did not lack in courage. Twice, she fasted for four days and nights alone without food in the desert mountains. She put herself through our month-long training course. Every day she underwent initiatory-style assignments in the foothills of the eastern Sierra. She went without water, slept in a cave, tracked herself through a volcanic wasteland, hunted cougar sign, looked for rattlesnakes without any clothes on. She was determined to understand herself, and to make changes in her life. Now she was off on a night walk, the object of which was to evoke the contents of her dark, or fall shield. For years, we had used this exercise to put the students in contact with the dark, inward aspects of human nature, the feelings, the memories, the self-consciousness of their souls. The darkness evoked dark memories. The fear of the dark evoked feelings of vulnerability. However jaded, civilized senses could be jarred into a state of alertness that bordered on intuition. To defend the threatened self, personal gifts were brought into play.

Not that there was any great risk walking around in the dark above the lights of our tiny town. The dark is unsurpassed as camouflage. The one who does not blind herself with a light has a distinct advantage over those who do. Without a light, a "civilized" human becomes diurnal, even when these "dark senses" are rusty from disuse. There was a remote possibility the student might run into a rattlesnake or be stalked by a cougar or see a car coming up the road. Hence, part of the routine of preparing Elise had been to face these possibilities squarely, and to help her equip herself with courses of action and prevention.

I left her standing there in the dark and drove home, ten minutes away by car. Meredith read and I wrote for several hours. Then we noticed it was time for her to check in, to let us know she had completed her walk. When she didn't show 15 minutes after the deadline, I jumped into the car and drove above town. I couldn't imagine what had gone wrong. At the turn off I noted that her car was still there. She must be somewhere up the road. I turned on the interior lights of the car, so that I could be seen as the driver, and proceeded slowly up the dusty trail to where I had dropped her off. No Elise! Dumbfounded, I started back, even more carefully this time, calling out her name. Cutting the engine. Straining at the quiet. No sound. In the headlights, her tracks led down the road toward her car. I decided to follow them. They led all the way back to her car. The car was gone. Mystified how I had missed her, I headed home. Meredith greeted me with the news that Elise had popped in ten minutes before to say good night.

The following day the council heard Elise's night walk story. Her eyes had adjusted reasonably well to the light. Aside from a few undetermined rustles in the bushes now and then, she had experienced no uncommon fear. She was feeling strong. But just before she got to the end of the walk, the headlights of a car turned up the road and came at her. Like a rabbit, she jumped off the road and hid behind a sage brush twenty yards away. The car came slowly up the road until it was adjacent to where she was hidden. Then it halted. The engine died. Two men got out and stood in front, their figures bright in the headlights. Their gaze was riveted on her.

She shrank back, quivering with fright, unable to think what to do. They seemed to be discussing what they were going to do when they got hold of her. Frozen in a kind of absolute fear, her mind went blank. Then a vigor coursed through her body, a feel of readiness, an animal-likeness. She thought, "If they take just one step toward me, I'm out of here. I'm gone so fast they'll never find me. I can see where I'm going. They can't. I'm quicker than they are." With a curious elation and self-confidence she arose from her hiding place and waited like a cat for them to make the next move.

At that moment, she saw another car, interior lights on, coming up the road slowly toward the idling car and its two inhabitants. She recognized right away that it was me. She watched as my car drove up to — and then *through* — the other car and the men standing in the road — all of which vanished, simply vanished. My car continued slowly up the road, interior lights and headlamps blazing.

Elise' fall shield, in concert with the natural psychosphere, had produced a state of non-ordinary reality which, though terrifying, had elicited strength and a kind of self-conscious power. She had discovered one of her finest gifts. By creating threatening scenarios — not illusions to her — she could heal herself. Her dark shield was gifted.

RITES OF VISION: The Vision Fast [8]

The time has come to confirm that you are no longer a child. You must be removed from the mothering arms of home, the reassurance of routine, and all that has been familiar to the emotional, reactive, comfort-seeking persona of summer. Innocence and trust must now be tried in the fires of initiatory experience. You will go alone, with an empty belly and a bare minimum of equipment, into the heart of wild nature, for four days and nights. There you will live with yourself in perfect solitude. You will surrender to the influences of the looks-within-place, the psychosphere, the soul of nature. In your outcast state you will find answers. You will drink at the springs of feeling and be filled with self-recognition. Returning to the elders, you will confirm your attainment of a new maturity.[9]

The Prostitute

She sat quietly in the circle, a little black teddy bear stuffed down into her tank top between her breasts. Its black, beady eyes glistened like tears in the hot sun. When her turn came around to tell us why she was going to live alone and fast in the desert for four days and nights, she looked up at us and out it came, honest as pie: "I sell my body for money. I don't want to do that and I'm going to stop it. For too long now I've been caught in a vicious cycle of doing things I don't really like to do. Sometimes I hurt myself really bad. I'm here because I really care what happens to me. I want to stop being self-destructive."

Her name was Dawn. She lived in a Santa Monica apartment and worked part-time at a health spa. Some of her time was spent entertaining marks. Her childhood had not been particularly cheery — a precocious child in a home broken by divorce. Her father, with whom she lived during her early teenage years, repeatedly "seduced" her into sexual acts. Her introduction to matters erotic in early puberty deeply marked her psyche with a seething inwardness and a vivid, almost hallucinatory fantasy life which, coupled with feelings of shame, revolved around an intimation that she knew how to please — and thus to exert a kind of power over — men.

It was also in early adolescence that she began to play games with words on the page, to make them do things, like painting pictures of what was happening inside her dark storehouse of memories and daydreams. The process of sorting through, depicting, and dramatizing — of defining the awful beauty of her rage and power to create — began to absorb her. After a couple years of working at it, she realized that life had dealt her an ace. She had the stuff to be a writer.

As it turned out, her mother had fasted in the desert with the School and considered the process beneficial. Anxious for her daughter's well being, she offered to pay for her enrollment in a vision fast course. For one reason or another, the idea appealed to Dawn. There would be a purging, a cleansing, a dying. She would go off to some godforsaken desert and come back clean. She would dance with the shadow of her father and return to a life that she had already decided she had to live differently. She wrote us a letter and nine months later went out with a group into the northern Mojave desert for four days and nights to live without food, company, or shelter.

It was late spring. The gusty spirits of wild flowers shouted on the land with yellow, purple, blue, crimson, and white. Zebra-tail lizards shot across the sands like camouflaged darts. Blurred by heat waves, the creosote green of the horizon melted and ran down into the brown earth. Another month and it would be too hot for an unshielded human. Flesh would crisp, boots sizzle. The frying pan smell of smoldering granite would choke the noontime air.

Mosquitoes clouded the ephemeral dampness of sunrise the morning she left base camp, pack on back, teddy bear stuffed into her shirt front, hair done up in a bandanna. No doubt that she was ready to go. She'd been ready for a long time. One last hug and a look into her dark eyes. They were bottomless.

Four hot days, four cool nights went by. The winds blew up canyon in the morning, down canyon in the evening. A mountain bluebird showed up one day, to the pleasure of those who stayed at base camp to watch and wait for those who were fasting. At night, poorwills cried on the creosote flats and kangaroo mice leaped around like overweight grasshoppers. A rattlesnake dozed in a lazy circle under a nearby saltbush.

The day after they came back from their fast, the whole group assembled in a sunny meadow beside a clear high sierra creek, at a cool 7,000 feet. Wild iris, Indian paintbrush, and purple and white lupine touched the bright green of spring with radiant color. We listened to stories, stories of what happened during those four hot days, stories of dreams, daydreams, encounters with non-human relatives, darkness, stars, and sun. We heard how lives unfolded within the microcosm of the initiatory passage. We heard the quiver in the voice, the words suddenly swell with tears. It was a good time, a hard time, an appropriate time to listen to stories of human nature.

Dawn's turn came around. There was not a soul in the group who didn't hang on her words. Everyone had seen her the morning she returned from the desert, looking fresh as a desert dandelion. She told her story with clarity and grace, and even with a touch of wonder, for most of the time she had been in a kind of seventh heaven. No, it had not been difficult. No, she had not felt hungry. She had not even been afraid. She had done nothing but had not been bored. She had simply "breathed it in." She went naked and got dirty and, since "I've never been made love to," made love to herself. She befriended a fence lizard who thereupon had climbed up on her leg and conversed with her about matters of great urgency. She deeply relished the feelings of emptiness, timelessness, and the subtle alterations of consciousness brought about by the solitary fasting.

She drew a circle in the sand, sat inside it, and told her father, her mother, her brothers, her friends, her customers, that she was going to die. She asked each one if he/she had anything to say before she died. She listened to their goodbyes and then said her own. One by one they "passed through" her, receding into history, into "the opposite direction of now."

That night, she had a dream: "I was handcuffed to a powerful black man. I was his slave; I did what he told me to do. Every year he removed the handcuffs for a little while. That was when I ran away, to a foreign country. For a while, I thought I was free of him, but one night he jumped out at me in a rage of crying and need. His rage was too powerful. I became his slave again."

Then she had a second dream. She was living in her apartment in Santa Monica and she looked out the front window and saw the black shadow of a man coming up the walk to her door. She felt a sudden panic. She was determined not to run away. She wondered, "Will I betray myself?" "Will I go into the dark again and hurt myself?" She knew it all boiled down to the question: "If he knocks, will I let him in?" Then she said: "All I have to do is wave at him through the window. That will make the black shadow go away." She waved. As Dawn told her story, I took notes and watched her face. I wondered if this lovely young woman knew what she was going back to. It would be a thousand times more difficult than fasting alone in the desert for four days and nights. That black shadow would no doubt come up the walk to her door. A wave from the window wouldn't keep him away. She would have to answer the awesome question: "If he knocks, will I let him in?" Simply, she was going back to face one of the profoundest of feminine dilemmas.

> "Let me in O precious woman,
> Let me in for heaven's sake,
> Let me in O tender woman,
> Ssssighed the snake."
>
> —Old Cajun ballad

When she got in her car to drive back to Santa Monica, she gave away her teddy bear.

Within a few days, we began to get letters from her. Here are a few excerpts:

I am NOT powerless! This energy, this intensity, this crazy whirlwind force that spins inside me like a top and demands personification, clarification, and creative outlet, I refuse to squelch down and be afraid of, as they do! I REFUSE to be ashamed anymore and I refuse to view the whirlwind as 'self-will- run-riot' that needs to be diffused. Since I fasted in the desert on the edge of freedom, I can wear my 'shame' as jewellery that adorns me. I can, because I can do whatever I want to do!

It was all very good and well to say the black shadow doesn't exist outside of me . . . . It was such a sane and rational and mature thing to say to show I'm normal. But I just SAID that. I'm not really normal, and the black shadow IS real. His eyes are very white. Just like images of fairies and wood sprites are very real when you . . . jump out of an airplane and the clouds are held up like little cherubs, as you fall screaming to the ground. . . .

The shadow is cunning. It knows if you secretly believe it is more powerful than you. It lies in wait like a poisonous vapor to mist on you if you have any doubt.

So far, I have faced my 'tests' with the real "black shadow." I know my strength and I'm 'O.K.' for now. You were right. You said that the primal scream from the black shadow inside would come when it saw me strong. . . . This little girl that's in my life now has been dry 12 days. She's the new girl at work. She smiles tremulously when I tell her that the craving DOES pass. She follows me everywhere like a puppy and says thank you a lot. . . .

There is no sin in what I did. . . except that the absence of love perpetuates more absence of love, especially my own love for me. I deserve to know I'm a great gal.

The letters keep coming. Exciting, disturbing, vital, fantastic, dramatic, profoundly sensitive — the effusions of unmistakable talent. We wonder, what shall we do with all these letters? In the meantime, we won't worry too much for her sake. How could anyone deny any experience, however perilous, to a true artist?

The Marathon Runner

Marvin was a tough nut, seemingly in perfect health. On his 50th birthday, he ran a 50 mile marathon, just to prove to all concerned that he was still full of spit and vinegar. When we asked him how his life was otherwise going (his wife, children, work) he glossed it all over with the same bravado. Everything was fine. He was riding the wave. He wasn't going to die for a long time. He was looking forward to fasting and time alone. He said he might even try a little running out there.

On the fifth morning, when the fast was over, everyone in the group returned to base camp but Marvin. We waited a while longer, then went to look for him. We found him at his place, lying in the dirt, his things scattered everywhere. His face was white as a ghost, his shirt covered with dried vomit. Shaking with fatigue and pain, he said he was too sick to come in. He said he had gone for a long hike on the second day of his fast. On his way back to his place he was hit by severe back pain and became sick to his stomach. The third and fourth days had been torture. He hadn't been able to keep any water down.

We gathered his things and brought him in on our shoulders. It took him several hours to come around. A physician, who happened to be one of the group, diagnosed his trouble. Extreme dehydration, due to water loss, and probable heart attack. Marvin refused to accept the diagnosis, protesting that his heart was fine. He blamed his condition on the fast and the hot weather and declared loudly that he wanted to have nothing further to do with this vision fasting stuff.[10]

Andrew's Mountain

A young man (18) came from Rhode Island all the way to Big Pine. He had just completed his first year in college at Wesleyan. A year before, his father had died. He was on his own now, and he wanted to celebrate his passage into manhood.

Andrew was a strong young man, intelligent, and idealistic. He was ready to take on the world with his bare hands and bare feet. Armed with the teachings of Castaneda, Black Elk, and assorted other shamans, he came for the BIG VISION — what he was going to do with his life. Of course, everyone in the group of young people was hoping for the BIG ONE too. But Andrew was a little more vocal about it. If talk could have summoned visions, he would have been richly rewarded.

As I remember, we honored his mystical yearnings, and we gave him our own definition of vision: "Something that has to be done." A work that has to be accomplished. We told him not to look too hard for angels when scorpions crawled underfoot. One of the elders suggested that he stay awake the final night and cry for a vision in the traditional way. This he resolved to do.

The area where we took the group was nestled on the northern flank of a high ridge in the Inyo Range called Andrew's Mountain. No doubt which direction our hero was going. Andrew went unto Andrew's Mountain, to seek a vision for his life.

Three hot, cloudless days later, Andrew returned from his mountain. With the others he crossed through the threshold circle and joined the world of basecamp. He seemed subdued, lost in deep thought. But on the ride home he talked animatedly. His experience had not been what he thought it would be. He had been bored, frustrated, and lonely. Nothing had happened. No vision had come to him. He wondered if something was wrong with him. He wondered if the Great Spirit had forsaken him. He wondered if this vision quest business was all it was cracked up to be.

The next day, with the others who had just returned, he told his story to the elders. The story in itself was a classic four shields story of the initiation of a young man into maturity.

He concentrated on his experiences of the last night. "It was agony," he said. "It was the hardest thing I've ever done. I had to do it all alone. Nobody was watching me. It was a test to see how much I could take. Staying up all night would prove that I was truly a man. I was determined to do it for myself."

As night fell, he entered the circle of stones he had prepared for his all night vigil. He sat down and waited. It was a warm evening. Nothing happened. It got darker. Just as twilight was fading a movement in the foreground arrested his eye. A silent, banded shadow was moving toward him. He nearly jumped out of his skin. He didn't know until later that it was a common kingsnake. He thought maybe it was a rattler. It was difficult to make it out in the gloom.

The snake seemed to be coming at him with conscious intent. For an instant he wondered if this was the vision he had come for. If so, he would need to watch and listen carefully to what the snake had to say. His overwhelming reaction was fear. "But I held my ground," he said. "I protected myself with the power of my quest."

Just inside the circle of stones, the snake stopped and assumed a defensive posture, its head held up and back, as if to strike. It hissed and held its ground. For a moment, Andrew and kingsnake regarded each other in the darkening gloom. Then the kingsnake moved off at an angle and disappeared into the surrounding cover.

In retrospect, Andrew wondered if he had blown the encounter. What had the kingsnake been trying to tell him? He pondered this question as the night wore on and the "agony" began. He stayed within the protection of his circle and prayed "O Spirit give me strength to make it through the night." Gradually the high desert air cooled. The high altitude night became downright cold. The stars rang down peals of brilliant hail. Andrew's prayer changed: "O Spirit, give me hope."

To pass the time he called all those he loved, living or dead, to come and be with him. He told them he was going to die and be reborn as a man. He waited for some cataclysmic event to deepen his feeling of dying. Nothing happened. He was simply an 18 year old boy-man, fighting to stay up through the night.

Twice he nodded off. He didn't think it was for more than a few minutes. Both times he had a dream. In the first he was fighting with a man who had come to kill his father. In the second a huge bear was frightening an old lady. But he knew the bear. He told the old lady not to worry, that the bear wouldn't attack her.

Gritty-eyed, he held on to wakefulness. Once again he changed his prayer. He prayed it over and over again, if only to keep his eyes open: "Father sun, please rise." Now it was very still and cold. The gloomy landscape stood out in sharp shadows cast by the rising crescent moon. And then, imperceptibly, without even a whisper, the curtain of night was drawing back.

Even as the theater of day was opening, Andrew was at a point of great desperation. All he wanted to do was lie down and sleep, to forget his resolve to become a man. That was when he saw the dirt on his hands. Light was coming. It was already there. "I never felt so good as when I saw the light in the sky," he said. "I was just so thankful that I had the strength in me to do it."

The council confirmed that Andrew had earned the right to call himself a man, and from then on they treated him like one. The test of manhood had not been designed to test his visionary, or nonordinary, abilities. The test had to do with values only true men manifest: patience, determination, hope, love, faith, and the powers of dreaming. The kingsnake was a powerful validation given by the spirit of nature. The kingsnake said, "Yo, brother. We are kin. But you go your way and I'll go mine."

Several days after, Andrew began to see that, in fact, the encounter with the kingsnake was profoundly meaningful to him. He would live the meaning of the encounter and thus uncover the mystery that lay embedded in the silent, banded shadow. He would look for the kingsnake in his daily affairs, in his life at College and with his girlfriend. Perhaps the kingsnake would appear in his dreams. Perhaps after the passing of many years, parts of him would become like the kingsnake. He fervently hoped so.

And so the council was reminded once again of the true value of initiations in the wilderness. The candidate comes face to face with the mirror. He looks into the mirror and sees self reflected. That reflection contains a great mystery.

RITES OF WALKING: The Walkabout[11]

Go alone into the wilderness for seven days and nights, following a pre-set course that leads you into an adventure that confirms your death to childhood and rebirth as a mature man or woman. With a minimum of food and shelter, you will have to exercise self-reliance, cooperation with nature, and a commitment to see yourself through hard times. You will follow a primitive road, walking at least 20 miles, camping each night at a new site a few miles down the road. Each day will represent a new ordeal in your initiation into maturity. When you emerge, you will tell your story in the elders' council and receive the empowerment that confirms your assumption of a new life state.[12]

Two Canyons

Handsome, bright, sociable, intense, politically astute, Derek seemed a good candidate for what he said he wanted to be some day — President of the United States. He would have made a good one. There was a serious side to him, a depth of character and soul unlikely in a boy-man of seventeen. After his first vision fast, he became obsessed with the desire to learn more about the process. He became one of our youngest "trainees." Everybody loved him. You couldn't help but love him. When he graduated from high school, he didn't go to college; he went to the Outdoor Leadership School in Colorado and became a wilderness leader.

Derek called one day and said he wanted us to get him ready and put him out on a Walkabout. He had grown some since we last saw him. He was considering a job directing a wilderness organization overseas. But something was troubling him. At first he didn't want to talk about it. Then he blurted out the truth, and with it came a copious flow of tears.

He said ever since he was a boy he had wrestled with the fear that he was homosexual. Although he got along well with girls, he wondered sometimes if he desired them sexually. And although he often felt estranged from "the guys," he was sometimes attracted by them. Certain recent events in his life had deeply confused him. The confusion had begun to torture him to the extent that he could not keep his mind on his work.

All we could do was to help him clarify his intent and prepare him for the Walkabout. He would start at Gilbert Pass. Seven days and nights later, he would end at the Eureka Valley Road. He would cover 25 miles and go without food, although there would be emergency rations and water at critical check points along the way. Each day would represent a different ordeal. The fourth day would be the "ordeal of the two canyons." On that day he would choose one of two canyons and explore it all the way to the end. The canyon on the right would be "heterosexuality." The canyon on the left would be "homosexuality."

We checked on him every day via notes left at stonepiles. On the eighth morning he appeared at the rendezvous point, filthy as a grub, his white teeth flashing in a welcome smile. He said he felt great. He declared himself ready to take his life on. We asked him which canyon he went into. He laughed, rolled his dark eyes. "Both," he said.[13]

RITES OF INTERMENT: Alone in the Earth

Leave your life behind and enter a dark place in the earth (a hole, cave, or darkened lodge) and stay there for 24-48 hours alone without food, water, or artificial light.[14] Take with you (the spirit or memory of) another person who has wronged you or you have wronged. Live with that person throughout the ordeal. Perhaps you will find a way to forgive or be forgiven. Pay attention to what you see, hear, and feel in the darkness. If you fall asleep and dream, remember the dream, for it will be relevant to current and future ways of symbolically characterizing yourself. If you wish, you may take a bundle of dried sage and a few matches to purify and bless your place of darkness or the "presences" that appear. You may also take a drum or a rattle or some other means of accompanying your chanting and singing. On emerging, tell your story to the elders' council. Then take up the new threads of understanding and stitch them into the embroidery of your life.[15]

The Philandering Ne'er Do Well

Twice he was hauled into court for not paying child support. He failed to fulfill his financial obligations because he was nothing but a hippie, a man without a stable address, income or assets who was wandering the earth seeking enlightenment with a guitar. The second time the judge told him he better seek employment or else. At that point, Mark ran away. Nobody heard from him, much less his ex-wife and young son, for several years. What was driving him? Anger, resentment, jealousy and anger at the woman who had left him and taken up with another man, and an intolerable guilt about how he had separated himself from his son.

As he wandered the American west, he had plenty of solitude and space in which to review the events that led to an ill-conceived marriage and the unexpected birth of a child. Back then he'd been a well-paid professional. Now he was just a wreck of a man afraid to face his karma — with a bitch for an ex-wife and a little boy with an absent father. He saw himself as just another casualty of the war between the sexes, a victim of the duplicity of love. He'd cynically "played the field." He'd loved them and left them, sampling like a connoisseur, working hard to distract himself from facing what he had to do.

It came to him one day that he had to go back, that there was no way out of the black hole but to wrestle with the monsters of the past. The realization that this was so came to him as a vast relief. Now he had somewhere to go. It was time to get on with his life, to claim his son and to be his father. He returned to the city where his son lived, cut his hair, got a job as a technical writer, and began visiting the boy, despite the fearful ordeal of being in a home where his own son called his step-father Dad. Soon after, he met a woman at work. The two became fast friends. In time, they fell in love. Even as the two lovers decided to live together, Mark's times with his son became more prolonged and frequent. The boy enjoyed living with his real father. When trouble erupted in the relationship between the ex-wife and the step-father, the son, with his mother's permission, came to live with Mark.

He showed up at the School. He said he wanted to go into the Earth Lodge. He wanted to review his past and to confirm the attainment of the new state of fatherhood. As we prepared him, he talked about his desire to cut away those parts of himself he detested — his pride, his tendency to avoid disagreeable situations, his inability to forgive his ex-wife, his hypocrisy. The list of "guilts" went on and on. It did no good to tell him that he was getting a hell of a lot of mileage out of his guilt. Better to let the dear man bumble through his psychological shield in his own way, and to trust the power of the initiatory process.

The night of the opening of the lodge arrived. With his sleeping bag, his jacket, a bundle of fresh sage, but no food or water, Mark entered the darkness of the lava cave. We shut him in with tarps held down by rocks, and left him there. One of the trainees would keep watch and sleep nearby. When morning came, he would be given light for a few minutes. At sunset, he would again be given a little light. And then the second 24 hour cycle would begin. Mark would again sit alone in the darkness, staying awake at night, sleeping by day.

Just as the setting sun was summoning the third night, the helper called Mark to come out. He emerged from the dark womb, his limbs stiff and uncooperative. He looked at the rest of us who had assembled for his "coming out." He smiled wanly and said, "I'm claustrophobic. Who are you?"

Later, he told his story to the council. The first night he thought he would go crazy with fear. He couldn't tell which way he was facing. He even began to wonder if he was upside down. To calm himself, he sang songs, any song that came into his head. For hours he rubbed his indifferent penis, vainly trying to change the movie — or seeking some kind of reassurance. Finally he fell asleep, only to be awakened by his helper opening the flap for the morning break.

Through the day and into the next night, he was able to review his past, remembering events almost forgotten, reliving moments he could never change. He got depressed. He sang a little bit. The idea came that he should do something to forgive himself. He thought, "If I make it through the night and get out of this hole alive, I'll forgive himself. At that moment, his son "came into the lodge." He wanted to know what his dad was doing there. Mark tried to explain, that he was trying to become worthy of being a father. The boy couldn't understand. "You don't have to do anything, Dad," he said. "I love you the way you are."[16]

RITES OF SWEATING: Lodges and Saunas[17]

At the door of the lodge you leave your life as a "child" behind. Stripped of your protective clothing, you enter the psychological world of naked feeling (fall shield), as represented by this dark place of anonymity. Here you sit with the others and become aware of your ability to endure the closeness, discomfort, heat, and blindness. There will be times when the child rages at the door, screaming to be let out, to escape to comfort and safety. You will take the rebellious child into yourself and comfort her/him. With the others, you will sing and pray for yourself, for them, for healing, for the good of the community, for the earth. You will discover that part of yourself that is humble, that is nothing, that can grovel unashamedly. You will learn how to transcend what you mistakenly believed to be personal limitations. Finally, you will emerge from the darkness cleansed, illumined, new born. Then you will enjoy a feast of acceptance and communion as an adult among elders.[18]

The Cry Baby

Larry (age 38) cried like a baby when his turn came to go into the sauna. He was afraid. He was genuinely afraid to such an extreme that he couldn't help but show it. In fact, there was some question in my mind whether we should let him in. I was afraid he'd throw a tantrum right in the middle of the first round. Undoubtedly, he was picking up on everybody else's fear too. He was the receptacle of collective anxiety.

The sweat would be hot, but not extreme. Larry's medical record was good. He had already proven himself to be physically strong enough to take it. He had just fasted for four days and nights in the Inyo Mountains during a series of violent thunderstorms. If he'd made it through that, he could make it through a couple hours in the sauna. His wails belied what he had just done. Surely he could see that.

All at once, the orderly procession into the lodge was entirely disrupted. We stood there looking at each other in dismay. Where had this little boy come from?

"What are you afraid of?" asked Meredith.

"I'm afraid of the dark! I'm afraid of the heat! I'm afraid of a heart attack!" At that point in time, he was afraid of *everything*.

His fear was great enough to warrant his staying out. I suggested the possibility to him. "You know, you don't have to go into the lodge. You can sit out here on the deck and sing and pray with us."

He looked at me with accusing eyes. "That wouldn't be a sauna," he sobbed.

"No," Meredith said, "but you would be with us almost as close as if you were in there with us. We'll hold hands with you through the walls. That's close enough."

You could see he was thinking about it. In the meantime, the others began to go into the lodge. One by one they disappeared until only he and I were left.

"Well," I said. "What do you want to do?"

He wiped his eyes and calmed his heaving breath. "I'm going in," he said.

The sauna was close and hot. The first round was probably the hottest. The rocks hissed and blubbered. Steam invaded the air with the odor of cedar and sage. The songs were good. The prayers were good. Now and then, people could be heard crying softly. When Larry's turn to pray came round, he prayed for everyone else in the group. He had to be prompted to pray for himself.[19]

RITES OF DREAMING

Go alone to a wild place with the specific intent to dream. Stay in that place, without food, for 24 hours. Sleep and dream. Be watchful for and record any dreams that may come, including daydreams, fantasies, reveries, out of body experiences, etc. When you return, tell your dreams to the elders. Elements of the dreams will help you to understand yourself and your mythical course.[20]

The Rape and Murder of Amy

A child of divorce, Amy had been raised by a loving mother in a small town where years passed without a cloud on the horizon, with scarcely a ruffle on the pond. At 18, she graduated from high school as class valedictorian. For a graduation present, her mother gave her the gift of a vision fast, a rite of passage celebrating the passage of young people into adulthood.

She was a lively contributing member of a group of eight young people, talking freely about herself, her life, and her future, which included plans to attend a large university on the east coast. A pretty, athletic girl, she said she had avoided "going all the way" with boys, yet confessed that she was hungry for love and relationship.

With the others, she crossed the threshold and lived alone for three days and nights in the Inyo Mountains. When she returned she told this dream to the elders' council:

> I was waiting at a bridge for my teacher to come. He was an old man with a white beard and white hair. When he came he told me there was a convention taking place and I had to go.
> The convention was happening at this huge old castle with elevators and revolving doors. There were people everywhere. I had to go to the restroom but they were all out of order. I had to take an elevator down to the basement, to the cleaner's quarters.
> I went into a stall but I couldn't close the door for privacy. I was trying to fasten the chain so the door would hold shut when a man with an evil eye peeked in on me through the crack. He slashed the chain and came into the stall. I screamed, but it didn't do any good. He held a knife to my throat and said he was going to kill me. I asked him why and he said he was angry and he wanted to take his anger out on me.
> Then he raped me. When he was done, he slit my throat. I just sat there crying with my hands at my throat, trying to stop the bleeding. He threw a sheet over me, and left me on the floor. Just then my mother and my two sisters came in to the bathroom. He pulled out a gun and shot them all dead.
> But I wasn't completely dead. I escaped to find an older woman who called an ambulance. I woke up in the hospital. There was a scar on my throat and a coyote was crying. I remember saying, 'I have to give up my need for comfort and security and trust.'

Amy's dream is a classic initiation scenario reminiscent of the mythic descent of the goddess Innana into the underworld. She undergoes the process of ravishment and dismemberment at the hands of a dark animus god and comes forth into womanhood bearing initiation scars. An older man and woman play the role of elders. Her family is rendered symbolically dead. Only she remains, with an injunction to face the hardships and dangers of adulthood.

Mark's Blob

A middle aged psychologist in the midst of a divorce, Mark had come to the four shields seminar to understand himself and his clients better. He was right on the cusp of change. His two children had gone off to college and his wife had moved out of the house in anticipation of the divorce. He was all alone in the house, and was feeling somewhat sorry for himself. He said he wanted to radically change his life.

On the second day of the seminar, participants were encouraged to go off alone and find a species that represented their dark, or shadow side. Mark went up along Big Pine creek and found a place to rest in a sandy area surrounded by granite boulders. Gently the breeze swayed the willows bordering the creek and the clear water sang a song of glaciers and purple sky.

But Mark never saw the beauty. His attention was riveted on the web of a spider, where a fly quivered, entangled. He watched the spider come out of hiding and repeatedly inject the shuddering fly with its venom, until the captive form was still.

He fancied himself the fly, caught in the web of his own karma, at the mercy of poisonous anxieties and fears. He was afraid of becoming frozen, stagnant, paralyzed. He was equally afraid of actually doing what was necessary to change his life.

In this frame of mind he dozed off in the warm sun. He dreamed this dream:

> I was in a house and there was a fire raging outside. Flames everywhere. But inside the house it was quiet, ominously peaceful. It was a familiar place, but strange at the same time. Everything was dusty, old, sleazy, dirty. Even filthy. And I lay down on this dirty couch and went to sleep.
>
> When I woke up the fire was still burning fiercely. It was like I was in a kind of hell. And then something emerged from under the couch I'd been sleeping on. It was a large, misshapen, vaguely human blob and it should have been scary but it wasn't. A part of me knew this thing well. . . .

Somehow I understood that this thing wanted to lie down on the couch with me and be close or merge with me or some such thing. And the fire was raging fiercely just outside the window and the dusty room was lit by an eery light. . . . The rest is kind of confused. But I think I let this ugly, awful thing lie down on the couch with me.

Then the dream changed abruptly. I was standing on a hillside with a small group of people. It was dawn. The sunrise was in our faces. They were ordinary people like you or me. But each one of them was very beautiful. We all shared some secret, some kind of mysterious love.

Abruptly I woke up. It took me a long time to adjust to where I was. The dream felt unusually powerful. Even now I can see the faces of those people on the hill. And I can still see clearly that poor horrible monster in the burning room. . . .

The mirror of the elders reflected their interpretation of the meaning of the dream. Mark had met his shadow side in that burning room filled with old, dirty, forgotten things. The blob was that dark part of himself that was the fly, entangled in the web of karma. His willingness to allow the blob to lie with him was a healing act of integration, which allowed him a glimpse of the joys of maturity and enlightenment. The fly and the blob on which it was feeding could live in peaceful coexistence in the country of self-acceptance. We even went so far as to predict that Mark would actually meet these faces in the sunrise of his dream. They represented the life that lay ahead.

ENDNOTES: SUMMER TO WINTER: THE RITES OF FALL

[1] Given the fact that universal rites of passage into adulthood are at present a cultural dream, and that modern children are still being reared with the notion that they are separate from nature, can we still discern possible ways that the child shield can be brought through the fall and into the winter? Indeed, there are many feasible ways, even today. If all these ways could be brought together into culturally sanctioned initiatory processes, we might have the beginnings of a new psychology of human nature. A new era would dawn. When the children reached adolescence, we would not wring our hands in despair.

[2] As in most passage rites, this "death" is more "psychological" than real.

[3] In the light of modern reality, however, most initiations into adulthood have been incomplete or abortive. It may take years for a modern adult, trapped in a complex of the summer persona, to finally attain a degree of winter maturity when, for so long, the child has chronically reigned supreme. This, and worse, is the price we pay for forgetting that the old ways are still within us, and that our self-thus is dancing to the tune of the seasons whether we know it or not.

[4] The walker must walk in a safe place apart from human predation and pack an emergency kit and at least a gallon of water. Someone should know where the walker is going and when returning. In some cases, a buddy might go along and remain all day at the point of origin. For a more extensive discussion of the therapeutic interpretation of a day walk or "medicine walk," see Foster and Little, *The Roaring of the Sacred River: The Wilderness Quest for Vision and Self-Healing* (Big Pine, CA: Lost Borders Press, 1998).

[5] The troubled child who vows to become an adult must leave the routines of the village behind and, like the child in the fairy tale, venture into the dark woods of destiny. At the end of the rainbow may be a pot of gold — or a wicked witch. Perhaps both. No doubt, the child will encounter the "psychosphere" — symbols, images, feelings, situations, and thoughts that compose a kind of microcosm of his life. The condition of aloneness and timelessness produces a constant self-consciousness. The fasting, coupled with a current crisis or problem, accentuates the inward state (fall shield). The "outer world" mirrors the "inward world." That is, the two worlds of self-thus cooperate to interweave a mythical tapestry that is the stuff of illumined adulthood. The "problem" also appears within the tapestry, usually in a minor motif, for the full story is much grander in scope, and can even presage, in broad strokes, a lifetime. Exercises such as these, when accompanied by the telling of the story to a council of elders, can be repeated

on an annual or bi-annual basis, and have a lasting effect on the mature life of the participant.

[6] In the foothills of the mountains behind our School there is a system of seldom-travelled dirt roads that are ideal for night walks.

[7] The child goes alone, without food or artificial light into the dark for one full night. There, where the eyes cannot see, she will learn to see with the inward eye. This initiatory exercise is of particular value to those whose "child" has been abused. The theme is how the traumatized child finds her way through the darkness and into the light of mature understanding, discovering means by which she is able to transform that which is feared into personal power.

[8] Through the years we have helped thousands of youth and adults through the vision fast, which involves four days of intensive preparation, four days of fasting in the wilderness, and three days of incorporation with the elders' council. See Foster and Little, *The Book of the Vision Quest,* Revised Edition (New York: Simon and Schuster, 1992).

[9] The moment the "child" steps across the threshold, the summer shield is harvested. The trees begin to shed their leaves, the stalk begins to wither, and the "adolescent" turns inward to prepare for the coming of winter. Alone in a seemingly indifferent wilderness, hungry and unshielded from the elements, the self translates the emotions of the child into deep feeling. From this vale of soul making, the mature self emerges. Sometimes, however, the mature one does not emerge. The youth falls into a black hole. The initiation is incomplete.

[10] Marvin was given a priceless opportunity to contemplate his own death. After 50 years, it was time to turn around and face it. But he couldn't. It didn't fit the boy's myth about himself. He ignored the lessons of the dark passage. We have no idea what happened to him. We never saw him again

[11] Though employed loosely, this term is intended to convey at least the spirit of the traditional Aboriginal rite: an individual or a group moving self-reliantly across the land through different regions of ancestral dream time. The particular initiatory process described here is but one modality among a host of possibilities. Walking time can be lengthened or shortened. Regions through which the walkabouter passes can be wild or rural. Different daily "ordeals" can be substituted — or removed entirely, insofar as the entire rite is itself an initiatory ordeal. Here at the School, the Walkabout follows rough mountain roads where, with the aid of 4 wheel drive, we can keep daily contact with the progress and safety of the walker.

¹² The child must embark on a quest for identity that confirms he is ready to assume (or reassume) the role of adulthood. The child must rely on his own ability without the aid of others. The mettle must be tested, the seed ground against the stone on the "threshing hold" to see if it will make good bread for the people (winter shield). The childhood fantasy journey to the sacred mountains must now be taken inwardly (fall shield), in the tangled, twisted forests of feeling, introspection, and self-consciousness, where nature clings to the eye like a mirror, and metaphors shine like beacons on a vast sea of feeling. Of course, the candidate will have to deal with events in the "outer world" as well, or he will not survive. He will have to look within at the consequences of his deeds, to see how they contribute to or sabotage his ability to survive the winter as an adult. A mythic map of the self's journey to the sacred mountains can be traced in the story told to the elders at the conclusion of the passage, when the walkabouter incorporates into adulthood.

¹³ The initiatory process was a vehicle by which the boy was conveyed into the closet of the dark shield, where hid the family secrets — the special attention of a beautiful, powerful mother, and the pathos of a loving but self-defeated father — as the invisible static of unrequited desire roared in the house. Ever the diplomat, Derek had united the mother and the father within him, and brought peace to his own house. Ten years later, Derek has graduated from the university in Environmental Studies and is married to a woman with strong, masculine appeal. She is absolutely beautiful. They are deeply in love. He directs an organization dedicated to the preservation of the American wilderness.

¹⁴ The dark place used by the School is a small lava dome with an entrance hole (looking something like a black, misshapen igloo). Small cracks that let in daylight and the entrance hole are easily covered up with tarps. An outside helper stays nearby throughout the ordeal.

¹⁵ Cut off from the light and denied food or water, the neglected child (of any age) becomes prey to the demons/angels of loneliness, many of which bear familiar names — boredom, anxiety, helplessness, depression. Against the dark screen of consciousness pass images, dreams, and profound feelings associated with the collective unconscious. Hallucinations sometimes intensify the experience. The presence of an "antagonist" evokes feelings of guilt, psychic pain, or revenge that call for mature coping skills. Prompted by psychological states she can hardly yet explain, the child cleaves to basic values exemplifying the winter

shield. The story of the inward adventure is told to the elders when the trial is complete and the "child" is incorporated as an "adult" within the community.

[16] Mark returned to his family as a confirmed father. It wasn't easy going. He made a lot of mistakes. But he hung in there and fathered as best he knew. The hippie boy who couldn't be tied down had become a responsible adult. His dark shield wanderings had rendered the boy into the man. His frantic search through women for a glimpse into his anima had brought him to mature love. His successful dance with the claustrophobic monster of karma in the earth lodge was, among other things, a demonstration of male maturity. He was able to face his past. He was able to understand that karma is not erased by feelings of guilt — which only compound the claustrophobia. Better to turn back and gracefully accept the burden. He was able to forgive himself. He was able to love his woman and his son.

[17] At the School of Lost Borders, a group sauna is held at the conclusion of every course. We do not practice any form of Native American sweat lodge ceremony, even though we've received considerable training in several forms. Our Anglo-European sauna is squared to the four directions and made of wood. The ceremony itself is divided into four rounds, each of which celebrates one of the four shields. Although the rounds are hot, they are not extreme.

[18] In the hot, primeval darkness, the spoiled child's anxiety rises to a limit. There seems to be no way out. He must search within and find the ability to surrender, to be helpless, or to call on the spirit for aid. He learns the rudiments of patience and how to transcend illusory self-limitations. The macho approach will not work. Sometimes, grovelling seems the only way to survive. Paradoxically, the child is being called upon to pray and sing selflessly for the healing of others and the earth (adult shield). At such times, the child, under the pressure of intolerable feelings, finds a kind of relief and pride in exercising the adult persona by taking part with the others. A sense of personal power emerges, nurtured by the mirror of darkness. The subsequent feast of thanksgiving with the elders is itself an appropriate elder's council, a means of taking on the social body again at a new level of maturity.

[19] Larry's way of dealing with his fears of claustrophobia might not have been particularly efficient, but when the chips were down, he would rather have entered the dark to be with the others than to be safe and alone in the bright sunshine. A boy voluntarily entered the dark passage. And a man gave the prayer.

[20] In open nature, the adolescent persona, especially when alone and fasting, is most receptive to ancestral dreams and images from the collective unconscious. Human soul corresponds with natural Soul. Human memory is aligned with natural memory. Practice in bringing the light of intelligence (winter) to bear on the shadowy world of the collective unconscious (fall) is necessary if the child is to become fully aware (spring). The dreaming child must attend the *abaton* of dreaming in order to become a responsible, skillful interpreter of her own dreams. Images, symbols, totems, spirit guides, allies, and the like compose a large portion of the mythic content of any life story. But first they must be interpreted and understood (winter shield) in elders' councils so that the new adult can understand and use them fully. Certain "children," particularly those who might tend to be angry, violent, or fearful, can benefit from repeated experiences with dream incubation.

FALL TO SPRING: THE RITES OF WINTER

You are a shade in the heat,
   You are a shelter in the cold,
You are eyes to the blind,
   You are a staff to the pilgrim,
You are an island in the sea,
   You are a stronghold upon land,
You are a well in the wasteland,
   You are healing to the sick.

You are the luck of every joy,
   You are the light of the sun's beams,
You are the door of lordly welcome,
   You are the pole star of guidance,
You are the step of the roe of the height,
   You are the step of the white-faced mare,
You are the grace of the swimming swan,
   You are the jewel in each mystery.

— Old Gaelic Prayer

THE MALADY

The adolescent (of any age) has fallen into the quicksand of feelings, and is depressed much of the time, a helpless victim, deeply wounded by love, assailed by doubt, addicted to guilt, narcissistic or suicidal, a rebel without a cause, beset by troubling dreams and self-consciousness, unable to kindle up a spark of creative insight, seemingly incapable of loving him/herself, and probably having difficulties integrating the anima or animus. Repeated efforts to extricate him/her from the black hole for any length of time result in full or partial failure. The opposite shield (spring) is undernourished and the adjacent shields (the adult and the child) are sucked into a psychological maw where everything is felt and nothing resolved.

THE RITES OF WINTER

The adolescent (fall) must be illumined (spring). But is it possible to illumine the dark shield of nature by directly moving it to spring? Not likely. The gateway to illumination is the adjacent shield of winter, the adult passage, the rigors of survival in a hard time, the commitment to the well being of others, work, study, application, order, self-control, self-reliance, and other attributes of maturity. These are the dimensions of the passageway between dark and light.

It is folly to imagine that fall can be brought directly to spring. The cycle of gestation would not be complete. The seed must be frozen into its purpose before it can burst its winter casing and shoot forth green fire. Direct sunlight hurts the eyes of a creature accustomed to the dark. Like a grub, the night being painfully twists away from the light. That darkness of psychological feeling in which the grub lives and feeds must first be changed into conscious direction. The mind must gain control. The time has come to be fully human, to build a life, to dance responsibly in the struggle to survive, to become a part of the design, not the virus, to get a hold on oneself.

Like a dwarf star with an all-consuming magnetic field, an exaggerated fall shield has sunken into the depths of itself. A person so constricted is not only a drag on himself, but a drag on the family and community. Prolonged and excessive self-absorption will wreak havoc wherever cooperation, willingness to work, and self-reliance are needed to survive the winter.

How much money does our culture spend every year to treat, rehabilitate, or escape depression? We who readily play the helpless victim, the depressed nonentity, the guilty masochist, the forever wounded, carry a dark thundercloud around with us wherever we go. Because we feel helpless to change the world or our condition, we cannot be counted on to contribute to the welfare of the whole. We must be brought out of ourselves. Confirmatory rites sanctioned by the community can lead us to enlightenment and spiritual health.

The adolescent (of any age) must, they say, "get a grip on himself." But in modern culture this is easier said than done. For one thing, there are no universally agreed upon standards of maturity. For another thing, mature behavior quite often goes unrecognized by the body social. Consequently, we find modern adolescents everywhere taking shortcuts to enlightenment. The fact that they cannot attain what they seek only drives them deeper into the exaggerated fall persona. This sense of despair — that the radiance of life does not come at their beck and call — can become self-destructive, even suicidal. Alcoholism, drug addiction, and masochism feed on feelings of unworthiness, frustration, and guilt. It is hard to swallow the truth: You cannot get there without becoming socially mature.

As summer weather blends into fall, so the child blends into the adolescent. The child shield (summer) can obstruct or aid the fall adolescent's progress through the passage of winter. All too often, the emotions of the child are negative, conditioned by suffering or pain. These negative emotions turn into negative feelings about self and the world — insensitivity, callousness, self-destructive ideations, cynicism, helplessness, autism, closed mindedness, shame. It is easy to see how the hurt child often gets no further than the swamps of introversion. How doubly difficult, then, to bring this confused adolescent (in which wallows an injured, innocent child) through the rites of winter to any kind of illumination.

Puberty, marriage, parenthood, divorce, midlife, retirement, death of a loved one, and dying are life transitions that call for community sponsored and approved rites that conduct the "adolescent" through the winter passage to the illumination of spring. The modern "midlife crisis," which exists because children were never initiated into adulthood, can fall under this category. Other winter rites, some of which already exist in one form or another, also require communal celebrations: induction into community subcultures, commencement, ordination, employment or cessation of employment, relocation, etc.

Changes in life status are invariably accompanied by fall shield disturbances. The adolescent finds it easier to withdraw into depression, helplessness, self-victimization, guilt. Perhaps she is living in the aftermath of trauma, shock, violence, death. Fear over an anticipated change in life status may have plunged her into a sea of apprehension. Guilt or boredom may entice her into the vicious circle of addiction. Feelings of alienation or estrangement, being on the outside of a privileged subculture, may brand her soul with loneliness, introversion, self-pity, paranoia, or depression. Negative self-images or the awkwardness of self-consciousness may form a nearly impervious shell of inwardness around her quivering yolk. In such eventualities, regardless of the adolescent's age, rites of the winter shield are called for.

The winter shield activities described below are part of the training curriculum at the School. They are designed to introduce adolescents (of any age) to elements of the winter passage. The spring shield is thereby nourished, for winter is the passageway between darkness and light. Each process is conducted as a rite of initiation — i.e., the severance, threshold, incorporation, and illumination phases are duly celebrated. All precautions are taken to insure the safety of these individuals in the field.

RITES OF SELF-TRACKING

Spend a week fashioning an object representing your self out of some natural substance. Go alone with that object into a natural place where there are no paths or familiar landmarks and your boot tracks cannot be seen.[1] Place that object on or in the earth and turn your back on it. Walk away from it without looking back for an hour. Then turn around, retrace your steps, and find the symbol. Note: The way you go about solving this problem will be the subject of a story you will tell to the elders. If you cannot find this symbol of yourself, then you must adjust to that fact and call off the search.[2]

The Man Who Found a Rattlesnake Instead

George, a middle aged married man who worked as personnel manager for a world wide natural foods corporation, came to the School to be trained in ecopsychological techniques. He was an apt and intelligent student who nevertheless wore a dark cloud under his hat. He had fallen in love with a woman at work and, after 15 years of marriage, was contemplating divorce. For nearly two years he had been living a secret, guilty, double life — outwardly the cheerful competent husband, inwardly the haunted, obsessed lover of another.

He spoke about the problem with the elders, seeking some way out of his dilemma. He loved his wife. He didn't want to hurt her. He loved his lover too. When he was with her, he felt years younger. The elders did their best to help him plumb the depth of his feelings and clarify his choices. Obviously, he had come to a crossroads. He could not be expected to confirm either path until he made a decision and faced the consequences of his action.

We decided George should go into the lava fields of Crater Mountain and track himself. This rite of winter would require a good dose of the rational shield, for the decision he was about to make about the future would have to be a mature one. He would go looking for himself — apart from his women, apart from the current predicament in which he found himself.

George was keen on the idea of tracking himself. He spent all day transforming a piece of desert driftwood into a beaded baton wound with bright yellow and red threads and adorned with a vulture feather.

The next morning we took him to the lava field, smudged him off, and he walked alone into the volcanic wasteland of his soul to track himself. He walked toward the dark flank of Crater Mountain, covering no more than a mile on the torturous, labyrinthine surface of the flow. Then he stopped, planted the bright symbol of himself in a crack, and deliberately walked away without looking back. For an hour he walked east, through the basalt outcrops and sloping scree of the flow, never once leaving behind a footprint in the obdurate basalt.

Then it was time to retrace his steps and find the symbol of himself. He was confident he would find it. But it wasn't where he thought it was. He walked further on, thinking he had stopped short. No sign. He backtracked, veered off to the right. Nothing. He veered off to the left. Nothing. It was nowhere to be found. He stood alone, surrounded by acres of jumbled rock. It had to be somewhere near. Back and forth he stumbled, certain it was just around the corner, over the next rise, just behind a bush. Nothing.

The noontime sun washed the lava flow with waves of heat. Sweat stung his eyes. Fighting a deep feeling of dismay, he looked until he was exhausted. Finally he rested in the shadow of a boulder. "What a mess I've made of my life," he thought. "I can't even find myself." He tasted defeat. His misery knew no bounds. He tried to think about the decision he was supposed to make. He was no closer to making it. "What a fool I am," he thought, "to have blundered into such a dilemma."

But he didn't give up. After a long rest he began looking again, crisscrossing the area in a deliberate, orderly fashion. Surely, he thought, he could catch himself in a net of his own making. All afternoon he toiled back and forth in the hot sun. By early evening he knew that his efforts were doomed to fail. There was nothing he could do but start back. Oddly, he felt relieved. He had given his best. The symbol was fated to remain somewhere out in the desolate flow. His inability to find it, given his current life dilemma, seemed strangely appropriate.

As he took a step he was instantly frozen by the angry buzzing of a rattlesnake. He looked down. It coiled at his feet, a taut, dust-colored length of poison, ready to strike. He stepped back quickly, out of range. "Who are you?" he asked in a quivering voice. "*I am what you are looking for*," came the answer.[3]

RITES OF SURVIVAL

For ten days you must put away all your technological toys except for a knife and an emergency kit and learn how to live as your primitive ancestors did. With the aid of a teacher you will learn the basic rudiments of stone age survival, mastering principles, techniques, and secrets known for untold thousands of years but almost forgotten by modern culture. You will build shelters, make fire without matches, find water, fashion hunting weapons of stone, wood, and sinew, twist fiber into cordage, weave baskets, hunt, skin, and preserve game animals, identify, gather and prepare wild foods. Before you are done, you will taste the fruits of the illumination that comes from knowing the all-sufficiency of nature.[4]

The Woman Who Couldn't Make Fire

Fresh from a middle aged divorce, Val was wallowing in self-pity. The man who had provided a great measure of stability and comfort was gone. Now she was drifting on a sea of regret not knowing who she was or what she could do. One of her girlfriends had enrolled in a survival arts course at the School. Val decided to tag along.

From the beginning, it appeared that the tools of wilderness survival were not Val's strongest suit. While attempting to pressure flake obsidian with leather and deer horn, her hand slipped and she severely cut her finger on a razor sharp edge. She cried a little, protesting that she would never make a cave woman. We bound her wound with a bandanna and set her to another task — twisting milkweed fiber into fishing line. Before long she had six feet of passable line, to which at one end we attached a sharp bone gorget. The other end was tied to a short willow pole. Voila! A fisherwoman!

The fishing idea appealed to her a good deal more than arrow-making. We showed her where to dig for worms with her stick. Voila! A worm! She was a little squeamish about threading it on the gorget but she refused help. Armed with baited "hook" she went down the creek to a deep, birch-shadowed pool where big German browns were reputed to hang out. The others, absorbed in various tasks, joked about having fish for dinner. A half hour later she was back, dripping wet. She'd fallen in. The pole and the line were lost. No, she hadn't caught a fish. She hadn't even had a nibble. She stamped her foot in impatience. "I'd never be able to survive in the wilderness," she declared. She volunteered to drive down to the little town and bring back dinner. But we didn't go hungry that night. One of the young men had very good luck with crickets.

The next day was fire-making day. All the materials were close at hand. Dead elderberry bark was gathered to carve fireboards and drills. I provided the stone sockets and lengths of thin rope for the firebows. We found tinder in cattail stalks, sage brush bark, and rotten cottonwood pith. It was a beautiful, dry day. Within a few hours, everybody had made fire at least once — everybody but Val. No matter how fast she spun the drill, no matter how perfect the tension of her bow or the notch in her fireboard, she could not generate a spark. Smoke, yes. She got plenty of smoke. Her arm ached. Her back hurt. The cut in her finger opened up. Perspiration ran from her forehead and dripped off her nose into the tinder. I advised her to lay off for a while. She went down to the creek to wash off, then came back to try again. Later in the day she became angry and frustrated with herself, and with the materials — muttering and cursing and throwing things around, like a spoiled brat. She sawed and swore. She went at it like the devil herself — and never made fire.

That night in the circle she talked affectionately about her ex-husband, remembering how she had always left household repairs and car problems to him. "I don't know the difference between a spark plug and a fan belt," she said wistfully. She deeply mourned her inability to use her hands. She had enrolled in the course because she knew she needed to learn to take care of herself. Now she felt appalled at the enormity of her ineptitude. But I for one was impressed. I had never seen such energy expelled to "get the hang" of something as I had seen this day. I was impressed.

The next morning we took up weaving. The group was swaggering a bit now that they had discovered there would be no starving. All but one had made fire. The creek was full of rainbows and German browns. A few were working on birch bows for their arrows. Now eager hands began to sort through weaving materials: cattail leaves, spike rush, strips of dried willow bark, slender willow tips. Everybody carved an awl. We demonstrated a few basic principles of weaving and showed them how to start a basket coil, how to splice in, and how to do the spiral stitch. It turned out to be a long day. Nobody could get it right — nobody but Val.

Before the day was over, Val had completed a small willow bark basket about the size of a large coffee cup. It was amazingly tight. It was woven so well that we smeared the inside of it with hot pinon pitch and drank water from it. A water-tight willow basket, on her first try.[5]

RITES OF OBSERVATION

Go alone into the wilderness for 48 hours with the intent to study a particular species and its relationship to the biosystem. Although you will have the opportunity to indulge your inner life and forget about the world you are in, you will not be able to abandon your intention — which is to examine the ways of the natural world. You will scrutinize a plant, tree, insect, reptile, fish, bird, or mammal as thoroughly as you can, noting its growth stages, how it propagates, defends, nourishes itself, how long it has existed in the evolutionary saga, how it is associated with other life forms in its habitat, i.e., how it "belongs." Lastly, you will observe the ways in which this species is related, in physical, psychological, mental, and spiritual ways, to yourself. When you return, you will share your discoveries with the elders.[6]

The Misfit

We found Carl in a "continuation school," one of those adjuncts to regular public high schools where students who don't fit for one reason or another are lumped together into the same bag waiting to be opened on graduation day. He was lonely, bored, under-achieving, alienated, and a computer game freak.

It became quite obvious to us that he was not moving gracefully through the passage of adolescence. He seemed to have gotten stuck just about the time he started to grow hair on his genitals. Withdrawn as he was, he nevertheless appreciated our attention. His parents appeared to be largely indifferent to him. He showed up unexpectedly one evening at a preparation meeting for a group of high schoolers going on a vision fast. We weren't sure he was mature enough, but we let him get involved. Passively, the group accepted him. When the time came to leave for the mountains, he was there.

It was early October. The high Mojave desert basked in the afterglow of Indian summer. Rodents and snakes were plentiful. Grasshopper snapped in the brush. The lizards were still out. Hawks, ravens and jays traversed the air by day, owls and poorwills by night. The summer had birthed a plentiful harvest. The youngsters fasted for three days and nights in perfect weather.

Carl returned early, on the morning of the second day. That was no surprise. Before he left we had told him not to be afraid of coming back early if he needed to. He said he'd been lonely and bored. He hadn't been able to think of anything to do. Most of the time he'd slept. Nevertheless, a day and night alone, without food, had done him a world of good. He was open, candid, even slightly proud. We did nothing to discourage his new sense of self-possession.

Instead we encouraged him to continue to demonstrate it by going out again to the perimeter of the camp, where he could be alone again but keep base camp in view.

"This time," Meredith said, "we will give you a specific thing to do, something to keep you from getting bored." "What?" he said, his eyes jumping with sudden interest. "Find, observe, and write about one species. Find out all you can about that one thing. Then come back and share the information with the rest of us."

He took his pack out to the perimeter, fifty yards away, and set up his tarp in plain view. Then he disappeared. We didn't see him again until late afternoon. That night we watched him hunched over a flashlight, writing something in his journal.

The third and last day he puttered around camp until noon, at which point he disappeared. He returned just before dusk. He wrote in his journal again. While I watched him, a coyote started yipyapping nearby, perhaps no more than a hundred yards away. Carl looked up briefly, then went back to his writing.

When he returned with the others on that last homecoming morning it was obvious Carl had changed. His gain in self-confidence was matched only by the excitement of his new interest, that "something he could do" to keep from getting bored. We are told Carl went off to the university, after which he became one of those heroes who venture into the Amazon to catalogue rare species.

What species did he find and study on that fateful vision fast? *Aphonopelma chalcodes*. The common California desert tarantula. He had come across a male looking for females. He followed the spider as it rambled around. He wanted to find out where big boy was going. When it became obvious that it might get dark before Mr. T found what he was looking for, Carl captured him in his day pack and took him back to his camp for further observation. The next morning he observed his captive for a while, testing its defenses and reactions with a variety of objects, including his fingers. Then he took Mr. T back to where he had picked him up and let him go again. When the spider got his bearings, he went back to his quest. Carl followed, at a respectful distance. The story was ended again by dusk. Mr. T did not find what he was looking for. But Carl did.

SELF-DESIGNED RITES

Plan your own ceremony using only the stuff of the natural world.[7] In order to do so, you must answer many questions. What would be the purpose of the ceremony? For what reason would the ceremony be performed? What goal would it accomplish? Would it be a ceremony marking a severance from a former state? Would it be a ceremony that mirrors the passage from a former state to a desired state? Would it be a ceremony confirming the attainment of a desired state? Who would benefit from the ceremony? How would you mark the severance, threshold, and incorporation stages? Who would witness the ceremony? When you are ready to perform that ceremony, share your intention with the elders. Then go out on the land and do what you planned to do. When the ceremony has been completed, return again to the elders with the story of its performance.[8]

The Forester

Bradley was the inheritor of 100,000 acres of land in the northeast whose trees had been logged for generations by his family. He was Chairman of an Atlantic states Forest Products Council and the former director of prominent charitable foundation. He was not your ordinary run-of-the-mill forester. He had the mind of a nobel prize winner and the soul of a poet. He was tough as nails and soft as a baby's butt. He had a lot of money and lived in a nice house, and he could get down on his belly and muck in the swamp. He was one of those who have been gifted with vision. Yet, like all the others, he was just another pilgrim on life's torturous road.

Bradley came to the School with a group of unusual people. For one thing, they had money. For another, they used their money to do good deeds. They belonged to a philanthropic organism that funded deserving projects all over the world. These unusual people fasted alone on the hard ground of the Inyo Mountain wilderness for four days and nights. They each had their own reasons for doing so. So did Bradley.

When he returned from the mountain of fasting his intent to further refine the way in which his land was selectively logged had been confirmed. And he was toying with the idea of dedicating a primeval 1200 acre plot of the ancestral land to Mother Nature, to whom he knew he owed his life and death. Never would a chainsaw sputter, or a dozer dig, on this land. It would be a "sanctuary." Humans could enter it on one condition — that they came to worship.

For many years Bradley had studied the ways in which humans perceived and interacted with the forest. He did not believe that the business and profit motive had to be inimical to conservation. To him, a business "dedicated to healing past abuses of the forest and working to increase its health and productivity" was simply good business. Modern forestry was actually "applied ecology." It was simply common sense "to maximize the land's productive value *over the long term*." "It should be much easier," he reasoned, "to *steer* the train of the free enterprise system toward greater environmental awareness than to try to stop it with rules and regulations."

In an address to the Nature Conservancy, he argued that we were "shifting . . . to a third age — an age of cooperation with nature. We're beginning to ask, 'What does the forest need to thrive?' along with 'What do we humans need?' . . . . And we are just beginning to engage in the humbling and challenging task of seeking to understand complex forest ecosystems and asking how can we meet our needs — our real needs — while ensuring the forest's ability to prosper."

Indeed, Bradley was a modern pioneer in forest "products," an industrial ecologist, and at heart a naturalist and a humanist. He could see that the kind of "re-visioning" of which he spoke "requires all the knowledge — and wisdom — we can muster. We need the insight of the rare plant specialist, along with the applied ecological understanding of the forester who works every day in the woods. We need the practical knowledge of the forest industry as well as the insight of cultures that never lost their connection with the earth."

Recently, Bradley fasted again. This time, he designed his own ceremony. He would go into the "sanctuary" and live alone without food for four days and nights. His reason for doing so would be to confirm his decision to forever preserve that plot of land as an haven of worship. It was springtime in the forest. The weather was gray and wet and the woods were alive with life. He found a camping place along the shore of Bittern Lake, in a bed of needles beneath a sheltering pine. Around him crowded the souls of birch, flowering popple, red maple, white pine, spruce. The first thing he did was to dedicate his time alone to "the healing of the northern woods — for their wise use and wise non-use," and to his wife and three children. And then he prayed: "To be. To be carried. To find the pulse again, To be."

It took him a long time to unwind from a hectic, stress-filled life. A few days earlier, he had been talking to the governor of Oregon. Gradually the black flies, the arbutus in bloom, the rain, the warblers, the loons, the mayflowers, and the merganser pair splashing in the cove claimed him and he began to reminisce about his job: "Not every tree is meant to be cut. . . . If the game were just economic value and maxing out advantage, none of us would be paid the salaries we are. We talk about the cost — really the foregone revenue — of not cutting late-successional trees — and it is significant. However, the scale shouldn't be calibrated to maximum extraction. We should embrace as part of our stewardship the 'cost' of maintaining some or all of Nature's parts."

One day on a stroll, he found an old fire ring. He debated whether to dismantle it. "No," he decided, "the land is saying, *Let it be!*" Other days, he watched beavers, shook his rattle to the pain of feeling distance with good friends, and prayed "How can I serve?" He wrote a letter to his family, to be read on his death. He remembered his lonely childhood, how he had been abandoned to the care of a governess. One night, he watched the stars come out and remembered all those who were praying for him. He wondered about his place in nature, as a human, and found himself differing from those "purists" who say humans don't belong, that they are a mistake, that they are incapable of cooperating with Mother Nature. "We are blind," he mused, "to Nature's forgiveness and hence unable to forgive ourselves. . . . But it doesn't mean that the whole race has fallen."

On the third day, he explored the confines of the "sanctuary," and wound up at the "heart" of an ancient grove of huge spruce interspersed with red maple, white birch, and fir. He understood the cry of the early loggers, to let "daylight into the swamp." A burned area "cried out" to him "to cut the birch and release the softwoods underneath."

But his purpose held firm. Standing among those hoary trunks he dedicated the ecosystem with the following words: "Not every stand is meant to be managed. Not every tree is meant to be cut. I intend this holy place to be a sanctuary, of and for Nature to do as she pleases." He asked the spruce tree: "Is what I'm doing right?" The spirit gave a "quick *yes.*" "Are you sure? *Yes.*" "Does it serve the ancestors? *Yes.*" It was all happening so quickly, like a kind of ancient magic. He asked for a personal "message." "Be," said the tree, with a dark, green, downflowing energy. He felt how difficult it was for him to "be" in that way. "How come it doesn't feel right?" "*Because.*" "Because why?" "*Because you're a doer.*" "How do I stop being a doer?" "*Be.*" "Be who?" *Be you. Be you. Be you.*"

On the last day he became aware that the fast had altered his consciousness. Lying in the needles under the sheltering white pine, surrounded by "familiar beings," "birch, loon, mayflower, bedrock," he mused: "There's no sound like the wind in the white pine. . . Wintergreen all around me. This is my land." He asked the spruce how he could best be with Barbara, his wife. *"Turn toward her and be fully present with her,"* was the reply. Every way he turned, there were spirits with clear words. Any direction he took, an inner lodestone pulled him back to the center. When the sun rose on the end of his time of fasting, he sang a prayer of thanksgiving:

> I came here exhausted, I leave restored
> I came here empty, I return filled
> I came here obsessed, I leave here centered
> I have been surrounded by love, and peace.[9]

RITES OF APPRENTICESHIP

You have decided to apprentice yourself to a work that involves the healing of people through interaction with nature. Although you have always loved being in the wilderness, you know very little about the old (or new) therapies of human nature. You go to a teacher, a medicine woman or man, a natural healer, a wilderness guide, an initiatory midwife, and learn to do the work yourself. You enter the traditional passage of apprenticeship.[10]

As an apprentice, you watch your teacher(s) closely and learn to do what is taught. You ask questions that help you to learn. You do not readily contradict your teacher's mastery of the subject matter or qualifications. You do your best to do the work required of you, and are open to the teacher's assessment of your abilities. For the duration of the apprenticeship, you sacrifice your own comfort in order to aid your teacher in the work. You do your best to live with the imperfections of your teacher and yourself. You do not become a burden, or hang around when you are no longer needed. As your skill increases, your teacher grants you a greater share of responsibility in the work. In time, both you and the teacher will know when the apprenticeship is complete, when you are no longer a student, but a colleague.[11]

The Medicine Woman

Obsidian was born in a large, lower middle class Catholic family in a run-down suburb west of Spokane. Early on, she developed a deep and abiding love for her natural environment. She also got involved with drugs and boys and secretly began to live outside the tenets of her childhood religion. When she graduated from high school, she went to work as a "go-go dancer" at a place called The Vault, where she was raped one night by a man she knew. Marriage to the wrong boy hardly solved the riddle of her future. The marriage lasted six months.

By then she was dropping every pill and smoking every joint in sight. She volunteered at a drop-in center for ex-mental patients. There she fell in love with one of the clients, a man named Destiny, and lived with him for five years. One day, Destiny simply announced "It's over," and walked out the door, never to be seen again. At that point, as she later put it, "I began to go crazy."

Still deeply involved with drugs, she answered a personal ad, "Looking for a Mate," in the Spokane newspaper. She wrote to the man. He was living in Fairbanks, Alaska. He wrote back. They decided to live together. But in the meantime, she had begun repeating the mantra, "God is within," a thousand times a day. By the time she arrived in Fairbanks, she was convinced she was "Jesus Christ incarnate." The attempt at relationship didn't work out. In two months it was over.

While she was with him, she "wrestled with the Devil" and came to the conclusion that she was not Jesus Christ. She fell into a subsequent depression that lasted for several years. The man drove her all the way to Spokane, via the Alcan Highway, and let her off at her mother's house. Struggling with her depression, she got her own apartment and found a full-time job at a community college nearby. She began to see a therapist. It was 1970, and the anti-Viet Nam war movement permeated the air. Influenced by a group of radical students, she joined the Communist Party and "began sleeping with any man I could find." Promiscuity and politics took their toll. Rage began to rise in her, rage so strong she thought she could kill. By then she was 25 years old.

Her interest in therapy led her to enrollment in a state college, where she jockeyed federal loans and part-time jobs into a degree in psychology. Gradually, her revolutionary fervor for communism was replaced by a fascination for expressive therapy, art, dance, and Buddhism. She had finally found an appropriate vehicle for the depression and rage that threatened again and again to overwhelm her. She danced her desire to kill. She screamed her outrage at men. It was a safe environment to let her feelings out. She whirled like a dervish until "I became the Devil himself, spinning through the world, touching everything and everyone with hate."

One day, shortly before she graduated, she had a dream in which she was a witch. She awoke realizing that she had danced her last dance. She had healed herself. "At that moment," she said, "I had a spiritual awakening. I realized that the world was Spirit. The earth was Spirit. I was Spirit." Her awakening was different than her delusions of Jesus and the Devil. Her feet were planted firmly on the ground. She was who she was, a witchy 30 year old woman with a dark past, a physical and psychological body, a mind — and a Spirit.

Without any formal training in art, she began to paint what she "saw" in her imagination. The scenes were almost always "primitive": bright antediluvian wilderness populated with symbolic creatures. She also began to learn gardening, an art to which she felt naturally adapted. She stopped sleeping around, and spent more and more of her leisure time alone in wild places. Prompted by inner urgings, she gobbled up books about American Indians and other indigenous peoples. On a journey to the Southwest, she went to a native gathering near the four corners area and was introduced to the sweat lodge and the pipe. The medicine pipe, in particular, affected her deeply. When one first came into her hands, she burst into tears.

She began to haunt "medicine wheel gatherings" held by Sun Bear at Vision Mountain near Spokane. There she met Joan Halifax, who invited her to come and tend the garden on her land in the mountains near Ojai. The land, dedicated to the teaching of values associated with Buddhism and native peoples, became her home for several years. Individuals and groups came from far and wide to attend seminars, workshops, retreats, or just to marvel at the beauty of its location. Obsidian supplied the kitchen with vegetables, fruits and nuts, attended the workshops, and, in her off hours, continued to paint.

Then one day a famous "medicine man" appeared, his "family" in tow. He brought with him strange and wonderful old teachings about the secrets of human and nature. He was an artist, a writer, a teacher, a philosopher, an actor, a visionary, a devil, a saint. Above all, he was a sorcerer, a man of great personal power. Though he was blind, he saw into people. Uncannily, he turned around, looked at her, took her by the arm and said, "I'll be seeing you later." When she asked him what he meant by that, he said, "Live with us. Keep our garden and cook our meals. In exchange, you can learn our ceremonies, our secrets — and you can paint."

Obsidian could no more resist the offer than thistledown a tornado. She loaded up all her belongings and went to live with the sorcerer in the foothills of the western Sierra Nevada. She joined the "family" as a crass beginner, apprentice fourth class. She washed the family's clothes, cooked the family's meals, recycled the family's garbage; tilled, seeded, weeded, and watered the family's soil. She grew the vegetables, the fruits, the legumes, the nuts. She raised, fattened, and slaughtered the chickens and the ducks. In exchange, she was allowed to take part in the ceremonies and learn the teachings of the sorcerer and his family. When she had time, she painted.

For eight years she lived with the family. For eight years she toiled and understood and lived close to the land. For eight years she lived the meaning of full commitment to a life of experiential knowledge. Gradually, her innate gifts came under her control: her imagination, her intuitive insight, her abilities to "see" the intent of words, and to dream the future.

After eight years, however, she was still apprentice fourth class. Just when she was on a roll, they'd bust her down. She'd pick herself up, get back in the saddle, start riding again. Wham! After a while, she began to get a little testy. She started standing up for her rights. That didn't help matters any. She became a trouble maker. She even had a couple run-ins with the "big boss."

One night Obsidian realized that she just didn't fit into the family any longer. She would have to go her own way. The family, however, didn't want to let her go. She'd become too important to them. Though she had reached a high level of competency as a ceremonialist, drummer, teacher, herbalist, sweat lodge chief, and artist, they needed her in the kitchen, in the garden, in the laundry. Her place was behind the mop. In any case, she didn't have the wherewithal to leave: no money, no car, no back pack, no suitcase, no future. She'd given it all to the family.

Ultimately, there was only one course of action open to her. Escape. One day on a trip to town with others, she slipped away to meet an old friend, who whisked her away in a car. Almost everything was left behind. She came away with her bag and the clothes on her back. At first, it was rough going. But others, appreciating her gifts, helped her out. Eventually, she returned to Ojai, where she was rehired as a gardener, resident artist, and "medicine woman."

It may be that the sorcerer had anticipated, even planned, her escape. It may be that he secretly pushed her to it. Certainly, she was ready to go to work for the larger community. She had learned a great deal as an apprentice with him. He had no right to bind her to him merely to increase his power. But had she learned enough? There was only one way to find out. Do it. "Demonstrate the vision on earth for the people to see." (Black Elk)

She came to study and participate in the initiatory process at the School of Lost Borders. Right away we realized she was no ordinary woman. She was a symbol-seer, a heart-reader. She could see words coming out of people's mouths in the form of pictures, objects and beings. She could feel what people wanted to say. An experienced shield-traveler, she could evoke the shields in others.

But the side of Obsidian that was the most fascinating was her spring shield, the heyoka-crone-artist, the divinely inspired, insane old woman (despite the fact that she was only in her early forties) who came forth when nobody else could think of anything to say. This was the spirit who inhabited her paintings, the clown who played with the light and shadow, the muse who gleefully spit in the face of God. When this side of her appeared, there was bound to be the kind of trouble that led to sudden enlightenment.

When her apprenticeship to the School was at an end, she decided to leave her community and move to the same valley in which we lived. She would live alone, paint to her heart's content, and occasionally guide small groups through passage rites in the wilderness. She would have to get a job — not an easy thing in a rural area with high unemployment — and make a home. For the first time in her life, she would be absolutely alone, left to her own devices, without a "family."

So she came to live here in the "deepest valley," in a small redneck town that knew her not. Her house was small and tidy. There was a marvelous garden in the back yard. People came to her, seeking understanding and wisdom. Above the front door, in invisible lettering, you could read the words: "Medicine Woman."

RITES OF CONFIRMATION: The End of Addiction

For too long you have felt victimized by your own deeds, addicted to patterns of shame, guilt, and self-disgust. No longer will you enlighten your own darkness with the aid of drug rushes that make you temporarily forget that you are, in fact, killing yourself. Perhaps you already understand that you cannot heal yourself without first accepting the truth that you are addicted (to whatever it is), that you love your life and want to live it, that you cannot salvage yourself without recourse to a kind of spiritual power. Alone or with the help of others, you begin to prepare to leave the addiction behind by watching your addictive behavior. You work hard to understand why you are addicted. You resolve to follow a course that leads to the end of the addiction. You envision life without this monkey on your back.

Not until you have taken firm steps toward your goal are you ready to participate in a passage rite in the wilderness that will test your resolve and confirm that you have symbolically attained a state of non- addiction. For four days and nights you will live alone, without food or adequate shelter, in the wilderness. Each morning you will arise to a day devoid of addictive behavior. You will drink plain water and flush the toxins from your body. Each night you will lie down a little emptier, a little cleaner. Gradually, your mind will clear. With clarity will come a new form of illumination unattainable with addiction. So you will signify that you have passed into a new life state. But your struggle will not be over, even after the elders have empowered you to live your life free of addiction. You must return with the illumination brought by your success and test it against the realities of your everyday life. You must find others who have freed themselves who know that freedom is won through constant self-control.[12]

The Love Slave

Melanie had been a love slave to a sadistic, rape-minded man. He tied her up in the bedroom and offered her to his friends, or even to perfect strangers. When she tried to leave him he beat her or subjected her to unspeakable indignities. Finally, he tired of her and threw her out. It took a long time to pick herself up. The short relationships she had didn't help much. She felt drawn into nightmarish sexual scenarios she felt powerless to resist. It was like a craving, an addiction to the very thing that was hurting her. Her therapist suggested to that she go on one of those wilderness trips where you have to live alone without food for four days and nights. "Just the thing for you," she said. "You'll learn how to take charge of yourself. You'll learn how strong you really are."

So Melanie showed up at our School and we prepared her to fast alone in the desert mountains. Right away you could see that she was very much like a little girl, and that she was seeing herself through the eyes of men who had only one thing on their minds. She needed special attention because she seemed to lack any ability to orient herself to the wilderness.

By the afternoon of the first day of her fast we knew something was wrong. She had not made it to the checkpoint (an easy hike from her place) to let us know she was O.K. We went to her place and called. The wind and a flock of pinon jays answered. From the looks of her camp, she had wandered off without her water, her daypack, or her clothes. We tracked her bootprints all over the area, calling like fiends. Darkness fell. We debated driving out a treacherous road in the dark and getting help, deciding to wait until daylight.

The next morning at dawn we gave it one last try, looking out from a high ridge as forms and colors stood out from the landscape in the rising sun. There she was! A speck of white way out there on a juniper tree. We headed out that direction, calling. As we approached, a figure stirred beneath the tree. It was Melanie, bare breasted, in panties and boots. She had spent the night buried in a bed of juniper needles. Her bra hung from the limb of the tree like a flag, a beacon, a symbol. "What took you so long?" she demanded.[13]

RITES OF CONFIRMATION

You are altering your life status. You are moving from one stage or phase to the next. You are changing worlds. And every time you change worlds, a part of you — the part that used to be — changes. And so you go into the wilderness alone, without food or adequate shelter for four days and nights, to confirm that the decision has been made, that the change of worlds has occurred, that you are ready to assume a new life status. For the confirmation to be meaningful, you will sacrifice a part of yourself (food, companionship, shelter). During the threshold time, you will perform a "death lodge" ceremony in which you will die a symbolic death, and be reborn to your new life.[14] When you return from the passage, the elders will listen to your story, mirror back its useful elements, and formally confirm that you have passed from the old world to the new.[15]

The Boy Who Was Raped by His Father

Warren woke up with a jolt, sweat pouring down his face. He had been dreaming that he was a little boy and that his father was raping him. He'd had this dream before. After several years of therapy, he even knew what it meant. The event had actually occurred, and more than once. Whenever he drank too much, his father had done things like that, flying into bestial rages, berating, beating and sexually abusing his wife and children.

He claimed that as a pubescent boy he was "overweight, with pendulous breasts. The boys and girls alike made fun of him. It was not until he was 17 that his body firmed and he grew into the man as he was at 51, lean, tall, with a nervous, intelligent look, an archetypal British major in a war movie. He was a successful editor, a loving husband, father of two healthy teenagers, and a nature guide for the Audubon Society.

He came to the School to confirm that he was no longer a victim of the painful memories of his childhood and adolescence. It was time to end his psychotherapy. He realized that he would never be able to rid himself of the memories. The scars would always be there. But they were "initiation scars," inflicted by a drunken inquisitor. He understood them now, had even been able to forgive his father before he died.

He went alone into the wilderness and fasted to confirm and to celebrate the fact that the painful time of retrospection was over. The fast was not easy for him. He suffered from the heat, the lack of food. But the hardship was countered by the wide-eyed wonder of the little boy, who had always gone to nature for solace and renewal. Afterward, he told the elder's council: "I've already created a meaningful life for myself. I can't spend the rest of my life digging around in the wound." He returned to his family and his work. Years later, his children gone off to college, he continued to refer to himself as "reasonably sane."[16]

RITES OF RELOCATION

You know the time has come to move — from one life occupation to another, or from one home to another. You are also aware that this relocation of body, psyche, mind and spirit will wreak a profound change in your life. You are, in fact, at a major transition, a crossroads, and you know the time has come to confirm that the new course has been taken, that the new life has begun. Therefore, you sever from your former home or occupation and you go into the wilderness and fast alone for three or four days and nights. When you return to the elders, you will tell the story of your passage through the threshold to the borders of your new life. They will validate your journey and empower your new life station.[17]

The Bad Girl

Laura's father was an orthopedic surgeon in the Marine Corps. He was big, with a square jaw and a crewcut. He lived for semper fidelis. He was American macho personified. Laura's mother was a professor of chemistry, absorbed in her research. Both were absent from the home much of the time. When dad was home and mom was not, he took out a good deal of his sexual frustration on his daughter. He abused her, physically and mentally, for ten years. He abused her so often she grew to hate him with a fury.

When Laura graduated, *cum laude*, from high school, the Viet Nam war was in full swing. She started college at Stanford, then fell in with the radical Student Nonviolent Coordinating Committee. She dropped out and began to study Lenin and Mao. She became convinced the only way was violent revolution. This led her to Black Power and Brown Power, to Huey Newton and Che Guevarra. She went to Cuba, lived with a succession of macho lovers, and learned how to fight guerilla-style alongside the men, how to clean, assemble, load, and fire automatics and semi-automatics, how to handle hand grenades and rockets, how to make and smuggle bombs. When she returned to the U.S. she went underground with a revolutionary movement called the Weathermen.

That was over twenty years ago. She grew tired of the revolutionary life. An inner voice called to her not to destroy but to heal. A few years later, she surfaced in the Los Angeles area as a pre-medical student at UCLA. She graduated *cum laude* and entered medical school at Johns Hopkins. She was a brilliant student, an apt intern, a sterling resident, and men were lured like bees to her pollen. She was soft-spoken, mysterious, her demeanor hinting of the shy little girl. But, as she told us later, she lured men to destruction. She ate them alive and spit them out in little pieces.

When we met her, Laura was a practicing family doctor in the Bay Area. She first came to the School to settle the dispute she was having with her father, once and for all. She would go alone into the wilderness and fast for four days and nights, and by so doing confirm that her father no longer had any power over her. We told her that it would be quite impossible for her to surgically remove her father from her memory banks. A far better intent might be to explore the darkness for the gift she already knew lay there, the impetus toward survival, growth, and freedom.

She returned from the wilderness with a new appreciation for her past, and could see clearly how the adolescent's reaction to and rebellion from her inner father-man (animus) had defined her adult life. But this adjustment in her father-perception only precipitated another crisis, this time in her winter shield — in her profession. She began to question whether or not she wanted to be a doctor, at least in the sense of "modern medicine." This question led her back to the School, a year later. She wanted to fast again, this time to confirm her decision to withdraw from the medical consortium in which she practiced.

When she returned from the wilderness a second time, she faced a difficult and challenging incorporation in the winter shield, as an unemployed, uncommitted M.D. First came the task of disengaging herself from her patients, many of whom had depended on her for years. This was painful and difficult. But it was nothing compared to the severance of ties with her colleagues. Their rancor and deception drove her to a kind of despair. Did she honestly want to continue in the medical profession?

Her doubts deepened when she met an older man, a natural scientist and writer, and they spent hours talking, hiking, travelling. She wondered if she were in love for the first time. The promise of a mature relationship tugged at her. All at once, questions about profession became secondary to the reality of love. They decided to take a whole summer off and tour the southwest together. Everything ran smoothly for a while until one morning, after a night of passionate love making, she woke up, looked at him, and proceeded to tear him apart, piece by piece. Valiantly, he attempted to understand what had come over her. It was too late. The damage had been done. He couldn't forget, nor could she.

She came to the School a third time. She enrolled in a training course that examined "adjacent season passageways": i.e., ways of guiding an individual from any given season to its opposite (as summer to winter) by way of the adjacent or intervening season (fall). She showed particular interest in the rites of fall. On the first day, we suggested she go alone into the nearby wilderness, get naked, and look for rattlesnakes (summer). That she did. On the second day we suggested she go back to the same place and take with her a person she had wronged. She was to be with that person, talk to that person, make it good with that person, so that she could die with a clean conscience (fall). That she did. On the third day we suggested that she do a self-tracking exercise up on Crater Mountain (winter). That she did. On the fourth day we suggested she wander and talk to the spirits (spring). That she did. On the last day she sang in the sauna and prayed for her father and the man she had recently wronged.

We didn't see her for another year. Then we got the news. She had ended her medical practice, at least for the time being. She had fallen deeply in love with a younger man who had fallen deeply in love with her. The two of them were getting married. They were going to raise horses on a small ranch in Utah. We met the young man. He was beautiful. He was devoted to her. Her blond face glowed with health and excitement.

ENDNOTES: FALL TO SPRING: THE RITES OF WINTER

[1] We are fortunate enough at the School to have a vast lava field nearby where this exercise can be undertaken to maximum effect. The field is like a labyrinth and, because it is all rock, does not retain boot prints. We give the student an entire afternoon to search for the symbol of self, with instructions to call off the search at dusk if the object has not been found.

[2] In this exercise the initiand enacts a symbolic drama in which the protagonist finds his self. Although the self is but a symbol — a stick, a stone, an effigy of feathers and string — the search for it becomes deeply meaningful. The basic question faced by the searcher is: Am I able to find myself in the midst of apparent chaos? As he continues to search, other questions arise: How do I find myself? How do I sabotage my attempts to find? What will I do if I don't find myself? How will I deal with disappointment? Inherent to the story is the way in which he navigates the apparent chaos. Is he a "dead reckoner?" Does he go about looking in a systematic fashion? Sometimes, the searcher "cheats" — for example, he looks for a prominent place, visible at a distance, on which to deposit the symbol of self — thereby guaranteeing that the object will be easily found. This means of dealing with the fear of "not finding" might indicate an adolescent who is not yet ready to accept responsibility for the kinds of personal enlightenment to which the winter shield leads.

The elders' task is to empower the method of seeking the self, regardless of the outcome. Dealing with disappointment can be a strong character builder. The magic is in turning the apparent defeat and loss into a significant step toward self-discovery. The magic wand is the empowerment of the elders.

[3] When George returned home he ran into another kind of rattlesnake. His wife had discovered his secret while he was gone. She was outraged and hurt. She gave him an ultimatum. Come to a decision within three months. In effect she was saying, "Go find yourself on the lava slopes of Crater Mountain." For three weeks he searched for himself. When his time was up, he had found himself. He told his wife the affair was over.

[4] Confronted by the specters of exposure, dehydration, and starvation, the helpless adolescent is forced to find the wherewithal within (fall shield) to turn the physical environment into hearth and home (winter shield), and thereby earn the illumination of a job well done (spring shield). Such experiences are of great worth to individuals who, because they are adrift on a vast sea of feeling and self-consciousness, lack the decisive action, will, and patience to get the job done. Those stuck

in the "victim place" (blaming everything and everyone else for their misfortunes) can also benefit.

There is probably no substitute for the acquisition of a skill which for so many thousands of years guaranteed the survival of the human race. The mastery of it brings a kind of enlightenment about the interactive cooperation between human and nature that cannot be gained any other way. Add to this enlightened understanding the joy of creating something useful with one's own hands.

[5] And so it was confirmed that Val had gifts that were of use to the people. She pulled herself out of the swamp of helplessness by proving to herself that she had the "right stuff." This she amply demonstrated during the week-long course. She has, in fact, adapted well to her single state and is currently involved in a serious relationship with another woman.

[6] This process calls for objective examination of the natural world, a "scientific" approach to understanding (winter shield). The rationale is to lure the exaggerated adolescent away from a steady diet of psychological states, to link her up with mental states leading to flashes of illumination and insight. The natural mind, in all its physical manifestations, attracts the human mind, for they are of the same self-thus. Exercise of the mind leads to the illumination of the dark recesses of the fall shield, and the entire system comes, at least temporarily, into balance. Of course, the initiand also reaps the benefit of living alone in a primitive manner in the very midst of what she is studying.

[7] It might be appropriate to require that the ceremony be at least 24 hours in length.

[8] Ceremony has always been a winter shield function. It is performed by that part of us that seeks to bring the people through the winter to the spring. It has design and structure, plot and denouement, theme and counter-theme, and is predetermined to bring mind into contact with Mind so that spirit may dawn. This exercise gives an adolescent (of any age) stuck in the fall shield a plan of escape from his own darkness. The elders empower the ceremony by treating it as "confirmatory" — i.e., its purpose has been accomplished. They say, "So be it."

[9] Sometime after the fast was over, Bradley commented on his experience: ""I followed my heart/mind/being and was guided to drop effort, to drop doing, to drop in and simply be — and inter-be. . . . I became myself without apology. I simply was, and the place was resplendent all around and within me. . . . The conversations I have recorded here [in his journal] are like fingers pointing at the moon, or milestones. They are not the journey itself."

[10] The therapeutic process of apprenticeship is related to the ancient Celtic rite of passage called *fosterage*. When he had reached the age of puberty, the boy was farmed out to a teacher, often a woman, where he was initiated into the arts of warfare, eros, and vocation. While he was thus employed, the boy owed his allegiance to his master or mistress and the household, and earned his keep both monetarily and domestically. By virtue of the passage of *fosterage*, the boy won the rights of adulthood, which included marriage, soldiery, and parenthood.

The old Celtic way is but one of many forms of apprenticeship, a passage to maturity as ancient as human culture. The adolescent must be removed from the child's world. The onset of fall shield fallowness, of inactive betwixt-and-betweeness, signals the need for the self-absorbed one to be sent away to a life heretofore foreign, where she or he can balance the abyss of self-consciousness (fall) with appropriate action, self-discipline, social responsibility, and the mastery of adult occupation.

[11] At the School, we honor the old traditions by calling our trainees "apprentices." The regimen is rigorous, requiring daily initiatory-style involvement with people and nature in the raw. Often, the apprentices are asked to hold back their personal feelings for the sake of learning and doing the work. They are expected to perform on-line, so that the work can go forward and the people can be served. If they have learned the craft well, they are encouraged and empowered to take what they have learned and use it in their own way, with their own style, theme and content. We do not want them to mimic us. If they have truly mastered the skills, then they have earned the full right to alter form and process as they see fit. We may not agree with the ways they have chosen, but we do not question their mastery of the skills.

Apprenticeship takes a lifetime. That which is learned, acquired, experienced, gradually forms a significant part of personal mythos, or life story, of the apprentice. As she defines herself, so she acts (as in "persona") and is. This human aptitude, to be who we want to be, is of the magic of spring.

[12] The threshold period ends with a celebration and a telling of the story. The final phase, incorporation, marks the confirmation of the emergence of a mythos in which life is now lived without the addiction. The "high" that accompanies incorporation is deceptive, for the person must now proceed on his own and come around to the summer shield of bodily cravings, childish temptations, and erotic ruts. Even if the initiation ultimately fails, and the individual is unable to incorporate the confirmation of the threshold passage into a body torn by temptation, there has been a partial success. He told the

story in front of the elders and has been enlightened, if only for a season. The rites of winter passage must again be made available to anyone who ultimately self-aborts the test.

[13] Melanie's shield system was damaged to the extent that she was unable to orient herself to her own wilderness. The victimized little girl became lost in the feeling of lostness, unable to care for herself, forgetting to look ahead to consequences. The way she was found (the bra-flag), symbolized other "rescues" in the past. A little girl (summer) who couldn't help herself (fall), she resented the fact that she hadn't been rescued sooner. Still, there was hope. Like a blind mole she had survived by burrowing into the earth. In her extremity she had turned to her underdeveloped winter shield for help. Her success at surviving had given her the brazenness to accuse me, the archetypal male authority figure, of dawdling.

The elder's council emphasized Melanie's ability to survive and honored her ingenious juniper bed. She became very high with a new-found self-confidence only to become deflated when she realized the next day that she would have to leave the group and go home. At that point, the little girl appeared and, with heart-wrenching pathos, pleaded to be allowed to live on our front porch.

She disappeared from our lives. We don't know what happened to her. She would have profited from a planned series of wilderness passage rites that gave her fledgling self-confidence more room to breathe. We do like to think that she has somehow survived, hopefully not in some underworld.

[14] See "Death Lodge" in the chapter subtitled: "The Rites of Spring."

[15] All life-altering decisions are made from the winter shield. Summer's child can't decide. Fall's adolescent, absorbed in the mirror of self-consciousness, must come out of herself to make the decision as an adult. Once the decision has been made, it must be backed by ceremonial action which, in effect, "makes it so." *Con* — "with," + *firm* — "hard," "rigid," "stiff," "dense." *Confirm* — "with firmness."

The decision is made rigid, dense, by virtue of the passage rite. It is the adult who undertakes the rite, and it is the adult who is illumined thereby. The indecision of the adolescent (fall) is resolved in the passage of con-firmness (winter) which opens up to spring.

[16] The little boy (summer shield) was raped. He survived the rape and the mockery of his peers by going deep inside himself as an adolescent (fall shield). Somewhere in the mire of anguish he found the stuff of maturity (winter shield). He refused to be a victim, learned to forgive, and thus integrate, his

past. The act of fasting in the wilderness connotes a healthy spring shield, as does ability to find meaning for himself in his life.

[17] The stuck adolescent cannot continue to live amid the chaos of an unorganized life without a sense of purpose or a means of obtaining the very sustenance that will enable him to survive the winter. "Get a job," "Change your job," or "Move to a new environment" are imperatives found in every modern culture. The initiatory nature of finding and securing employment or another home (meeting new people, impressing them, fitting in, mastering new skills, etc.) often frightens the adolescent, who can become stuck in paralysis or avoidance. Rites are needed by which he can confirm a move, new employment, or new friends and co-workers.

Rites of vocational change or relocation are particularly appropriate in midlife crises when the old job or environment no longer meets the needs of the "adolescent" who has finally become aware of attaining adulthood. It may appear as though all other options have narrowed down to a dark passage without an end. At such times, spiritual illumination is desperately needed. The only way to earn passage there is through the adjacent winter shield. Training, apprenticeship, preparation for a new vocation more worthy of an elder can be undertaken. These rites must include confirmation that a new life station has been assumed.

WINTER TO SUMMER: THE RITES OF SPRING

> Yes, and was it not perhaps more childlike and human to lead a Goldmund-life, more courageous, more noble perhaps in the end to abandon oneself to the cruel stream of reality, to chaos, to commit sins and accept their bitter consequences rather than to live a clean life with washed hands outside the world, laying out a lonely harmonious thought-garden, strolling sinlessly among one's sheltered flower beds. Perhaps it was harder, braver and nobler to wander through forests and along the highways with torn shoes, to suffer sun and rain, hunger and need, to play with the joys of the senses and pay for them with suffering.
> — Herman Hesse, *Narcissus and Goldmund*

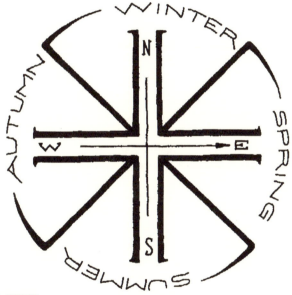

THE MALADY

The adult is frozen into the roles, poses, attitudes, values, and myths of adulthood, and rarely shows any other face. He/she is overworked, absorbed in the role of mother or father, unmoved by sex, unable to play, overrational, lost in thought, caught up in dogma, formality, abstraction, cynicism, duty — cold as an icicle. Work or relationship related stress is held in like steam in a pressure cooker. A facade of respectability, responsibility, untouchability, capability, is coldly maintained. The self avoids the dark shield by turning feeling into mental processes, profession, or routine. The little boy or little girl of the summer shield is undernourished, unacknowledged, and unseen.

THE RITES OF SPRING

Behind every over-compensating adult there is a hurt or starving child. Unless the child is nourished, unless the emotions spurt unimpeded, unless the body comes alive, unless the juices flow, unless the terrible burden of responsibility is relinquished, unless mortal instincts rage, there will not be balance within the shield system and the family or community may be in for hard times. Only when the child is nourished can the adult become whole. She must embark on a journey to childhood via the passage of spring.

A person cannot stay in the shield of maturity indefinitely. Nor can the laws and regulations of wintertime forever oppress the freedom of the people. The icy grip of winter must thaw. The adjacent spring shield is the gateway to the world of summer. There must be rites of spring so that the children may be affirmed, the adolescents may feel, the adults and elders renewed. There must be rites to confirm that "the law" has been turned upside down, that there has been a veering away from the long night. The inevitable light has appeared. The sun rising toward the zenith is proof. The blood that ran from the wound of the sacrificial goddess or god has reappeared in the greening of vegetation. There was no death after all — only a change of shields.

For thousands of years in pre-Christian cultures, the gods and goddesses associated with the seasons were killed and resurrected in rites of spring:

> The killing of the god, that is, of his human incarnation, is . . . a necessary step to his revival or resurrection in a better form. Far from being an extinction of the divine spirit, it is only the beginning of a purer and stronger manifestation of it . . . . [and] is regarded as a means to promote and quicken the growth of vegetation. For the killing of the tree-spirit [or god] is associated always (we must suppose) implicitly, and sometimes explicitly also, with a revival or resurrection of him in a more youthful and vigorous form.[1]

Traditional celebrations surrounding the death and birth of incarnated deity ran the gamut from effigy to human sacrifice, from sexual abstention to sexual license, from fasting to gross overeating, from social order to chaos. Everything deeply sacred could become deeply profane. Everything deeply profane could become deeply sacred. Under the aegis of the dying, resurrected god/goddess of the spring shield, mortal and immortal were a sacralized unity. Spring passed into the body of summer, the holy child, the holy instinct and emotions, the holy blood pumping, the holy erotic impulse. The spirit infused all mortal forms with grace. ("Everything that lives is holy!" — Wm Blake). The child of the people was nourished and balance was restored to the collective shield system.

How does one attain the threshold of enlightenment? There are, of course, many disciplines, faiths, and "isms" designed to do so. But a shield stuck in the winter may, like the Pharisee, know only too well the discipline or technique, and not the enlightened spirit inherent in the form. It may be necessary to "trick" the winter shield into dying so that spring can come — for without death there can be no birth.

Perhaps it is the trick itself, the mysterious flip-flop inside the seed, that breaks the rigid hold of winter. How can there be fire when the earth is cold and dark? Yet there is a spark, and the spark yearns to be a great fire blazing in the east.

Though you enter by way of death, you leave by way of birth. Indeed, this is the profoundest teaching of the seasons, of the earth, and of all our brothers and sisters, regardless of species. Hence, spring shield rites of regeneration always involve separation from the life of the adult, from the orderly realms of the rational — separation, in fact, from all other humans. In a solitary natural place the death passage is encountered as darkness. At that moment, the descending fall shield and its opposite, the rising spring shield, come into a harmony of balance. The center of gravity shifts inexorably toward the spring as gradually the outlines of the birth world are illumined by dawn.

Although contemporary culture lacks in sheer numbers of "mature" adults, there are many courageous men and women who, suffering the slings and arrows of lives lived for the benefit of others, have been trapped by various aspects of the winter shield. Take, for example, the plight of the single low-income mother with children. The initiations of childbirth, marriage, separation, divorce, or desertion have always been accompanied by one of the most fundamental aspects of the winter persona — motherhood. Encompassed by an incredible variety of personal, domestic, and cultural difficulties, her winter shield can become exaggerated to such an extent that she faces an imminent breakdown. But she cannot break down. The children must be cared for. She must be mother.

The middle aged man at midlife crisis, married since he was twenty-one, watches his last child leave home, and falls into a depression. But he cannot allow his depression to exist, for that would be admitting to himself that he has some reason to be depressed. He has no reason. He has a good job, a devoted wife, two lovely children, a nice house, a new car — what more does he need? He ignores the incipient depression and keeps on doing what he has always done to survive. Finally, he will retire. With no meaningful work to do, he will waste away. After his death, his children and wife will remember him as distant and cold.

Men and women such as these, and many others stuck in the winter shield, have availed themselves of the School's services. They tended to characterize themselves as "living too much in my head," or "the perfect mother for too long," or "burned out at the job," or "isolated in an ivory tower," or "an empty shell, the fire and passion gone." The conditions of modern life make it far more difficult to maintain the burdens of adulthood. The absolutely necessary task of caring for others and oneself has become an obstacle course through regions with names like "Technological Tension," "Lack of Meaningful Human Contact," and "Gridlock." Even those with more than respectable shield systems suffer damage to the winter shield simply by "trying to do what's right."

Those who came were ready to undergo the rites of spring. The ice floe was breaking up. It was time to feel again, to remember how to play, to earn a new lease on life, to let the little kid laugh again. But the adult wasn't able to just run to the summer and play. First, she had to be reborn, enlightened, illumined, enter the spirit world, envision life's purpose, know herself to be of nature. Only then could the adult take on the mantle of childhood.

The rites of spring described below have been offered at one time or another at the School. The activities were initiatory in form and always held in a natural place. Although they were designed for exaggerated winter shields, they were also of benefit to the summer and fall shields. Every exercise was prefaced by a period of severance and concluded by a period of incorporation with elders. The mid-phase, the threshold, involved an ordeal designed to evoke the spring shield. Usually, the ordeal involved fasting, seclusion, and exposure in a natural place. As with most initiatory rites, the natural setting was of absolute importance. The dance of day with night, light with darkness, body with Body, soul with Soul, mind with Mind, and spirit with Spirit, brought the student through death to the rebirth of the child.

RITES OF COMING FORTH FROM DEATH

For too long you have held your rigid, rational, controlled pose of maturity. Your body screams for sensation. Your children say, "Come and play with us." You've grown so cold and numb you don't know if you will ever feel again. You want to come down from your ivory tower and traffic in the streets of mortality. But how? You feel awkward, out of place in the warm, self-indulgent climes of the south. You're not sure how you'd handle it. Maybe you'd make a fool of yourself. What would happen to your carefully plotted ways and means of holding your life together? You know you must let go. You might as well die as keep going on this way — the same old resume, copied a thousand times.

So you leave your tilled fields behind; you put your affairs in order; you write your will; you exit your former life; you go off to die. You go to a place in the wild, where you can be alone for a period of four days and nights, because you know you will die alone someday, in the wild of yourself. You go without sustenance because you know that where you're going you'll need a different kind of food.

You enter the death lodge.[2]

When the people in your life see that you have entered the death lodge, they know that the time has come to say their goodbye for the last time. One by one they come (in memory), asking to be forgiven, or to forgive, or simply to bid you farewell. This will also be your last chance to say a clean goodbye to all those who composed the symphony of your life. One by one you dance with them. One by one you let them go. Those who cannot forgive you, or those you cannot forgive, will be encountered as some form of obstacle during the death passage. When all have come, you close up the death lodge. Then you take the next step.

You enter the purpose circle.[3]

You go alone to the exact place in which you have chosen to die. Now you are completely without physical assistance. You have crossed the boundary of rational control. Now you are at the mouth of the death passage that leads to birth. All day you pray and sing to those powers and presences in your life, asking them to help you die. Slowly, night falls. In the darkness you pray and wait. The death passage lies dead ahead, where the karmic monsters of your former life lurk in illusory shadows. Here in the circle of your life's purpose, you hold true to that which you sense is your destiny.

You enter the passage.

With the coming of midnight, you die. You must be ready to face the destiny you have forged in your former life. Memories, dreams, temptations, feelings of discomfort and futility, masks and faces of the past, drag you backward through the passage. If your life has been good, and if you love your own soul, you will accept these illusory karmic monsters as your lot. You will not allow yourself to be frightened into a premature birth. Doggedly, you follow your purpose.

You enter the birth world.

Inexorably, the aim and direction of your purpose resolve into the blinding light of the rising sun. The death of your former life has given way to birth. All is holy; all is aflame with the glory of life. Nature is but a mirror of the newly born. *Is* the newly born.

You're not a baby. You're an adult, with an adult life to return to. A thought gives you pause. How do I want to live this life I now enter, as if for the first time? Will I live as the person I was when I entered the death passage? You may even ask yourself an even deeper question. Am I still in the death passage? Am I not encountering the karmic monsters of my former life? Am I not dancing with them on the great ballcourt of existence for stakes of life and death? You hasten to greet your life.[4]

The Man Who Rehearsed His Own Death

Charles and his wife Sybelle came to a vision fast training. They were creators and directors of an initiatory-style therapeutic program in the Southern California area. They were convinced a four day fasting retreat in nature would enhance their program. A more charming middle aged couple could not be found. They were also tense, having just faced a big scare. Six months before, Sybelle had been told she had stomach cancer. But there had been a subsequent remission. She still wasn't certain the cancer had left her body. Because they were so deeply committed to each other, the fear of death had shaken them to the roots.

Sybelle wanted to confirm that she was free of cancer. We encouraged her to identify with the signs of life around her during her time of fasting, and to do those pleasurable things which best expressed the needs and instincts of her body. We discussed her pending incorporation (when the fasting was over) as a woman who had formally confirmed that she was without cancer.

Charles' intent was as challenging. He had danced so thoroughly with the threat of his wife's death, that now, he said, "I want to experience my own death." We carefully reviewed the four initiatory death-steps leading to rebirth: Decision Road ("I'm going to die"), Death Lodge ("Goodbye to all my loved ones"), Purpose Circle ("Alone, I face death"), and Ballcourt ("I dance with the karmic monsters of my former life"). A former Christian minister, he balked at some of the terminology, but he got the general idea. Dying a good death had a great deal to do with how he would be reborn. Dying well meant, in fact, living a good life. Had he lived a good life? Yes, but he had hurt those who were closest to him. We suggested that he do whatever was necessary to give and get forgiveness before he entered the Purpose Circle the last night of his fast, so that he could die cleanly and enter the Ballcourt, where, in birth, he danced with the karma of his former life.

When they returned from their threshold fast, Sybelle looked absolutely wonderful. There was color in her face and a spring in her step. Charles, on the other hand, was exhausted. He had been up all night in his purpose circle, practicing his death. After a good meal and some rest, he seemed good as new. Something rare glittered in his eyes.

In the elder's council Sybelle and Charles told their stories. It had not been easy for Sybelle. For four days she had danced with desert heat in the skimpiest of shade. Nausea gripped her, relented, gripped her again. At night, in the silence, she could feel her heart bouncing in her chest like a ping pong ball. Through it all, she felt an underlying assurance of peace and certainty. She thought of her husband, fasting nearby, and was overwhelmed with love and gratitude for the way he had stayed with her through the crisis. Toward the end of her fast, she ceased to wonder if the cancer was still there. It occurred to her that she had begun to assume she was clean. She attributed that assumption to the wisdom of her body.

As he had hoped, Charles thought a lot about death. He reviewed his past life, said goodbye to those he had offended, or had offended him. He let them all go and entered the purpose circle of the last night. He'd found a rusted, old tin can, filled it with sand, and fashioned a makeshift rattle. He stood up in his purpose circle and shook his tin can rattle and declared his intent to die. But he could not escape his memories. He realized he would die with these memories. He would carry them through the death passage to the other side.

He paused in his story, looked up, said, "You know what? I'm a lucky man. All my major dreams have been fulfilled. Every one. Everything I set out to do, I did. In my own eyes, I guess, I'm a fallible kind of hero."

A mischievous look danced in his eyes. He produced his tin can rattle, stood up, and began to declaim:

> I grew up in the slums of St. Louis — and I survived!
> I became a man who ministered to thousands!
> I graduated from the Lutheran seminary with a Th.D.!
> I graduated from the University of Missouri with a Ph.D. in sociology!
> I fell in love and got married and had two children!
> My wife was the most beautiful woman on earth!
> My children were the most beautiful children on earth!
> We made it through hard times, through the valley of the shadow of death!
> I made enough money to take care of my own!
> I was respected in my profession!
> I helped many people bind up their wounds!
> I have made my peace with all those I have offended!
> I am a man who is ready to face his own death!
> I have given my body to be burned!
> I have given my spirit to the darkness!

His voice cracked. He bowed to everyone and sat down. A year later, Charles was stricken unexpectedly with bone cancer. He was dead in three months. He died at home. I called him a couple days before he crossed over. He was too far gone to pick up the phone. But Sybelle says he smiled when he heard who had called. He was in his purpose circle. The time was midnight. He had turned to face the east. He was getting ready to dance the dance of karma on the Great Ballcourt of birth.

RITES OF PRAYER

You have done everything you possibly could to be of help to your loved ones and to the word. But having done your best, you realize your best was not enough. You feel emptied of all emotion and feeling, having worked so hard you are nothing but a shell of meaningless activity enclosing a void of nothingness. You have lost your faith in anything or anyone. God has died.

The time has come to go alone to the heart of nature and to do something so seemingly useless and futile as to pray. You leave the everyday world of emptiness and striving behind and go to a wilderness place where, for three days and nights without food, companionship, or shelter, you spend the majority of your time praying. Perhaps you have a specific reason to pray — or many reasons. Perhaps you have no idea what to pray about. All you know is you need to pray.[5]

The days and nights will slowly pass as you pray for yourself, for your mate, your children, your friends, your people, your community, your earth. The spirits of the wild place in which you live will watch and listen. You will call them in and pray to them. Pray to fly, ant, bird, mouse, blade of grass, flower, tree, sky, cloud, mountain. Pray to the spirit within you. Pray to your sacred ancestors. Pray to people you know. Pray to god or goddess. Pray to nothing at all. Pray about what is closest to your heart. Unburden yourself of all those things you have been holding in for so many years. When you lie down to sleep, pray to the stars. Make of your very dreams a prayer.

Pray without ceasing. without hope, without doubt, without fear, without question. And when your time in the sacred world of prayer is ended, return to the elders and tell your story to them. Tell them what you prayed for. Tell them about the answers that came to you because you prayed. Allow them to empower the regenerated child who returned from the sacred mountain of prayer.[6]

The Jew Who Prayed for Palestine

It was not as though the prayer Alan prayed was new to him. He had prayed it since he was a boy. The prayer had to do with his homeland, the Jewish nation, his people, and their so-called enemies. The prayer was for peace in Palestine, for an end to the ceaseless rounds of atrocity and retaliation.

A wealthy American-Jewish philanthropist, Alan had given his life to the pursuit of Arab-Israeli reconciliation through a foundation that he himself had set in motion. The foundation worked throughout the world to create small enclaves and retreats where Arabs and Israelis could meet to share issues of mutual concern. Through the years, the foundation had been traumatized seemingly hundreds of times by acts of terrorism and political duplicity on both sides. Many times his only recourse was to throw himself into the arms of God. His strength was gone; his hope was lost; every shred of faith in human nature was shattered. He prayed to the mercy of God for the faith to continue.

As Alan knew, desert religions such as Islam and Judaism rested on mythical traditions of vision fasting teachers and prophets. When he was given an opportunity to follow their ancestral example, he couldn't resist the invitation. But there was a conflict in his schedule. One of his lifelong dreams was about to become a reality. The leaders of the Palestinian and Israeli nations were coming together in Washington to mutually ratify a treaty of peace that would finally give full sovereignty to the Palestinian people. Because his foundation had played a major part in the forging of the accord, Alan was being asked by the Secretary of State to attend. The dates, however, conflicted with his vision fast.

Alan's ultimate decision affords considerable insight into the man he was. He decided his presence at the peace accord would not be so important. All the bigwigs would be present, the presidents, the premiers, the potentates, the secretaries of state. Let them be the ones to speechify and posture. He would go off into the wilderness, like some minor prophet and starve and pray to God for what would happen after the pact was signed. Surely, the success of this venture was in His hands.

A thin graying man in his fifties who lived and worked in Manhattan, Alan had never slept on the ground before, nor had he ever fasted for more than two days. Despite four days of sunlit meetings, his face was stark white as he awkwardly shouldered his pack and set off for his fasting place on the western verge of the Inyo Mountains. We had few doubts about his ability to do this thing. His commitment to the process was impeccable.

In the same group there was a father with a 12 year old son. While the father was fasting, the son prepared and went out to be alone for 24 hours. Just after dusk, the boy got lonely and began to wail and cry out to his father. We who waited at basecamp heard his cries. They reminded us of the cries Alan was making to his God. I went up through the dark trees and snags to find the boy. When I got there, his father had already found him.

Alan returned with the others after four days and nights of fasting. The story he told to the elders' council did not concern itself with God's answers to his prayers. He had prayed formally, again and again, for the mercy of God. Like the Psalmist, his prayers seemed unable to penetrate the sounding brass foundations of Heaven. But he lifted his eyes to the mountains, from which came his strength. He knew that his strength was in the Lord who had created heaven and earth. He became weak and very small. In the darkness he wrestled with his version of the angel of God, and he felt his limbs grow sore and numb. In his distress he found a gift. It was a special blessing to all those to whom he returned.

That same day he came down from the mountain, the School received a call from the office of the Secretary of State. The lady respectfully asked to speak to Alan. I told her Alan was 8 miles away where there was no phone, that he had just finished fasting in the wilderness for four days and nights. There was a slight exclamation and a long pause. Then she asked me to convey to Alan the message that they were holding a place for him in the front row of dignitaries at the signing of the peace accord. When would that happen? Tomorrow afternoon.

I drove up as fast as I could to the upper campus to convey the news to Alan. He was in the bath house, taking a shower. When he came out, all scrubbed and ruddy-faced, I told him about the invitation. He laughed with a certain impish delight. "I'm staying right here," he said. "These people [meaning the group] mean more to me than heads of state. I want to listen to their stories." As he turned to go I noticed how well Alan actually fit his body. He moved with an odd grace. But he was limping slightly — probably where the angel of the Lord had touched his thigh.

RITES OF HEALING

Someone you care for very much is sick, and you're at your wit's end about what to do. Maybe you have hurt your mate, friend, or colleague very much, or he has hurt you, and your mind keeps flopping over the same familiar ground like a flat tire. Perhaps a dear one has died in a sudden, violent, or accidental manner and you can't shake the thought that her spirit is not at ease. So you take that "lost soul" with you on a healing journey to the heart of the wilderness.[7]

You leave your ordinary life behind and set out on a journey to the sacred mountains. The entire journey will be a prayer. You will not be alone. The spirit of your "lost soul" will accompany you in the form of a symbol which you will carry everywhere. For three days you will live alone without food or shelter. You will seek to do that which will effect healing in the "lost soul." Yours will not be an easy task. It may even involve considerable suffering on your part, perhaps an empathetic sharing of the condition which you seek to cure, possibly even a kind of death. In dreams, trance-states, or other forms of altered consciousness, you will see through the eyes of spirit what you can do, or what you have already done by your actions. With ceremonies you have designed to affect the healing, you enter the naked heart of spirit.[8]

Quest to Heal a Father

Nicolai's father had heart trouble. It happened suddenly, without warning. His heartbeat stopped altogether, and then started again, after 60 frightening seconds — but it beat too rapidly. Fingers of pain groped for his chest. He felt weak and faint and out of breath. It had happened before. The doctors prescribed pills but were unable to ascertain the actual cause of his distress. It sometimes happened in his sleep. There were times when he could hardly make it up the stairs to his apartment. He had begun to live in constant fear of death.

About this time, Nicolai, a Swiss medical student, studied the four shields with us during a training seminar in Germany. The subject of a healing journey for the sake of his father came up toward the end of the training course. We talked about how he might do it. He returned to his native Switzerland with a plan.

Two years later, we received a letter from him. He had in fact enacted a healing journey for his father. "To my surprise, it made a lot of sense to him. His only fear was that I would contract the disease instead. I told him I would put the disease in my medicine pipe with the tobacco and transform it to ash."

During the Easter holidays Nicolai met his mother and father in the mountains, where he had planned to enact the ceremony. His intention was to ascend a nearby mountain, where he would fast for three days and nights so that his father could be healed: "I asked him to check on me with binoculars every day at a certain time and to make a small fire and burn the things he didn't want in his life anymore. I also asked him to come and help me down the mountain after the third night in case I felt really weak — so that we could end the ceremony together."

Nicolai set up his camp in a dry, sheltered place a half mile from a cabin where his father stayed. By the second morning he felt weak and dizzy. Walking the few yards to a nearby streamlet exhausted him. He spent most of his time "just sitting, sometimes thinking of my father, more often not thinking about anything — just sitting, looking at the ground." He slowly became aware of a difference in the light: "different from the way it is at this time of year, not a very dark blue but somehow faded, with a tinge of yellow. And the sun was more piercing."

On the second day he became aware that his father was watching him with binoculars. He began to walk down toward him, then realized that would be inappropriate. From a distance he looked down on the tiny dark speck against a white patch of snow. "He stood there a long time before turning back toward the cabin." That night the temperature plunged. Wherever his breath touched his sleeping bag, ice formed.

The third morning he struggled stiffly into the wan light of a cloudy day. The wind was freezing. He huddled in his down parka, looking at the ground. After several hours he realized that all that time he had been looking at an ant hill. "They were busy working, working, working to rebuild their home after winter. They never paused for a moment." Again he felt the eyes of his father upon him. "He watched me for a long time. I could feel his caring. I could feel him sharing my time alone." He smoked his medicine pipe as he had promised. He stuffed his father's irregular heart beat into the bowl and smoked it down to ash.

That last night it turned warm and began to snow softly. Very early in the morning he heard his father's dog barking down below. His father was coming up through the new-fallen snow to greet him. He'd expected he would stop short of the steep part and wait for Nicolai to come down. But it sounded like he was coming all the way. Nicolai stood up to welcome them. "I felt good, not dizzy at all anymore. Filled with a feeling of soft power." Never had his father looked so good, and none the worse for wear after his climb. "It was good to hug my father, to drink some tea, and talk. . . ." "Before leaving we smoked the pipe together, which a year before I couldn't have offered and he probably couldn't have accepted."

As they descended the mountain Nicolai noticed that the snow was rapidly melting. The sun was breaking free.[9]

RITES OF SPIRIT

Weary of the rational control in which your discipline or world view holds your mind, you want to go back there again, to view the world through the eyes of childhood. You set out for the wilderness to be alone with the spirits of nature for a few days. To clear karmic accumulations from your mind, you go without food, shelter, or identification books (hand lens and flashlight excluded). You enter the wild with few symbols of that rational persona you are leaving behind. During this threshold time you will seek to acquire adventures with the spirits of various or particular species, learning your own way of opening channels of communication.[10]

When you return, you will be looking at the world through the eyes of the child. In the elders' circle, you will tell your story. The elders will carefully bring the child with the spiritual eyes back into your body.[11]

The Woman Who Hated People

As a girl, Emily wasn't interested in girl's things: boys, dresses, dolls, and the like. She collected insects and studied the behavior of animals in the wild. In school, her subjects were mathematics, physics, and biology. She spent countless hours alone in the deep woods, turning over rocks, looking under rotting logs. A loner, she made a living doing odd jobs for Fish and Game or collecting species of plants for botanists. As the years passed she became a great authority on high desert botany, particularly mycology.

Her forays into the wilderness engendered within her a mystical love for the wild and its creatures — and a great disdain for the human species. She hated to come back to her town, to its noise pollution, drunken neighbors, and places of commerce. One afternoon while she was at home cataloging specimens, two teenage boys across the fence decided to test their new boom box by pumping up the volume to the max. Enraged by the thunderous cacophony, Emily ran out the back door, picked up a rock, and threw it over the fence in the general direction of the sound. The rock hit one of the boys in the head. Fortunately, he was not permanently injured.

Indeed, Emily was a misanthrope. She avoided most people because she disliked them. They did not share her values. They had little or no respect or interest in their natural environment. Her dislike of the human species finally became so acute that she doubted that she could be what she professed to be — a Pantheist (pan-theism — "divinity in all"). The crisis went like this: The Great Mystery lived in everything; ergo it lived in humans too. Emily, however, strenuously doubted that god could live in humans. And if god did not live in other humans, god did not in live in Emily.

She enrolled in a spirit quest at the School and went into the Last Chance Range with a small group to fast alone for four days and nights. Her intent was to confirm that she did — or did not — define herself as a Pantheist. Although she was accustomed to being alone in the desert for extended periods of time, she had never gone without food, or just sat on a rock for four days to find out whether the spirit of nature was — or was not — in her.

She returned with an answer. The Great Mystery of Nature lived in humans too.

It may be that the little girl got very hungry, even afraid, and that the adolescent felt all alone. It may be that in her own darkness she felt the stirrings of a higher power. There were human tears in her eyes as she stood in the threshold circle and the strong odor of sage smoke welcomed her back into the society of homo sapiens.[12]

RITES OF ART

The wellsprings of creativity seem to have gone dry. You stare at the empty canvass, the blank page, the unplayed instrument. Where is the desire to fill it with images of regeneration? You feel so old and full of care. The innocence and spontaneity of childhood seem so far away. Were you ever truly young? Were you ever truly loved? Were you ever truly alive? Is it possible that you were never meant to be a writer, a poet, a musician, an artist? The thought fills you with despair.

You leave your care-filled life and go alone, without food or shelter, to seek vision in the wilderness. For several days and nights you live with your emptiness in an environment teeming with spirits. There, with no mortal presence to see or listen, you practice your art. Hungry, lonely, uncomfortable, forgotten by the human world, you draw, paint, compose, write, sing, make music, or otherwise dedicate your hunger to the spirit of nature. Of course, you are free to do absolutely nothing.

Dreams may come. Images, symbols, and understandings from nature will compete for your attention. Sunlight, wholesome air, the silence, the call of birds, the music of insects, will gradually, quietly engage your spirit. At night, the sound of your rattle will flame out from your arm; the heartbeat of the drum will set the rocks and trees to dancing. The song of your voice will pave a road for spirits to travel. Poems will fly into the open, like quail bursting from cover. In the dark of night, in the glare of noon, in the lengthening shadows of dusk, the Muse called Gaia will stalk you.

And when your time alone is over, you will return to celebration, feast, and an elders' council, where you will share your stories, your art, your songs, your dreams with those who value and respect what you have done, and will do, in the name of the sacred Muse.[13]

"I'm On My Way to the Place of the Spirit One"

Kate was small and slender, with long chestnut hair. She could have been the teenage girl next door, though there were marks of middle age in her sweet face. But when she took up a guitar and sang her songs she was anything but a teenage girl. She was a true-to-life entertainer, cut from the mold of Baez and Collins, with albums all over the market. And when she sang in person, her fans flocked from all over the world to hear her.

She never disappointed her fans. She was certain to give them what she was famous for, something pure, something refined by adversity and dedication to truth, something of value to the heart. Her voice was soft, like bird fluff, smooth and sweet, with a hot little bite. She sang about love, about the land, about pollution and greed, about relationships, about growing older, about the emerging woman, about common working stiffs like you and me. You could always hear her music on public radio, where they weren't so afraid to broadcast songs that told unpopular truths.

Kate showed up at our School in Marin County one day and declared that she was ready to go out and fast on the mountain. "I'm dry as a bone; I'm burned out," she said, referring to current conditions in her life — a hectic schedule and the end of a love affair. The wellsprings of her creative life were blocked by "too much work and too much grief. And too many songs that won't come."

So early one morning she walked off alone into the sunswept desert of Joshua Tree National Monument, carrying her meager pack and an old guitar. She found a canyon and a soft place to sleep. For three days and nights she lived there, without food or companionship. When she returned on the fourth morning, her face was dirty and her jeans were caked with dust. She looked tired and at peace. There was a twinkle in her hazel eyes. She told her two guides, Sunwater and Adele Getty, that she'd written a couple new songs. Would they like to hear them?

It must have been a couple years after that when her newest album, "Give Yourself to Love," with her autograph and thanks on the cover, arrived in the mailbox. It was absolutely beautiful. I was particularly entranced by "Desert Wind":

> What can I say? You said it all.
> Your words ride on the desert wind,
> Telling me about tomorrow,
> How a heart can love again.

But the last time we saw her was when she came through on her way to New Mexico to sing at a benefit for American Indians. Just before she left, she went out to get her guitar from the van. There, in our humble living room, she strummed and sang "Brother Warrior":

> We are crying for a vision that all living things can share.
> And those who care are with us everywhere.

Then she drove away. It wasn't too long after that we got a late night call from one of her close friends. Kate was dying of leukemia. We reacted with disbelief. She had always seemed so vibrant with life and soul. We prayed for her then. We prayed like crazy. But there was nothing anyone could do. The Spirit she loved most was determined to call her home. In six months she was gone.

I know the songs will exist forever. But something in me still refuses to be consoled. It was a poet who died. I still imagine Kate sitting alone and hungry out there somewhere in a sandy wash, hunkered down over an old guitar:

> I'm on my way to the place of the Spirit One.
> Grandfather hear me now I am on fire.
> Let the sun dance guide my feet to your desire.
> — Kate Wolf, "Medicine Wheel"

RITES OF MEDICINE POWER

You know that the mystery of self is connected with the mystery of earth. And so you undertake an initiatory experience in the wilderness which introduces you to "medicine power." Under the supervision of a medicine teacher or guide, you go alone without food, company, or shelter, to a wild place where you live for an extended period — four to seven days and nights. Your sole intent is to confirm the reality of a "medicine helper," the spirit of the wind, the tree, the mountain, the bear, the coyote, the river. Surely you are doing nothing more than your great great ancestors did thousands of years ago.

Knowing that such power does not come without your willingness to sacrifice, you forego comfort, security, and physical sustenance. The fast only makes your senses more acute. The loneliness only whets your appetite for spirit company. The exposure only opens you to the fears in which your "helper" dwells.[14]

The Lady in the Coyote-Tail Hat

Kit was a lovely young woman who had fallen head over heels into a romance with anything that was American Indian. A big city girl (San Francisco) she didn't get out here much, but when she did, she always had a feather stuck to her head band, a crystal in her fringed, calf skin pocket, and a gorgeous beaded medicine bag for a pipe that had been given to her by a young Indian male enamored of her charms.

We had seen a lot of people like her down through the years. Sometimes it was difficult getting through the outward trappings to the deeper soul. But we tried to serve her well. She was, after all, a genuine person. She was like a little mouse, busily poking her nose into a multitude of holes. Sooner or later something would jump out and grab her nose. That's the way she learned.

When she came to the School to vision fast, she claimed to crave "medicine." The fact was, her head was already full of medicine. Too full. She had read all the latest books. She had memorized the healing wheels, the Indian zodiac, which animal helper went with which kind of personality, how to make medicine with prayer ties, prayer arrows, and smudging feathers, what colors went with what directions. She had done a considerable amount of guided shamanic fantasizing and in a trance had met the Grandmothers and the Grandfathers. She could explain the dynamics of crystal healing and invoke the six directions and powers with ceremonial prayers. And she could smoke her medicine pipe in the Arapaho way because it had been blessed by a Cree medicine man.

With such a headful of "medicine" she didn't seem to need extra. But here she was, going out on the sacred mountain to fast for more medicine power. She seemed genuinely disappointed to find that we didn't practice Indian ceremonies and began to look slightly askance at our "pan-cultural" ways. She was delighted, however, to return from the fasting time with the tail of a dead coyote. This was just the kind of validation she had hoped to find. When we saw that coyote tail we held on to our hats.

Right away she started asking questions about Coyote. We weren't too hot on answering. Secretly we'd been hoping she'd come back without so much medicine mania, looking for new ways of validating herself. We shouldn't have been so disappointed. She had brought back precisely what Mother Nature thought best for her — the Trickster.

The old Paiute Indian doctor in our valley says that coyote medicine is not good for anyone under fifty. He says the young ones can't handle Coyote. He says Coyote will twist them and turn them and flip them upside down. He says sometimes Coyote will cause the young ones to die. Kit didn't know about that. We warned her that she had Coyote by the tail. She looked at us mysteriously and said she could handle it. She produced her new hat, the tail dangling from the brim.

Within a year or so she had been sexually accosted at work and had fallen in and out of love several heart-breaking times. She lost her job twice, had a near fatal car accident, and her apartment was burglarized. Her faithful dog died and her best girl friend refused to talk to her any more. The final twist? She got pregnant, with a man she didn't love.

When we saw her again she was not wearing the hat. It was, however, in the trunk of her car. She looked ten years older. Soul was in her face. Initiation wrinkles. Not a feather or a crystal could be seen. "I've come to bury the coyote tail," she said.

ENDNOTES: WINTER TO SUMMER: THE RITES OF SPRING

[1] Sir James Frazer, *The Golden Bough: A Study in Magic and Religion* (New York: Macmillan, 1963), p. 349.

[2] Usually the drama of the death lodge takes place on the third day, allowing the previous two days of fasting to take their toll. The purpose circle occurs on the fourth day and night. Midnight on the morning of the fifth day, the initiate reaches the "singularity" of birth. The death lodge can be any natural enclosure or niche in a wild place.

[3] Traditionally, the initiand stays here through a long dark night, surrounded by a circle of stones aligned to the four directions.

[4] The general idea is to bring about an altogether harmonious turning from winter to spring, from death to birth, from mind to spirit, from rational to irrational, from thought to imagination, from seeing to Seeing, from finitude to infinitude. Only then can the body of the child begin to grow in the mind of the adult; only then can the summer rage and swarm.

The rites of birthing in the wild, as described above, are of particular value because they merge human and nature. Immersion in the natural elements naturally evokes the eastern shield. The mind of the adult, exaggerated in part by the technological enclosures of modern life, ceases to be of primary importance. Time assumes a languid aspect. Life is measured by the passage of night and day. Gradually, the spiritual aspect of nature comes to the fore, activated by fasting and isolation.

The body shield also plays a significant part in the process of dying and birthing, for the body of the initiate must continually be in contact with the body of nature. Physical discomfort alone can pull the fastidious mind from its castle.

The dying that occurs at the absolute zero of the night is symbolic and psychodramatic. And the quality of the death is relative to the quality of the person who enacts it. But even those lacking in intent and imagination can greatly benefit from the process. Plunk an exaggerated adult shield down on the earth alone, without food or shelter, for four days and nights. Take away all that symbolic superstructure. The chances are still very good that when the person returns from the experience, almost immediately you will see the child shield. The elders must be ready to empower that child, to plan with her a seasonal life in which the summer waxes and grows strong.

[5] The prayer quest is an ideal initiation rite for suicidal people who have not

only fallen into the black hole of feeling, but have intellectually assented to the fact that this is so, and have convinced themselves that there is no way out. Such a quest is not a cure-all, however. The ability of the individual to be healed of suicidal ideations is directly related to the quality and seriousness of her/his praying. If a person is suicidal because he/she has not tried very hard at living, then she/he might not be a very committed supplicant.

⁶ Loneliness, an empty belly, and exposure to the natural elements, lend great poignancy to this exercise. The spirit is lured forth from the exaggerated mind, where form and structure have grown weary of carrying all the weight. The idea, of course, is to break down or frustrate mind power by putting the self through the "irrational" act of prayer (i.e., moving from the winter shield to the passage of spring so that the mind's opposite, the child, can be nurtured). It is not easy for the rational mind to stoop to prayer. Yet it is the mind itself that must consent to the act.

In Judeo-Christian mythology, prayer is considered to be nothing less than conversation between human and divine. The night before he died, Jesus prayed in the Garden of Gesthemane, a very human prayer — that his destiny be taken from him. His prayer was answered at Pentecost, when his resurrected spirit returned to physical bodies in the form of tongues of fire, and his people were renewed. Even so, the Plains Indian vision quester prays to the Great Spirit on the sacred mountain of the vision quest. Nothing fancy — just a human prayer — that his burning thirst be slaked, that his emptiness be filled, that he not have to die this living death — so that his people will prosper. With the renewal of the people comes the renewal of the self. And the path of renewal is always through the healing passage of the spring. Once the great wheel turns toward spring, it cannot reverse itself. If spring comes, can summer be far behind?

Prayer is a passageway from the mind to the body. The mind finds the words to evoke spirit. The spirit finds the ways to activate body. Hence, the act of prayer has a salutary effect on all forms of physical dis-ease and sickness. It makes changes in the physical world occur — even, as from the vulva of spring, all the children crown and begin to grow.

⁷ In a series of preparatory meetings (severance), the journeyer equips herself with a "plan" that will be enacted during the threshold phase. This plan will include intellectual assent to an inescapably obvious truth — that what I do affects another, even when I am not in that other's presence. Even so, the intricate, interconnected spirit web of nature (plus body, psyche, and mind) in which humans share, stirs us, moves us in mysterious ways that only love can fathom.

When the journeyer, accompanied by the "lost soul," enters the incorporation phase, the elders take special care to "ground" him in the personal and social body. It is not good for the person to be off in the spirit world when cars are moving down highways at 60 mph and people are being people. The healing process is not complete until the spirit enters the body (summer shield). The child must be nurtured with acceptance, love, and bodily necessities. It is as if he has returned newborn.

[8] The journey to redeem the "lost soul" is, of course, a familiar motif in the mythology of almost every culture that ever existed. There is no reason to assume that this quest is any less pertinent or powerful than it has been for a hundred thousand years. Another name for it is "shamanic journey." The "savior," "doctor," medicine person, or concerned other is willing to go to great lengths to discover the healing secret and affect the cure.

Many at our School have undertaken such healing journeys, not as "shamans," but as ordinary people. Their experiences have underscored the obvious: real healing can be accomplished in this way. The "lost soul" is deeply touched, even healed. The quester is healed as well. The most effective healing is accomplished by individuals who genuinely care about the welfare of their people, and who do not fill the process with arrogance or pride. They see themselves in the "lost soul" and deeply appreciate the "human condition." Their compassion extends to all life.

[9] Was Nicolai's father actually healed? One might confidently say that there was a healing in the psychological, mental and spiritual shields. There was a balancing within the shield system. The jump in health of the other three could have affected the health of his body shield. At any rate, Nicolai's father is alive to this day.

[10] If this is done to acquire "medicine power" from a particular species, that power must be directed to the benefit of the people.

[11] Those who come to the School often ask for instruction in "intuitive cognition." This is a delicate subject. The real objective is to help the student to find her/his own way. We offer a variety of ways, letting the student chose which one. Of course, there are many books that give in-depth instructions on how to reach the spirit world. Students are asked to be aware that there is not an "only way." Rather, there is "my way." We tell them what we know about the spirit world — that the spirit cannot be apprehended apart from the being, the entity, the physicality of it.

Any foray into the spirit world necessitates a "coming down" into the social body. If this descent is not accomplished, the student may wander with the spirits indefinitely, like a hippie lost in an LSD trip. This incorporation of the spirit into the body, and the body into the social body, can a dangerous enterprise. Once activated, the spirit shield can dominate the whole system. The self can hold itself back, disdaining to enter a dog-eat-dog world of competition and survival on a physical level. The elders must watch closely to see if the returnee is accepting the conditions of the body. A lot of nurturing, social and physical contact is applied. Often, a sweating lodge ceremony, without clothes (or a minimum of clothes) is held. Excessive sweating automatically brings body awareness. A feast (activating the body by putting food into it) is an almost universal way of bringing spring to summer.

[12] The one who went into the desert was a girl who had never properly become a woman. The girl had to go live in adolescence for a while, in self-consciousness and doubt. She had to put aside her flimsy facade of intellect and logic and live like any other human under the sky. Immersed in the human condition (fall shield), her humanless universe (winter) dissolved, and she found a sense of identity with her own species. She engaged with the Great Mystery of Nature (spring). The woman who returned saw her place among the people. She was a Pantheist.

[13] This is an old cure-all. But it sure beats going on a tear, beating the wife (or husband). slowly drowning in stagnancy, or waking up drunk in an all-too-familiar cage. Change the environment, change the perspective, add a big dose of nature. Artists have perennially taken vacations or retreats — to the seacoast, the mountains, the desert, the arctic. Invariably, they take their trade tools with them — the pencil, the paper, the instrument, the paintbrush. The beauty and power of art have always come from the profoundest solitude, loneliness, vulnerability, and hunger, often bodily hunger, as well as the hunger to encompass the four fold enterprises of human self-thus.

The net result of the wilderness quest for the muse is the emergence of summer's child, innocent, emotional, wild-eyed, sensual, alert — with all the powers of the summer shield. This child, of course, must return to adult life, to profession, family, and the mature expressions of love. The "grind" is waiting. There may come another time when it will be necessary to return to the spirit quest for the company of the wild Muse.

[14] Those who have undertaken such quests for "medicine" at the School invariably return with a new sense of how they can go about their work. Usually, they exhibit a sharper attunement to the natural world — on all levels, but

especially the physical (south shield). Questing to find the spirit in physical form, they have fallen in love with both. The new-born child who returns is also older and wiser. He is less afraid to enter the darkness of inwardness, for that is where the memory of the "medicine power" can be found. The feelingful aftermath of disappointments, defeats, and unforseen accidents becomes a source of personal power. Because the secrets of this power are not leaked out all over the place, the power is contained and fermented in the cask of the soul. In the service of humanity, it makes the finest wine.

Those who quest to confirm the reality of a "medicine helper" need never see that particular spirit "in the flesh." The spirit sought will appear in many forms, many presences. In traditional cultures, the mere act of fasting to confirm, confirms. For example, the old Paiute "Indian doctor" in our valley decides he is ready to use humming bird as one of his healers in the sweat lodge. He fasts four days and nights on the mountain to confirm that hummingbird is indeed his helper. When he returns, there is no question. It is so. Hummingbird is his helper, and will come to help him in the sweat lodge.

There are many, however, who seek to wrest medicine power from a futile life filled with futile ambitions. One does not necessarily acquire "medicine power" by virtue of a few day's fasting. Such mysteries of the spirit are not easily plumbed — and never plundered. Many glibly boast of their medicine power. That is because they are afraid that they don't have any. Those who truly possess medicine power are continually occupied with its use in the service of others. Because this power has been recognized by others, they don't have to tell anyone it's there. They "do" it. They demonstrate their vision — on the earth — for the people to see. As old Sun Bear put it, their medicine "grows corn."

SPRING TO FALL: THE RITES OF SUMMER

> Keep on,
> *Keep on*, he signals, *follow me!* He guides him
> In flight — O fatal art! — and the wings move
> And the father looks back to see the son's wings moving.
> .... And the boy
> Thought *This is wonderful!* and left his father,
> Soared higher, higher, drawn to the vast heaven,
> Nearer the sun, and the wax that held the wings
> Melted in the fierce heat, and the bare arms
> Beat up and down in air, and lacking oarage
> Took hold of nothing
> — Ovid, *Metamorphoses*

THE MALADY

All is sweetness and light. The earth is always smothered in wildflowers. The sun is always coming up and never going down. The butterfly flits from flower to flower, sky dancing, reviewing past lives, astrally projecting, channeling, altering consciousness, shamanic journeying, consulting crystal balls, swept up in pie-in-the-sky dreaming. The feet dangle inches above terra firma. Who cares for the things of this world when the riches of the invisible world call like sirens? The opposite west shield, the dark soul, is undernourished. The exaggerated spring shield is protecting itself from the dark, which hurts its far-seeing eyes. The innocent summer shield, the child, has been drawn into a fascinated alliance with angelic beings and refuses to learn or grow up. The adult shield, its rationality sublimed away by the light, lacks self-control or real work to do. Healing must take place in the opposite fall shield. The illumined one must face the darkness behind the light.

THE RITES OF SUMMER

For spring to become fall, it must first pass through summer. To reach the dark shield, the illumined one must become a child, live in the physical world, and experience the lessons of the body. Only then can the one whose eyes are blinded by the light attain the illumination of darkness.

What has expanded must become constricted. What has been spiritual must become psychological. What has been god-conscious must become self-conscious. This cannot occur until spirit (spring) is willing to descend into the body (summer) and take on emotions, sensations, the law of the jungle, the survival of the fittest, the erotic instinct, the maze of materialism, and all the monsters of childhood.

The rites of summer lead to the incorporation of fall. But before the fruit can be harvested (fall), the sprout (spring) must grow up into body (summer). The spirit must be infused by the characteristics and identity of its species. If the vision is to be realized in the dark, it must take on the corpus of the earth. The vision must be oriented to the body and to the inward self before it can benefit the people. The road expansiveness must take to constrictedness runs through the physical world. The road from dawn to dusk runs through the day. The road from imagination to memory runs through a land called sensation. The gravitational field through which innocence falls toward experience is the animal world of instinct (summer). The fuse through which love for god or goddess is transformed into love for self is called eros (summer).

The exaggerated spring shield doesn't want to pass through the body of summer because trauma resides there. The child is hurt, angry or afraid. In order to survive, the child has invented various means of avoiding the here and now of sheer physical existence. That may be why the adolescent is so undernourished. On the other hand, the child may be in collusion with the spring shield in an attempt to escape the torturous realities of life. Childlikeness is often associated with illumination.

The child pockets the vision like a gold coin and goes about the business of entering the initiation time of adolescence. Experience is the key. First, one is innocent. Then one knows. The spirit sprout must be tested by the cold winds of experience. "Throw him in the river who [says he] loves water." (William Blake) Perhaps the inflated visionary will realize he can swim.

Another kind of stuck spring shield is in collusion with the winter shield. The high priest (winter) is married to the divine (spring); the nun (winter) is married to Christ (spring); theology (winter) is married to faith (spring); the intellect (winter) is married to the artistic (spring). The marriage tilts the wheel toward winter-spring. The imbalance can only be righted when the "enlightened one" deigns to get his hands dirty in the marketplace of the body. Then the feeling-starved adolescent of fall will finally take a look at those dirty hands. Ivory towered or cloistered tenders of the vision are of little benefit to their species unless their vision is tested by the brute fact of mortality (summer) and incorporated into the holy Mecca of the soul (fall).

Spring must return to its source, the black hole of fall. There is nourishment there, in the falling leaves, in the settling of dusk, in the fading of innocent days. But there is power in memory. Truth lies in the wound, in the hurt — in the guilty, anxious, helpless, painful, psychological truth. Without this dark star of truth and the winter it engenders, there would be no dawning in the spring. The "shaman's secret," the philosopher's stone, the Alchemist's gold — they all tell the same old story. The secret lies in the base metal, in the dark night of the soul, the opposite side of the tracks, the ugly sweating walls, the stark shadows cast by the overabundance of light.

Rites of incorporation into the fall shield involve a severance from the state of illumination. The point of severance should be marked by ceremony involving elders and witnesses. The visionary has turned his back on the sacred mountains and returns to the haunts of humans, to communities, neighborhoods, malls, freeways, barrios, pay toilets, and red light districts. Now he must find the sacred mountains inside. Ahead lie the regions of the body, senses, and instinct — the threshold of childhood. Without undue delay, the initiate must be reintroduced to the pleasures and pains of *samsara*. Of course, such rites do not formally exist in contemporary culture. Perhaps the existence of what the law calls "vice" reflects the human need for them.

Rites of incorporation into adolescence do not exclude the adult shield of winter. Adults must periodically undergo these rites simply to keep their shields balanced. Those who claim to have "found it" can become amazingly complacent and hypocritical. It is important that they remember their own mortality, that they acknowledge their bodies and a myriad of sensations, emotions and feelings to which humans are subject, that they struggle with the monsters who guard the gates of self-acceptance and love. Of such stuff are mature adults composed.

Many grownups hover in the ether zone just outside the body of summer, frozen into the posture of "I'm just about to jump in." It may be that for years they have explored countless methods for attaining enlightenment and now, their head echoing with sacred resonances, they are about to embark on a course of action, a commitment, a jump into the real life muck. There they teeter for years, just about to let go. Verily, such as these will die convinced that their lives were wasted. Their fear of testing their life myths against the realities of life in a naturalistic world (summer) comes from an undernourished adolescent who doubts self.

The summer shield is of course an integral part of any initiatory experience in nature. At this very moment, a group of trainees from the School are fasting in the mountains outside our town, It is mid- September and the weather has turned uncharacteristically rotten: thunder and hail storms, rain and wind. Their only shelters, eight and a half by eleven foot tarps, flutter in the storm like wounded butterflies. There is no way to escape the wind. Initiation in the wild is *always* an intensely physical experience. The body lives in the Body for a period of time. The body aches and shivers and hungers. In the quiet of night, the heart beats against the breastbone like a drum. The ears strain for the slightest sound. A rustle in the bushes tickles the hormones. Adrenalin sings in the blood.

Usually, an exaggerated spring shield will succumb to that kind of physicality because the animal body must survive.[1] And the actions of the animal body naturally lead to the inward consciousness of the fall shield. Down through the years, many stories told in the elders' council at our School involved this movement from an exaggerated spring persona — through the body — to the psyche-land of shadows and feelings.

RITES OF SUMMER

You can see very clearly what needs to be done — even what you can do. But you cannot bring yourself to do it, to apply your insights and understandings to practical means. You hold back, acquiring even more illuminations, hoping that their sheer weight will force you to "walk the vision with practical feet." Others around you seem to have their feet on the ground, striving to do their part, while you live in a rarified atmosphere where there is no bloodshed, no struggle, no doing of the thing that has to be done.

You decide to free yourself from the spell of bloodless enlightenment and put your body on the line. You plunk your butt down in the dirt of some remote but very real wild place and for four days you live there — in the summer time, when every living thing is raging to survive. You undergo the trial of the body. Your shelter is minimal, your purchase precarious. You take whatever nature brings you. You live in your body, in the body of Nature. You exist in the sheer physical presence of self-thus. For the first four days you live alone and fast. On the last day, just before sunset, you eat.[2]

When the threshold period is over, you bring your animal body back to the people (the social body), and the council of elders, where the story is told for the edification of all. Naturally, the story contains not only elements of the body shield, but of the psyche, mind (and spirit) as well. Your senses have given birth to feelings, your emotions to memories. Your body is healed and its inner life breathes freely. The elders confirm your passage. They may suggest that you celebrate the rites of summer annually within a program of on-going self- therapy.[3]

The Anorexic

Claire lived in a very private world. It glowed with a kind of spirituality and included many others like her. In a manner of speaking, she was a saint, starving her way out of this world and into the next. She would not eat meat or chicken or fish or any dairy product. She turned away from nuts and seeds and grains. She positively abhorred sugar. A tiny pile of rice, a slice of tomato, maybe the tip of a carrot, and a bottle of Perrier — this was her entire food intake in a day, if she was hungry. Her body fat was all but gone. Glycogen and muscle were going too. Gradually, inexorably, she was starving her body to feed her spirit. She was subliming away into Paradise.

Claire was an only child. Her father was a busy lawyer. Her mother ran a clothing store. They were formal and strict with her, and at an early age instilled in her the drive to excel and seek perfection. She was a blond, pretty little girl, albeit a bit inward and quiet. But when she reached puberty, the carefully maintained family structure began to crumble. Her parents became alarmed when she shut herself away in her room and began to wear black. Her mother, in her attempts to control her, became a tyrant. Her father backed up her mother. They didn't realize that Claire was simply "individuating."

Inwardly, she was rebelling against her mother's iron fist. One of her favorite forms of silent protest was her refusal to eat. This refusal accomplished two goals: it defied mother and was a way of losing weight. She thought she was too fat anyway. And even as she began to lose weight she still considered herself to be too fat, and the reason why she was fat was because her mother kept trying to put food into her.

At this point in her adolescent development, Claire began to seek help in her efforts to resist unpleasantness at home. She went to her spiritual self, her righteous self, the "illumined one." By the time she was 18, she was on a spiritual quest to starve herself to death. By then she knew only too well that in order to live she must eat. The great spoken and unspoken command at home was EAT!

The pressure of mortality was so intense Claire chose to be rid of it rather than to turn and face the real monster — her inner feelings about what she was doing to herself, her conscience, her consciousness of the eyes of her mother and father and friends looking at her. Claire stood at the edge of an ocean of feeling. The fear of jumping in was killing her.

Claire decided to go on a vision fast. Her therapist had recommended it. She was attracted by the "no food" taboo, and by what she thought would be the spiritual payoff — a vision. At the time, she weighed 95 pounds. We didn't think she would be able to carry a pack. We were wrong. She proved to be strong enough over the short haul. She moved meticulously, like a long-legged insect, picking her way through the sage and prickly pear. When the moment came to step across the threshold into the "sacred world," she was ready.

For three days and nights she lived alone, without food, amid the dust and rubble of the desert mountains. Nobody told her to eat. Technically she was forbidden to do so. Gratefully, she embraced the spiritual bliss of not eating. Just to make sure she didn't leave her body for good, we checked on her welfare every day. She seemed weak and tired, but she was hanging on.

A huge thunderstorm rolled in on the second day. The wind howled through the thick junipers and the grass danced crazily. Lightning licked the ground. Thunder boomed like the crack of doom. Rain fell in a sudden intense squall, then was gone. The air brightened. The clouds rolled away from a deep, clear sky. The girl who was starving her body to feed her spirit wept under her tarp like a little girl. She was afraid of getting wet. She was afraid of dying alone because no one loved her. She was afraid of anorexia.

The last day she got sick and vomited green bile. She felt miserable and all alone. She felt something else, like a craving for something pleasurable. She remembered the tiny bag of lemon drops she carried in her emergency pack. In case she needed energy. She popped a lemon drop. Nothing had ever tasted so good. She realized that she was violating her sugar taboo, and was not surprised that she didn't care.

Much of her last day was spent consuming the rest of the lemon drops and remembering things that had happened at home. She began to feel angry and resentful. The more she savored the lemon drops, the more she was able to see herself as her parents were seeing her. She did not like what she saw. She was ashamed, resentful and bitter. All at once, sainthood was forgotten. She saw that what she must do was to get strong enough to leave home.

When Claire returned to basecamp on that final morning, she was ravenous. She ate too much and suffered for it. We joked with her about the consequences of eating. But the challenge was there. Getting back into her body would be difficult. It would take a long time. Meanwhile, she needed to find love. We took the group to a hot springs, where everyone sported about in their bathing suits. Claire wore her wasted body self-consciously but she did it. By showing so much of her flesh, she was making a statement. She was confirming her right to be in her body.[4]

RITES OF PRIMAL EMOTION

"The body likes fear. The body likes the darkness and the wind."

— Don Juan (Castaneda)

Secretly, you might be willing to admit that you'd rather not dirty your hands with shadows, that you are quite comfortable, thank you, living in the sweetness and light. So you keep your mind busy with "soul mates," "old souls," "past lives," and never hear the termites gnawing away at the foundations of your mortal existence. But when your airy edifice crashes down around your ears and for a moment you actually eyeball the ruins of your life, you realize something in you has got to change. The time has come to undertake the rites of primal emotion that will lead you to the source of wholistic enlightenment — the dark shield.

So you enroll in a ropes course, or you learn how to rock climb, or you fast alone for a couple days in a canyon near a mountain lion den. You get that old adrenalin pumping and you get back into your child shield. The body, with its senses, urges, and primal emotions, will automatically link you to the memories and consciousness of the fall persona. The messes you have made of your life will invade your feelings and your conscience will whisper urgent messages in your ear. There will be balance between soul and spirit, between the dues that bring the blues and the heart that sings.

Later, in the elders' council, the story of your quest for the land of shadows will be accepted and empowered. The elders may recommend further participation in the rites of primal emotions.[5]

The Woman Who Crossed the Log

At our "upper campus," a huge Ponderosa pine fell across the creek many years ago. Now nothing is left but the bare, weathered trunk and its stubbly limbs. If they are careful, people can negotiate the log without undue difficulty, avoiding the snags and cracks along its uneven length. 10 feet below, birch-lined Big Pine Creek rages in foaming rapids. If you fell in, it probably wouldn't kill you, but it wouldn't do you much good.

Barbara, a married woman of 40 preparing for a four day/night fast, took one look at that log and her mouth went dry. Her knees wobbled and sweat trickled down her back. "No way," she said. She stood there, swamped in a sudden, deeply painful dilemma. She couldn't do it. She was afraid. She was looking squarely at her Nemesis.

It didn't help to watch the others frisk across with nary a hitch. How was she going to get to the meeting place? One of the women came over to help. After an extremely painful moment of indecision, Barbara accepted her offer. Clinging to the woman for dear life, she inched across, a dangerous counterweight to her helper's poise. At one point, they both almost went into the drink. Somehow they made it. Later, she told the group what she had done. Many applauded. Some offered advice: "Don't look down!" "Take your shoes off!" "Don't think about it. Just go ahead and do it." "Go back and do it again." She considered going back, trying it again. It was too risky. Besides, she had other things to think about — like the reasons why she was going to live without food in the desert for four days and nights.

Barbara was married to a man who was obese. The passion was gone, if it had ever been there, and making love was a kind of ordeal. Still, she loved him deeply, and was quite stunned to discover that she was entertaining passionate thoughts about an unmarried man with whom she worked. Nevertheless, she did nothing to betray her marriage vows. Years passed. She immersed herself in the study of spiritual disciplines. She took up yoga. She spent hours in a state of non-attachment.

Meanwhile, the marriage inched on like a rusty wheel in deep sand. When she arrived at the School, Barbara was holding tightly in one hand to a single, tiny thread of marital commitment. The other hand was holding fast to the gurus. She was not looking up ahead. It was too frightening.

She went alone into the desert mountains, where the wild creek that flowed under the fallen Ponderosa had disappeared into hot winds from the southwest that washed the ridges with currents of incandescent light. She walked up the dry canyons, the silent, brooding arroyos, the craggy slopes covered with grasshoppers screaming for the faintest taste of water. And all the while the sacred river was roaring in her soul. She wrote in her journal: "I want to be able to go across that log alone. . . . I really believe I'm going to make it over that log."

Her return from the fast confirmed that she was ready to try the log again. The girl had become a woman, by the right of initiation. In order to celebrate that fact, while a woman friend stood watch, she slipped out of her clothes and, stark naked, inched unaided across the log.

The spiritual woman (spring shield) faced the challenge of her body, to feel its needs and to savor its appetites. That evening, during the sauna ceremony, she danced in the hot darkness, whirling like a dark Spanish shawl.

At that point, we began to talk to her about "bridges" instead of "logs." She seemed to agree. In her journal she wrote, "Lots of bridges to cross, though fearful I go." She went home and asked her husband for a divorce. He agreed.

It did not go easy for her. She encountered many of her own shadows. Nine months later, she was back again at the School, attending a seminar on the four shields of sexuality.

Once more, she confronted the log. At the back of her head she heard "Pachelbel's Cannon" unfolding. She breathed deeply, and slowly, very slowly, crossed the "bridge."

That same week, hurrying to get to a meeting, both hands loaded down with bags, with flies buzzing in her face, she crossed the bridge without thinking.

RITES OF SENSUALITY

> In Heaven you have heard no marriage is,
> No white flesh tinder to your lecheries,
> Your male and female tissue sweetly shaped
> Sublimed away, and furious blood escaped.
>
> — John Crow Ransom, "The Equilibrists"

You realize you are ready to release yourself from your vows. You are ready to forsake the chapel, the prayer book, and the kneeling stairs.

And so you go alone to the sensual heart of nature and undergo the passage rites of summer. You go without food, so that your body can hunger, not simply for spiritual food, but for meat and drink. You go without shelter, so that your body can hunger for a roof and a bed. You go without company, so that your body can scream for the touch of others. You go without clothes and roll in the dirt and filth, so that you can wash yourself clean in the pure, glacial river. You shampoo your hair with soap root and smoke it with the odor of sage and wild mint. You fondle your toes, your legs, your belly, your buttocks, your genitals, your armpits, your eyes, nose, ears. You lie in the open and make love with the sun. You give yourself to the greater Body. You call in fantasies and dreams. You imagine and remember the face of your anima/animus. You ask yourself why, in Buddhist Tantric rites, the devotee partakes of the "five forbidden things" — wine, meat, fish, parched grain, and sexual intercourse.

And when the threshold time is over, you return eager to partake of the great feast of summer that awaits you. The elders will hear your story and mirror back to you the meaning of what you have done and the shadows that will come to life in the shield of your "dark side."[6]

The Minister Who Couldn't Go All the Way

Carelton came to the School to fast in the open desert and affirm ("confirm" as he put it) his relationship to the Holy Spirit. A minister with three children, he was nearing the time of midlife crisis. For twenty years he had ministered unto his Presbyterian flock through lean times and flush times. Now he was tired. He needed to reconnect with the Source of all energy.

He joined a group of others which included a slender dark-haired woman of 35 named Maria. The two of them immediately became friends. And because they were camping in the same place, they began to see a good deal of each other. Carelton was very aware of appearances, and did nothing to reveal the fact that he was falling into passionate love with Maria. And she with him. To outside eyes, it was all very platonic. Nobody thought "romance." Friendships are typical in the days before the threshold fasting time begins.

Nobody but Maria knew the pain the poor minister of God was feeling at this unexpected turn of events. He loved his wife and family dearly. His parish was his entire world. In the council, he reaffirmed his love for his wife. He spoke of her in endearing terms. He also spoke of his work, the people who had, by the grace of God, been healed, blessed, found faith. He took his work very seriously, as he did his relationship to God the Father, Son, and Holy Spirit. But as is often the case with those who walk the spiritual path, the illumined one cast a dark shadow. Even as he walked toward the dawning light, the darkness came up from behind to meet him.

The night before we journeyed to the mountains the rain clouds climbed down the peaks and relieved themselves on the campground. It was a very wet night. The bottom of Maria's tent flooded. Carelton invited her into his tent. She accepted. They spent the rest of the night talking and listening to the rain tattooing the synthetic roof. Mostly, they talked about their romance, how much they wanted to make love with each other, what they lusted after in each other, why it would be a terrible thing to do, why it would be a wonderful thing to do. IT hung between them, an unanswered question, until, in the early morning hours, the rain stopped and, in spite of themselves, they dozed off for a while.

They didn't actually "do anything." They just did it a thousand times in their imagination. And when it came time for everybody to go off into the high desert mountains to fast and be alone, they went out as "buddies," separated by half a mile of juniper-pinon woodland and connected each day by a walk to the stonepile, where each left a sign of well being. If he got up on the ridge above his camp, Carelton could see her place in the distance. If she went to the end of a copse of pinons, Maria could see his place. Given their proximity to each other and the events of the preceding days, what do you imagine the two thought about out there while they were alone and hungry?

The mornings were hot and dry, with cooling breezes every afternoon. Thunderstorms threatened, then slunk away to find other haunts. The nights were cold and clear, resplendent with stars. The new moon hung like a jewel over the peaks of the Western Divide as they flushed rosily in the early light of dawn. The sage meadows exploded with high summer life, dusty hoppers, vivid dragonflies, sweat bees, basking lizards, ground squirrels, deer mice, kangaroo rats. Flocks of pinon jays terrorized the tree tops. You could feel a kind of urgency in the air, an urge to indulge the skin, to sweat, to go bare, feel the earth-kiss, smell the sage, roll in the dust, wag your naked bum at the trees. "Get into your body," said Phoebus Apollo. "Let go of everything but your body."

Carelton lived in this sweet hell for four days and nights. Every day he went up on the ridge and spied on her with his binoculars. Most of the time, she was nude. He wanted so badly to see her up close, to touch her. He also wanted so badly to be faithful to his marriage vows, to go back to his people with a clean conscience and new found energy. Was God testing him? He remembered Christ's temptation in the wilderness. All the kingdoms in the world if he would only bow down and worship Satan. Well, he was going to resist the temptation, like Jesus did. Now, where did he put those binoculars?

To be sure, Carelton was not Jesus. He was only human, like any other man. He didn't have to condemn himself. He didn't have to decide that lust was profane and abstinence was sacred. After all, he had fathered three children. He didn't have to decide that his vision fast was a failure. He didn't have to tell Maria, when they came together at the end, that it was over, that they shouldn't see each other anymore. And he didn't have to keep it all under his minister's hat, and not tell anyone what had really happened.

To the dismay of everyone, he left early, before his story was ever told. We tried to find out what was going on with him, but he evaded, dodged, and was gone without a hug, leaving Maria behind to tell her story. Gradually, the outlines of his story appeared in hers. No matter how unintentionally, Carelton (and Maria too) had celebrated a rite of sensuality. The holy minister had not confirmed his connection to sacred chastity. He had confirmed his connection to eros.

Like Arthur Dimmsdale, the minister went back to his home and parish. He put up a brave front but there was a skeleton in the closet of memory. He tried to keep the door locked. He wanted to hide this profanity away, to keep it out of the sacred. But the closed door kept luring him back into the shadows, back to the secret sin. It was as easy to go back there as it was to pick up a pair of binoculars.

Within a few years, he had a torrid affair with a young and willing parishioner. He went all the way with her and awoke in a new world. In this world the sacred was profane and the profane was sacred. And the sighing of his beloved was the Word. It wasn't long before Carelton was a divorced man — and an ex-minister of the Gospel.

RITES OF THE BODY

Go naked, alone, without food, to a wild place, and surrender your nakedness to Nakedness. Walk about looking for rattlesnakes and other symbols of fear.[7] Give yourself unshielded to the body, soul, mind, and spirit of nature. Give yourself to the wind. Surrender to your own sensuality in the presence of danger. Take careful note of the memories of people you already know or dream of. When the time of nakedness is complete, tell your story to the elders.

The wild child learns to wear clothes. The adult has to learn to take them off, for she is aware of the consequences. Removal of clothing for a full day and night lures the initiate into the self- conscious realms of the fall persona, where self-acceptance and love dwell. The extreme embarrassment that prompts most children entering puberty to become very private about their nakedness indicates the inner presence of a growing anima or animus, a dark god or goddess who watches and desires. The growing child must be given to that dark deity as symbolized by the natural world. Nakedness in nature evokes self-acceptance on a primal level. From this self-acceptance comes attributes of the winter shield: true modesty, mature sexual love, the ability to parent, and a deep reverence for all naked, fierce, vulnerable entities (spring).

The Woman Who Was Afraid of Rattlesnakes

Mary Lynn did not want to undergo the rites of nakedness. At first she acquiesced; on second thought, she realized everything within her was rebelling against it. An attractive woman in her late 30s, she had come to the School because she was in a "crisis of loneliness."

Mary Lynn's husband had died in an automobile accident five years before, leaving her with two children. The tragedy had stunned her to the core. A cheerleader just out of high school, she fell in love and married him. He was two years older, an engineering student at a state college. It was a happy marriage, "an improbable romance." The family, living in a suburb of Los Angeles, was close-knit. And then one night on his way home from work, he was rear-ended in the fog. The fairy tale was shattered forever.

The little girl of her was angry at her husband for dying, and she grieved fiercely and endlessly for him. After a long period of paralysis, during which time her mother kept the children, she found work at a posh restaurant, waiting on tables. She made enough money for her family to get by, but ran a gauntlet of propositions from "contemptible men" every day. Since her husband had died, she said, she had not dated a man. She had no desire to. Yet she was lonely, so lonely she almost didn't care about living.

The morning her day of nakedness was to begin, she glared at us so hard she could have knocked us over. "Do I have to do this?" she demanded. We told her she didn't have to do anything she didn't want to do. She stalked off saying she wasn't going to do it. But when the time came and she was alone, she did it.

The day was hot. Several members of the group went down into the thick willows and birches along a wild stretch of the creek, hiding themselves in green watery dens of naked solitude. Others, Mary Lynn included, went up into the jumbled hills and ridges of granite, where the sun beat hotter and the only shade to be found was on the north side of boulders. Ever so slowly, the sun inched across the blazing blue. In the coolness of evening, they returned, looking none the worse for wear.

A few, Mary Lynn included, joked about sunburn in private places. There was a marked change in her demeanor. The next morning in the elders' council she told the story.

Fully clothed, she had wandered about for an hour or so in abject fear of stepping on a rattlesnake, cursing us for talking her into it. Then it began to get hot. She found a reasonable hunk of shade and rested, drank some water, and poked into all the nearby holes with a long stick to see if snake was around. Finding that nothing was bothering her but the sun and the wind and a few flies, she stripped down to the buff and laved her skin with sunscreen.

She was startled at the whiteness of her body. At first it revolted her. Her body was ugly. She hadn't been taking care of it. An ant scuttled over the rock toward her leg. She was afraid it would sting her: "I felt like a piece of bait." She stood up and the blood rushed from her head. For a second she thought she heard the buzzing of a rattlesnake. She decided to move. She stuffed her clothes in her day pack, took her water and her snake stick and went looking for a better place.

The sun tingled her shoulders and breasts. The breeze tugged at her hair. As she walked, she began to feel stronger, meaner, not quite so helpless. She had her sun hat. She had her snake stick. She poked it here and there as she walked. Finally she came to a semi-circle of shaded boulders in the midst of which squatted a large flat rock, like an altar. A perfect place to spread out her mat and give herself to the sun.

As she reclined, letting the sun lick her flesh, she realized she couldn't let go. She couldn't give herself to the sensual sensations of her body. Something in her was "uptight." The thought made her angry. Only too well she knew what it was. Her man had been a jealous, passionate lover. She had stayed away from other men because she loved him and would do anything to please him. When he had died, she shut her sexual needs into a little box and hid it in the attic.

Later that afternoon, she had dozed off into dream in which she was entangled in writhing snakes. She awoke with a start and found herself looking at her belly and pubic hair. Overwhelmed with feelings of vulnerability, she jumped into her pants, only to feel guilty about breaking the clothing taboo. After a while, she got naked again. She wondered vaguely if she could masturbate to any fantasy other than one involving her dead husband. The thought was disturbing but intriguing. She decided it was actually possible. She let herself imagine another lover.

Mary Lynn had to go into the shadows of fear, anger, vulnerability, and self-disgust in order to discover that her husband was truly gone. Her fear and subsequent dream of snakes was linked to the little girl's initiatory fear of being intimate with another lover. What she found in the self-consciousness of nakedness were two elixirs that could revitalize her life: eros and self-acceptance. The elixirs were not found in great quantities. But they were there.

Two years later, Mary Lynn finally let go of her loneliness and fell in love with a man 15 years her senior. He too was a passionate lover, and he was not jealous of her former husband. The decision to marry him, she said, was "a sober decision, from the head as well as the heart." Besides, he was a good stepfather to her children.

THE RITES OF KARMA: The Great Ballcourt

You ask yourself, "Why do I keep avoiding the consequences of my deeds?" You spend an inordinate amount of time thinking up things to do just to keep from remembering. It may be that you have been punishing your body unconsciously because you blame its behavior. Maybe you're letting your body waste away because you are too busy feeding your little projects. You cry "Joy! Joy!" and stay away from those who block your access to the light. But memories are beginning to plague you unmercifully. You know you should turn and face them, but you hold back.

Finally you obey inner promptings and undertake a passage rite in the desert wilderness.[8] For four days and nights you live alone without food or adequate shelter. You do, however, take along a special item of equipment — a ball.[9] And whenever, wherever you go, the ball goes with you — not tucked under your arm, but on the ground, propelled by your foot. You cannot pick it up. You must not touch it with your hands.

You can, however, move the ball with any other part of your body, including mouth and nose, if that's of any help. For four days and nights you live with that damned ball, and with all the crazy places it chooses to go. You cheer it, you curse it, you wish it would disappear. No matter how carefully you aim, the slope, the declivity, the rocks, the vegetation, the wind — the vagaries of your foot — all conspire to bedevil you. You are forced to live with the karma (consequences) of your ability to kick that ball. You are forced to confront your shadow. And shadow accumulates shadow. Before the four days are over, you are, like an ancient Mayan hero, shadow dancing on the great ballcourt of the underworld with the consequences of your deeds.

At both gates of the threshold you will dedicate your ball to your worthy opponents, the lords and ladies of karma who author and control your destiny.[10]

Coyote on the Great Ballcourt

There was a 51 year old man who conducted people through the mazes of wilderness initiations. He worked with a partner, his wife. Together, they spent a good deal of time in the bright light of illumination. You might even say that they got pretty sunburned at times. Soul-sick people came to them with life questions that could only be answered with fasting, prayer, loneliness, faith, and imagination. Only too well they knew the dangers of staying too long in the shield of illumination. The longer they lived in eternal spring, the blinder they became to the reality of their own shadows.

Every February the man and his wife went into the desert to fast and pray for those who would come to them throughout the spring, summer and fall. The time had come again for them to dance with the shadows of memory.

All winter he had been working on a book that probed the limits of his imagination. He was bone tired of reaching for the illumined phrase, the poetic metaphor, the transcendent wisdom. He wanted to leave the realms of the empreyan behind. He wanted to get back into his body and remember once again that he was mortal, helpless, and nothing but a lost soul like everyone else.

His wife agreed. This year's schedule promised to be gruelling. Again and again they would be called on to listen patiently, empathetically, and to respond with inspired understanding. It was time to formally confirm their readiness to get on with the work by taking the passage that leads away from the light.

They decided to play for stakes of life and death on the Great Ballcourt. They would go wherever the bouncing ball led them. They would have nobody to blame but themselves for the events they set in motion. The lords and ladies of karma would be watching. If they played well enough, they would be given permission to continue for another year. Their heads would not join the others on the heap of skulls — at least not yet.

Marilyn Mountain, a close friend, helped them to clarify their intent and then drove them out early in the morning to the ballcourt site, an enormous stretch of desert pavement in the northeast sector of Termination Valley. With a heavy heart, the man kissed his wife goodbye, hoisted his gear, and walked out into the southwest flats. His wife went off in a northerly direction. They would not see each other for four days and nights.

The area into which he went was open and, except for the gullies, largely free of any brush higher than a couple feet. Cover was hard to find. After some looking, he found two dark boulders, varnished black by sun, wind and rain. Between them there was a narrow space just large enough to accommodate his sleeping bag. Home. He plunked his pack and water down and inspected the immediate area. He took out his ball and inspected it. A yellow nerf ball, about soccer size. Its synthetic makeup seemed out of place in this stark landscape. A sacred ball. The symbol of the consequences of his deeds. He rolled it around in his hands, as if to savor it. For the next four days he wouldn't touch it with his hands or fingers.

From his pack he extracted a small bundle of dried sage tied up with red string. He lit the tip of the sage with a match, let it burn for a minute, then waved the fire out. He rolled the ball around in the pungent smoke and asked for a blessing from the Lords and Ladies of Karma — not to win, because he knew he never could win — but to dance well. The smoke enveloped the ball, bathing it with the prayer. Then he tossed the ball to the ground. It bounced once, cleanly, came down on a protruding rock and bounded off at an angle. The slope, being slightly downhill, drew the ball further down toward a shallow gully 30 yards below. The ball picked up speed as the grade steepened, bounced off another rock and bounded down the gully until it disappeared from view.

"Oh shit," said our hero.

Thus his dance with karma began. Wherever the ball went, he went. Wherever he went, the ball went. The two were inseparable, though not necessarily companionable. The ball didn't always want to go the way the man wanted to go. And the man didn't always want to go where the ball wanted to go. They were at odds a good deal of the time. The success of any attempt to go anywhere always came down to one obvious cause — the kicker, "the one who kicked the ball." The psyche, mind and spirit of the foot that kicked the ball. The act of kicking. The relative angle of impact. The relative velocity of the foot-swing. The approach and the follow-through. The attitude and focus of the foot, its state of mind, its feelings, its awareness of spirit.

Equally important in this dance of cooperation of man and ball was the Great Ballcourt. The playing field, the desert pavement, and the conditions of weather and time. The surface, the slope, the gully, the cut bank, the obstacle, the bush, the cholla cactus, the wind, the fox hole — anything within reach of the sacred ball.

The man soon learned that he could exercise only the grossest kind of control over the antics of his ball. He could make it move. Once he had it moving he could nurse it into a general direction. That took a great deal of effort. And once he had it moving out in front of him, he had no power to make it stop. He could only mitigate its impact.

After the first day he had to sit down and take stock of the situation. He had three choices. First, he could continue to do what he had done today — that is, he could keep going to places where his ball wanted to go. Second, he could refuse to go anywhere, thereby ducking out on his promise to play well on the Great Ballcourt. Third, he could kick the ball somewhere, leave it, go off and do something without its constant presence, then come back give it another kick, go off, etc., etc. Although this would be a form of cheating, it would not constitute an outright cop-out.

He thought about his wife. Undoubtedly, she had run into the same problems. He imagined how she had dealt with them. Knowing her as he did, he figured she probably had a wonderful day. "I can't let this frustration get to me," he decided. In the morning he would look more closely at the problem.

He didn't want to be a quitter, or a cheater, but he had to admit that the easy way was always a part of his thoughts.

The second day was windy and cool. The man decided to take his ball on a long trip. Because he was beginning to feel weak, he would go slow. His actions would be deliberate. He would concentrate on the terrain ahead, and avoid subtle traps. He did not want to repeat the mistakes of his first day. He had no stomach for pulling his ball out of tight spots with his teeth. As he wended his erratic way across the open desert he saw how necessary it would become to accept the consequences of his kick, to submit to the rules of the game, to enjoy playing for the sake of playing, to appreciate the outcome — and above all, to honor his ball.

But actually surrendering to his karma was another thing. The obstinate boy of him was all too readily angry and impatient. It was easy to blame the ball. "The ball went there. I didn't intend it to go there. It's the ball's fault." Savagely, he took out all his frustration on the ball.. It came down in a creosote bush. He spent ten minutes digging it out. At one point he realized his anger was draining him of vital energy. He lay down with his ball in a sandy hollow and took a nap.

The third day the wind blew cold and the sky turned milky white. It looked like a storm was coming in. His body felt cramped and chilled. His empty belly rumbled and groaned. He felt a vague fear in his gut and loneliness for his woman. He wondered how she was doing, if she was keeping warm, if she was still kicking her ball around. As the day warmed slightly, he decided to take his ball out to the dirt road a half mile to the east. He'd kick the ball up the road. It ought to be easier out there, where the rocky surface had been graded for cars to pass. And it was easier, until he hit an upward grade. The ball kept rolling back to him. He kicked hard, aiming for the top of the grade. He didn't make it. The ball rolled backwards at an angle and fell off the road into a tangle of spiny hopsage. As he moved to retrieve it, he realized how sick and tired he was of having to kick that ball around. On his way back to his camp, he came within an inch of picking the cursed thing up.

On the afternoon of the fourth day the cold wind died and it started to rain softly. He erected a small tarp over his pack and sleeping bag, roping the grommets to the boulders and nearby bushes. When he finished he was bone tired. He was glad that the last day had come. By tomorrow afternoon he would be warm and dry. A pang in his heart reminded him of his wife, He always missed her most when the weather was miserable. He knew she could take care of herself. But he worried about her anyway. She'd said something about forgetting her mittens. The rain was turning to sleet. He dived under his tarp and hunkered down in that limited space, listening to the frozen rain slap against the tarp with a sharp, lonely sound.

Suddenly, a voice, clear as crystal, spoke into his ear. "What about your ball?" The voice didn't startle him. He'd heard it before. He could see the ball from where he sat. The outside rind had been eaten away by three days of contact with the desert pavement. "A little bit of rain won't hurt it," he said. The voice answered clearly, without hesitation: "You haven't played on the Great Ballcourt today." He groaned loudly. "It's raining. It's cold. I've had it with that ball." "No you haven't," replied the voice. "It's time to take your ball for one last ride."

The man cursed and did nothing for a long while. Then, still muttering to himself, he started putting on his long underwear, his wool shirt and pants, his sweater, raincoat, cap, and mittens. Thus fortified, he stumbled into the open and numbly began to kick the ball. He didn't have any destination in mind. He just wanted to fulfill the vow he had made to the lords and ladies of karma. He had vowed not to play to win, but to play well.

As he moved around, he began to warm up. The sleet was hardly a bother. It fell softly with a faint tinkling sound. He ventured farther out on the pavement. And as he kicked the ball, images of those he loved came to his inner eye. His wife, his sons and daughters, his brother and sisters, his mother and father, his friends and colleagues. He began to dedicate each kick to one or another of them. Meredith — whack. Selene — whack. Christian — whack. Keenan — whack. Shelley — whack. Kevin — whack. Out across the desert he strode, kicking the ball for his loved ones. Sometimes the ball would veer off into a trap. Then he would go get it, his breath frosting the air. He would say, "This next one is for Christian and it's going to be perfect." Then he would kick. Sometimes the ball rolled clear of any entanglements. Wherever it went, he followed with a strange kind of joy.

During the night, the sleet turned to snow. It fell softly for hours. When he awoke to the first light, everything was white — the mountains, the alluvial fans, the ridges, the arroyos, the pavement, the bushes, the cacti — everything. Shaggy, sleepy-eyed, and sore, he stared in wonder. Brr! It was cold. He was going to have to pack everything up and go to meet his wife. Marilyn would be waiting by the truck to take them home.

He started to get up, then stopped. A dog was sitting beside the entrance. A dog? What would a dog be doing out here? Big pointed ears. Sharp muzzle. Bushy tail. No, it couldn't be. Yes, it was! A coyote! An honest to God coyote. How long had it been sitting there?

"Be casual about this," he thought. Moving slowly, he stuck his head out from under the tarp. Panting softly, tongue lolling, the coyote watched him, apparently surprised to see this face appear at the door. For an eternal moment, the two stared at each other in speechless wonder. What should I say? the man thought. He groped for a word. "Good morning," he stammered. "Would you like a cup of coffee?" The coyote cocked his head, stared back scornfully. Coffee? Come on, get serious. How about ham and eggs? "Sorry old boy," the man replied. "I don't have anything to eat. I'm as hungry as you are. How about a ball instead?"

He nudged the ball out into the open. The coyote jumped back, as if to flee, then, seized by curiosity, went over to investigate. It lay there, a worn, yellow thing, in the snow. He sniffed at it, turned back to look at the man. Then, for whatever reason, he pawed at it. The ball rolled a few inches. He pawed it again. The ball rolled a little further. He nudged it with his nose, kicked it with his paw. It rolled over the edge of the gully and began to gain speed on the downslope, skipping through the dry snow. His magnificent tail waving high with glee, coyote dashed off after it. He met up with it down the gully in a shower of mud and snow. The two wrestled for a minute. The ball slipped free, then bounded further down the gully and out of sight, coyote hot on its tail.

For a moment, the man couldn't believe what he had just seen. His ball was gone. Coyote had it. He wondered what the Lords and Ladies of Karma would think of that. As he packed up his gear he thanked them for granting him another year to dance on the Great Ballcourt. Soon, he would see the love of his life. The dance would begin again.

But wouldn't you know it. Coyote had his ball.

ENDNOTES: SPRING TO FALL: THE RITES OF SUMMER

[1] On rare occasions, people have been known to escape into a bodiless world of spirit, splitting off from the intolerable reality of their situation like Gothic saints roasting in the *auto da fe*. Obviously, among people with such tendencies, experiences such as the vision fast are not beneficial. Hide-bound "saints," super-aesthetes and "starry-eyed flakes," because they ignore the fire they may be roasting in, are a real and present danger in the field and must be danced with in another way.

[2] The aim is to intensify the body's craving for food — and then finally to feed it. Of course, the initiand lives in a place accessible to daily checks on his/her safety and well-being.

[3] The rites of summer are indicated for individuals in danger of "losing touch with reality." This tendency can be caused by a multitude of factors — addiction, traumatic memories in the fall shield, dissociation from work and other winter shield responsibilities/duties, or an over-zealously followed spiritual or artistic discipline. There is always a possibility that such individuals are already incapable of living in wild nature for five days and nights without injury to themselves. In the field, these people can be monitored daily.

A few days are hardly sufficient for a lifetime. An exaggerated eastern shield can quickly rob its opposite western shield of memory and the moth can again be drawn to the flame. It is important for those who tend to get stuck in the spirit shield to annually undertake the rites of summer. Over a period of years, spring persona imbalances cease to exist. More "earthy" attributes appear in the self — and the psychological complex, formerly ignored, starved, or manipulated by the spirit shield, grows into depth of character.

[4] Claire went home to her parents and her last year of high school. She became more openly hostile — and slowly began to gain weight. It took a long time. She did get away from home. She went off to college, where she met and fell in love with a young man her own age. At that point, she began to eat regularly, though she continued to refer to herself as "fat."

When she was able to access the feelings in her dark shield — the vast ocean of the psyche — she was finally enabled to jump in. Here in the deeps where soul is formed, she became aware of her plight. The road back to health led past the front porch of her childhood home.

[5] Rites of primal emotion enacted in the wild are an effective means of bringing physicality and feeling to a shield system bent on getting and staying high.

At the School, these rites take various forms. Usually, they are geared to the needs of individuals (not groups), and are conducted only when the person agrees to undertake the regimen. Certain wilderness areas contain suitable risks to physical safety. These risks are usually more perceived than actual, such as the presence of mountain lions or rattlesnakes; exposure to certain climatic conditions, such as excessive heat (Death Valley), high altitude cold (the High Sierra), or precarious hiking (log river crossings, canyon and peak climbs, night walks on uneven terrain, etc). All exercises are framed within the four part dynamic of passage rites — severance, threshold, incorporation, illumination.

Once the person is able to "get into the body," the shadows of the psyche appear. When verbalized, these shadows take an active role in the therapeutic process. The elders' council reflects how the memories and secrets of the dark shield can be a source of personal power.

[6] In the primitive terminology of the four shields, there must be a balance and a tension between self-indulgence, introspection, self-control, and spiritual expression. The rites of sensuality are but a passage for the spirit to the inward realms of fall. Likewise, Eros the immortal must pass through the body of the physical world in order to reach Psyche who lies as if dead on the gloomy steps of Hades. The darkness, the memories, the feelings, the motivations must be evoked, revived, enlivened, if true balance (between east and west, soul and spirit) is to be achieved. Rites of sensuality in the wilderness evoke not only the body, but the shadow. The shadow is nourished. Balance returns to the system.

[7] Needless to say, being naked in nature does not mean being heedless of the dangers. The student is conducted to a safe wild place where other humans are not likely to be encountered. Boots are required for walking and moving about and clothes are in a day pack. In most places the actual possibility of encountering a rattlesnake is remote. The fear is largely primal, and firmly imbedded in the summer shield.

[8] Flat, open desert playas, sandy flats, fanglomerate, and No. 2 desert pavement are indicated. Regions with cryptobiotic soil are not indicated.

[9] The only kind of ball that has proven to be satisfactory is a soccer sized nerf ball. The others are too easily punctured, too heavy, too light, or of awkward size. After four days of kicking, even a nerf ball loses some hide.

[10] This initiatory exercise, fancifully named "The Great Ballcourt," serves a dual function: first, to convey the initiate from the east shield to the south; and

thence to the west shield. In a metaphysical sense, the athlete (body shield) who dances with her karma (psychological shield) on the great ballcourt of life is, in fact, also the spirit (spring shield) dancing the death-passage dance into the body (summer shield) as described in the Tibetan *Book of the Dead*. Always, the stakes are for life and death. At any time, karma can kill, or give birth. It all depends on how well the dancer kicks the ball.

The elders' council encourages the expression of feelings and memories that arose during the threshold time. Whatever came up is beneficial, is a gift of change and re-balance to the shield system as a whole.

THE YELLOW BRICK ROAD

> The gods you weep for will return as ghosts.
> The old order of ancient days shall reestablish itself.
> Earthquakes prophesy the revolution.
> Underneath the Arch of Constantine a swarthy sibyl slumbers.
> When she awakes the gate will crumble.
>
> — Gerard de Nerval, "Delfica"

> Bears in the back yard, lions in the park, beavers in the swimming pool — has Mother Nature gone wild?
>
> — T.V. News Anchor woman

After one of the most difficult winters anyone can remember around here, spring has just arrived with cold rain and thunder clouds. Three times the normal amount of snow fell. At velocities rarely recorded, the arctic winds blew ceaselessly through the valley. White-outs obliterated the roads, causing car crashes and loss of life. Blown off course, light planes went down in the impassable mountains above us. Several people, including a couple of German tourists, died of hypothermia. One night, one of our cats died on the back porch. We found him the next morning, stiff as a stick of firewood.

Winter didn't forget to pay a visit to the gardens of health. Just after Christmas, the flu virus struck town, leaping from house to house with contagious speed. In hot little rooms closed off against the biting cold, the virus bred. It seemed to spare no one, grandmother, father, child. Nauseated, aching, feverish, shaking, sweltering, coughing, bed-ridden, the people suffered, some of them for weeks at a time. A few of them died. Most of them went to weary, overworked doctors, who prescribed the indicated antibiotic. Most of them got better, eventually. Flu vaccinations saved many of the elderly. If there had not been medical services, a much larger number of the inhabitants of our valley would have succumbed to the virus. Of course, the people suffered from more than the flu. Arthritis, rheumatism, chest colds, ear aches, respiratory ailments, heart attacks, falls, burns, carbon monoxide poisonings, automobile accidents, frostbite were also common.

A significant number of our neighbors suffered from the effects of Seasonal Affective Disorder (SAD). The absence of light was hard to bear. It paralyzed them, turned them into vegetables, forced them to wallow in their own puddles. They hardly got out during the day. At night, they lived by the illumination of artificial light and the TV screen. Some of them became depressed and suicidal. They tried to fill the long nights with diversions. But the diversions were boring. Always the same programs, news, videos, music on the radio, parties, people. Alcohol, the drug of preference, flowed freely, and, according to the local paper, was responsible for stabbings, shootings and car accidents.

I remember taking a walk one crisp night, looking up at the stars, realizing how vulnerable the people of our town were in the implacable grip of winter, especially the young children and the old people. The nearest doctor, a mere fifteen miles away, was unreachable if the highway were snowed in or washed out. What if the electricity, the phone service, and the medical helicopters from China Lake, 130 miles away, were suddenly rendered inoperable by extreme climatic conditions? What if, in the midst of the severest weather, hurricane force winds (also not impossible) ripped the roofs off our cozy little homes? What if a 7.2 earthquake, such as the one that hit our valley in 1872, were to occur in the fault underlying our town? And what if, at the same time, a deadly virus was jumping from body to body like a flea in a dog pound?

All at once I felt exposed, weak, irrelevant, a little boy lost in the streets of an incomprehensibly huge and indifferent universe of tomorrows. I wondered, what would I, could I, do in the face of extreme crisis? Not much more than any other bloke. Maybe less, considering my age. I turned and headed for the warm hearth of family and home. That night I crept into bed and held the warm torso of my wife against my breast. I thought, "Maybe if I go to sleep tomorrow will never come." Of course, I knew better. I just wanted to be a craven coward for a while.

Still, there are many of us, even in this little redneck town, who listen to what nature is telling us about the future. We seek to fabricate a life in which our fragmented identities are healed and our children are reared in hopeful and meaningful settings. To us, "prevention" is the only solution. We know that the cure begins with the recognition of who we are, a species of "self-thus" that seems bent on destroying itself. If we can begin to study, with all of our shields, the nature of which we are composed, we will begin to live according to the seasons of life. We will begin to bring our children through the fall passage so that they will survive the coming winter.

STANDING IN OUR TRUTH

Today a woman in our training program, a tall, intelligent, national park ranger, who mediates disputes between ecologists and ranchers, spoke up in a manner forbidden by her profession. She couldn't hold it in any longer. She took sides, bitterly deploring the ways in which people stubbornly continue to degrade the land. Then she began to cry quietly, heartbrokenly. After a while, she quieted. She said: "Maybe I shouldn't do this work anymore." We saw it happen in her shields. She went all the way around the wheel. The irrepressible little girl of summer couldn't hold her emotions in check. The inward adolescent of fall felt a keen empathy for the plight of the earth. The trained diplomat of winter could no longer stuff feelings and emotions into the bag marked "impartial." Winter thawed into spring. She saw where she stood on the issues she was attempting to mediate. And then, emotions distended the face of the little girl shield.

It might not have been appropriate at that moment to tell her that her shield system was healthy, but it was. All four shields were there, in tensioned wholeness — the emotion, the feeling, the thought, the illumination. Her response was entirely appropriate. First the child reacted, then the adolescent empathized, then the adult held it all under control — until it all broke down in the pulverizing light of realization.

Needless to say, there are many of us like this tall woman. Though battered and tired, we continue to stand in our wholeness. No one would ever accuse us of being perfect. The idea of "perfect," after all, is relative to the culture that defines it. But we are *basically* balanced, *basically* grounded and whole, *basically* in tune with the changing seasons of human life. Even now, many of us are attempting to weave our threads into the unfinished tapestry called "Our Ecological Future."

One fact is certain. Summer is over. The human race collectively stands on the brink of the fall passage of initiation. Adam and Eve are about to be expelled from the Garden of Eden.

A lady from the New Age once chided us for being so "pessimistic." "The human race will be fine," she said. "Love will prevail. Love is letting go of fear. The people will let go of their fear and learn to love." I deeply hope so. For if love is to prevail, it must begin by facing its fear. It must turn to face the darkness with trembling legs. It must grow up, become mature, adult. Only then will love save the children.

No matter how we twist and turn in the arms of Mother Earth, the threshing floor is dead ahead. We are compelled to enter the temple of the soul, where conscience, guilt, and complicity lie in wait to thrash the seed from the chaff. Some of us kick and scream and blame everybody else for rubbing our noses in our own mess. Still, we are inexorably dragged toward the threshing floor, without even the sense to recognize that we are, in fact, in an initiatory mode of existence, and that there are few elders at the other end of the passage waiting to receive us.

Our initiator is the earth, our only home, our body, soul, mind, and spirit. It is not the same earth our sacred ancestors knew, but one we ourselves have altered. Some alterations may not be permanent, especially if we disappear from the scene.[1] Some alterations, however, are significant enough to bring us to the brink of Fall. We will cross the threshold largely unprepared to face the conditions we will find there. The initiatory taboos of this liminal state will be three, the same basic three that have always marked the passage of humans through nature — hunger, exposure, and loneliness. Fear will be there too, and feelings of guilt and despair, and memories of the way it was. The ghosts of our ancestors will haunt our dreams. Lost in the darkness, many of us will feel powerless to act and victimized by our own impoverished visions.

Those of us who emerge from the darkness of initiation into the gray light of winter will not be paralyzed. We will be the ones who stand tall in our truth and take appropriate action to save the people. We will give our lives for the welfare of future generations. Those of us who languish and complain in the dark, the victims and the victimizers, the boys and girls who turned away from the passage — will become at-risk. They will not pass the test of the threshing floor. Big winds will blow many of them away. Yet many of us will survive. Enough to make a start.

It will go better for us if we spend more than a little time studying the old ways by which our kind managed to survive for so many thousands of years. But then we will have to manifest what we have learned within the context of modern culture. This will not be easy.[2] Changes bring stress. Inertia dies hard. Our childlike culture is deeply mired in notions of technological perfectibility.[3] This naive faith in tooling betrays the lack of confidence we feel in our own human nature, and amounts to an alarming devaluation of our sacred ancestors, the "savages" which we far too often thank God we are not.

Yet we *are* those savages. The current suit of clothes we happen to be wearing cannot hide who we are. We are summer continually growing into winter via the passage of fall. We are children continually growing into maturity via the passage of initiation. The savage rites of passage must return, not merely to our consciousness, but to our muscles, psyches, and imaginations. We must do what our ancestors the savages did. We must bring up our children in the ways of our nature, so that our kind will survive.

COMING OF AGE IN A SMALL TOWN

Some time ago, I tried to interest the educators of our valley in our youth program, a rite of passage that invited high school graduates to fast alone for three days and nights in the nearby wilderness in order to confirm their passage from high school into life as adults. The response was almost nil. Almost noone saw the appropriateness of offering the students something *real,* something that might prove their mettle as grownups, offering complete freedom to explore their abilities, gifts, and dreams, that would tug at their gut and pump their adrenalin and bring them face to face with the heart of wild nature.

Perhaps some of those youth educators did recognize the worth of such a program, but they simply could not be held liable for any kind of activity that starved the children. School officials could not be officially associated with such a scheme. What would the parents say?

Indeed, what would the parents say? Doubtless, some of them would be interested, intrigued. These would probably compose a minority. The majority would refuse to allow their children to participate in such a hare-brained risk. Never having had to face themselves alone and empty in the wild of nature, they wouldn't want their children to do it. To them the risk might seem no smaller than the other illegal rites of passage their children were using to attain adulthood. Drugs, drunken parties — and now this? Starving in the mountains for three days? Other parents would reject the idea outright because it would smack of paganism, environmentalism, or even cultism.

Here in the valley, where rural conservatism rules, the kids seem no different than their counterparts in the city. There might be differences in certain *preferred* rites of passage, legal or illegal, but styles of dress, lingo, rock stars, and partying are very much the same. Small gangs have formed even in our small town, pop. 1500. Kids seem to be kids, everywhere. When they reach puberty, they start looking for ways to initiate themselves. These ways often contain danger because rites of passage always contain at least a perceived risk. What they do is invariably asociated with what is considered "mature" or "forbidden" behavior: drinking alcohol, handling and shooting guns, driving powerful cars, having sex, experimenting with and sometimes becoming addicted to, drugs. If the adults do it, then it must be a way to maturity.

Peer pressure is equally strong. "Join me." "Find out what it is." "We'll be soul-mates in this." "Let's do something that will cause a powerful bond to exist between us, a secret laugh between you and me." "Let's know certain things our parents don't." "Let's do it together and find out who we are."

To an adolescent, the drive to individuate is the same drive that causes the tree to shed its leaves in the fall. This drive is a form of memory. It is as though it has been engraven in our genes. The child must pull away from the parents and go with the others his or her own age into the initiation grounds. The child must seek to find ways that make him/her fully adult and independent of childhood influences. The child must become a person in his or her own right. The time has come, as it comes in nature, to go inside, to prepare for the winter, to brush up close to death, to explore the limitless regions of the psyche.

In our valley, the parents want their children to grow up to be like them. They want them to acquire the same values, the same ethics, the same political outlook, the same outward behavior. They do not understand this crazy individuation concept. Yet they will tell stories until they are blue in the face about how it was for them when they were growing up, and how they had to do this or that to become their own man or woman. They might insist that they don't want their children to go through that.

This inability to recognize the value of the rites of passage into adulthood is innocent enough. Because their own passages through adolescence were not confirmed by a body of elders or by the community at large, they do not see the value of requiring it for their children. They love their children. They would never want anything bad to ever happen to them.

We'll keep trying. After all, we've only been living in this valley for 17 years. Gradually, the reality of what we do here will seep into the consciousness of our neighbors. Some will be outraged. Some will just put us down as harmless nuts or flakes. Some will think about what might be good for their children, and for themselves. Some may even decide to ask their kids if this might not be a bad thing to do when they graduate from high school. Three adolescents from our small town have already fasted for three days in the nearby mountains. Others are bound to follow.

THE YELLOW BRICK ROAD

In *Child of Fortune,* the brilliant science fiction novel by Norman Spinrad, an ideal future is envisioned for the human race.[4] After a series of devastating wars and the near-fatal despoilation of the environment, the "Arkies," a ragtag bunch of neo-hippies of trans-ethnic origins launched themselves toward the infinite stars. For centuries they existed in their dilapidated biospheres, wandering along infinite paths of space, called "yellow brick roads," seeding untold worlds with their offspring. The many cultures coalesced into a "consensus reality" in which war no longer existed and all languages merged into a universal "Lingo."

The discovery of the artifacts of an ancestral race that had migrated through the stars brought a startling revelation. Others had come this way untold centuries before. These legendary strangers called themselves "We Who Have Gone Before." Among their artifacts was found the secret of the "Jump Drive," a means of traversing empty distances between the stars in the blink of an eye.

Contact with "We Who Have Gone Before" initiated the Second Starfaring Age — and gave birth to a cultural conviction that all too many adolescents in all too many worlds had never passed through the "Chaos."

> They were born, they were acculturated, they were schooled, they took up their adult stations in life, passed through an ill-defined period of mid-life angst, resigned themselves to old age, and died, without ever walking the Yellow Brick Road, indeed without ever understanding what it was that they had missed in their lives.

And so the universal "Wander Year" was decreed for all adolescent children reaching the age of 18. Against the background of the Second Starfaring Age the wander year tale of the 18 year old heroine unfolds: "Once within our time, on a planet not so very far away. . . ."

The legend of Moussa, or the "Pied Piper of the Bloomenwald," is too marvelous to describe here. It follows the classical dynamic of a rite of passage — severance, threshold, and incorporation. Her threshold wanderings through the sensual venues of Edoku (Xanadu) and the beautiful but deadly Bloomenwald (labyrinth of initiation) acquaint her with the fullness of womanhood and her destiny. She emerges from the terrifying jungle as a woman ready to fulfill her personal mythos with visionary action.

The polemic of the novel is clear. When modern humanity discovers its ancient link to We Who Have Gone Before, the children will inherit their collective myth — the myth of the wander year, the pilgrimage of the four seasons — and a new history, a new evolution, will begin. Not I. Not *my* personal history. But ours. *Our* personal history, *our* myth, *our* destiny, realized, as it always must, through our children. We the children are our only hope. We are the future. The Pied Piper of the Bloomenwald sings for all of us:

'Follow . . . yellow . . . sun . . . road. . . children . . . .'

We cannot allow ourselves to be drawn into mindless sensuality. It is a trap. Turn away from it and enter the labyrinth leading to adulthood. Follow the Pied Piper and her ragtag band of children:

> 'Follow the sun, follow the yellow!'
> 'Children found!'
> 'Follow Yellow Brick Road!'

Follow the path of the sun. Follow the turning of the seasons. Follow the road of initiation. Escape a mindless death and be reborn as a woman or a man in the brightening dawn.

This is our myth. The myth for our children. The myth from "We Who Have Gone Before." This is our inheritance, our legacy — our salvation. We must not turn away from the gift. Our story must prevail, regardless of the cost. Thus far, the cost has been great. Because they have nowhere to go, no road to follow, no sacred grail to seek, the children are not growing up. They toy with the earth. They prey on their own species. They are out of balance. They cannot exercise control. They cannot love their people.

The cost may grow to immensity before the myth of the children prevails. But surely it must. There are those of us who *know*. We will launch ourselves into the Chaos, following the starways blazed by We Who Have Gone Before.

SPREADING THE WORD

We were not trying to avoid a filming. The right opportunity had simply never arisen. For years we had talked about how important a step it would be to reach a much wider audience with a message that would spark a revival of interest in the old ways of bringing up our young. We knew that if a rite of passage such as the vision fast were to be brought back into our culture, it would have a profound affect on the way we collectively handle those "difficult years" of adolescence. Not that we considered it to be *the* answer. But it was, without doubt, a piece of the answer.

When Kim Shelton of Two Shoe Productions (and a graduate of our training program) asked us if she could film a youth vision fast, we looked her in the eye. Did she really know what she was talking about? Yes, she thought she understood the difficulties, but she was ready to begin tackling them one by one, including funding. She had been through this process before. She had three award-winning documentary films under her belt already, and would probably make more. She wanted to know if we were willing to go ahead with the project. I looked at Meredith. She looked at me. It would be a rite of passage for us too.

We put it on the schedule for the summer of 1995. A 10 day vision fast for youth. Four days of intensive preparation, three days alone and fasting in the desert mountains, and three days of story-telling in the elders' council. Parents of the young candidates are invited to participate in the incorporation phase. (By the way, the entire rite of passage will be filmed. Don't come if you are not willing to face the camera.)

To be honest, we had our doubts. We had no idea how the presence of a camera and microphone might affect the re-enactment of this ancient rite, which, to our knowledge, had never been filmed before. We wondered if the kids would feel inhibited, self-conscious, or reticent to talk about those matters that were closest to their hearts. We wondered what our own reaction might be, and if the filming schedule would upset the tempo and the timing of the rite.

We initiated a series of soul-searching discussions with Kim, who remained optimistic. She had no plans to interfere with the unfolding of events. She merely meant to be there with a camera man and a sound man to record it all. "People get used to the camera," she said. "After the first day, nobody will notice." We weighed the possibility that the sacred rite might be profaned against the possibility that millions of kids might watch the vision fast on T.V. Kim took the stance of the artist. "Real profanation," she said, "would be if we filmed and edited it badly." In the end, we had to agree. After all, we had given our life to the proposition that someday a meaningful rite of passage such as this would be an ordinary part of teenagers' lives.

In the meantime, young people began sending us letters of intent. Jeff (17), a tennis player from a broken home in Colorado. Alden (17), linebacker on the Longmont high school football team. Chad (19), a Portuguese-American Indian street brawler from the suburbs of Denver. Christina (16), a troubled Filipino-American girl from a small town in Iowa. Skye (19), a snowboarding honors student from Oregon. Kaya (16), an adventure-loving junior in high school from Montreal. Sean (16), a mystical, dreaming, home schooled student from Northern California. Before we knew it, we were one over our limit of six participants per course. We tried to hold the line, but two more popped up and we couldn't ignore them. One was John (17), a hometown boy who approached me one night at a high school basketball game and said he wanted to go on a vision fast because he knew it would be good for him. The other was

Selene (17), the class valedictorian at Big Pine High School. We had to sign her up too. She was our daughter.

So we ended up with nine participants, six of whom were from broken homes. More than a handful. Fortunately, four trainees would be there to help us out: Pam, a therapist from Vermont who worked with young people; Sandra, a woman from New Zealand with credentials in the School of Hard Knocks, who wanted to work with abused adolescents; Flynn, a college teacher from Vermont who wanted to bring the vision fast into the curriculum; and Joya, a woman trained with the Bear Tribe, a friend of Christina's mother. In all, nine kids, four trainees, two teachers, three film people, and Win Phelps, a dear friend who leads people on vision fasts and directs programs on commercial television. Seventeen people in all.

Meredith and I like to work with small groups. Rarely are we comfortable with a crowd. We looked forward to the youth vision fast with a certain amount of dread. When Kim arrived with Tim, the camera man, and George, the sound man, two days early to check out our meeting place, we realized that their presence would not be as unobtrusive as we had thought. Our usual meeting place (a sunny glade beside the creek) would not be suitable for filming. It was too bright. The shadows would be too hard. The sound of the creek was too loud. We would have to meet further from the creek, in an area shaded by willows and birches. Unfortunately, the area they chose was quite small. How were we going to cram seventeen people plus camera and sound equipment into such a space?

Severance

The ceremony began a little late that first morning. Everybody was there but John, who hadn't showed despite his promise the day before that he would be at the meeting. The kids were already accustomed to the camera. It had been there to greet them when they arrived. It had followed them around as they set up their tents and ate dinner together that night. To our surprise, everybody fit into the new meeting place. It was a little tight, and we had to share it with thousands of lady bugs just emerging from hibernation in the grass on which we sat. As the meeting proceeded, the bugs crawled on our skin, hair, clothes, a legion of harbingers sent by the earth.

Everyone formally introduced themselves to the group and we got down to the business of outlining the day-by-day itinerary of the rite of passage. The camera watched like an independent head, its dark, glossy lens roving here and there, stopping at whoever was speaking, then restlessly moving on.

Not only did we quickly forget that it was there, but we learned not to see it even when it jumped up and stared us in the face.

That afternoon, we began the first of a series of interviews with the participants, including John, who had decided to rejoin the group. Each of these interviews went an hour and a half, and covered whatever the candidates wanted to talk about. We "tracked" them through the streets of their lives, going as deep as they wanted to go, sometimes gently probing to see if they were willing to go deeper. Usually, we tried to touch upon such topics as father, mother, school, friends, the neighborhood, self-image, dreams, fears, personal myths and values, love and sex, drugs, plans for the future, and whatever they might want to say goodbye to. Specifically, we concentrated on their intent. That is, what they were confirming by going out into the wilderness alone without food. We wanted their reason, their intent, to be crystal clear.

Thus began a series of "elders councils," the elders in this case being the teachers, the apprenticed teachers, and the old friend/consultant Win. The youngest was in her early thirties, the oldest 58. The elders sat with each candidate in turn; they listened and asked questions. One of their functions was to "screen" the kids in terms of their ability to survive the rigors of the solo fast. The elders were there not to judge, but to help them realize their intent.

From the beginning these councils were filled with the stuff of adolescent human nature: the rage of Christina at her father, the sadness of Jeff at the death of his older brother in an alcohol-related accident, the tears of Skye, weeping for no reason he could articulate, the quiet burning of Chad, who had been stabbed in the head at a party and by the skin of his teeth lived to tell the story, the pain of Selene, leaving parents and a narrow but comfortable small town and going off to college in New York, or the honesty of Sean, who confessed he had never cried, never "let go."

All the while, the camera and the wires and the pocket mikes were in attendance, unseen but for concerns about who sits where and who gets wired. Our fear of the filming apparatus proved groundless. Spontaneity flourished. The kids showed no fear about getting at their deepest feelings, and sometimes went a lot deeper than they thought they could go. In terms of the film, they became actors in their own drama. They explored their own "character" and "played" themselves with consummate skill.

During the morning meeting of the second day, we presented the "four shields," relating it to their bodies, psyches, minds, and spirits. They understood immediately what we were talking about. Alden, speaking for the others, identified the initiatory shield as the "dark days we've been going through. It helps to know," he said, "that there was a reason for all that kicking and struggling." In the afternoon, the elders prepared the kids to live alone safely without food with minimum impact on the environment. The meeting, which covered equipment needs and the entire range of environmental and psychological hazards, took nearly four hours. At the break, the kids jumped into the creek. Energy was high. The group was beginning to cohere. Through it all, the camera watched. Already the regimen was taking its toll on the camera and sound men. Tim's back was killing him. George was having a hard time sleeping.

The morning meeting of the third day involved a study of ancient pancultural symbols, ceremonies, and ways associated with the vision fast: the death lodge, the purpose circle, the power place, the calling song, interspecies communication, the rattle and the drum, the all-night vigil, the meaning of vision, and the effects of fasting. In the afternoon, the elders reconvened for another interview-screening session. More tears, more laughter, more pathos.

John was the last to be interviewed. He appeared restless, ill at ease, unsure of his place in the group. It looked as though he might be stoned on something, maybe speed. No doubt he was frightened of the prospect of fasting alone for three days and nights in the Inyo Mountains. He covered up his agitation with vows of commitment to the process. This would be his way of leaving childhood and his parents' divorce behind, he said, of getting ready to enter the Navy. In all, a gruelling interview. Some of the elders were concerned about his drug use. He admitted he took drugs, but said at the moment he was clean. We wondered if his somewhat manic behavior might not be related to his continual diet of candy bars and twinkies.

By the end of the third day, the kids had become a vital group. They journeyed to a nearby hot springs, sans camera or microphone, and soaked and talked until late into the night. Although this part of the therapeutic process was not captured on film, this sharing of feelings and experiences was of vital importance to each of them. They were one, united in common purpose by their commitment to the process.

The fourth morning everybody, including film crew, packed up for the journey to the vision fast area in the Inyo Mountains. This logistical challenge was further complicated by the absence of John, who had not arrived by the time the vehicles were packed and ready to go. We cooled our heels for a half hour, wondering what had happened to him. Just when we had written him off as a no-show, he appeared, protesting that he had been detained by a Navy recruiter.

The drive to the vision fast area took an hour, the last several miles accomplished by four wheel drive vehicles. The site was spectacular. In juniper-pinon pine forest at 8,000 feet, we looked west across the valley to the snow-streaked summits of the Sierra Nevada range, over 14,000 feet high. Today the kids would go out in pairs to find their fasting places, which were to be less than a mile from base camp. Each would stash two gallons of water at their place. On their way back, they would set up a stone pile where, each day of the fast, they would leave a note telling their buddy they were all right. Thunder clouds were building overhead. Rain seemed immanent. The mood suddenly quieted. For a long time, nobody said anything. Finally, Jeff and Alden shouldered their day packs and their water, and went out looking for their places. The others soon followed.

From the moment we arrived in base camp, Tim was active with the camera, watching faces, bodies, the approaching storm. George held the mike boom above our heads. With its wind protection fringes, it looked like a long handled mop. By now, the film people had been sucked into the drama. They had become as much a part of our group as we were of theirs. They had taken it upon themselves to play their own parts within the elder's circle. One of the finest moments had come when Jeff was talking about his inability to let go with girls because of the "armor" that protected him. The headless body behind the camera suddenly spoke: "Armor is nice. But you can't make love with armor on."

That last night of the preparation phase the entire company formally met around the fire. Tomorrow their fasting alone time would begin. The candidates were asked to tell the elders what to pray for them while they were alone. The darkness closed in. The faces glowed like specters as they spoke quietly, earnestly. We sang together for an hour with rattles, drums, and sticks, inventing words and melody as we went. Then it was time to go to bed. Although the storm had not materialized, clouds still threatened. Thunder rumbled in the distance. We had erected a large tarp to show the kids how it was done (they were allowed tarps but not tents). That night, all nine slept beneath the tarp.

Threshold

The morning dawned clear and hot. Packed and ready, the young people held hands with the elders, then one by one stepped into the threshold circle, where Meredith sent them off with the acrid-sweet blessing of sage incense. The camera and the mop were there, catching the expressions, the nuances of dress and conversation, the goodbyes, hugs, and tears. Then out across the sagebrush flats the questers went in pairs of buddies (and one triad), traversing the high ridges, disappearing into the shadow-folds of the pinon-juniper woodlands.

The elders and the camera crew breathed a great sigh of relief. They had earned a little R&R. But shortly after noon of that first day, our quiet routine was interrupted when first John and then Christina returned. This unexpected turn of events sent the film crew scrambling for their gear while we elders shifted back into compound low. We had known that it wouldn't be easy for Christina and John. We hadn't realized how quickly trouble would come. Christina was weeping copiously. How could she have known how painful some of her feelings would be? She was in a rage at her father. With her permission I played her father in a kind of psychodrama that, with the help of Pam and Joya, expressed these feelings in extremis. That night, she went to sleep exhausted, declaring she was still fasting, and that in the morning she would return to her fasting place.

John said he was done. He said he sat out there for a couple hours, tried to take a nap, then realized he "really had to come back." No, he wasn't scared. No, he wasn't lonely. No, he wasn't hungry. Even as he protested that he felt just fine about coming back, he looked like a recruit condemned to do latrine duty forever. His decision was accepted at face value by the elders, though they did their best to help John clarify exactly what was going on inside John. Finally he came clean. He was hungry; he missed his friends back in town.

The second morning of the threshold phase, Christina went out again. We then convened a short meeting with John and asked him if he would be willing to go back out, this time with food. He jumped at the suggestion. Yes, he would like to try again. By the time John headed out, Christina had returned. Her pack was lost. She'd put it down while she looked for a different place to sleep. She'd found the place, but now she couldn't find the pack. Win and I went out to look for it. Her pack was retrieved and she said goodbye to us for the third time.

That afternoon, the film crew went out looking for "the mirror of nature," i.e., the natural world in which the candidates were seeing themselves reflected. They found it everywhere, in the wind, in the shadows, in the lizards, the cactus flowers, the limbs of trees, the shapes of stones, the cipher of animal tracks in the sand. The camera, equipped with a magnificent zoom lens, roamed the ridges, identifying tiny patches of blue tarp a half mile distant. It zoomed in on the eastern crest of the Sierra Nevada, where Split and Birch Mountain and the Palisade glaciers beckoned like giant ice cream cones through heat waves rising from the meadow.

By evening, neither John nor Christina had returned. The trainees rested after a busy afternoon establishing the exact locations of fasting sites. The film crew climbed to a high promontory to capture a spectacular sunset. By the time they returned, it was dark. Poorwills called from the open meadows, and owls whispered softly in a spangled sky.

The third and final day brought the gnats, invisible bits of air that, according to local legend, "inject their victims with cobra venom." People had to cover up, or slaver on repellent. The morning was still and hot, the shrill of locusts echoing down the canyons. John reappeared just after breakfast. "I've come back to stay," he said. "Now, what's for breakfast?" We looked at him closely. What had come over him? Something had changed. What we were seeing was that, in his own eyes, he had finally done something significant. He had lived alone for one afternoon and one night. He had acted with great courage. He had succeeded at something that was important to him. He hugged everyone with gusto. He even swaggered a little. The sleek box with the glowing lights and the long-handled mop pressed in close to record it all.

Most of that last day the film crew was out in the field, poking into holes and crevasses. I drove back to town to bring up the parents of several of the kids, who were arriving that day. The plan was to get them to base camp, where they would stay the night and, in the morning, be there to greet the returning questers. I returned with the parents to the news that Chad had come in just before 6:00. I was surprised. Chad was strong and had certainly been keen on fasting. "Why did he come in?" I asked. "He just said he got what he came for. His time was up. He looks just fine." "What about Christina?" "She's still out there." "Did they catch Chad's return on film?" "Yes."

That night around the fire, the parents discussed their "children." There was pride in their voices — and an honoring. We suggested they acknowledge this shift in maturity by rewarding their son or daughter some new privilege or responsibility, some lasting token or symbol of their individuation, a visible sign of their severance from childhood. For the next three days, the parents would sit with the rest of us in the incorporation, or story-telling circle. They would have the opportunity to respond to their childrens' stories.

Out in the darkness the kids were calling to each other. It was their last night of fasting and aloneness. Their voices sounded strong.

Incorporation

They came in two by two, walking slowly, carefully, burdened by their dusty packs. Their eyes were bright and brimming with tears. Before anyone could touch them, they had to cross the border of the sacred world and stand again in the threshold circle. Meredith issued a challenge. Were they ready to live the maturity they had confirmed? One by one they stepped into the circle — and then into the hugs of fellow questers, parents, and elders. To anyone on the outside, it would have been a strange sight. On the back side of nowhere, 27 people milling about, embracing, laughing, clowning, in the midst of which could be seen a man with a great camera for a head and another man in a headset, holding aloft a black mop. Those of us in the crowd paid no heed to such incongruities. There was no film. All the questers had returned, and the sun was rising triumphantly in the eastern sky.

The group came back into itself like a quiet river pulled down through rapids. The simple break-fast was so brilliant with talk and good cheer that time seemed agitated, speeded up. In a nearby clearing we formed a large circle and each member of the group was given a chance to thank the earth for safely holding us. And then all too soon it was time to turn our backs on the mountains of vision and reenter the body of the world. The story telling council would convene the next morning. We packed up the vehicles and swept the area clean. In an hour we were at the river, four thousand feet below. We stopped there, for it was a natural incorporation boundary. All those who had fasted jumped into the slow current, to clean the dust of nostalgia from their pores, and to turn and face the body of the world which they had earned by virtue of their quest. The river was swollen with melting snow. Mosquitoes hung like bits of fluff above the flow. The sun shouted down with 100 degree heat. The kids whooped and hollered and paid the mosquitos no mind. Meanwhile, the camera man's helpless legs were attacked by a thousand needle pricks as he held steady, recording the flash and shout of movement and mood.

Returning to the campground, we set up again beside the roaring creek. Now the encampment included the tents of the parents and the children. Although the youngsters had been counselled to spend some time alone in solitude preparing their story for the councils of the following days, they could not bear to be apart. They socialized (high intensity) until it was evening and time for the traditional feast.

Six months later, as I review the videotape and audio transcript, I am most impressed by the three days of elders' councils when the candidates told their stories and the elders and parents responded.

No doubt, what we had here was a significant growth event in the lives of these adolescents, activated by their decision to test themselves in a wilderness rite of passage. What we also had was a model for what could happen in any neighborhood or community, in any city. The youth could be the kids living down the block and the "elders" could be aunts and uncles and significant others who saw them every day. The "elders" had witnessed and found meaning in this real-life drama of maturity and self-discovery. The community would prosper from the contributions brought back from the lonely vigil in the wilderness.

I could talk about John's story, and about his father's tears of insight as he heard John tell of his tentative success in living alone, without his dad. I could talk about Christina's courage, her dream of running free in the wind, and her mother's response, so pure and true the heart trembles. I could talk about Chad's vision of the shadow of death, or Jeff's conversations with his dead brother, or Alden's calling to be a leader, or Skye's sadness for his mother and father, who sat before him, separated by divorce, but united in their pride. I could talk about the elders' responses to Selene's tale of inner struggle and frustration, and the tearful blubberings of her mother and father, or I could talk about Sean's tale of the owl and the Ace of Wands and the medicine blanket given to him by his mother, a "medicine woman" in her own right. I could talk about the Kaya story, subtitled "What is Beauty," and the corresponding beauty of her mother and her little sister, who for the occasion, had decided to be a boy named Sam. I could talk about the painful ecstasy of letting go of children who are no longer children — or the dawning of maturity in the eyes of a home town boy.

Only Alden claimed to have experienced an "easy" fast: "I wasn't hungry, I wasn't thirsty, I was just so happy, just being, simply being." His friend Jeff, on the other hand, had thought seriously about coming in every day. Chad had been haunted by flashbacks to his near death experience. He came to terms with it when he realized his shadow was death. And since he couldn't do anything about his shadow, he just had to let death be. Christina had wept and screamed until she felt too exhausted to walk. Still, she made it to the stonepile to check on her buddy. At one point, Skye had wept uncontrollably because he felt so lonely. John had actually started to walk back to town, a distance of some 20 miles (as the crow flies), until he saw the folly of his actions. Kaya had encountered a rattlesnake just after she'd taken off her clothes. Selene had struggled all night with the pain of leaving a happy childhood. As the sun rose on the last morning, she vomited bile. Sean had endured a gigantic boredom only to come to the conclusion that "Nothing was going to happen unless I made it happen." His realization is the very essence of the meaning of "vision."

Although the camera did not accompany the young people on their wilderness ordeal, it was present throughout most of the rite. Over 50 hours of videotape and a thousand pages of audio transcription contain the priceless record. On the other hand, the film does not depict the great exhaustion of the crew as the rite came to a close on the last day with a ceremonial "coming out" sauna for young people, elders, parents and kids. It does not depict the painstaking manner in which Kim and her cohorts were able to create real and artificial "shade" for 28 people, especially at high noon. It does not show the professional agony of standing, or squatting, or scuttling back and forth, or the monotony of incoming and outgoing tapes and batteries. Tim claimed it was the hardest and most rewarding shoot he'd ever been on. George, his nerves tried to the limit, had broken through into emotional areas he hadn't felt since childhood. Kim was haggard, tired to the bone, but animated by intimations of success. She had accomplished what she had set out to do. She had made her dream a reality.

The film is unique in contemporary therapeutic circles, a sound example of applied "eco-therapy." The methods and the teachings are ancient, and the emotions and the feelings are for all time. In this incipient work, human and nature combine to make art. The relevance of a wilderness rite of passage will be known in the twenty-first century.[5]

The history of the School of Lost Borders points towards such a future. When many years ago we began the work, there were very few colleagues. Now there are so many we cannot keep track of them. In the early days we were "tree huggers," "pagans," and the like. Now we speak at conferences and universities and our training schedules fill a year ahead of time. A cultural revival of wilderness passage rites has occurred. The revival threatens to grow, for it is an integral part of a larger whole that is now being called "eco-psychology." As the movement grows, it will be stereotyped by the media. But the movement will persist, for at its core will be the authentic and irreplaceable initiatory experience. Ever-so-gradually, the subject will become respectable. Leaders will emerge, indeed, are already emerging from the deserts and the forests and the mountains of the world. People will go out on their land to be alone, to fast, to wait in the silence for confirmation. Shields will be healed.

The movement will not last, however, if it is not accepted and nourished by the people themselves. If it becomes just another mode of "therapy," it will develop into a vehicle for professionals and may never put down roots in the common soil of our culture. It must come rather from the desire of parents to initiate the children, and from the children to be initiated. It must spread from family to family, from house to house, from block to block, from neighborhood to neighborhood. It must be securely rooted in community, in the shared understanding that at life transitions and crises we must go alone and empty to the wilderness so that new life status may be confirmed and imbalances in the community righted. It must be nourished by the wisdom of visible elders (not invisible "seniors") who, by the rights of their own life experiences, hope to leave an inheritance for our children.

Am I dreaming? Ask the mountain lion who roams the streets of our little town late at night, when only the dogs are awake. Ask the black bear who ambles down the canyon along the creek, sampling campsite trash cans as he goes. Ask the raccoon climbing the fence of our neighbor's chicken yard. The TV anchorwoman is right. Nature is going wild. It has always been going wild. It is we who are becoming tamer — and tamer — and more frightened and helpless, until we, like the Bear in the famous children's story, swallow the lie that we are just a silly man who needs a shave and wears a fur coat.[6] There must be changes. The stress of these changes can no longer be avoided. The gaudy riot of summer is over. The chill of fall is in the air. Initiation time is at hand.

ENDNOTES: THE YELLOW BRICK ROAD

[1] "It's not the earth that's in jeopardy, it's the middle class Western lifestyle.... The earth will live on until the sun dies — it's just a question of whether we'll be a part of its future." Lynn Margulis, *Talking on the Water: Conversations About Nature and Creativity*, Ed. Jonathan White (San Francisco: Sierra Club, 1994). Philip Slater puts it in another way: "If humans are in fact incapable of transcending the ecological circuitry in which they are embedded, then the cause for gloom vanishes.... Nature still heals itself — humans are still embedded in their ecosystem, despite their grandiose fantasies, and subject to its processes...." *Earthwalk*, p. 162.

[2] "If it is true that modern people desire a new relationship with the natural world, one that is not condescending, manipulative, and purely utilitarian; and if the foundation upon which the relationship is to be built is as I suggest — a natural history growing largely out of science and the insights of native peoples — then a staggering task lies before us." Barry Lopez *Crossing Open Ground*, p. 202.

[3] "A utopia detached from these twin pillars — a sense of human nature and a sense of the precivilized past — becomes a nightmare." Stanley Diamond, *In Search of the Primitive*, p. 208.

[4] "A Historie of the Second Starfaring Age," (Bantam Books: New York, 1985).

[5] Bullfrog Films, P.O. Box 149, Oley, PA 19547, Fax (610) 370-1978, www.bullfrogfilms.com. A study guide written by Steven Foster accompanies the film.

[6] Frank Tashlin, *The Bear That Wasn't* (New York: E.P. Dutton and Co, 1946). The bear continues to accept the lie that he is not a bear until the first winter snow convinces him of his true nature.

APPENDIX

I. SHIELD IMPERSONATION

II. THE FOUR SHIELDS OF A WOMAN

III. THE FOUR SHIELDS OF A MAN

I
SHIELD IMPERSONATION

> Who has not sat,
> anxious, before the curtain of his heart?
> — Ranier Maria Rilke, *Duino Elegies,* IV

In the contemporary world, the human response to its own nature has been reinterpreted by the mass media. Daily, hourly, momently, the culture is exposed to a massive array of self-representations. Our ways of expressing ourselves are documented, scrutinized, rhapsodized, and satirized according to stock formulae. We see how the jaw is clenched in anger, the brow frowns in concentration, tears are choked off by a swallow, or the eyes averted in anticipation, fear, or uninvolvement. As these and a thousand other images have bombarded us, they have become the standards of expression, a subtle "Miss Manners" for the world of interrelationship. The culture is informed as to how happiness, guilt, and sorrow are "done" — their duration, expression, and appropriate intensity. We have come to a time when, if we do not "put on the proper act," we cannot always define ourselves as happy, guilty, or sorrowful. Too often our behavior is dictated by the media metaphors. We are losing the ability to differentiate between artifice and authenticity.[1]

This is a fine turn of affairs, considering that before the mass media existed, the only "entertainment" was enacted on the stage of nature. In those days, Miss Manners was formed by the relationship between human and nature, and the media was archaic human drama, otherwise known as the early or ancient "theater."

SEASON AS MASQUE

Any inquiry into the meaning of human drama begins long ago with the time of the year when the goddess or god died or descended into the underworld. Sometimes this happened in the fall, when it became obvious that the life force of summer was dwindling. Sometimes this happened in the spring, when it became apparent that the life force had been reborn. Whenever it happened, there was a communal ceremony or rite celebrating the passage of life from an antecedent to a subsequent state of nature. Naturally, the people themselves associated the passage of this life force through the earth with the miracles of rebirth, growth, change, and maturity. In fact, their own rites of initiation were based on this seasonal rhythm. It was quite impossible for them to escape the cyclical forces they saw everywhere around them, and in themselves.

And so theater was born. The growth, demise and reappearance of vegetation gave birth to deities who became actors in human tragedy. Likewise, the all-too-mortal behavior of these same deities gave birth to satire, and subsequently to comedy. All that was needed was a stage and people to impersonate the deities and/or supernaturals responsible for the rhythms and changes of the life changes they sensed in themselves. In the iconography of preclassical Greek masks, Napier finds three kinds: those that were used in conjunction with the worship of vegetation and fertility spirits, such as Dionysus, Artemis, or Demeter; those that were used to depict death, such as the Gorgon head; and those depicting nature spirits, such as satyrs and centaurs. All three categories represent the forces of wild nature as mirrored by human nature.[2]

The Dionysian rites of Hellenic Greece were divided into four phases: *agon* (contest), *pathos* (inner suffering), *threnos* (lamentation), and *anagnorisis* (resurrection). These correspond to the four seasons: agon (summer), pathos (fall), threnos (winter), and anagnorisis (spring). Tragic drama is incomplete without all four. In *agon,* the hero/heroine/deity is ensnared by his/her emotions, instincts, or erotic impulses. A conflict with an antagonist develops in the outer world which, as the season changes, is mirrored by the inner world. Summer gives way to *pathos,* to inner suffering, to the dark and unknown regions of the soul, to self-consciousness of the human condition. Lamentation, *threnos,* is the function of maturity, which is to give form, meaning, and purpose to the human condition through mature action, to comprehend the conflict of psyche and spirit, body and mind, to bury the dead, and to prepare to die. Death itself gives birth to *anagnorisis,* resurrection. Funereal forms are broken by the miraculous upthrusting of new life. The hero/ine's "fatal flaw" (mortality —*agon*), produces an inner awareness/suffering (*pathos*), which becomes a life lived, a decision made, an understanding (*threnos*), that leads inevitably again to resurrection (*anagnorisis*).[3]

Mask. French, *masque;* Spanish and Portuguese, *mascara;* Arabic, *maskhara;* German, Dutch, and Danish, *maske;* Swedish, *mask;* Serbian, *masca;* Russian, *maska.* Mask: "A disguise that transforms the wearer, hides or heightens his personality, or identifies him with the character of the mask. Costumes, gestures, and actions conform to this character, in order to produce a definite result."[4]

To the audience, the mask or character worn by the actor becomes a bigger than life but nontheless "real self." The people deeply empathize with the fortunes of the enacted character. The illusion of reality projected by the mask becomes reality. Willingly they suspend their disbelief; they experience *agon, pathos, threnos,* and *anagnorisis.* They cry and laugh, suffer and die with the protagonist. So deeply do they accept the "deception" that they are even capable of undergoing transformational catharsis.[5]

The actress, however, is merely "acting," hiding behind the mask of the role. Her "real self" is masked. To effectively play the character, she must project elements of her "real self" through the role-mask to the audience. She must dig into her own emotion, feeling, thought, and imagination and bring up the stuff of reality with which to suspend the audience's disbelief. Her mask, then, is a means through which her "real self" expresses itself in order to trick onlookers into believing the character is real, and that they *are* that character.

Many questions arise about the "real identity" of the self when the mask is put on. Those who have done so will usually attest to a feeling that the wearing of the mask is actually less concealing and more revealing of the self, more genuine than the normal "mask" the self presents to the everyday world. In this sense, what is ordinarily concealed is revealed through the mask. The "mask" behind the everyday mask emerges, expresses, and acts. One of the important functions of the mask, then, is to enable the hidden self behind it to more fully realize itself.

The seasonal masks of the self lurk behind our everyday masks. Again and again they emerge, express, personify, act. As we instinctively grow through the drama of the seasons, the child of the natural self dons the summer masks. The adolescent of the natural self dons the masks of fall. The adult of the natural self dons the winter masks. The regenerated self wears the masks of the spring. Indeed, there is nothing alive on this lifeboat earth that does not wear these masks and dance in this same masquerade.

What is the ultimate goal of this masquerade? Perhaps the most important reason why the natural self dons the four seasons/directions masks is because it seeks to fully grow into itself. In this it is no different than the sprout of grass, or any other life form. Surely, it is the function of all life to grow into the fullness of what it is, to complete and to fulfill the cycle. If the sprout of grass should, in its grassy self-thusness, live to become fully complete, how can we, from our own spiral of completeness, deny it that great destiny?

The sprout of grass will put on its summer mask. It will hardly be aware of who it is because it is forgetting who it was. But soon it will grow strong and green, turning inward toward the night and remembering who it is (fall) as it bears fruit, parents children, gets ready to die (winter) so that it can come forth in the spring. It will seek to grow into the completeness of its purpose. "Completeness" in human terms? Completeness in natural (self-thus) terms. In these terms, a blade of grass is no less Buddha-like than a two legged human —

and no more. What's reflected in the Buddha's mask? How human nature completes herself.

SEASON AS PERSONA

> Like an outstretched arm is my call. And its grasping
> upward open hand stays before you,
> open, as safeguard and warning,
> you unseizable one, wide open.
>
> — Rainer Maria Rilke, Duino Elegies, VII

Rilke's "call" would not be an inaccurate way to charactize the basic function of the healthy human psyche. The self must both express and defend itself, and at the same time give itself to growth: "grasping, onward, upward . . . wide open." The self must "enact" its nature — and survive, not only to live but to undergo successive initiatory experiences by which it attains new levels of maturation. This enactment of its nature, this "grasping upward open hand," is what Dr. Jung called the "persona."

Persona. From the Latin *persona* , "a mask worn by a player, one who plays a part, a character or capacity in which one acts"[6] — or enacts. In the ancient festivals celebrating seasonal return and the death/birth of the gods and goddesses, the persona was a mask or costume employed to convey and amplify an actor's role to the audience. In the earliest dramatic festivals, the persona was often one of the four seasons or a seasonal/nature deity. Thus, with the concept of persona, we add the idea of "person" to the idea of "seasonal mask." We are proposing that four "persons" or personas are worn by any human player in "All the World's a Stage."

We are always impersonating our nature, for that is how we enact our nature. It's difficult to buy that "I'm always real" stuff. We're only as real as we are able to impersonate our selves.

Impersonation. From the Latin, *im* + *persona.* "To invest with a personality; assume the person of."[7] In a basic sense, person and impersonation are one and the same. And the better impersonations we become the better we survive as "persons," grow, and fulfill our destiny in the four acts comprising "All the World's a Stage." The more totally the actress *becomes* the part she plays — i.e., becomes aware of the person she enacts — the more complete the drama, the more transforming the tragedy, the richer the character. To impersonate, then, is to act: "*L. actus*: doing, playing a part, dramatic action . . . to perform."[8] The persona is the mask of the one who acts, the impersonator, the performer, the one who sets things in motion, the "carry outer" in the four seasons masquerade.

This impersonation business gets real interesting when, with the aid of physics and microbiology, we look behind the impersonation of the physical world (summer shield) to another impersonation, until we come up with more impersonations (masks, illusions) than you can shake a stick at. All such attempts to ascertain the "true nature of things" terminate in uncertainty. We wind up observing our own human nature observing nature. The heart of nature cannot be pierced with objectivity. Let those who lust after the "true nature of the physical world" join forces with those who lust after the psyche, mind, and spirit of the natural world. Then we will get somewhere.

Jung defined the "persona" as "the form of an individual's general psychic attitude toward the outside world."[9] His persona surrounds the ego, casting a kind of veil between the ego and the environment, and is composed of four "psychic functions": feeling, sensation, thought and intuition. These four aspects of the persona, similar to aspects of the four shields described in these pages, constitute "a compromise between individual and society as to what a man should appear to be."[10] The Jungian persona, then, was the form (mask, act, role) assumed by an individual's psychic compromise with the demands of the environment.

Four shield theory agrees with the use of the term persona, but differs from Jung in the word "compromise." Because the human natural self is of the same stuff as the environment, there is no compromise — only cooperation, the kind of cooperation that springs from all parts interacting to form a whole: "The outer and the inner are one, a unitary movement, not separate but whole." Ideally, there can only be cooperative expressions (impersonations) of the four aspects (seasons, directions, masks, faces, shields) of the One, which, like the ying-yang, or day and night, comprise the one whole called human-nature, the whole that seeks, by masking, by impersonation, by self-expression in the great cooperative drama, to fully complete itself.

Put yourself in the moccasins of your sacred primitive ancestors. Winter is coming. By sheer faith you hold to the hope that the season of chill will pass. The people of your little community share your faith. And now you all must do what winter has told you to do for untold millenia. You pick up your things and leave the heights of the mountains. Like the animals you hunt, you go down into the valley, or into a cave, a semi-permanent shelter, a protected declevity. Like migrating seeds, you burrow into the cold ground and wait for the warm winds to flow again. In the time of the big snows, you rest. You sit around the fire and tell the stories that keep the people together. You cooperate with the will of self-thus. You conserve your energy and resources, even as winter itself hoards and harbors.[13]

Expression. The pressing outward of the mask, the "act," the manifestation of the persona, the casting of the subjective self into the objective world, projection. Through expression we become aware, by giving our self to the environment. Expression — as in acting, as in drama or comedy; as a means of impersonating the environment (such as animal camouflage, display, posturing). Expression — as in the theater of nature, the masks, the clothing, the dance, what's being performed, the script, the "grasping, open, upward" game:

> O body swayed to music, O brightening glance,
> How can we know the dancer from the dance?
>
> — W.B. Yeats, "Among School Children"

There can be no "compromise" between persona and the outer world, between the dancer and the dance of nature, for there is no basic antagonism — only an illusion of separateness, only a psychic assent to a basic misconception that human and nature are not cut from the same cloth.

Even today, we can find ceremonies practiced among "primitive" peoples where humans and animals blend into the indivisible "self-thus" of human nature. When the shaman or medicine doctor dances as an animal, the animal dances as a shaman. Such shape-shifting does not spontaneously occur in modern humans who do not live close to nature. How are we caged ones to know the who, what, how, where of the animal we are? Still, there are clues — in the identification of self with an animal, in animal dreams and daydreams, and in walking reveries, especially when they occur in nature. Impersonation is a form of expression by our natural persona. Impersonation comes instinctively to us. It is the means by which we have always cooperated with nature.

SEASON AS SHIELD

> shield. "Old English, *sceld, scield.* Article of defensive armour; protection. [See also *heraldry, coat of arms, escutcheon.*]

Shield, as we define it, is worn like a persona or "persona-lity" by a player in the seasonal drama. Like the ancient ceremonial shields, on which were painted heraldic symbols of the bearer's medicine powers, the seasonal shields serve the natural self in four ways: 1. They protect the life of the human wearing them, concealing vulnerability by putting on the appropriate mask/shield. 2. Thus protected, the natural self is empowered to express the shield. 3. Defended and expressed, the self acquires power to survive, to grow in body, psyche, mind, and spirit, to turn in balance with the seasons of life. 4. The shield interacts with the community at large, and so benefits the players/audience in "All the World's a Stage."

Every shield wears a different design, or impersonation, and is an unique depiction of the self behind the shield. Although designs between shields can be strikingly similar, there are always subtle differences, for no two shield systems are alike, not even if they happen to belong to congenital twins. If I were to compare the summer shield of my wife with that of my own, I would find different symbols, insignia, or heraldry inscribed on hers than on mine. Yet her symbols and my symbols would be related — if only because they are both derived from childhood. The shield designs and the hands that painted them would be different. The canvas, the shield's composition and the paint would be the same. The child that I am would look different from the child that she is, but both of them would be children.

Let's go a little deeper here. How, in fact, would we even be able to see what is inscribed on our shields? Obviously, we don't carry around a painted shield inscribed with our own insignia for all the world to see. Ancient people often did, but it's hardly practical now. Nevertheless, the unique character of our shields is apparent — in behavior, emotion, feeling, thought, imagination. The heraldry is composed of the expressions, the "acts" and actions, the revelations of the natural self seeking to become fully aware of its life function by impersonating itself. In this case, the summer shield is a vehicle of self-protection. The natural self protects itself by impersonating the child. Look to the mask. Look to the impersonation. Look to the actor; look to the act. Look to the dancer's nature; look to the dance of nature. The sacred shield insignia are there.

THE MEDICINE SHIELD

> Then Sweet Medicine Came to the People. . . . And the First Shields were Built. People Began to Write their Names for Everyone to See. And he Put each Man's Medicine Upon that Man's Shield. The Truth of Each Man's Inner Being was Put Upon his Shield. And the People Began to Seek their Medicines. As they Sought their own Names, they also Found their Brothers and Sisters.
>
> — Hyemeyohsts Storm, *Seven Arrows*

A study of the "medicine shields" of American Indians and other "primitive" peoples reveals a profound understanding of how masking and the dramatic impersonation of human-nature served as vehicles of self-defense, personal health, and "medicine power." Fashioned of the stuff of the material world, imbued with powers won from initiatory experience, symbolized by the laws and forms of human interrelationships with nature, and infused with the immanence of spiritual power, the shields both defended the wearer and expressed the wearer's "medicine."

Let's take a look at the medicine shield worn by the legendary Odysseus, the one depicting the goddess Athene in the form of the grey eyed sea owl. To the modern scientific mind, it means little but superstition. To the mythologist, it is an ancient symbol of cooperation between human and nature. To the collective oral tradition that was Homer, the shield was a rich source of material with which to fashion life meaning.

The season is winter. Lightning, thunder and hail ravage the deep. The ship of the people founders. Who among them can insure survival? The children? The unitiated adolescents? Only the initiated ones who, like Captain Odysseus, have been to Hades and back, only those who have been cast adrift and found their way home. Only these are capable of enacting the daily work-dramas of subsistence.

Thus the people who insure the people's survival pay homage to the figure on the captain's shield: Athene, the grey-eyed patroness of species survival: goddess of wisdom, the arts, the sciences, agriculture, navigation, ship building, horse taming, pottery, the olive tree, arithmetic, architecture, democracy, the law, etc; Athene, man-born from the head of Zeus, the chaste goddess of mind, of intellect, of work, of craftsmanship, of intelligence and all it spawns; Athene, goddess of the winter shield, who appears among the people as Mentor, the elder.

Is it any wonder that the wiley Odysseus, the archetypal, initiated seafarer, would bear the shield of Athene, that he would honor her above all others, that he would call on her for help whenever he got into a jam? He couldn't always depend on the irrational child of himself. And the inward adolescent, the psyche and its tricky anima, were incapable of decisive action. To fully live the purpose of his life, he needed the goddess of male aldulthood. And so it happened that again and again the sensual, willful, angry boy who was Odysseus was rescued by the man who was Odysseus, the man whose intelligence and "wits" were symbolized by the goddess his shield impersonated.[14]

THE SEASONAL PERSONAS OF MODERN LIFE

Models of psychological health are based on the exigencies of living in contemporary culture/civilization. That is to say, modern psychotherapy is the study and treatment of caged humans, captivated in part by the modern productions of human time/space, who, like the poor bear in the story, *The Bear that Wasn't*, have been seduced into a life separate from their true home. We also must not forget that the modern psychotherapists who study humans are also caged.

To this captivity, add the absence of seasonal rites of passage, the destruction of intelligent culture by the media, the stresses of living, getting along with others, and working by the clock, the constant tugging of addiction, the terror of random violence, the slow deterioration of our right to seek solitude, the rapid disappearance of wilderness, and the sense of helplessness that creates more "security" and more isolation from our true home. Any caged psychotherapist, confronted by such a stew, could easily forget that, despite our captivity and the lie it perpetuates, we are still of nature. But it's true. The forgotten ancestors still live within us. We will continue to wear the shield- personas of the four seasons of life — even if the masks are a gross parody of the real thing.

The big difference between today and the good old days has to do with the fact that the conditions under which we live have changed. The demands on the circle of the natural self have altered our life expectancy, our perceptions, our awareness of time, our values, mores, and institutions. Modern human life is fragmented, disjointed, complex, and layered like an onion. Much or most of it is cluttered and in various stages of repair. We each have our own versions of the cage. Check it out. The cage is around us. Ask yourself how much of it is devoted to being at ease. How much of it is devoted to distraction? Meanwhile, the seasons pass. Winter is a flick of the thermostat. Spring is a perfect soufflé, fresh from the microwave. Summer is the hum of an air conditioner. Fall is Monday Night Football.

But the fact is, that as the seasons passed, we've had to deal with crises, accidents, changes, whether we wanted to or not. Again and again we were forced abruptly to face the truth. Nature loves change. Everything, everyone, and every state, passes. "All is vanity." Innocence must fall from the Garden of Eden. The job had to end. The lovers had to part. The wrinkles had to form. Death had to arrive out of nowhere. The shield-persona had to turn to meet the crisis. But alas! the shield that turned to meet the crisis was the wrong one. The self had become stuck in the persona-role of the innocent child of endless summer, or in the black hole of fall, or in the cold logic of the winter adult, or in the endless sunrise of spring, and could not dance gracefully with the crisis.

It's not easy for people living in the modern world to don the persona-shield appropriate to the circumstance. Because we are accustomed to functioning in more or less the same way regardless of season, and because we have abandoned the seasonal rites of passage, we have lost contact with what is already there — the steady, balanced, wheeling of the cycle drama of life. We experience physical, psychological, mental, and spiritual difficulties moving from childhood to adolescence to adulthood to rebirth from death. Often we have to be dragged screaming into our own sunsets because our eyes have become unaccustomed to darkness — or we turn our backs on our own dawnings because the light hurts our eyes.

Though the ancient seasonal drama has been distorted, obscured, and displaced, bit and pieces still remain. The modern self still puts on persona-shields — as if they were roles in some forgotten drama. Inappropriate as the masks may sometimes be, at least they are still there. Unfortunately, some no longer defend/express themselves with more than one shield-mask. Their seasons have ceased to come and go altogether. The day is always fall — or spring — or winter. In others, the self wears only two seasonal masks. In still others, three. Usually, you can find humans with four intact personas that have nevertheless been damaged, some slightly, some moderately, some badly. These latter somehow manage to maintain themselves, with a greater or lesser degree of balance, amid the conflicting tides of stress typical of modern living.

The ancient paradigm holds true. If we have been beguiled into living in cages, at least we have the power to unlatch them from the inside, to change the character of our roles in the life drama. We need but to walk outside to discover what time of day or season prevails. And there is nothing in our modern technology that is not from, and of, nature. Though it seems that we are but distantly linked to the natural sources of our survival, threads of DNA still bind us to our brothers and sisters, and to the ancient seasons. Like all the others, we come and we go. "We are all earthworms," Ann Sexton says, "digging into our own wrinkles." And the earth is our only home.

ENDNOTES: SHIELD IMPERSONATION

[1] Cf. Kenneth Gergen, *The Saturated Self: Dilemmas of Identity in Contemporary Life*.

[2] David Napier, *Masks, Transformation, and Paradox* (Berkeley: University of California Press, 1989), pp. 52-3.

[3] Echoes and reflections of this form can be found in traditional dramas from traditions as diverse as the Zuni *shakalo*, the Thracian carnival, the Rumanian *calusar*, the Iroquois False Face seasonal dances, the Portugese *mouriscadas*, and the English May Day dances, all of which celebrate seasonal return. The players or dancers often wear masks that impersonate deities, spirits, demons, seasons, vegetation, and animals who guard the passage from one life season to the next. The impersonators earn the right to impersonate — to wear the mask — by virtue of their dedication to the rites of seasonal return.

[4] *Standard Dictionary of Folklore, Mythology, and Legend*, Maria Leach, Ed. (San Francisco: Harper and Row, 1972).

[5] Cf. Aristotle's *Poetics*.

[6] *Oxford Dictionary of English Etymology*.

[7] *Ibid.*

[8] *Ibid.*

[9] Jolande Jacobi, *The Psychology of C.G. Jung* (New Haven: Yale University Press, 1973), p. 27.

[10] C.G. Jung, *Theory of Types*, Vol. 6 (Bollingen Series, Princeton University Press, 1971), par. 801.

[11] J. Krishnamurti, *Krishnamurti Himself: His Last Journal* (San Francisco: Harper and Row, 1987), p. 130.

[12] Four shields theory also differs from Jung by conjecturing not one but four personas that blend into each other as the earth blends around the sun. Each persona wears the seasonal mask appropriate to itself. Each mask projects and sheilds the natural self with expression. Nor does the ego inform all four psychic functions from the center of the persona, as in Jung's metaphor. In shield theory, the ego is a part of the summer complex and is found, even as the

child is found, in all phases of human development, including, of course, the other three personas as well. The self-thus that is at the center of the four shields circle cannot be identified with the ego. It is the still point at the center of the turning world, a concrete abstraction if you will, an energy with an awareness of life, that turns always at the center of the shielding that is the fourfold expression of itself.

[13] When did it occur to us that we didn't have to migrate, that we didn't have to cooperate? Where did we get the idea that we could work out a "compromise" with nature? Did the cows and horses we gradually domesticated tell us this? Did our bulging sacks of potatoes tell us this? When autumn frosted the air, we didn't exactly do what the wind said. We compromised our original pact with nature. We stayed right where we were. Of course, there were certain disadvantages to staying put. We had to work up a whole series of new technologies to deal with problems caused by not obeying the will of self-thus. Our values changed too. Things and domesticated animals took on increasing value, as survival insurance, as status. We began to birth larger families. The communities grew in size. We protected ourselves with the fear of knowing that we had compromised with our environment and our nature. We began to forget the old migratory path of the seasons.

[14] This same goddess became the teacher of Telemachus, son of Odysseus, in the guise of Mentor, old and trusted friend, man of wisdom and maturity (winter shield).

II
THE FOUR SHIELDS OF A WOMAN

> The good news is that we can make the necessary corrections and return to our own natural cycles again. It is through the love for and the caring for our natural seasons that we protect our lives from being dragged into someone else's rhythm, someone else's dance, someone else's hunger. It is through validation of our distinct cycles for sex, creation, rest, play, and work that we relearn to define and discriminate between all our wild senses and seasons.
>
> — Clarissa Pinkola Estes, *Women Who Run With the Wolves*

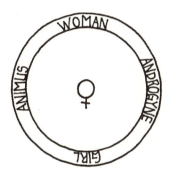

In the sacred teachings of the Northern Cheyenne, there are but two commandments: "All things are born from the woman" and "Nothing shall harm the children." The two are related. If the children are harmed, the women who give birth to them are harmed, for the children and the women are of one body. The Cheyenne were not just talking about human children and human women. Their two commandments refer to all things, to the whole that is Grandmother Gaia herself. She gives birth to it all. She is the Mother of human nature. And nothing must be allowed to harm her children in all of their manifestations: physical, psychological, mental, or spiritual. That is the truth of the matter, and that truth defines humankind's awful predicament. The children are being harmed.

When nature, human or otherwise, is tampered with, the entire living web of things is disturbed. Grandmother Spider senses each quiver or quake in the web. She knows if anything is harming her children. Any harm to her web is harm to herself.

Considerable injury has been done to the four shields of the modern woman by a patriarchal culture alienated from nature. Nevertheless, the basic vitality of her shields persists into modern times. It is still possible to find women with healthy shield systems — "healthy," though often battered by self-initiations and weakened by the illusion of separateness from nature. It is still possible to find women whose deepest knowing — that the web has been disturbed, that the children have been harmed — constantly informs their being.

If basically whole, the woman has at any given time all four faces, or personas. She has the body, senses, instincts, primal emotions, erotic urges of summer's little girl. Psychologically, she is the self-conscious, feeling, individuating, animus-shadowed adolescent of the fall. As a mature adult, she is the full woman, the rational professional, the competent volunteer, the nurturing mother, the concerned matron, the grandmother, the wise teacher, and the white-crowned elder of winter. Spiritually, she is enlightened, creative, intuitive, and wild as the winds, the goddess who happens to be a woman, and she wears the regenerative shield of the spring.

SUMMER

> . . . . there is no end,
> believe me! to the inventions of summer,
> to the happiness your body
> is willing to bear.
>
> — Mary Oliver, "Roses"

The sheer physicality of the woman, her genetic makeup, her bones, organs, nerves, brain, muscles, flesh, the totality of her bodily capabilities and existence, her physical environment, her feminine instincts, her senses, her genetic susceptibilities, her physical illnesses, her reactive emotions, her unique sensual chemistry. The innocent, trusting one, the little mouse, the one who doesn't look ahead to see where she is going because she is so absorbed in what's under her nose.

She is organically related to the physical forces of nature. Her body is composed of fertile earth. Her placenta is of the sea. Her eggs come and go with the tides. Her vagina opens on a sacred black hole in space.

If the girl-in-the-woman is loved and parented apart from cultural-sexist distinctions, she will be able to be fully who she is, to live freely within her body, to express her emotions, and to stand with her senses wide open. She will be naturally uninhibited, sexually curious, and unconsciously sensual. She will enjoy getting dirty, singing, dancing, playing house or baseball or tag. Wild animals will be her special friends. When she is angry, jealous, or afraid, she will express herself, innocently, reactively. She will hug, kiss, and otherwise display affection, and will welcome the exchange. Though her dreams sometimes may be nightmares, "evil" will come but briefly to her consciousness, for she is cared for by her parents and believes in magic. She will be fond of games and play and laughter, seeking fun and entertainment wherever she can find it. Her face is flushed, her cheeks rosy; perspiration beads her forehead.

THE CONTEMPORARY SUMMER SHIELD

She may not be happy with or even want to live in her body. She may be unable to express her emotions, or she may express them inappropriately. Her natural defenses could be inoperative, or her senses under wraps. Many of the ways in which she expresses or obtains affection could be manipulative and self-serving. She could be afflicted with various disorders related to pain, fear, anxiety, malnutrition, with many a conditioned flinch in her neuromusculature.

She may not be ready to enter the dark inwardness of adolescence and turn away from psychic fears that invade her memory. The initiatory passage may not appeal to her.[1] She may hold on to various symbols and situations offering security, comfort, ego-gratification, and the like. She may languish and play the victim. Squabbles with peers for parental love and approval (never properly granted) may develop into jealous, self-defeating battles and intrigues with family, mates, or peers in the work place. Repressed anger may appear in the diatribes of the "bitch."

She may be swayed by feminine summer shield symbols in the culture that represent the desire to acquire material wealth and status, and emphasize outward display, youthful beauty, and a life of sensation. The beautiful young princess spends her entire life in the kingdom of summer. Her prince is virile and handsome. He whisks her away to a life of passionate luxury untouched by sorrow or toil. They give birth to little princes and princesses who grow up to be perfect too.[2]

Aphrodite rules the summer shield of a woman, assisted by Cybelle and a number of other love goddesses, none of whom were famous for their intellectual or professional qualities. Their immortality lay in the body of summer, in the beauty of the flesh and the lust of the senses. Fidelity, morality, commitment was unknown to them. Drawn eternally to the source of attraction, they were little girls inhabiting luscious bodies that never wrinkled. In the mythical parlance of modern culture, Aphrodite has become the film actress, the entertainment diva, the model, the play girl, the porn actress, the high school cheerleader, the prostitute, the girl in the perfume ad. Not only does she stay perfect forever, but she exists to please men (or women), is always in the mood, and never has to deal with pregnancy, periods, or menopause.

Granted, this little girl is supposed to grow up. Sooner or later she will encounter the shadow in herself and others. On an innocent romp through the pastures of flesh she will fall and wake up at the bottom of a black hole. But will she emerge from the hole? And if she does, will she be the wiser? Will she recognize the black hole as her ally? Or will she be so frightened she'll never go near a black hole again?

She must find ways of initiating herself into womanhood. Her very survival depends on her ability to confront her own fears and gain strength from them. If she continues to depend on her parents to keep the jungle from entering her cozy childhood, she may forever remain the sweet American princess who never became a queen.

FALL

> I stepped from plank to plank
>   A slow and cautious way;
> The stars about my head I felt,
>   About my feet the sea.
>
> I knew not but the next
>   Would be my final inch, —
> This gave me that precarious gait
>   Some call experience.
>
> — Emily Dickinson, "I stepped from plank to plank"

    The little girl enters adolescence, a time of inwardness. It comes on almost overnight. One day the little girl is there. The next day the door to her room is shut tight. She has gone inside herself, like sap into a tree, and has begun to explore her inner self in preparation for her life as a mature woman. She has entered the fall shield, the transition state between child and adult, the twilight zone known among anthropologists as the "threshold" or "liminal" phase of human growth. At this point she will turn away from complete identification with her parents. With the aid of inner resources engendered in her childhood, she will begin to identify herself as a unique individual apart from her home-womb.

    If she is loved irrespective of cultural mores, she will be given the freedom to explore and come to terms with herself — to "find herself" as the saying goes. She will be allowed to experiment with how she is seen by others, spending considerable time in front of mirrors, trying on various social personas or roles to find that "personality" or character appropriate to her inner truth. She will seek those experiences that dare her to risk, to hazard herself, to test her own mettle, to make a real story of her life. She will identify with others involved in the same process. Social interaction with peers will be important to her, although much of the time she will feel on the "outside," different from her friends, a stranger even to herself. Reactive emotions and sensations she experienced as a little girl will become conscious feelings and sensibilities tucked away in a box marked "secret."

    She will explore the mansions of memory and soul. Her dream life will expand to encompass adult situations, cultural conflict, and the human condition. The consequences of her deeds will begin to haunt her, and she may wistfully remember the innocence and irresponsibility of her childhood.

Her sexuality will take on profoundly inner dimensions, the physical act becoming psychological, feelingful, "more than just lust." Love for self and others will stir in her heart, even as she realizes neither she nor her lover are perfect. Her romance with her animus (inner man) becomes evident. In her inwardness she will be profoundly aware of her father, and other men, watching her. Often she will look at herself, even define herself, through their eyes. If her father loves her and allows her to freely individuate, her animus will be basically healthy, helping her to accept, admire, and love the self she is seeking. If her orientation is gay, she will still have a strong relationship to her "inner man," which in a variety of ways will affect her behavior, particularly the ways in which she perceives and interacts with her lovers and men in general.

She will undergo experiences that develop soul, character, and inner conviction — though many of these "experiments" go against the grain of her upbringing. Some of them may render her extremely vulnerable, or bring her to the brink of despair. The consequences of her deeds will teach her how to pull herself up by her own bootstraps, how to alchemize darkness into light.[3]

She will explore her own psyche by entertaining ways of conferring maturity on the little girl. She will mark the end of the liminal period of adolescence by assuming the life station of an adult woman through rites of marriage, childbirth, motherhood, or profession. She will emerge from the threshold with self-acceptance and a unique individuality tested by the inner fires of personal experience, having honed the fundamental tools necessary to continue her inner quest through life. She will take her place beside her mother, beloved stranger and teacher. If all goes well, her father and other shadow men will live within her, a steady source of encouragement and approval.[4] The maturational processes of the psyche will have brought her to full womanhood.

THE CONTEMPORARY FALL SHIELD

The little girl may not want to grow up, or she may be inhibited, or stunted. She may become a mother before she is mature enough to be one. She may become a "misfit" who rejects or rebels against society or parental authority until she destroys herself. She may become the perennial victim — or the perennial avenger. She may become the anorexic unconsciously seeking a self-deserved suicide, or an uninitiated naif claiming to be a real woman.

She may become a martyr who barters spousal abuse for security. She may become a pampered, spoiled tart of the leisure class, or a desperate, undernourished little Nell of the ghetto. She may become a masculine amazon who eats men for lunch, or an over achieving superstar stifling suicidal ideations with popular success. She may become the "dutiful daughter" whose comfortable life leads to the brink of complete breakdown.

The trauma runs even deeper. Dissociation of the feminine from nature has done great harm to the psyche. Without nature-based rites of passage, little girls become mothers who cannot impart psychic oneness with nature to their children. Natural solitude, wildness (their own wildness), and aloneness are frightful rather than healing. The little girls are captured by the artifices of civilization, lulled into a sense of reality dangerous to the well being of the species and the planet. When they are unable to deeply, experientially connect with their wildness, they remain little lambs, ripe for predation.[5]

So-called initiatory experiences offered to a young woman by our culture to mark her attainment of womanhood are hardly sufficient. They neither prepare nor confirm her maturity. The onset of menses is rarely celebrated by anything more than a box of tampax. Loss of virginity is all too often an embarrassing secret never imparted to the mother or the women elders. Commencement from high school has little to do with the actual achievement of adulthood. Considering the parental-authoritarian manner in which most public high schools are run, rebellion against high school might be a surer means of exploring the richness of the initiatory shield. Yet high school, and all the social activities associated with it, are often the only culturally validated initiations available to most adolescent girls.

The shadowy thresholds of rock concerts, weekends away from home, parties while the parents are gone, and reckless experimentation with sex, drugs, automobiles, and weapons, convey the initiatory flavor, but almost invariably fail because there are no elders to validate the attainment of mature insight.[6] A girl cannot confirm another girl's attainment of womanhood. Sometimes these shadowy initiations, especially those that are blatantly illegal, scar and wound and traumatize to such an extent that the "initiated one" attains the new life station of outcast, outlaw, or felon. Other young women, however, learn from their experience, and acquire depth of soul thereby. But it always begins with adolescent fascination with the initiatory shadow. This fascination is an essential part of feminine development.

The adolescent-in-the-woman, the one-who-initiates-herself, never disappears from a woman's life. She exists in every woman at initiation time. She is the one undergoing a profound growth-event. If all goes well, she will learn from the experience and achieve a sense of new life status. Often, however, she will have a neurosis or two, or will be even more heavily wounded. She can be the undecided one, powerless to decide and act; the self-effacing one who has trouble liking herself; the hidden one who entertains ideations of suicide; the depressed one, the lonely one, the addicted one, the one who eats, sleeps, drinks, diets, or shops to fill her emptiness. She can be the stagnant, enervated one,[7] the rebellious daughter, the prisoner of abhorrent animus-memories, or the victim who blames others for her condition. And though she may wear such a face, she is not always powerless to help herself. Through the years she has found ways to psychically survive. These ways often wear the face of wariness, neediness, melancholy, or self-dislike.[8]

Inanna/Ishtar, Persephone, and other goddesses of the seasonal underworld descent rule the initiatory shield of the fall. Their seasonal male counterparts (Tammuz, Orpheus, Dionysus) symbolize the animus, "the god within the goddess" of the west. Inanna's overpowering desire for her "dark god" compels her to descend to the deepest levels of hell, and to undergo the death and dismemberment of initiation, in order to rescue him. This need to preserve and nurture the animus is psychically related to the preservation of feminine wholeness. The woman needs the man within as much as the man needs the woman within. One of the most fundamental goals of the initiatory process is to give the initiate access to the power of the animus.[9]

The animus is the key that unlocks the fully mature woman, gay or straight. As these dimensions of the animus blend and balance within her, the initiated woman finds harmony, purpose, and direction.[10]

Failure for one reason or another to engage with one or more faces of the animus can result in an incompletely realized life. Lord knows, there are plenty of reasons why men, particularly fathers, are to be feared, hated, reviled, avoided, repressed, ignored. The little girl-in-the-woman can suffer much at the hands of men who are themselves uninitiated little boys capable of the worst kinds of reactive violence. Nevertheless, development and integration of the inner man is essential to the adolescent's attainment of mature womanhood, regardless of sexual preference. The father must somehow be "redeemed."[11] This integration often begins with profound expressions of rage and grief against men, particularly the father. As her acceptance of the masculine within her grows, so increases her ability to accept herself, to play, to create, and to interact with loved ones in a wholistic, nurturing way.

Modern culture is not a particularly helpful place for a woman to go about fashioning a whole animus, thereby freeing herself to become fully mature. It helps if she can find examples of mature males. But if the woman herself is immature, she is not always likely to find a mature male who can help to heal her animus. And if she does find one — a rare commodity these days — she may not be able to appreciate what she has found. Large numbers of women spend a great deal of their lives turning away from the winter face of their animus (the husband-king-father), thus remaining stuck in the swamps of the fall shield.

WINTER

> Let us thank Almighty God
> For the woman with the rod.
> Who was ever and is now
> Strong, essential as the plow.
> She shall goad and she shall drive,
> So to keep man's soul alive.
> Amoris with her scented dress
> Beckons, in her wantonness;
> But the wife drives, nor can man tell
> What hands so urge, what powers compel.
>
> — Anna Wickham, "Creatrix"

The winter shield of the woman is her mind, her rational self, the way she governs her body, soul, and spirit, the way she orders her life, her considered actions, her sense of the appropriate, her value system (convictions), her understanding, her wisdom, her adult social status (motherhood, wifehood, matehood, professionhood, elderhood), her service to others, and her "abilities" to undertake projects of any kind and see them through to completion. The passage of thousands of centuries of winter have engendered such attributes within her. Without them, the people would never have survived.

Passage to the winter shield marks the little girl's attainment of maturity. The self-serving summer and the estranged fall have, by dint of initiation, come to the regions of the north. Winter winds howl in the trees. The women see to it that the children are not harmed, that the community remains balanced, harmonious, and purposeful. To that end, they conduct rites of passage for women at the transitions of life, to insure that their mothers, sisters, and daughters will always be free to fully realize their feminine potential within the circle of life. These rites will culturally define "what womanhood is" and so guide and direct feminine youth toward the full realization of their nature.

The winter shield of the woman manifests outwardly to her children, family, friends, and community. The self-love of the fall shield has matured into love for others. Above all, there is a concern for the children. This concern, if it extends to the environment, is vital to the health of all the people. In the winter shield, the woman takes her place beside her own mother, as a woman in her own right, unique, and free to live her life as she sees fit. She can see her mother as a fellow human being, with gifts and weaknesses, dreams and disappointments. By the natural right of initiation, the separation from her mother is complete and sanctioned by the community. The quality or worth of her unique "womanliness" or "femininity" is not questioned.[12]

Ideally, the woman of the winter shield manifests signs of maturity in every aspect of her life. She has become capable, responsible, self-contained, a harmonious blending of the girl and the adolescent. She plays many roles with grace and conviction: lover, partner, mother, professional, friend, diplomat, manager, teacher, counselor, healer, volunteer, adventurer, poet, warrior of peace, matron, midwife, witch, elder, crone — not to forget the little girl and the adolescent. She is capable of decisive action, when needed, and does not faint dead away in the face of crisis, as Southern belle-girls were wont to do. She is no stranger to hard work. She seeks to order chaos, to bring harmony, balance, and mutual accord.[13] The center of her purpose is anchored to her relationship with self-thus. "All things are born of woman." She is of the earth; she is the earth.

Ethically, the winter shield of a mature woman has depth. She is not a rigid or moralistic parrot, an innocent child obeying by rote, or a flat surface on which truth hits and glances off. If she is "the law" in household or community, her law contains emotion, feeling, and soul. Her judgments never lack compassion and her mind can be changed. She nurtures herself and her loved ones, not because it is correct to do so, but because she loves them, as she loves life, with that maternal love that keeps the children from harm.

As the woman grows older, she continues to be of great importance to her family and community. She continues to grow in psyche, mind and spirit through initiatory experiences (growth events) from which her child shield does not shrink. In this way she confirms the attainment of progressively more mature life stations. As she ages, her summer and fall shields, the girl and the adolescent, body and soul, remain fresh and active within the seasons of her days.

The mature woman does not discard sensuality, sexual passion, or the "withness" of the body. As the woman's beauty matures and changes with menopause, the little girl within her adapts to and cooperates with the alterations of time. The adolescent initiate of the fall shield continues to gather memories and dreams, to feed the soul's mortality with imaginings of eternity. She continues to court experiences through which she can become conscious of herself, sometimes by dancing with her ever-elusive animus. Her seasons pass, not in a linear fashion, but gyre-like, a circular rising, circling, always adding depth and volume. This series of initiatory steps (circling through summer, fall, winter) leads to new beginnings in the spring.

Having loved, nurtured, and given of herself to the inevitable ravages of time, the woman at midlife has attained a mature understanding of her life's purpose. She knows how to add body, soul and action to her vision. She is better able to serve the human community at-large, and the mothering earth. Her vision is confirmed by participation in rites and mysteries which bring her to the new life status of "elder."

Because elderhood itself is an initiatory process leading to a death (a birth) in the spring, the feminine mysteries are means of marking progress through the stages of menopause and aging toward the highest levels of crone-attainment. By virtue of her initiatory experiences, the woman takes her place among her sisters in an elderhood of midwives. Together, they become responsible for the yearly enactments of passage rites for the female children. As a respected teacher and counselor, the elder sits in attendance at communal celebrations of transition, exercising her acumen and compassion for the good of her people. She becomes a kind of mouthpiece for the collective wisdom of all those generations of women who have gone before. Even as her vision has grown outwardly, toward others and the earth, her character has deepened, widened, enriched itself through inner experience. She has acquired the kind of soul necessary to midwife initiates and the dying into their new worlds.

The elder will not allow herself to be "put out to pasture" until death looms and she turns her gaze to the eastern horizon. She will continue to represent and express the wisdom of all those who will not squander their children's inheritance. Even at an advanced age, she will continue to indulge her little girl shield, whenever appropriate, and to explore the initiatory darkness of her adolescent shield. Her death will be the fullest expression of her body, soul and mind. As death approaches, her presence will radiate the light of the spirit shield, which soon will take precedence over all. Her dying will be a blessing and a teaching to her family and community. Death will be her finest giveaway.

THE CONTEMPORARY WINTER SHIELD

Relatively few women in this modern world ever attain the fullness of the winter shield. Our society and the basic family unit have been badly damaged, not only by male domination, but by the illusion of separateness from nature. The shield systems of most women bear many a trauma scar never assimilated by healing passage rites. Significant numbers of little girls have taken short cuts to a poorly clarified "womanhood" for which they were never properly prepared, defining themselves as women when, in fact, they were badly initiated girls. Others turned back from the fall passage, having tested the water with their toe, finding it too cold, too hot, too uncomfortable. And when winter came, they preferred to think that it was still summer. Only after reaching middle age did life offer some of them unsolicited initiatory experiences that awakened the slumbering woman.

The woman's mind is made mature by the full participation of summer and fall, body and soul. When body and soul are injured or malnourished, the mind is affected. Many a woman bears the scars of traumas never examined, acknowledged, or assimilated. The scars are deeply imbedded in their fall shield, the place of feeling and memory. Many women feel crippled by these scars for an entire lifetime. They fail to recognize that the scars are, in fact, signs of the deepest mysteries of womanhood, gifts of power and healing. They turn away from the self-confirmation of maturity and wallow in the blackness of victimization and incapacity.

Still others are "scarless," having serenely sailed through adolescence as "Daddy's girl" or "Mama's clone." Perhaps they tested the dark waters of initiation with a toe, and retreated hastily into a safe world where it was not really necessary to individuate from mother and father. Although many refer to themselves as "women," they are unacquainted with the grief and depth of soul. Lacking in character and dimension, they are often devoid of empathetic interest in other ships outside their safe little harbor. Their intelligence lacks character; it rarely develops into wisdom. With the coming of fall, they exclaim over the changing colors of the leaves, but they continue to live as if it were summer. When winter howls down around their eaves, they lie under tanning lights and schedule another facial.

Some women don't even think they have a mind, convinced by male cultural conditioning that they are indeed little girls and should stay that way. Others know they possess great qualities of mind, but in many cases the inward adolescent dares not express it for fear of consequences. Still others express their mind *ad nauseam*, but it is the mind of an uninitiated girl. Many other symptoms of undernourishment of the mind, often directly attributable to male cultural domination, are seen in the isolation of women, in their loneliness in or out of relationships, in loss of solidarity with their sisters, in oppressive standards of feminine beauty exaggerated by the difficulties of aging, in the bi-level work force, in the need to balance work and domestic life in unequal marriages. Even when they are involved in personally fulfilling work, they often feel harried and isolated.[14]

The mind of the mature winter shield is in rapport with the natural order, where the great majority of female vertebrates live according to the dictum, "Nothing shall harm the children." The fact that the children are being harmed in great numbers, is testimony to the widening rift between the mind of woman (and man) and the mind of nature. Women are not fully taking possession of their ability to insure that the children and their earthly inheritance are secure.[15] Environmental degradation and overpopulation are stark examples of the harm that has come to the children, as are the absence of sanctioned passage rites into womanhood.[16]

It is quite common to find the woman hiding behind the shields of summer's girl and fall's adolescent, afraid to come out and do what has to be done, to face responsibility, duty, and the need to self- sacrifice. Under pressure, she may panic, become hysterical, violent, passive, undecided, purposeless, helpless, a victim. She may confuse her values, or lose sight of her center. Love and creativity, her greatest gifts, may be squandered on her body, material security, or on her own feelings. She may not be able to love maturely because she was never loved, or she has confused it with sex, or she cannot love herself.

It is also quite common to find the little girl hiding behind the skirts of the woman, afraid to come out and face the stranger. Like a puppet master, she guides the woman's every move, feeling, and thought. A competent, seemingly impervious facade does the bidding of a girl whose ego swallows all. Beneath the exterior lurks a volcano, earthquake, or flood, a scornful cynic, or a competitive, vengeful predator motivated by fear and pain. Such a woman is capable of murdering her children, destroying anything or anyone who stands in her path. The keyboard of her mind is in the hands of a dangerous, irrational juvenile. Intolerance hides behind a shield of respectability. The "spiritual correctness" of a zealot hides the smugness of a little girl who was once afraid, but now has "found it."[17]

Exaggerated winter shields are quite common among modern women. Perhaps to escape the little girl's pain, or the adolescent's "sin," or the plain reality of her life, the woman lives almost exclusively in the world of duty, responsibility, orderliness, rationality, and work. She loses herself in routine, regimen, discipline, volunteerism, spending most of her time caring for others. She never has time to play. Some accuse her of coldness, remoteness, or lack of feeling. Her defenses, however, are not without their weaknesses. Her nature dictates that there be transitions, crises, deaths and rebirths. Sooner or later she will suffer a "breakdown," a "burnout," a life-threatening illness, a psychotic episode.

The little girls hiding behind and manipulating the winter shield of the modern woman prefigure a bleak future. The endless summer is a dead end. Ineffectual attempts to control their destinies via their bodies, their emotions, and their material things will result in frustration. The embryos will remain in the placenta.[18]

The mythical goddesses of the winter shield are those who symbolize the full potential of womanhood, as exemplified by motherhood, wisdom, and the preservation of social structure. The Gnostic Ptolemaeus considered Sophia to be the intermediary between the soul of the world and the world of ideas; i.e., the gate-keeper between the fall shield and the winter. As the story goes, she was originally a part of "primordial man." But she abandoned him, and man cannot be saved until he finds her again.[19] In her classical Greek form, Sophia was Athene, the goddess of wisdom born from the head of Zeus.[20] She stood above her city, Athens, her shield uplifted, her spear at the ready. In China, Sophia/Athene was celebrated as Kuan Yin, goddess of mercy and wisdom, protectress of children, bringer of rain. She was born from a tear shed by the Buddha at the spectacle of suffering in the world. Among Christians, the goddess became Maria, Mother of God, patron of the lost, protectress of the children, healer of the sick, guardian of marriage. Whatever form the goddess took, she was revered by women and men alike, for she represented the full blooming, the complete maturity, the awesome dimensions of the feminine mind that always brought the people through the winter.

Sophia has survived to modern times. Here and there, such completeness of the winter shield can still be found. Invariably, these women who stand so strongly beside their mothers and grandmothers and great grandmothers have lived a life filled with initiatory events. They dared; they risked; they looked into their own darkness; they tilled the soil called soul. And because they had soul, their minds had something on which to grow.

For the most part, however, the setting forth of the modern girl upon the perilous seas of modern life is uncertain at best. The initiatory experiences leading to maturity are still there — some legal, some illegal — but the old midwifery is gone. The rites are gone, the elders are gone, the sanctions and the confirmations are gone. The sisters and the daughters and the mothers and the aunts and the nieces and the grandmothers can't agree on what to do. Is it any wonder that the little girl would simply rather that it stayed summer all year round?

SPRING

> Light are the petals that fall from the bough,
> And lighter the love that I offer you now;
> In a spring day shall the tale be told
> Of the beautiful things that will never grow old.
>
> — Anna Wickham, "The Cherry-Blossom Wand"

The spring shield seems almost the "odd one" in the seasonal cycle. The girl of summer, the adolescent (and animus) of fall, the woman of winter — these three together would seem to constitute the tale of a life, a triangle of completeness. But then comes spring.

So, who is spring? Spring is who the little girl, the adolescent, and the woman become. You can't exactly see her. But you can't SEE without her. If you go up to the gates of death and look with the eyes of faith into the dark, you might catch a glimpse.

The spirit shield is the mature woman's "reward." It is what life inevitably brings her to. It is the fruit, the issue of labor, the grail at the end of her quest of discipline. The summer shield is the girl who is the woman. The fall shield is the adolescent who is the woman. The winter shield is the woman who is the woman. The spirit shield is the transformed one who is the woman. And it is the passageway between the old woman and the little girl.

Donning the spring shield frees the spirit from the limitations of body, psyche and mind. The old forms of the winter are shattered by the explosion of birth. Imagination flows through the breach and engulfs the gloom with light. The woman steps across the threshold of maturity and becomes the goddess, the illumined one, the miracle-worker, the doer of magic, the artist, the poet, the muse, the "perfected work." In a healthy shield system, this state is common. Spring represents a full fourth of the shield system. It occurs constantly in the life of any mature woman whose little girl hazards the initiatory darkness.[21]

In an ideal culture, there would be many windows through which the spirit shield of the woman could be seen affecting her behavior and the world around her. The gifts of the spring would stand clear in the creative lives of women everywhere. Because modern culture is not enriched by the full force of feminine creativity, views through the windowpanes are murky — but not without hope. There are millions of housewives who bring the sacred into their homes. There are all those who nurture their children and their mates with creative, unconditional love. There are those genuine voices of the feminine "consciousness raising movement"; the brilliant works of feminine novelists, playwrights, poets, artists, film makers, actresses. The revival of covens, "women in the wilderness," earth healers, feminine reverends and priests, medicine women, and the like, indicate a quickened interest in the spiritual aspects of feminine self-thus.

The seasonal return to spring requires that the woman take the risk of stepping beyond her previously ordered and rational existence. If death is, after all, but a seasonal return to birth, then she must be willing to step across the border. This final step is accomplished with the whole, healthy assistance of the other three shields. Indeed, spring would not exist without the other seasons. Nor would the other seasons exist without the eternal emergence of life. The woman surrenders by allowing her destiny to pull her toward intuitive regions. Here the mind and its laws are but the frozen soil from which spring the fires of spiritual delight.

The spirit shield is most clearly seen in all the ways women express the healing impulse. If all things come from the Mother, then it is the mother (winter shield) who brings all things to term (spring), even those whom she chooses to abort. This mothering impulse, typical of the feminine gender, leaps out from her like a spark, a stitch, a caress, a prayer, a song of praise, yearning like a lover toward the body of nature. Many women, from housewife to CEO to nun, are aware of this, and they express this healing proclivity to loved ones and the community at large.

THE CONTEMPORARY SPRING SHIELD

But how many more women live lives of quiet desperation, sublime ignorance, or narrowness so extreme as to run always on a single track? The conditions of modern life often do not breed women with imagination, or women whose spirituality runs deeper than doctrine or form. If the little girl never fully matured, how can she be expected to attain a mature enlightenment? How can she celebrate the goddess within herself? How can she regenerate herself? How can she tell her own story, reinventing her destiny even as she matures year by year? How can she be aware of her purpose or mission in life? Where is her vision? How can she ever know the truth of the poet's prayer to the Spirit: "Nor ever chaste, unless Thou ravish me"? How can she face death with nobility of spirit?

The specter of a future unfolding without the full expression of the feminine spirit is grim indeed, for one of the four faces of the feminine is divine. Under the aegis of this shield, the woman knows her own body to be no less sacred than the mysterious universe.[22] This knowing in itself is a potent form of insurance against the pending ecological crises of the 21st century. For if her body is sacred, so is the self-thus of which it is made. The sacred bond between human-mysterious and natural-mysterious must be maintained, nourished, and worshipped if the children are to survive.[23]

Over-nourishment or exaggeration of the spring shield, however, will accomplish little. A woman's light must be balanced by her darkness. In this balance there is a power of self-acceptance unknown to those who dwell eternally in the light. Self-acceptance is of the soul. It is found lurking in the dark places of the psyche. Women who hide in the light, live apart from their bodies, flit from psychic flower to psychic flower, or avoid doing anything that might dirty their karma, are of little use to their people or their earthly home. They are so buoyant with light they cannot stomach their own darkness. The balanced woman "walks the mystical path with practical feet."[24]

The spirit shield is animated by the feminine version of the Trickster, the upside down woman, the backwards lady, the tooth-cunted woman, Madam Coyote — representing the sudden flip-flop of spring. Forms and traditions are overturned; ethics and morality are swept away. What was, is not. What was not, is. The electron jumps out of its orbit. A surge of energy is released. And a new element is born.

So spring comes to a woman, unleashing energies within her both unexpected and healing. Traditionally, women have been known to go crazy during the rites of spring, dancing with abandon, making love to strangers, spitting on the high priest, dressing like a man, etc. The Trickster within the woman knows that in the spring, sacred and profane are one and the same. The goddess herself is a turd. And a turd is the goddess. The beauty of the mature modern woman is that she knows this trickster, this fusion of sacred and profane within her. She is familiar with the upside down, Zen world, where everything is holy and not holy, seen and unseen, carnal and spiritual. She considers it a measure of human life, and a reward for loving the Spirit in all things.

Long ago, our teacher taught us that the deity of the woman's spring shield was a beautiful boy with golden hair. We have come to know this figure as "the feminine muse." This god, or spiritual agency, helps to balance the shield system of a woman, who has a masculine psychic agency in her fall shield (the animus).[25] An appropriate mythical figure for the woman's spring shield might be Apollo, the beautiful sun god of poetry, music, healing, ceremonial purification, and the wisdom of the oracles. His oracle at Delphi, the most famous in the classical world, was delivered by the Pythia, or Pythoness, an intoxicated high priestess. What came from the mouth of Apollo-Pythia was then rendered into hexameter verse.[26]

The Apollo-Pythia metaphor is wondrously suggestive. The east shield of the woman is the omphalos, the navel of the world. After bathing and drinking from the Castilian Spring, the woman goes to her center, her omphalos, where she is possessed by the godlike Muse. There she dances with him, as Psyche did with Eros, and their movements seduce the light, the symbol, the image. She becomes the entranced instrument, the Pythoness, upon which the erotic plays. The music, the poetry, the vision that flows from her is for the benefit of the people. She is our high priestess, our prophet, and our bard.

And she is our Spirit Mother. "All things are born of woman," say the Northern Cheyenne. Her spring shield is the agency through which all things appear. From the Spirit they come, and, as spring turns toward the summer, the body of nature forms anew. The underworld journey is completed, only to begin again with the blood, the muscle, the nerve, the genetic encoding of the little girl. And because the spirit is, from the beginning of time, in the little girl, in the baby dolphin, in the baby lizard, in the baby worm, in the sprout, in the sapling, in the fledgling star, the spirit will seek itself through the seasons of body, soul, and mind. By virtue of the processes of birth, growth, maturation, decay, and death, the spirit will find herself again and again.

CONCLUSION

> No alchemy and mystery is this,
> no cross to kiss,
> but a cross pointing on a compass face,
> east, west, south, north . . .
> the book of life is open,
> turn and read. . . .
>
> — Hilda Doolittle, "Erige Cor Tuum Ad Me In Caelum"

What will become of the four shields of women as our culture crosses the threshold of a new century? The outlook is bleak. The children are dying in unprecedented numbers. They are too many, too hungry, too neglected, too wounded, too often poisoned by the environment, too much at the mercy of an immature adult world to make it on their own. Adolescents run lawlessly through the streets, unchecked by absent fathers and heedless of despairing mothers. The environment reels under the impact of human abuse. Fanatics and dictators command billions of childlike adherents. You can still find uninitiated boys at the helm of the good ship homo sapiens. Concerned women, far outnumbered by the unconcerned, are divided over what to do. Many prophesy a human twilight, another Middle Ages, where the "haves" harry the "have nots" and "ignorant armies clash by night." Will the women of the future find ways of attaining the kind of maturity that will enable our species to nourish itself and survive, if only by the skin of its teeth?

The uninitiated girl who plays at being a woman is no more capable of planning for the future than she is of turning and facing the monsters that dwell in the outer limits of her fall shield of initiation. The darkness of the 21st century yawns like a curse, like a deserved punishment. Surely, our species faces a monumental challenge. Those who survive will be those who are willing, no matter how reluctantly, to turn away from endless summer and face the threshold within, the initiation-place of the human race, where the seed will be beaten from the chaff. The girls who are willing to face themselves in the vale of soul-making may survive. If they do, it will be because they became women.

In the meantime, the requirements of feminine maturity (severance from the summer, threshold passage through the fall, incorporation in winter as a woman, regeneration in the spring) will not change. Will culturally sanctioned rites of passage into womanhood, elderhood, cronehood, return to the next century? Only if the conditions of life require that neighborhoods and communities adhere in love and understanding to the old ways of bringing up the little girls and boys. Only if the illusion of separation from nature disappears, and the people cleave to the self-thus of which they are composed.

It is imperative that this happen. Our survival depends on it. Women must *will* it to happen. The definition of womanhood *will* again include the ancient myth:

> And then the girl left her father and mother and her family and faced the dark, inward journey of initiation that passed through the regions of the soul, the dark gods, feeling, and self-consciousness. In that place she was made into a woman. When she returned, it was winter. The people were starving. The children were dying. She took her place as a woman among women, beside her mother, her grandmother, and her great grandmother. She fed the children. She lived to complete her earthly purpose and nurtured those she loved. When spring came, she was enlightened.

ENDNOTES: THE FOUR SHIELDS OF A WOMAN

[1] The initiatory passage of a woman is often mythically phrased as an heroic journey. See Sylvia Perera, *The Descent of the Goddess: A Way of Initiation for Women* (Toronto: Inner City Books, 1981). Also Frances Vaughan, "The Heroic Journey: A Symbolic Context for Psychotherapy," *Voices: The Art and Science of Psychotherapy*, Spring, 1988, Vol. 24, No.1.

[2] Cf. Anne Rice's pornographic *Beauty Trilogy*, a gross south shield parody of the little girl's fairy tale.

[3] If her parents or the community attempt to protect her from her own darkness, she will be denied those initiatory elements that lead to maturity. She will remain a girl, or *puella aeternis*.

[4] See Victoria Secunda, *Women and Their Fathers: The Sexual and Romantic Impact of the First Man in Your Life* (New York: Delacourt Press).

[5] Cf. Clarissa Pinkola Estes, *Women Who Run With the Wolves: Myths and Stories of the Wild Woman Archetype* (New York:Ballentine Books, 1992). "If a woman does not look into these issues of her own deadness and murder, she remains obedient to the dictates of the predator." (p. 12)

[6] One of the striking differences between primitive initiations and modern self-initiations is that in the former the secrets are the property of initiates and elders alike. In the latter, the secrets are held only by the initiates.

[7] In *Women Who Run With the Wolves*, Clarissa Estes eloquently describes the natural state of the woman who is bogged down in her fall shield: "When creativity stagnates in one way or another, there is the same outcome: a starving for freshness, a fragility of fertility, no place for smaller life forms to live in the interstices of larger life forms, no breeding of this idea to that one, no hatch, no new life. Then we feel ill and want to move on. We wander aimlessly, pretending we can get along without the lush creative life, but we cannot, must not. To bring back creative life, the waters have to be made clean and clear again. We have to wade into the sludge, purify the contaminates, reopen the apertures, protect the flow from future harm." (p. 301)

[8] According to Gloria Steinem, *Revolution from Within: A Book of Self-Esteem* (Boston: Little, Brown and Company), modern women need encounters with the "inner child" (or adolescent) in order to bring about a "quiet revolution" of self-worth that may ultimately change the world.

⁹ The way in which a young Aborigine girl loses her virginity graphically underscores the basic need to implant within the candidate for womanhood, a powerful, positive, psychic image of the male: 'One day soon after her marriage ceremony the girl may go food collecting as usual with the older women. She is seized by a group of men, sometimes including her future husband and several others who are in the kin category of brother. During the seizure she addresses all these men as 'husband,' and they have intercourse with her, often gathering the semen and blood mixture and drinking it. . . . The defloration rite seems severe from a Western perspective; however, from early childhood Aboriginal girls look forward to this initiation, viewing sexuality as a joyous, integrated part of life." Lawlor, *Voices of the First Day*, p. 205.

Obviously, the intent of the ceremony is not merely sexual. Several significant functions are served. The girl sees herself through the eyes of the men closest to her childhood, and her husband. Their eyes tell a story of love, approval, desire, trustworthiness, intimacy, and friendship.

¹⁰ Estes, *Women Who Run With the Wolves*, on the function of the animus: "He brings ideas from "out there" back into her, and he carries ideas from her soul-Self across the bridge to fruition and "to market." Without the builder and maintainer of this land bridge, a woman's inner life cannot be manifested with intent in the outer world." (p. 311)

¹¹ See Linda Leonard, *The Wounded Woman*, pp. 148-164.

¹² In a review of Radclyffe Hall's *The Unlit Lamp*, Vivian Gornick claims ". . . an important shift in interest is now taking place from fathers and sons to mothers and daughters. This view includes but subsumes the testimony of mothers and sons. Our necessity, it seems, is not so much to kill our fathers as it is to separate from our mothers, and it is the daughters who must do the separating." Ms. Gornick continues: "The writer knows what really goes on between a mother and a daughter when the daughter wants to live not the given life but a free life, one that won't repeat the mother's life. That's *true* separation." But without a culturally acceptable means of separating, the resulting battle is often carried on with great inward violence: "The most ignorant among us knows murder will not accomplish separation. You can't kill your mother because there is no mother to kill. It's the mother within who's doing all the damage. That's a piece of shared wisdom now, something the culture knows down to its finger tips." *New York Times Book Review*, Nov. 22, 1987.

¹³ Note the reaction of the traditionally male-dominated military to feminine ways of ordering chaos in Brian Mitchell, *Weak Link: The Feminization of the*

American Military (Washington D.C.: Regenery Gateway), when he asserts: "The lack of discipline among men is itself the fault of a feminized force, a force that fails to instill discipline during basic training because of its be-nice-to-privates approach to attracting and managing troops." (as quoted in the *New York Times Review of Books*)

[14] See Anita Shreve, *Women Together, Women Alone: The Legacy of the Consciousness-Raising Movement* (New York: Viking).

[15] Cf. Suzanne Gordon, *Prisoners of Men's Dreams: Striking Out for a New Feminine Future* (Boston: Little, Brown and Company). Ms. Gordon issues a plea for women to rededicate themselves to the emotional and the domestic by calling for grass-roots action on parental leave to care for new-born babies, subsidized day care, decent public education, a national health program, national pension and vacation policies, and affordable housing.

[16] Not to mention religious nationalism and fundamentalism. See Robin Morgan, *The Demon Lover: On the Sexuality of Terrorism* (New York: W.W. Norton and Company). She quotes a Middle Eastern woman who received a hysterectomy after giving birth to 28 children: "I will not give birth only to see my children kill and die. *My body is not a weapons factory.* It is *my* body."

[17] One is reminded of feminine "fundamentalists" such as those who seek to compel other women to choose Jesus, or Islam, or breast-feeding, or motherhood, or heterosexuality, or homosexuality.

[18] More often, one finds women in various stages of self-initiation, some more advanced than others. Look at the face of the "woman" in your town. Do these faces actually reflect the woman? Or do they look like girls in various stages of self-initiation?

[19] Cirlot, *A Dictionary of Symbols* (New York: Philosophical Library, 1962).

[20] Athene's mother, if she had one, was Metis, swallowed by Zeus because he was afraid she would give birth to a son who would be greater than he (Hesiod). Zeus got more than he bargained for — a daughter who became greater than he, at least among humans. Whereas Zeus could deliver the thunderbolt, Athene delivered the plow, the rake, the yoke, the bridle, the olive, the numbering system, the flute, the chariot, the art of navigation, the ship, the shoe, the township, the state, and every occupation in which women were employed.

[21] "... a woman's creative ability is her most valuable asset, for it gives outwardly and it feeds inwardly at every level: psychic, spiritual, mental, emotive, and economic. The wild nature pours out endless possibilities, acts as birth channel, invigorates, slakes thirst, satiates our hunger for the deep and wild life. Ideally, this creative river has no dams on it, no diversions, and no misuse." Estes, *Women Who Run With the Wolves*, p. 299.

[22] See Sherry Ruth Anderson and Patricia Hopkins, *The Feminine Face of God: The Unfolding of the Sacred in Women* (New York: Bantam Books, 1989). Also Kim Chernin, *Reinventing Eve: Modern Woman in Search of Herself* (New York: Times Books, 1988).

[23] Contrast this to the Christian notion (St, Paul) that the body is mortal, corruptible, and the source of sin and the Devil.

[24] This expression has been attributed to Angeles Arrien.

[25] Gender-wise, the south and north poles are feminine (girl and woman). The western and eastern poles contain a masculine counter-balance in the inner archetype of the animus (fall) and the "beautiful boy with golden hair," the muse of spring. This would hold true for gay women as well. Women who attempt to substitute the animus and the "god" with animas and goddesses run the risk of becoming all yin, nothing but feminine. When this happens, the woman may become incapable of empathetic feeling or creativity among any but her own congregation. She may even go so far as to deny yin-yang as a fact of her own engendering.

[26] "Every artist is androgenous ... it is the masculine in a woman and the feminine in a man that proves creative." May Sarton, *Journal of a Solitude* (New York: W.W. Norton, 1973), p. 141.

III

THE FOUR SHIELDS OF A MAN

> The head Sublime, the heart Pathos, the genitals Beauty, the hands and feet Proportion.
>
> — William Blake, *Marriage of Heaven and Hell*

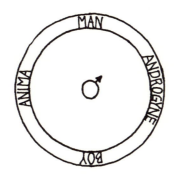

The sorcerer who gave us the two great commandments of the Northern Cheyenne — "Everything is born of the woman" and "Nothing shall harm the children" — was himself a man. This conviction he so reverently held is, I think, a profoundly important article in the faith of most men. Most men *do* acknowledge that all things come through the woman. They *do* care for the welfare of the children. Unfortunately, their uninitiated behavior often belies their convictions. Women are all too often objects of hostility and resentment. And the children are being harmed.

We modern males suffer most cruelly from the absence of culturally sanctioned rites of manhood. Deep inside this most grievous wound, our little boy kicks and screams in the muck and laments his inability to live his own truth, to be the hero, the lover, the king, the magician he knows himself to be. No wonder. The culture we have fashioned robs us of our ability to live our own myth. Social roles requiring responsible manhood are too readily filled with uninitiated boys. The roles themselves are tailored and modeled by the same kind of boys. Where are the elders? Where are the men who are fully male, fully human? They exist, but the numbers are regrettably small.

It is not easy nowadays to reach full masculinity. Some of us don't even try. A kind of stubborn energy within must persist in driving us down paths that are darker, less travelled, tragic, forbidden, that again and again demand a bigger self. By "self" I do not mean just the physical man (summer shield), but the psychological man (fall), the rational man (winter), and the spiritual man (spring). All three have the potential to grow whenever the little boy, for one reason or another, chooses the initiatory passage.

Actually, modern culture provides plenty of passages. Any red-blooded boy looking to prove himself, will have no trouble finding them. The trouble is that most of these ways are not sanctioned by the community or celebrated in rites of incorporation. We suffer through self-initiations that never confirm the attainment of a new life or a new level of awareness, that never end with a beginning. The severance, threshold and incorporation stages of our self-initiation can only be self-marked, self-validated. Without a body of witnessing elders we must confer manhood on ourselves.

I grew up in the deserts and suburbs of Southern California during World War II. The dreams of the four children were haunted by Hitler, the Nazis, the "Japs," air raid sirens, "blackouts," and the mournful tallying of casualties on the evening news. Our family was fundamentalist Protestant. My education was WASP. I graduated from high school with a diploma in Republican Americanism and entertained conflicting dreams of becoming an NBA basketball player or a missionary. My adolescence did not present me with much in the way of initiatory experiences. The rites of passage were typical of the subculture in which I had been nourished: "conversion," baptism, driver's license, the car, the prom, varsity athletics, graduation from high school, employment at a local aircraft factory, and one forbidden beer party. At the age of 18, I was obsessed with the idea of finding out what sin was all about. But I turned away from the fall passage, afraid of the wrath of God.

My first meaningful rite of passage occurred on my wedding night, at the age of twenty one. I lost my virginity. If my bride wasn't turned on, I was at least innocent of any guile. I had nothing to go on, except what I had heard in locker rooms or had stolen from forbidden books. I distinctly remember going to the window of the motel the next morning and looking out at the Pacific Ocean. The future stretched before my eyes, deep, hidden, vast, disturbingly attractive. I was going to find out everything I didn't know, take what I hadn't been given. At that moment, I severed from my mother and crossed the threshold into an initiatory state of being (fall shield) that lasted fifteen years, that included two marriages, several cohabitations, countless affairs, five children, a

Ph.D., several professions, a couple hundred LSD trips, a time when I thought I was a goner for sure, a couple nights in the poky, three childbirths, one abortion, the loss of all material possessions, and a year of desert solitude.

The good Christian boy did some self-initiating. Because his culture didn't offer him much in the way of the attainment of maturity, he bungled his way through the darkness of the threshold like a blind burglar, breaking rules and hearts, shattering symbols, preconceptions and habits, stricken with guilt and remorse. It took him a long time to fully grasp the meaning of the story he was living. When he finally did, he incorporated himself as a mature adult male.

I tell you this because I am a typical product of non-existent initiation rites in America. To describe in general the four shields of the modern male, I need only draw on my own experience. Though I cannot speak for all men (such as those growing up in urban jungles), I can speak for many. My own experiences on the streets of San Francisco and Los Angeles have convinced me that all males possess some version the four shields, regardless of station, ethnicity, region, or sexual preference.

SUMMER

> In the sun that is young once only,
> Time let me play and be
> Golden in the mercy of his means . . . .
> And nothing I cared, at my sky blue trades, that time allows
> In all his turning so few and such morning songs
> Before all the children green and golden
> Follow him out of grace . . . .
>
> — Dylan Thomas, "Fern Hill"

The summer shield of the man is the body of the boy and all that it constitutes, including the environment. All the technological gadgetry, the buildings and the bombs, are also his body. There is nothing in the physical world that is not his body.[1] He makes a lot of mistakes, just playing around with his body. That might be expected, considering the fact that he is only a boy. And since he so often appears to be in a state of rebellion against a mother from whom he was never formally severed, he resents her telling him what to do.

Because the body of the boy is also the body of nature, it is of elemental stuff, of Mother DNA and Father Sperm. Without the body and the sperm of summer's boy, the man of the winter shield would not labor — as all men must labor — to give birth in the spring. There would be no children. Without children, life itself would not exist. The physical male is as profoundly important as the physical female. And both are of the body of nature. And whatever the body of the boy does to the woman or the man, is also reflected in the body of nature.

The sexual play of the "boy-in-the-man," regardless of his sexual preferences, is generated by his genetic makeup, his hormones, his environment, and the presence of other bodies (summer shield). In this sense, the boy is innocent of deceit. He is "playing," manipulated by the pleasure principle and the instinct to survive on a biological level. He is no more guilty of cunning than the dolphin or the snail. The boy-in-the-man shield, however, lacks the inwardness and feeling of the adolescent-in-the-man, or fall shield. He also lacks the self-control and experienced intelligence of the man-in-the-man (winter), or the spiritual ecstasy of the shield of enlightenment (spring), which is the boy-adolescent-man-enlightened.

Therefore, the boy must not be allowed to enter the matrimonial state (gay or straight) until he has earned it by right of initiation, until he is able to recognize and feel the consequences of his sexual behavior. He must be allowed to experiment and to satisfy his curiosity in communally acceptable ways.

Of course, the boy shield of summer is more than just toys and sexual behavior. If raised in a loving, nurturing home that prepares him for the rigor of adolescent rites, he exercises his freedom to explore, to taste, to test his strength, to flex his ego, to merge with "the green fuse that drives the flower." He is inquisitive, athletic, inventive, competitive, affectionate, animated by forces of gravity, inertia, friction and electro-chemical magnetism. He has not yet identified nature with "mother." He careens about his natural environment like a young bull butting heads with every tree. Sensually curious, he is capable of innocent acts of dominance or cruelty with other life forms. Typically, he lacks a certain ability to look out for himself. Limits must be set to his behavior until he is ready for the initiations of adolescence. These limits are a source of security and he identifies them as mother and father. In his dreams and fantasies he consorts with animals and demons, fights battles, and vanquishes evil with magic.

The male ego is of the summer shield — and is associated with the need to survive. It cries with the voice of necessity to be fed, to be cared for, to acquire, to possess, to be the one and only. It cares little for those not associated with the filling of its greedy maw. The ego's most cherished prize is to be loved, and will forever try to find ways to get it. The kind of love that it seeks depends to a large extent on the kinds of love it has received.

The ego, too, is innocent. It is but the emotional magnetic field of the body, fluctuating, changing, as it moves through the seasons of self-thus. Where the boy goes, the ego goes. And the two of them get into their share of trouble — necessary trouble, of course, if the ego is to learn. The learning of the ego of summer becomes the psyche of fall's adolescent.

THE CONTEMPORARY SUMMER SHIELD

If the boy (in-the-man) was not loved, or loved conditionally, or raised and nurtured within a repressive value system, or abused physically or sexually, or not exposed to the natural vicissitudes of boyhood, he might not be fully able to be who he is. He could be uneasy in, or afraid of, his body, or distrust his senses, or be susceptible to bodily illness. His natural defenses could be chronically down, or up, or dangerously lying in wait. He could be afraid of his emotions, or unable to express them. Because he never severed from his mother and father in rites of passage, he might lack self-discipline or the ability to take care of himself. He could be sexually inhibited, exaggerated, or twisted. Down deep in his neuromusculature, the boy-in-the-man of modern times could be afflicted with a variety of disorders related to childhood pain, fear, anxiety, malnutrition, and abuse which, combined with the body's susceptibility to illness, could plague him throughout his life.[2]

If the boy (in-the-man) was nurtured by American culture, the chances are fairly good that he has been conditioned to avoid experiences that depress or deprive his ego or his appetites. He is liable to be selfish, materialistic, untried, and lacking in the ability to perceive the consequences of his own deeds. He might prefer to take his thrills vicariously via spectator sports, movies, etc., and then again he might be the kind who acquires thrills like trophies, sky diving, mountain climbing, trekking, and the like.[3] The chances are very good that he will mask his fears of being victimized with the cult of "macho," an "act" typical of uninitiated boys.[4] Sexually, he may tend toward aggressive as opposed to diplomatic behavior, seeking to dominate, dehumanize, and gratify primary urges through conquest — all the time blithely oblivious to the brutish nature of his conduct.

The ways in which the boy (in-the-man) survived his childhood are often glaringly evident in the uninitiated male. If he got his way by throwing a fit, he will be prone to fits. If he reacted to crisis with panic, he will be prone to panic. If he banged his spoon and screamed for his mother when he didn't get what he wanted, he will tend to do the same thing when he "grows up." If he bullied others or ran away from trouble, he will retain his bullying or fearful ways. Modern culture is full of such boys. The thin veneer of a vaguely earned manhood will not hide the truth that what is lacking is the ability to be self-aware. Such self-awareness is only earned through the initiatory experiences of the fall shield, experiences which the boy never had — or if he did have them, he was given no cultural understanding of them.

Boys cannot initiate boys any more than girls can initiate girls. Urban youth gangs are obvious testimony to that. Although membership in the Crips or the Bloods is filled with heavy initiatory experiences, including almost daily confrontations with death, the transitional process into manhood is rarely completed. Severance from the mother is never effected. Sanctioned status within the "hood" is never conferred by the elders because there are no elders, or very few.[5] Those who are of elders' age are all too often uninitiated macho fathers and uncles who know no better way. As the gangbangers age, they continue to live in their summer persona — if they survive. Adult status is never officially conferred on them. They are allowed to be "reformed" or "corrected," but they are never fully incorporated into manhood.

So many boys (in-the-men) fall easy prey to the media and the popular culture. Entire lives are wasted acting out roles that sink into the meaning of things no deeper than a cork. The stud, the status seeker, the playboy, the who-knows-whoer, the celebrity imitator, the glory boy, the tough guy, the hard body, the sporting man, and so on, appear to be intent on evading the gates of initiation, and the darkness of their own souls. They are content to play in their safe worlds of summer and to consider this play to be a valid sign of maturity.[6] The modern media shows little sign of redefining its popular symbols of "manhood." Those who grow too old to fit the style drop from public view.

The great god Pan rules the summer shield of a man. Among his cohorts are Cupid (of the bow and arrow), Sir Lancelot, Hercules, Cuchulain, and all the athletic, romantic young gods of legend and lore who were known for their strength, courage, and passion, though not necessarily for their intelligence. Their immortality lay in their lust, their vigor, their magnetism, their fiery blood. Their emblem is the phallus, symbolizing the animal magic of male sexual potency. Drawn by their bodies toward lust, war, and personal glory, these young immortals never lose their ability to get it up. In the mythos of modern culture, Pan and his kind have become the macho film heroes, the sex idols, the sports stars, the guys in the perfume ads. They come and go, depending on age and demand; they spring forth perennially, always fresh, lusty, and invulnerable.

Nevertheless, the beautiful, potent young man that we are must inevitably grow up and discover that every woman does not fall at his feet, or that every foe does not flee before his vanquishing sword, or that every contest is not his to win. Sooner or later we will awaken alone, forgotten, rejected, ignored, disliked, on a road leading nowhere. The innocent romp through the pastures of flesh will have taken its toll — in memories, regrets, wounds, wrinkles, doubts, diseases, anxieties, guilts. Will the beautiful young man then look at his own ugliness, his own despair, and recognize it for what it is — his ally? Or will he turn away from his own soul and preoccupy his now aging body with the same old rounds of sensual thrills and pleasures? Will he refuse to contemplate his own black hole of initiation?

Our natural environment bears the scars of the boy-in-the man's immature behavior toward his woman (mother) and his body, both which belong, not only to him, but to self-thus. His uninitiated play can be unthinking, violent, and deadly. He bites the tit even as it feeds him. He likes to play dangerously, and has no stomach for consequences. His toys pile up, the discarded ones outnumbering his current favorites. Bored, he looks around for something better, something more "virtual," something with a real kick to it, something to prolong the orgasm. How easy it is for him to ignore the door marked "initiation." Who wants to suffer? Who wants to be alone? Who wants to face the dragons of manhood? Long live summer!

FALL

> The job of the initiator, whether the initiator is a man or woman, is to prove to the boy or girl that he or she is more than mere flesh and blood.
>
> — Robert Bly, *Iron John*

With puberty come the hormonal changes that tease the little boy inward, toward the development of self-consciousness, memory, feeling, and soul. These, along with the body, compose the psychic placenta from which the mature man emerges. In primitive cultures, this change from the summer of life to the necessary fall, was attended by communally designed and sanctioned initiatory rites into manhood.[7] In some cultures, these rites lasted for years, in others, for a year or two, or for a season. The boys were removed from their mothers and fathers and home (severance) and, in a natural place, conducted through an initiatory regimen in which they endured hardships involving physical pain, loneliness, privation, exposure, and fear (threshold). During this time they were instructed in the ways of men and nature — mythology, laws, codes of conduct, values, taboos, sexuality, roles, dreams, totems, names, and the like.[8] More often than not, the initiatory process was designed to experientially effect some kind of "death" to childhood and a resurrection into life as a man.[9]

When the initiation was complete, the candidates were officially presented to the community as adult males, with all the rights and privileges of same (incorporation). Their new status was not questioned by their parents, or by anyone. Having earned and been granted full adulthood, they were expected to conduct themselves as such. They could hardly do otherwise, for they had been "transformed" by their rite of passage. Nor was it a static kind of manhood that was attained. The process of "making the man" continued for a lifetime as the younger man passed through successively higher initiatory stages culminating in elderhood and death.

In modern times, the community does not provide such rites of passage. The adolescent boy must fend for himself. If we have been loved and encouraged by our parents and family in such a way as to prepare us to face our own shadowy psyches, we will gain a sense of maturity from self-initiations that will ultimately lead to manhood. We must be allowed to experiment with self-definitions or myths and to seek meaningful ways of risking, or hazarding ourselves, to test our mettle. Our need for secrecy and apartness must be honored.[10]

Invariably, the adolescent of us will come face to face with evil or "sin," and will question its relationship to himself. He is likely to investigate the realms of the "taboo." Suicide, incest, rape, drinking, self-mutilation, drug-taking, homosexuality, and other forms of "antisocial behavior" may interest, even fascinate him.[11] No matter how lovingly he has been raised, he may need to open the doors marked "PRIVATE." Real monsters lurk here — depression, guilt, obsession, addiction, and the irreversible consequences of his own actions.

Gradually, men will develop those "deep" qualities identified with character or soul. Our dream life will expand to include unconscious scenarios rising from the collective unconscious. As the demands of adult life vie for our attention, we may wistfully wish we were carefree children again. Our sexuality will take on self-conscious dimensions. We will become aware of ourselves as "lovers," sensitive to the emotions, feelings, and psychological states of "thou." Thus, we will come to see that we (and our lovers) are not perfect, that love is filled with the pain of rejection, loss or regret. The quality of our love will be profoundly related to our relationship to the "woman within," our anima, which in adolescence is vividly colored by the influence of our mother. We will feel her eyes on us, watching us, assessing and defining us. Because our mothers have loved and respected us, including the sexual beings we have become, we will be able to sever, individuate, become our "own man." We will be able to accept ourselves, and be capable of loving another.

No doubt even this ideally-raised adolescent boy will poke his nose into trouble, or experiment with experiences that go against the grain of his upbringing.[12] He may come nose-to-nose with death, or nose-to-nose with himself. More often than not, it will be the consequences of what he has done that awaits him beyond the next bend. He will learn to accept karma, and to recognize in failure and despair a gift, a teaching, a knowing. The day will come when the self- initiating adolescent recognizes that he is ready to assume the full status of manhood. This may occur when he finally is able to see that his father is just another man, and that, by rites of initiation, he has earned the right to stand beside his father, co-equal and free. At that point, he has incorporated himself within the winter shield of the full man.

THE CONTEMPORARY FALL SHIELD

When we shift the focus to modern traumas of incomplete or aborted self-initiation (boys who stay boys. or boy-men who got to adolescence and stayed there) we see that we are dealing with a paternalistic culture in which there are no culturally sanctioned passage rites into manhood — or womanhood. Most families are managed by uninitiated parents, grown up little boys and girls who were never ready for the supremely mature step of co-rearing children. The boy-in-the-man or the adolescent-in-the-man has real difficulty coping with the bewildering responsibilities of manhood. All-too-often he ignores his duties as father and husband, or loses himself in dark forests of guilt and remorse.

The trauma runs deep. Uninitiated or incompletely initiated boys or can be seen everywhere: in the man who spends a lifetime in search of personal pleasure, gain, or glory; in the man who becomes a father only to reject fatherhood; in the man of the "double standard" (I can hurt you but it's not fair if you hurt me); in the star athlete who cannot control his temper or his tongue; in the circles of power composed of "good ol' boys"; in the man who becomes alcoholic and commits suicide; in the man who blames everyone else for his troubles; in the man who is afraid of intimacy with women or men; in the fanatic behind the intolerant or terrorist act; in the man who cannot admit he is wrong; in the soldier who knowingly kills innocent people; in the man who worships the cult of the body; in the man who plays the role of hypocritical Pharisee.... there are many more.

The culture must take the boy away from his childhood and begin a series of initiatory experiences in nature that culminate in the attainment of adulthood. Our culture does nothing. The boy languishes at home, torn between wanting to get the hell out of there and needing the safety and financial security of parents. He develops a secret life of language and experience that he shares only with uninitiated peers. There are few elders to guide him, if he should even want their guidance. All too often, school (education) is nothing more than a glorified prison doing its best to smother the flammable energy of adolescents in the process of self-initiation. As at home, an underground life of initiation develops, usually of a social nature — sexually mature and physically capable boys and girls, trying to "grow up."[13]

Initiations in the "shadow zone" of rock concerts, beer parties, "lost weekends," drugs, cars, guns, whore houses, etc., might have great potential if there were elders to help validate the attainment of mature insight. But a close buddy to whom one confides about losing one's cherry is no substitute for an elder who officially validates and confirms the authenticity of a growth event. No doubt, many forays into the shadow zone are disastrous or deadly. If the boy has not been prepared from boyhood to undergo the initiatory process, he may very well become lost. Indeed, the fear of rites of passage, so pervasive in our culture, springs in part from the horror stories about young men or women who broke the law or met their end in the dark passageway. But the question remains. If we will not provide our boys with real initiatory experiences, how can we prevent them from initiating themselves?

The experience of self-initiation is often profound.[14] There can be a kind of wounding, a psychic hurt. If the boy cannot face that pain, he will turn away, and the purposes of the initiation will be thwarted. If the adolescent gets lost in the pain, the purposes of the initiation will also be thwarted. Without effective elder-midwives, there are many casualties. Disturbances in the fall shield are usually easy to spot. Indecision, powerlessness, playing the victim, depression, self-dislike, melancholia, guilt, addiction, shame, are typical. More dangerous are suicidal, violent, or homicidal ideations nursed secretly within and building up, like the contents of a pressure cooker: "Expect poison from standing water" (Blake, *Marriage of Heaven and Hell*). Inevitably, the contamination leaks from its container.

Dionysus, the inward, feminine god of death, dismemberment, and resurrection, rules the fall shield of the adolescent-in-the-man. From his festivals rose the Greek concept of tragedy — the rending of the goat god, the blameless boy snatched by his father from the ashes of his mother.[15] The concept of cutting back, pruning, wounding, is central to the initiatory process. Without the initiatory scars, the mature man is incomplete. But the pruning hook of fall uncovers a death-gift realized in the spring: the blossoming of new growth.

Another legendary figure springs to mind. Sir Percival, the self-initiated knight of despair who quests hopelessly for the Grail and finally settles on an answer to the question: "Whom does the Grail serve?"[16] Raised as an innocent hick and a defier of God, it is Percival who suffers separation from his wife, who wanders incoherently for years, who finally learns the lessons of human sympathy and becomes the Grail King.[17] It is Percival who rides up to the ruins of his dreams at midnight in a dry and thirsty land and fancies he hears the sound of dripping water.[18] He is the blind knight who sees inwardly, who contends with his own darkness until he develops a sixth sense, until he catches the end of the thread of maturity leading out of the labyrinth.

The mythical feminine counterpart to the god/hero of the fall shield, the anima is an important part of the initiatory complex of that shield.[19] Like the young Dionysus, every boy, regardless of sexual preference, must be initiated into the mysteries of his feminine nature. As all "masculine" life in the natural world contains the "feminine" (note opposing "dots" in the yin-yang symbol), so the growing boy must be introduced to the feminine within via loneliness, exposure, and initiatory intercourse. The man must have access to the power of the feminine within him, or he is not fully mature, not fully capable of empathy with self, others, or his True Mother, the natural world of self-thus.[20]

In other words, the anima is the key that unlocks the fully mature male, regardless of his sexual preference. This key has four dimensions, all of which are evident in a bewildering variety of shades, combinations, dimensions, faces.

The persona of the summer shield is that of the orgiastic feminine, the flesh-and-blood "sex queen," the "Venus." The persona of the fall shield is that of the dark lady, the succubus, the "Tooth Mother," the fatally beautiful witch who turns men into pigs. The face of the winter shield is that of mate, wife, queen, the fully mature woman. And the face of the spring shield is that of the spirit lover, the Muse, the incandescent goddess of inspiration who dances on the eastern rim of the world. As these dimensions of the anima blend and balance within him, the initiated man finds harmony, purpose, and direction.

Modern culture is not a particularly helpful place for a man to go about fashioning a whole anima. Many men suffer from an incompletely realized inner woman. If they are uninitiated boys, their animas may lack dimension or depth. Boys never severed from their mothers are likely to develop a rebellious attitude toward the winter aspect of their anima. Adolescents who have never completed the passage to manhood are likely to be swallowed alive by the fall aspect of their anima. Neither the boys nor the adolescents are ready to assume their rightful place as worthy mates and kings to the anima's mature face. Of course, it may be difficult to find a woman wearing winter's face in a culture full of uninitiated girls. The anima can be badly undernourished if the boy-in-the-man has rarely seen a fully mature woman.

WINTER

> Death and life were not
> Till man made up the whole,
> Made lock, stock and barrel
> Out of his bitter soul . . . .
>
> — W.B.Yeats, "The Tower," Part III

Passage through the fall shield of initiation leads to the boy's attainment of maturity. The self-serving summer and the estranged fall take on the winter shield of the man. In this cold, bitter season, the people look to the man (not the boy or the adolescent) to bring them through. The community must keep its balance, working together peacefully to survive. The men see to it that the children are not harmed, that the work is done, that the family units stay intact, that the laws of the human remain in accordance with the laws of nature. The men also see to it that the boys are initiated into manhood. These rites of manhood will culturally define "what manhood is" and so guide and direct the masculine youth toward the full realization of the responsibilities and privileges in the human community.

The winter shield of a man is composed of the boy (summer), the adolescent initiate(fall), and the man who has been made via the initiatory process (winter). The full man is also enriched by the spirit shield of spring, to which I will subsequently refer. The male winter shield is manifested outwardly, to his family, friends, community, and the laws of the universe. The flesh-love of the summer and the self-love of the fall have been transformed by initiation into the life-sustaining expression of other-love. Above all there is an abiding concern for the well-being of the children. When this concern is extended to the natural environment — to "give back for what you have taken" — there is health for the human biosystem — and for the earth.

In the winter shield, the full man stands beside his father, as a man in his own right, with all the privileges and responsibilities of manhood. Compassion for his father has taken the place of rancor or rebellion. His father no longer has power over him, for he, like his father, carries the wounds, the initiation scars. Having been separated from his mother by the rites of initiation, he is no longer her "little man" but his own man. His mother stands alongside his father in that winter shield, but she is a woman in her own right, not just a reflection of the adolescent's anima. When all three stand together in their full maturity, the family unit, the fundamental building block of society, holds firm against the seasonal storms of existence and ever grows into the fullness of its purpose.

Ideally, the "initiation-made man" of the winter shield manifests signs of maturity in every aspect of his life. He is what the fall turned the summer into. He is considerate, rational, responsible, a synergistic sum of the innocent child and the mortal adolescent. He has earned many roles. As his life matures, he will play them: lover, partner, father, friend, professional, diplomat, teacher, healer, volunteer, artist, warrior, initiatory midwife, magician, elder, "aged one." He is capable of decisive action when needed. He swallows back the panic, hysteria, and reactive violence of the little boy and does what is necessary. He is no stranger to hard work, seeking always to bring order to chaos, harmony and balance to discord. The center of his purpose is anchored to the laws of nature. He knows he is *of* the earth, that he *is* the earth.

As the man of the man grows older, he continues to be of great value to his family, community, and earthly home. The growth-events (initiations) of his life increase his value, defining soul and character. The adolescent (in-the-man) faces his own darkness, remembers his wounds, and matures thereby. The number of winters he has lived begins to show on his head. Though he ages, his summer and fall shields, his boy and adolescent, his body and soul, remain fresh and active within the seasonal cycles of his days. His senses remain open, his sexuality intact (more or less), his body still craving the sun and wind. His psyche continues to gather memories and dreams, to feel its mortality, to become conscious of itself, to make love to the ever-elusive anima. Again and again the boy and the adolescent become the man, and the seasons pass, not in a linear fashion toward the entropic goal of death, but gyre-like, a circular rising, coming back on itself, back to winter, and then to spring. World without end.

At midlife, having loved and fathered and given of himself, he has come to a fuller realization of his life's purpose. His vision is capable of comprehending and serving the community-at-large in some capacity vital to its continued existence. This vision is confirmed by participation in passage rites that mark the attainment of new life status as an elder among the other male elders, a brother in the brotherhood, a member in good standing in the fraternal order of midwives. He and his brothers are responsible for the yearly enactments of passage rites for the male children. As respected teacher and counselor, he sits in attendance at communal celebrations of transition, exercising his gifts of communication, reconciliation, and compassion for the benefit of the entire community. His primary role is to instill in students and initiates the collective wisdom of those who have gone before. Without his wisdom, the children will not survive.

The elder will not allow himself to be "put out to pasture" until death looms, at which point he will withdraw from active service to the community, giving himself time to turn his gaze toward the east, the rising sun and the coming of spring. The boy, the adolescent and the man will still be strong within him as he awaits his appearance in spirit form. Death will be the fullest expression of his body, soul, and mind, a teaching and a blessing to his family and community. Death will be his finest giveaway.[21]

THE CONTEMPORARY WINTER SHIELD

Unfortunately, the modern picture is far from ideal. Few men in this culture ever attain the full promise of the winter shield. This fact is perhaps our deepest, most unspeakable wound, for it amounts to saying that our fathers neglected fatherhood, elderhood, and the care and upbringing of their sons. Our uninitiated boy fathers toyed with the inherent mind of nature and made tools of mass destruction. They quarreled with each other and expressed their anger in wars that murdered and maimed the children.[22] Worst of all, our boy fathers perpetuated the lie that we were not one with the earth.

The shield systems of most modern men bear many a trauma-scar never occasioned by initiatory rites into manhood. One of the basic sources of the initiatory process, the need to know oneself instead of wonder about, has driven many men unconsciously toward manhood. But the experience hasn't always led to actual self- knowledge. Because the fathers and the elders were not there to confirm the meaning of the experience, self-knowing slipped away, like a thief into the night. And it was back to square one — still bearing the unexamined initiatory scar.

Still others are "scarless," having tested the waters of initiation with a toe, only to draw back from an experience that would be too uncomfortable and seemingly unnecessary, considering the vast tide of material diversions. Many of them refer to themselves as "men," but they are unacquainted with the grief of the man, the deep soul of the man.[23] They fall short of empathy, and character. When the trees shed their leaves (e.g., midlife), they paste artificial leaves on their limbs and call it summer. And when the north wind covers the world in white, they fly to West Palm Beach and call it summer. The winter shields of these are skinny and malnourished, no matter how well-fed their bodies might be.

In others — too many others — initiatory scars rankle and stink, and the harder the adolescent (in-the-man) tries to keep them hidden and unspeakable, the more they break out, like boils or disfigurements. These are the adolescent boys who are truly dangerous, to themselves and to others. They are out of balance, obsessed with that dark thing within them. They have gone inside themselves and have drawn the blinds. This preoccupation with the pain, or the perceived ugliness, causes them to grow twisted, grotesque, criminal, psychopathic.

The dark shield of fall has become so heavy that the wheel of human seasons may never shift to winter.

When the body and the soul are malnourished, the mind of the man (winter shield) is affected. The damage takes many forms. Many men are convinced they have no mind. "It's too complicated," they say, and leave thinking and rational action to the "experts" who think and act for them. The "experts," on the other hand, are too often unknowingly manipulated by their own boy or adolescent shields, and the mind which they express and act upon is motivated by egotistical, materialistic, or psychological needs. These men may express their mind *ad nauseam*, but it is the mind of uninitiated youth. The results of cultural domination by males without healthy or mature minds can be seen in the current status of women — and men. Mature criteria of "what constitutes a man" have been eroded by a mass media dominated by boys-in-the-men. Modern men are experiencing difficulty standing their ground and saying who they are, for they lack the self-assured knowledge of the initiated soul.[24]

The mind of the winter shield is the mind of self-thus, the invisible glue that holds the living earth together. In accordance with the laws and orders of nature, the man acts appropriately and with forethought. If the children are being harmed, the man seeks to save them. So dictate the laws of human nature. The species must survive. Overpopulation, starvation, war, genocide — these are all concerns of the male winter shield, for they threaten the lives of the children. Likewise, environmental pollution, resource depletion, social distress, fanatical religion, epidemics and diseases, and the use of destructive technologies, to name a few, are his concern. Obviously, most of the males in our male-dominated culture are not taking a stand. The reason why is clear. They are boys, and they are not taking good care of their bodies.

Little boys hiding behind the winter shield of the modern male are all-too-often puppet masters, pulling the strings of the man, causing him to behave in ways that feed his infantile needs. The smooth facade that muffles the bulging caldera, the time bomb, the latent fit of violence is not, in fact, a form of control, but a mask donned by the boy or the adolescent to gain his own ends. Since the boy was never severed from his mother, much of this manipulative behavior involves projections of his mother into the women or men in his life.

Flimsy facades of manhood can be dangerous, particularly when rebelliousness against the mother (or both parents) takes the form of criminality or fanaticism or political/military action that threatens the wellbeing of women and children. When violence breaks out, the boy's attempts to control himself through the winter shield break down. The shield has not been made a strong enough container (via rites of passage) to hold its volatile contents. It is not the true man who breaks down, but the boy's and/or the adolescent's role-play of "the man."

Exaggerated or "stuck" winter shields are also common among modern males whose initiation scars have never been ritually confirmed by the culture. To escape from the pain of an abusive childhood or the quandaries of unacknowledged self-initiations, the boy became prematurely old. He lost himself in work, intellectual pursuits, systems, dogmas, theologies, self-disciplines, routines. He accepted responsibility as though it were God himself. Such men rarely indulge the body of the child, or the feelings of the adolescent.

"Workaholics" can be remote or absent fathers and cold, inaccessible lovers-statues sculpted by rational control. Undernourished as the opposite summer shield may be, the boy is not dead. He is often revived by the transitions, crises, and accidents of normal life. The rigid self-discipline of the winter shield breaks down under the onslaught of tragedy. The man suffers a sudden burnout, a life-threatening illness, a neurotic or psychotic episode. The boy appears, screaming with anger.

The mythical gods of the winter shield are those who symbolize the potential of manhood as exemplified by fatherhood, elderhood, wisdom, and the preservation of the people. Zeus, patriarch of the Olympian gods, might qualify, if he did not behave so often like a child. Hermes, the communicator, the god of wit and commerce might qualify, if he were not such a mischief maker. Jehovah, father creator, might qualify, if he hadn't been a bachelor, and so cruelly jealous of his children. One of the better models would be ancient Egypt's Thoth, the record keeper, the creator and orderer of the universe, the god of wisdom and learning, order and measure, the masculine counterpart of Sophia or Athene. Other mythical or semi-legendary figures come to mind. Homer's Odysseus is a particularly full depiction of the winter shield of a man — the man-father who lives by his wits, who, despite all temptations, setbacks and detours, finds his way back to wife and son. Kings Arthur and David are excellent examples of the relationship between the man and his environment, or the mind and the body, or the man and the boy. Both depict the profound influence of the anima (Guenivere, Bathsheba) on the overall health of the king and his kingdom.

Undoubtedly, there are genuine men in this world, with well-developed winter shields. If there were not, our species would already be extinct. By virtue of the self-initiatory process, they were able to validate themselves as true men. With such as these, and their feminine counterparts, we will attempt to survive the oncoming winter of the 21st century.

In the modern male, a mature winter shield has the feel of compassion, reconciliation, commitment, coherence, and balance. It is of the same stuff as the mind of nature, the mind of men of old, the mind that interrelates and governs the whole. The laws of this mind, such as the laws of seasonal change, constitute a wisdom by which nature (and human nature) regulates and nourishes itself. The real man is attuned to this, and turns his attentions to the well being of his loved ones and the natural environment to which they owe their lives. Because he has earned his soul, he can look to the past, he can remember. And without regret or nostalgia, he can learn from the past and apply what he has learned to the future.

Of course, the summer shield is never absent from such a man. He has a playful, sensual, emotional, egotistical side. He is proud of his body's strength and beauty, proud of his erection, proud of his expressions of love. He is not impervious to pain, and not afraid to show his fear, anger, or hurt. At times, the boy can overwhelm the most mature of men, and the balance shifts to the physical excesses typical of the summer shield. But the winter shield will soon gain control of the dance of the shields before any real damage is done. The man knows the boy shield must be indulged if growth is to be healthy. He also knows how and when to put the boy in his place so that the man can do his work.

Above all, the mature modern male is enlightened. That is not to say he is like the Buddha, or Jesus, or some kind of saint (although that is always possible). His kind of enlightenment comes from wholeness and completeness, a balance in which the boy, the adolescent and the man are given full and appropriate expression. He finds comfort, even joy, in knowing that the greatest expression of his life will be in death. He also knows that death always returns to revivification, to imagination, to spirit. He is not a "religious" man, but a spiritual man who realizes that the deepest truths of deity reside in that union of sacred and profane called human nature, that this union exists in him, and that winter always comes round to spring.

SPRING

> O how can I explain
> It's so hard to get on?
> when these visions of Johanna
> keep me up past the dawn.
>
> — Bob Dylan, "Visions of Johanna"

Spring comes forth from winter like fire from ice. The rigid forms of the rational mind, like a flimsy dike, burst asunder in the onrushing flood of birth. Old age and the rigidity of winter death melt away. Birth, the wellspring of the spirit, bubbles forth. The boy, the adolescent, and the man are fulfilled and reinvented through the vaginal eyes of the Imagination.

The spirit shield is our reward, the enlightenment earned by the initiatory process. It is the fruit of our labor, the grail waiting at the end of the discipline of wholeness. The summer shield is the boy who is the man. The fall shield is the adolescent who is the man. The winter shield is the man who is the man. The spring shield is the transformation that is the man, and is the passageway from the old man to the little boy, from the spirit to the body.

The rites of spring set the spirit free from the limitations of body, psyche, and mind. More succinctly, they are the synergistic sum of the other three shields. The initiated boy-adolescent-man becomes the god, the illumined one, the healer, the magician, the artist, the poet, the muse, the "perfected work." Although the spring shield is present in almost every one of us from the moment of birth, it is never capable of full expression until the boy has fully become the man.

Our winter shield labors to give birth to the enlightenment of spring. This labor is a kind of childbirth. The contractions and involutions of the mind push out the new-born impulse into a world of spirit, where it becomes the impetus for many forms of healing expression. Our spring shield, then, is a means by which the pregnant man "comes to term."[25] This process involves the initiatory copulation of body and psyche (sensation and memory) to germinate the thought-egg in the placenta of the mind. The children birthed by our minds can be found in the sacred writings and teachings of human history, in our rites of passage, in our artistic expressions, our inventions, our medicine, our music, theater and dance.

If we lived in an ideal culture where rites of passage into manhood were the norm, the spring shield of men would be obvious. There would not be varying gradations of "having it" or "not having it." Every one of us would experience and express himself as spirit. The healing impulse would be an inseparable part of our way of life. The "sacred" would live in the home, in the marketplace, in the body, soul, and mind of men. Our children would be nurtured with spiritual (as opposed to dogmatic or "religious") values, with unconditional and creative forms of love. Our social problems would be treated with enlightened understanding. Our culture would be deeply enriched by the spirituality of every man.

THE CONTEMPORARY SPRING SHIELD

But we live in the modern world. The spiritual (as opposed to religious or dogmatic) is conspicuous by its absence. The Holy Spirit, who in ancient times lived in all forms of self-thus, is scarcely seen these days. The "scientific method," espoused by minds unbaptized by the initiatory process, will not grasp the spirit's validity. The Big Lie (that human and nature are separate) has further debilitated the spirit shield by postulating that nature is not "spiritual." Without his vital spirit-link with nature (his own nature) the modern male (i.e. the uninitiated boy) will continue to treat nature as he all-too-often treats his own body, with undisciplined ignorance and a kind of contempt, as a plaything, a tool of anger, or a septic tank.

Without the mature enlightenment of full initiation, the modern male is incomplete. How can he regenerate himself? How can he celebrate the god within himself? How can he find his life story? How can he reinvent himself as he matures towards the ultimate birth? Where is the vision that will save the children and heal the biosphere? When will he assent to the vision of the poet?

> But when I breathe with the birds,
> The spirit of wrath becomes the spirit of blessing,
> And the dead begin from their dark to sing in my sleep.
>
> — Theodore Roethke, "Journey to the Interior"

I'm reminded of the lives of men from whom the spirit has fled, the slaves to the mirror, the lonely drinkers sitting on barstools, the devotees of drug-induced tranquility, the long distance swimmers of trivia, the men of greedy briefcases and schedules, the prisoners of cheap thrills, the condemned of the ghettos, the boys spellbound by "the rocket's red glare," the tongue-tied ones whose bodies so easily erupt into violence and murder. The specter of a future unfolding without the full expression of the masculine spirit is grim indeed. The spring shield of a man is divine, and it is not easy to contemplate a 21st century without human gods.

The modern world has also bred another phenomenon — the uninitiated boy who, to avoid his own darkness, hides in the light. Too much light without corresponding darkness breeds disconnection, rootlessness, overweening failure. There is perhaps nothing so ineffectual as a man with an overabundance of vision who cannot, or will not, flesh it with the practical. Such vision has no soul. It is incapable of penetrating the darkness, or illumining the evil that lurks in the psyche. A man who hides in the light, who flits from illumination to illumination like a butterfly, suffers from spirit bloat. Buoyant with light, he floats free of mundane concerns and rises too close to the sun — or, mistaken for a hostile aircraft, is shot out of the sky. The true visionary keeps his feet on the ground, and gives his life to the practical attainment/expression of the dream.

A traditional element of the spring shield of a man, largely absent or forgotten, is the Trickster, representing the sudden flip-flop of spring, when the winter-rigid forms of winter are contravened by the improbability of new life. In times gone by, the trickster of spring was celebrated in festivals and rites of spring. Coyote, Raven, Magpie and their friends possessed a man, unleashing energies within him both unexpected and healing. At such times it was customary to enact the Trickster, to go crazy, to dance with abandon, to lose all common sense, to make love to strangers, to dress like a woman, to spit on the high priest, etc. At such times, the Fool and the Magician, the profane and the sacred, were one.

Nowadays, the Trickster has devolved into laws and ordinances designed to curb the divine insanity of spring. "Sacred" and "profane" can be seen as artifices created by boys afraid of the initiatory darkness. Never the twain shall meet, even though they are both inseparable from self-thus. How many men in this schizophrenic world still recognize that god is a piece of shit — and that a piece of shit is god? How many still celebrate the upside-downness of life, the reversal of fortune, the existential death, the twist of fate, the holiness of the not-holy?

Long ago, our teacher told us that the creative source of the spring shield of a man was a beautiful girl with golden hair. He called her the Muse, and she is whatever the individual man conceives of her. According to the Greeks, the Muses were the offspring of Zeus (winter) and the goddess Memory (fall). Phoebus Apollo brought them from their home on Mt. Helicon to the springs at Delphi, where he tried to tame their wild frenzy with his lyre. Even so the muse of every man, regardless of his sexual orientation, whispers and screams into his lyre, his flute, his drum. And no matter how many poems, how many songs, how many dances reverberate from the plucked string, she is never tamed.

The mythical personification of the spring shield, then, is a wild, powerful spirit of the imagination, a "daughter of the earth and air" who animates and inspires a god's instrument. The god arranges the inspirations of his Muse into verses, melodies, visions. He is her "medium," her servant. But he must not presume to possess her. Thamyris made that mistake. He thought he could make better music than the Muses. Counting on his skill, he bet a chance to enjoy each of them individually against whatever they cared to do to him. He lost. They blinded him and broke his lyre and left him sitting alone by the side of the road, where the wind blew his songs away.[26]

The relationship between the Muses and the earth is unmistakable. Their name originally meant "mountain goddesses." Their ability to prophesy the future was based on the ways pebbles danced in the wind. Their symbol was the winged horse, Pegasus. Natural landmarks such as Pieria, Mt. Helicon, the springs of Hippocrene and Aganippe, Mt. Parnassus, and the Castalian springs at Delphi were home. One went to a place on the earth to be with them, spirit to spirit. That's how the songs came — from the achingly beautiful feminine spirits of the earth, through the man-god's instrument. Man-god and goddess were one in self-thus.

No doubt, there are many men in the modern world with healthy spring shields who live with the Muse on a daily basis. It matters not whether they are gay or straight. These are the "spiritual men," the men who, regardless of their religion, celebrate the spirit within themselves and nature. These are the enlightened ones, the ones who know that if they wait up through the night, the dawn will break upon them like the voice of the Muse. Men like any other men, they are nevertheless gods, immortal in spirit. No one knows this better than they, yet they are ever ready to traffic in the marketplaces of the body. In their eyes the material world is no less sacred than the world of the spirit. In the end, they give their bodies to the spirit world, knowing that the spirit will return again to the body of summer.

An enlightened man cannot be known from his vestments or his position in life, and rarely from the ways he behaves in the public eye. If he is truly enlightened, his other shields are also healthy, enriched by initiatory experience. The lusty boy of summer, the inward adolescent of fall, and the mature man of winter are all evident, and all under the orchestration of the spirit. Such a man you might be tempted to call "fully human." You could be right — if "fully human" means balanced, whole, attuned, and manifest (as opposed to repressed). If such a man is contained like a cistern, he also overflows like a fountain. If he is a fool, he is also wise. If he is a mouse, he is also an eagle. A willing guest at the banquet of love, he will also go without food and pray alone in the wilderness of his heart. In the excess of sorrow, he will laugh. In the excess of joy, he will weep.

I have known such men in my life. Rarely were they the ones singled out by the media or the values of my culture. The enlightened man doesn't advertise much. He simply *does*. His actions wear the vestments of insight and are reflected by the beauty of his natural environment. As a father, his doing glows with healing impulses. As a lover, his doing tricks the sacred from the profane. As a worker, his labor never lacks the creative spark. As an elder, his wisdom bodes well for his grandchildren and the community at large. Such a man might almost be called ordinary, if ordinary refers to what ordinary does when it is complete. Yoke such a man to vision, and you have what the human race will never be able to live without.

More often, I have known men who have only tasted of enlightenment, as if it were a rare wine, men who have merely flirted with wholeness. Until passage rites are reintroduced to our culture, most of us will suffer from malnourishment of the spirit shield. And as the spirit of man suffers, so suffers the living organism that is our only home.

CONCLUSION

> What do you think has become of the young and old men? . . . .
> They are alive and well somewhere,
> The smallest sprout shows there is really no death.
>
> — Walt Whitman, "Song of Myself," 6

What will become of our four shields as our culture crosses the threshold of a new century? At the present time, nothing but further fragmentation and degeneration seem certain. The children, the future of our species, are dying in unprecedented numbers. Matricide, genocide, ethnic intolerance, blind nationalism, religious fanaticism, poverty, over-population, ecological ignorance and exploitation are common. Many of us are waging wars over gender, custody, sexual preference, abortion, and equality. Technology, the media, and the conditions of every day life are reinforcing the illusion that we will somehow magically survive. Many of us who rule the heap do not seem to be any closer to enlightenment.[27] The laws we mandate to protect ourselves from those we fear do not kill fear. Nor are we able to recognize the part we have played in the creation of the swamp in which we wade.

The uninitiated boy who plays like the man is no more capable of planning for the future than of facing the darkness of the fall shield of initiation. Surely, times of trial lie ahead. We face a monumental initiatory challenge. Those of us who survive will be those who are willing, no matter how reluctantly, to turn away from the endless summer to engage the dark visage of fall, the time of testing, the "thresh-hold" where the seed is beaten from the chaff. Those of us who are willing to go into our own darkness may survive. If we do survive, it will be because we have become men.[28]

But what of culturally-sanctioned rites of passage into manhood, into elderhood? Will they return in the 21st century? Only if the conditions of life require that neighborhoods and communities adhere in love and understanding to the old ways of bringing up the boys and girls. Only if the illusion of separation from nature disappears and the people cleave to the self-thus of which they are composed.

It is imperative that this happen. Our survival depends on it. We must see to it that the definition of manhood includes the myth:

And then the boy left his mother and his family and faced the dark, inward passage that led to the Greater Mother. In that place he was made into a man.

When he returned, it was winter. The people were starving. The children were in great peril. He took his place as a man among men, beside his father, his grandfather, and his great grandfather. He helped save the children. He lived for the welfare of all. When spring came, he was enlightened.

ENDNOTES: THE FOUR SHIELDS OF A MAN

[1] The summer shield is the material world, or body, of the man, including all the technological (material) extensions of his body. Unfortunately, the little boy doesn't take very good care of his body. That is the responsibility of the man. But the man isn't there to take care of the boy's body because the little boy hasn't yet become the man. He is still living with, or rebelling against, his mother. Or absorbed in the drama of proving he is a man. Or helplessly adrift in a sea of initiatory memories and feelings. Or meticulously avoiding emotion or feeling, considering such to be childish or weak.

[2] The violent side of the boy-in-the-man who was never initiated is a typical spinoff in a culture without universally sanctioned passage rites into manhood. If the boy grew up in a family where violence was a means of loving, he will also be prone to violence, and abusive to those closest to him. When violence is bred into this boy, whether by family life, media, or peers, it remains, unless cast into the transmuting fires of initiatory self-consciousness. The torturer, the gangbanger, or the rapist, has no control over instinctive emotions such as love, hate, or fear. He escapes the self-consciousness of the initiatory state by veering into the savage jungle of the body, where predators roam. But the jungle is devoid of self-transformation. The predatory act is secret, barely conscious, locked away from view. The jungle thickens. Initiation is nowhere in sight.

[3] "A man who plays with life will never get anywhere; a man who cannot command himself will always be a slave." (Goethe, "*Annonce*")

[4] The question arises as to whether the "macho" is found in primitive cultures where rites of initiation into manhood are common. It would seem that certain elements of "macho" are indeed found in primitive, initiated men. The little boy-in-the-man likes to strut his stuff, even when he is an elder. He makes light of physical pain, revels in his physical strength, and displays courage in the face of danger. What makes primitive "macho" different from modern American macho is that the primitive man is far more complete. He is also inwardly sensitive, capable of deep empathy, and gentled by the anima within — all earmarks of the initiatory process. As a mature man, he has learned to constrain the egotistical struttings of the little boy, and allows him to be "macho" at appropriate times. *Voices of the First Day: Awakening in the Aboriginal Dreamtime*, by Robert Lawlor, contains many priceless descriptions of primitive, initiated male behavior. See also Colin Turnbull, *The Human Cycle, The Mountain People, The Forest People.*

⁵ Note the apparent failure of Baden-Powell's initiatory vision of the scouting movement. Though the Boy Scouts was, and is, an important means of introducing boys to nature, the initiatory process (the class and merit badge system) has little to do with the actual making of men. There could be no validation of manhood by elders because the elders themselves were uninitiated boys. The Boy Scouts are, in fact, excellent examples of prolonged childhood. *Peter Pan* was Baden-Powell's favorite play. See Tim Jeal, *The Boy-Man: The Life of Lord Baden-Powell* (New York: William Morrow and Company, 1990).

⁶ For a sensitive feminine evocation of the problem of boys who stay boys, see Beth Nugent, *City of Boys* (New York: Alfred A. Knopf, 1991).

⁷ These rites have existed from ancient times because the people saw what happened when the boy reached adolescence. Almost overnight he changed. One day he was playing with the other kids. The next day he had disappeared inside himself. He could no longer be trusted to follow the rules of childhood, or to identify himself with his parents. On the other hand, he could not be trusted to act like a man. He had entered an in-between state, had become a kind of question mark. He could be dangerous to the community, hanging out there with the other adolescent boys. Lord knows what he might do, in his clumsy attempts to individuate. Innocent summer had come to fall. It was initiation time.

⁸ An excellent account of Aboriginal male initiations ("the oldest people") may be found in Robert Lawlor, *Voices of the First Day*, p. 184 ff. Of particular interest is the role of women in these masculine rites, for example, when the men come to take the boys away: "Deciding when to seize a boy finally lies with his mother or female relatives, although it is the men's duty. The women may choose to delay or hasten initiation if they feel it may benefit the child." In a more pervasive sense, Lawlor asserts that the highly secret male initiation rites would not exist without feminine approval: "The secrecy and exclusiveness of male religion depends on the conscious pretense and theatrical deception provided by the women." This consent of women is absolutely necessary if the boy is to leave his earthly mother and cleave to the power of the universal feminine.

⁹ Michael Meade: "A double ritual is enacted. Because the search for a new identity must begin with the loss of the previous identity, the initiate is, on the one hand, emptying himself of childhood in order to open himself to manhood; he is making room for the next stage of life. On the other hand, the culture is also stripping him of his identity as a child. In other words, the youth

lets go of the previous stage of life and has it taken away from him. He participates in giving it away, and he suffers the loss of it." *Men and the Water of Life*, p. 240.

[10] Allowing the young man to make mistakes on his own is, indeed, a difficult task for parents, particularly given the real dangers of modern culture. Many were the nights I paced the house at a late hour while my sons were off pursuing their own myths. Their efforts (and my loss of sleep) were ultimately rewarded by a few minor infractions of the law, nothing too significant, and increased self-reliance, self-confidence, and self-knowledge.

[11] "Something extreme must occur in order to deepen one's connection to life, warmth and beauty. Each youth looks for that extreme occurrence and will drive horses and cars full of horsepower as fast as possible to break through to that place. They will explore the depths of the earth and fall into great depressions in order to enter that cave." Michael Meade, *Men and the Water of Life*, p. 221.

[12] Some might argue that service in the military, or going off to war, might serve that purpose. Warfare and being a soldier, however, are primarily manifestations of the summer, or boy shield. Attainment of manhood is not the primary aim of the military, or of any war. If it were, great emphasis would be placed on the teaching and development of soul, mind and spirit, apart from the merely physical training of the "good soldier." And when the hitch was over and the inductees were officially incorporated as adults (which they are not), they would fully take on the roles of true men, which is to serve their people (which they do not). Of course, there are exceptions. The armed services have been known to produce complete men. For these men, the armed services were a means of self-initiation.

[13] The "fire," as Michael Meade calls it, cannot and must not be denied. "The fire must be acknowledged and the risk accepted in each individual and each generation if both individual and culture are to thrive. Each generation enters the fires of change; denying or avoiding the risk of it increases the fire faced by the next generation." *Men and the Water of Life*, p. 219.

[14] The adolescent-in-the-man, the one-who-initiates-himself, never disappears from a man's life. Although modern rites of passage are largely self-induced, they still evoke the fall shield. All profound growth-events reside here. The boy-in-the-man is plunged into an experience of his existential condition: his

loneliness, his separation, his inner darkness, his mortality. Robert Bly (*Iron John*) calls it "the Drop Through the Floor, the Descent, the humiliation, the 'way down and out.'" Symbolically, the naive boy dies into the helpless, self-conscious, isolated adolescent. And the adolescent dies into the man. Yet they do not die, but remain in the man, as his summer and fall shields.

[15] When seven months pregnant, Semele, the mortal mother of Dionysus, begged her lover, Zeus, to show himself to her in all his glory. When he did, she was burnt to a crisp. Zeus rescued the child Dionysus and carried him in his thigh until he came to term. Hence the epithet, "twice born." The myth is a parable of the male initiatory process. The father must take the child from his mortal mother and nurse him to a second birth as a man. The initiatory process involved being treated like a girl, transformed into a sacrificial kid, and resurrected as a god who traveled the world, spreading the cult of the vine. See Ovid, *Metamorphoses*; also Homer, *The Seventh Hymn*.

[16] Strongly recommended: *He: Understanding Masculine Psychology*, by Robert A. Johnson (New York: Harper and Row, 1974). Also by the same author, *The Fisher King and the Handless Maiden* (Harper San Francisco, 1993).

[17] See Wolfram von Eschenbach, *Parzifal*.

[18] T.S. Eliot's *Wasteland* is a powerful and prophetic exploration of the fall shield of human nature. Note particularly his allusive use of the Grail legends.

[19] Michael Meade: "Someone once asked, 'Is she a woman? Is she a part of him? Is she a goddess?' And the answer is, yes. For some find it in a woman, some find it in a place inside themselves, and some touch it in some event in great nature. Some find it in a man. Some find it in meditation and contemplation, and some find it riding a ship on the sea. She is in the beauty that's in the eye of the beholder. She is in the beauty that's in the eye of the lover. She is the wonder made up in the individual soul." *Men and the Water of Life*, p. 274.

[20] The older men are responsible for the initiation of the younger men. But women are not entirely without their part in the ritual drama of the threshold. Robert Bly, *Iron John*: Access to the Hairy Man (the true man) is gained by the key that lies under the mother's pillow. The internalized mother, then, guards the initiatory secret which cannot be revealed until it is stolen from her by acts of severance and experiential intimacy with another who is not-mother. Loss of virginity is tantamount to stealing the key from the mother's pillow. It opens

the cage of the true man, who stalks off with the boy into the wilds of the true Mother, otherwise known as "self-thus."

[21]
> Through winter-time we call on spring,
> And through the spring on summer call,
> And when abounding hedges ring
> Declare that winter's best of all;
> And after that there's nothing good
> Because spring-time has not come —
> Nor know that what disturbs our blood
> Is but its longing for the tomb.
>
> — W.B.Yeats, "The Wheel"

[22] William Golding's *Lord of the Flies* comes to mind: a parable of what is happening today in a society where the boys must initiate themselves. With no adult elders to control their behavior, or confirm the validity of search for manhood, they can only validate themselves. Boys validating boys as "men" only results in a physical struggle for summer shield needs. The law of the jungle prevails.

[23] Good examples of "scarless men" can be found among Protestant Christian men who as adolescents never truly doubted their "faith." Such men were never severed from mothers, parents, or home. They grew up to be carbon copies of their own uninitiated mothers and fathers. Hence they are boys masquerading as Christian men, espousing a morality that has never been tried, professing a grief they have never felt, and evangelically parading a truth they have never earned. True, the various denominations do conduct rites of passage for their young (baptism, confirmation, church membership) but only for the purposes of incorporation within the congregation. These rites do not introduce the candidate to their dark sides or to the world-at-large.

[24] Michael S. Kimmel explores the concept of the "good enough man" of modern culture in *Staying the Course: The Emotional and Social Lives of Men Who Do Well at Work* (New York: Free Press).

[25] In this fashion, Zeus gave birth to Athene, the feminine counterpart to Thoth.

[26] The Muses never forsake those who seek them with a graceful heart. They

were the ones who collected the remains of the dismembered Orpheus on the island of Lesbos and brought them home to the foot of Mt. Olympus.

[27] Robert Moore and Douglas Gillette refer to these kinds of "men" as the "'puerarchy' (i.e., the rule of boys)." *King, Warrior, Magician, Lover* (Harper San Francisco, 1990), p. 143.

[28] "Our effectiveness in meeting these challenges is directly related to how we as individual men meet the challenges of our own immaturity. How well we transform ourselves from men living our lives under the power of Boy psychology to real men guided by the archetypes of Man psychology will have a decisive effect on the outcome of our present world situation." Moore and Gillette, p. 145.

BIBLIOGRAPHY

Anderson, Sherry Ruth and Hopkins, Patricia. *The Feminine Face of God: The Unfolding of the Sacred in Women* (New York: Bantam Books, 1989).

Arrien, Angeles. *The Four-Fold Way* (San Francisco: Harper, 1991).

Asimov, Isaac. *The Human Body: Its Structure and Operation* (New York: Houghton Mifflin, 1963).

Bass, Rick. *Winter: Notes from Montana* (Boston: Houghton Mifflin, 1991).

Bateson, Gregory. *Mind and Nature: A Necessary Unity* (New York: Bantam Books, 1979).

Bear, Sun; Wind, Wabun; Shawnodese. *Dreaming with the Wheel* (New York: Simon and Schuster, 1994).

_____. *The Medicine Wheel* (Englewood Cliffs, NJ: Prentice Hall, 1980).

Betwixt and Between: Patterns of Masculine and Feminine Initiation. Edited by Louise Mahdi, Steven Foster, and Meredith Little (La Salle, IL: Open Court, 1987).

Biedermann, Hans, *Dictionary of Symbolism* (Meridian, 1994).

Blake, William. Blake: *Complete Writings.* Edited by Geoffrey Keynes (London: Oxford University Press, 1966).

Bly, Robert. *Iron John: A Book About Men* (Reading, MA: Addison Wesley, 1990).

_____. *A Little Book of the Human Shadow.* Ed. William Booth (San Francisco: Harper, 1988).

_____. *The Sibling Society* (Reading, MA: Addison Wesley, 1996).

Bowman, Douglas C. *Beyond the Modern Mind: The Spiritual and Ethical Challenge of the Environmental Crisis* (New York: Pilgrim Press, 1990).

Brennan, Martin, *The Stars and the Stones: Ancient Art and Astronomy in Ireland* (London: Thames and Hudson, 1983).

Briggs, John and Peat, F. David. *Turbulent Mirror: An Illustrated Guide to Chaos Theory and the Science of Wholeness* (New York: Harper and Row, 1989).

Bryce, Derek, *Symbolism of the Celtic Cross* (Samuel Weiser, 1995).

Campbell, Joseph. *Hero With a Thousand Faces* ((New Haven: Princeton University Press, 1970).

Campbell, Joseph, Ed. *The Portable Jung* (Middlesex, England: Penguin Books, 1971).

Cajete, Gregory. *Look to the Mountain: An Ecology of Indigenous Education* (Durango: Kivaki Press, 1944).

Chernin, Kim. *Reinventing Eve: Modern Woman in Search of Herself* (New York: Times Books, 1988).

Christie, Anthony. *Chinese Mythology* (Middlesex: Hamlyn, 1968).

Cirlot, J. E. *A Dictionary of Symbols.* Translated by Jack Sage (New York: Philosophical Library, 1962).

Collins, Marie, and Davis, Virginia. *A Medieval Book of Seasons* (London: Sidgwick and Jackson Limited, 1991).

The Complete Grimm's Fairy Tales (New York: Pantheon Books, 1972).

Crossroads: The Quest for Contemporary Rites of Passage. Edited by Louise Mahdi, Nancy Christopher, and Michael Meade (LaSalle, IL: Open Court, 1996).

Davies, Paul. *The Mind of God: The Scientific Basis for a Rational World* (New York: Simon and Schuster, 1992).

Devall, Bill and Sessions, George. *Deep Ecology* (Salt Lake City: Peregrine Smith, 1985).

Devereaux, Paul, Steele, John, and Kubrin, David. *Earthmind: Communicating with the Living World of Gaia* (Rochester, VT: Destiny Books, 1989).

Diamond, Jed. *Inside Out: Becoming My Own Man* (San Rafael, CA: Fifth Wave Press, 1983).

Diamond, Stanley. *The Invisible Pyramid* (New York: Scribners, 1970).

Diamond, Stanley. *In Search of the Primitive* (New Brunswick: Transaction Publishers, 1993).

Dillard, Annie. *Pilgrim at Tinker Creek* (New York: Harper and Row, 1974).

Dossey, Larry. *Recovering the Soul: A Scientific and Spiritual Search* (New York: Bantam Books, 1989).

Eaton, Evelyn. *The Shaman and the Medicine Wheel* (Wheaton, IL: Theosophical Society, 1982).

Eisley, Loren. *The Invisible Pyramid: A Naturalist Analyzes the Rocket Century* (New York: Scribners, 1970).

Eliade, Mircea. *Rites and Symbols of Initiation*. Translated by Willard Trask (New York: Harper and Row, 1958).

Ecopsychology: Restoring the Earth, Healing the Mind. Edited by Roszak, Gomes and Kanner (San Francisco: Sierra Club, 1995).

Erickson, Erik. *Childhood and Society* (New York: W.W. Norton, 1963).

The Essential Rumi. Translations by Coleman Barks (Harper San Francisco, 1995).

Estes, Clarissa Pinkola. *Women Who Run with the Wolves* (New York: Ballentine, 1992).

Foster, Steven and Little, Meredith. *The Book of the Vision Quest* (New York: Simon and Schuster, 1992).

_____. *Lost Borders: Coming of Age in the Wilderness: A Handbook for Youth Entering Adulthood* (Big Pine, CA: Lost Borders Press, 1998).

_____. *The Roaring of the Sacred River* (Big Pine, CA: Lost Borders Press, 1998).

_____. *The Trail to the Sacred Mountain: A Handbook for Adults at Significant Stages of Life.* (Big Pine, CA: Lost Borders Press, 1996).

Frazer, Sir James. *The Golden Bough: A Study in Magic and Religion* (New York: Macmillan, 1963).

Freud, Sigmund. *The Future of an Illusion.* Edited by James Strachy (Garden City: Doubleday, 1946).

Graves, Robert. *The Greek Myths,* Vols I, II (New York: Penguin Books, 1953).

Getty, Adele. *A Sense of the Sacred: Finding Our Spiritual Lives Through Ceremony* (Dallas: Taylor Publishing, 1997).

Grof, Stanislav. *Realms of the Human Unconscious: Observations from LSD Research* (New York: E.P. Dutton, 1976).

Halifax, Joan. *The Fruitful Darkness: Reconnecting with the Body of the Earth* (Harper San Francisco, 1993).

Hall, Manley. *The Secret Teachings of All Ages* (Los Angeles: Philosophical Research Society, 1969).

Henderson, Joseph. *Thresholds of Initiation* (Middletown: Wesleyan U. Press, 1967).

Hesse, Herman. *Narcissus and Goldmund* (New York: Farrar, Straus and Giroux, 1968).

Homer, *The Odyssey*, Translated by Robert Fitzgerald (New York: Alfred A. Knopf, 1961).

Ingerman, Sandra. *Soul Retrieval: Mending the Fragmented Self* (San Francisco: Harper, 1991).

Jacobi, Jolande. *The Psychology of C.G. Jung* (New Haven: Yale University Press, 1973).

James, E.O. *The Ancient Gods* (New York: Putnam's Sons, 1960).

James, William. *Varieties of Religious Experience: A Study in Human Nature* (New York: Mentor Books, 1958).

Jeal, Tim. *The Boy-Man: The Life of Lord Baden-Powell* (New York: William Morrow and Co., 1990).

Johnson, Robert. *The Fisher King and the Handless Maiden* (Harper San Francisco, 1993).

_____. *He: Understanding Masculine Psychology* (New York: Harper and Row, 1974).

Jung, C.G. *Psyche and Symbol.* Edited by Violet S. De Laszlo (Garden City: Doubleday, 1958).

_____. *Psychology of the Unconscious.* Translated by Beatrice M. Hinkle (New York: Moffat Yard, 1916).

_____. *Theory of Types.* Vol 6. (New Haven: Princeton University Press, 1971).

Kalweit, Holger. *Dreamtime and Inner Space: The World of the Shaman* (Boston: Shambhala, 1988).

Krishnamurti, J. *Krishnamurti Himself: His Last Journal* (San Francisco: Harper and Row, 1987).

Kurtz, Ron and Prestera, Hector. *The Body Reveals: An Illustrated Guide to the Psychology of the Body* (New York: Harper and Row, 1976).

Lawlor, Robert. *Voices of the First Day: Awakening in the Aboriginal Dreamtime* (Rochester, VT: Inner Traditions, 1991).

Leopold, Aldo. *A Sand County Almanac* (New York: Ballantine, 1970).

Leonard, Linda Schierse. *The Wounded Woman: Healing the Father-Daughter Relationship* (London: Shambhala, 1983).

Lilly, John. *The Center of the Cyclone* (New York: The Julian Press, 1972).

Liungman, Carl G. *Dictionary of Symbols* (W.W. Norton and Co, 1991).

Locke, Steven and Colligan, Douglas. *The Healer Within: The New Medicine of Mind and Body* (New York: E.P. Dutton, 1986).

Lopez, Barry. *Crossing Open Ground* (New York: Vintage, 1988).

Loos, Linda. *Sitting in Council: An Ecopsychological Approach to Working with Stories in Wilderness Rites of Passage* (Institute of Transpersonal Psychology, Ph.D. Dissertation, 1997).

"Lost Borders: Coming of Age in the Wilderness," A video film by Kim Shelton (Olney, PA: Bullfrog Films, 1998).

Lovelock, J.E. *The Ages of Gaia* (New York: W.W. Norton, 1988).

Maslow, Abraham. *The Farther Reaches of Human Nature* (New York: Viking Press, 1971).

Matthews, Caitlin. *The Celtic Tradition* (Rockport, MA: Element Books, 1991).

McKenna, Dennis and Terrance. *The Invisible Landscape: Mind, Hallucinogens and the I Ching* (New York: Seabury Press, 1975).

Meade, Michael. *Men and the Water of Life: Initiation and the Tempering of Men* (Harper San Francisco, 1993).

Metzner, Ralph. *The Well of Remembrance* (Boston: Shambhala, 1994).

Millman, Dan. *The Warrior Athlete: Body, Mind and Spirit* (Walpole, N.H.: Stillpoint Publishing, 1979).

Moore, Robert and Gillette, Douglas. *King, Warrior, Magician, Lover* (San Francisco: Harper Collins, 1990).

Moore, Thomas. *Care of the Soul: A Guide for Cultivating Depth and Sacredness in Everyday Life* (New York: Harper Collins, 1992).

Napier, David. *Masks, Transformation, and Paradox* (Berkeley: University of California Press, 1989).

Nugent, Beth. *City of Boys* (New York: Alfred A. Knopf, 1991).

Oliver, Mary. *American Primitive* (Boston: Little, Brown and Co: 1983).

Osherson, Samuel. *Finding Our Fathers* (New York: Fawcett Columbine, 1986).

Ovid. *Metamorphoses*. Translated by Rolfe Humphries (Bloomington: Indiana University Press, 1967).

Perera, Sylvia Brinton. *Descent to the Goddess: A Way of Initiation for Women* (Toronto: Inner City Books, 1981).

Pound, Ezra. *Selected Poems* (New York: New Directions, 1957).

Puer Papers, Ed. James Hillman (Dallas: Spring Publications, 1979).

Rees, Alwyn and Brinley. *Celtic Heritage: Ancient Tradition in Ireland and Wales* (London: Thames and Hudson, 1961).

Rilke, Rainer Maria. *Sonnets to Orpheus*. Translated by Stephen Mitchell (New York: Simon and Schuster, 1985).

_____. *Duino Elegies* (Berkeley: University of California Press, 1961).

Roethke, Theodore. *Straw for the Fire: From the Notebooks of Theodore Roethke* (New York: Doubleday, 1974).

Roth, Gabrielle. *Maps to Ecstasy: Teachings of an Urban Shaman* (San Rafael, CA: New World Library, 1989).

Sarton, May. *Journal of a Solitude* (New York: W.W. Norton, 1973).

The Seasons of a Man's Life, Ed. Daniel J. Levinson (New York: Knopf, 1988).

Sexton, Anne. *The Awful Rowing Toward God* (Boston: Houghton Mifflin, 1975).

Sheldrake, Rupert. *The Presence of the Past: The Habits of Nature* (Rochester, VT: Park Street Press, 1988).

Shepard, Paul. *Nature and Madness* (San Francisco: Sierra Club, 1982).

_____. *The Tender Carnivore and the Sacred Game* (New York: Scribners, 1973).

Slater, Philip. *Earthwalk* (Garden City: Doubleday, 1974).

Snyder, Gary. *The Practice of the Wild* (San Francisco: North Point Press, 1990).

_____. *Mountains and Rivers Without End* (Washington D.C.: Counterpoint Press, 1996).

_____. *No Nature* (New York: Pantheon Books, 1992).

Some, Malidoma Patrice. *Ritual: Power, Healing and Community* (Portland: Swan/Raven and Co, 1993).

Spinrad, Norman. *Child of Fortune* (New York: Bantam Books, 1985).

Standard Dictionary of Folklore, Mythology, and Legend. Ed. Maria Leach (San Francisco: Harper and Row, 1972).

Stevens, Wallace. *The Collected Poems of Wallace Stevens* (New York: Alfred A. Knopf, 1961).

Talbot, Michael. *The Holographic Universe* (New York: Harper Collins, 1991).

Tashlin, Frank. *The Bear that Wasn't* (New York: E.P. Dutton and Co., 1946).

Thoreau, Henry David. *Walden and Other Writings*. Edited by Brooks Atkinson (New York: Random House, 1950).

Tulku, Tarthang, Ed. *Reflections of Mind: Western Psychology Meets Tibetan Buddhism* (Emeryville, CA: Dharma Publishing, 1975).

Turnbull, Colin. *The Human Cycle* (New York: Simon and Schuster, 1983).

Turner, Victor. *The Ritual Process: Structure and Anti-Structure* (Chicago: Aldine, 1969).

Van Gennep, Arnold. *The Rites of Passage.* Translated by Gabrielle Caffee and Monika Vizedom (Chicago: The University of Chicago Press, 1960).

Von Franz, Marie Louise. *The Feminine in Fairy Tales* (Dallas, Tx: Spring Publications, 1972).

_____. *Projection and Re-Collection in Jungian Psychology* (LaSalle, Ill: Open Court, 1980).

Watson, Lyall. *Dark Nature: A Natural History of Evil* (New York: Harper Collins, 1995).

Watts, Alan. *Nature, Man and Woman* (New York: Vintage, 1970).

Weiner, Bernard. *Boy Into Man: A Fathers' Guide to Initiation of Teenage Sons* (San Francisco: Transformation Press, 1992).

Wheelwright, Philip. *Heraclitus* (New York: Atheneum, 1957).

White, Jonathan. *Talking on the Water: Conversations about Nature and Creativity* (San Francisco: Sierra Club Books, 1994).

Whitman, Walt. *Leaves of Grass* (New York: Modern Library, 1892).

Wilbur, Ken. *The Spectrum of Consciousness* (Wheaton, Ill.: Theosophical Publishing House, 1977).

Williams, Terry Tempest. *An Unspoken Hunger: Stories from the Field* (New York: Vintage Books, 1994).

Zimmerman, Jack and Coyle, Virginia. *The Way of Council* (Las Vegas: Bramble Books, 1996).